Creator: Marimo Ragawa

SBM Title: *Baby & Me*

Date of Birth: September 21

Blood Type: B

Major Works: *Time Limit, Baby & Me, N.Y. N.Y.,* and *Shanimuni-Go* (Desperately—Go)

Marimo Ragawa first started submitting manga to a comic magazine when she was 12 years old. She kept up her submissions for four years, but to no avail. She decided to submit her work to the magazine *Hana to Yume*, where she received Top Prize in the Monthly Manga Contest as well as an honorable mention (Kasaku) in the magazine's Big Challenge contest. Her first manga was titled *Time Limit*. *Baby & Me* was honored with a Shogakukan Manga Award in 1995 and was spun off into an anime.

Ragawa's work showcases some very cute and expressive line work along with an incredible ability to depict complex emotions and relationships. Some of her other works include *N.Y. N.Y.* and the tennis manga *Shanimuni-Go*.

Ragawa has two brothers and two sisters.

BABY & ME, Vol. 10
The Shojo Beat Manga Edition

STORY & ART BY
MARIMO RAGAWA

English Adaptation/Lance Caselman
Translation/JN Productions
Touch-up Art & Lettering/Vanessa Satone
Design/Yuki Ameda
Editor/Shaenon K. Garrity

Editor in Chief, Books/Alvin Lu
Editor in Chief, Magazines/Marc Weidenbaum
VP of Publishing Licensing/Rika Inouye
VP of Sales/Gonzalo Ferreyra
Sr. VP of Marketing/Liza Coppola
Publisher/Hyoe Narita

Printed in Canada

Published by VIZ Media, LLC
P.O. Box 77010
San Francisco, CA 94107

Shojo Beat Manga Edition
10 9 8 7 6 5 4 3 2 1
First printing, October 2008

store.viz.com

Shojo Beat

BABY & Me

Vol. 10

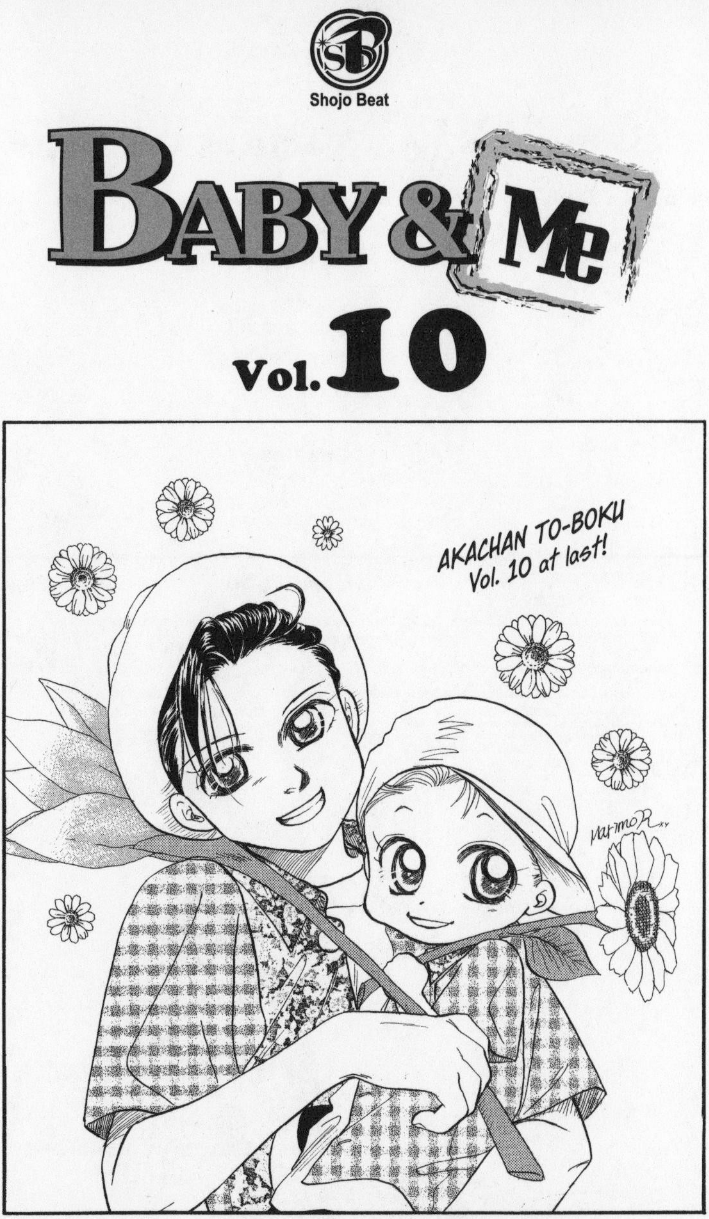
AKACHAN TO-BOKU
Vol. 10 at last!
MarimoR

Story & Art by Marimo Ragawa

Baby & Me

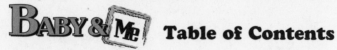

Table of Contents

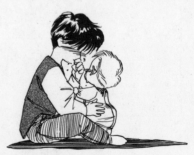

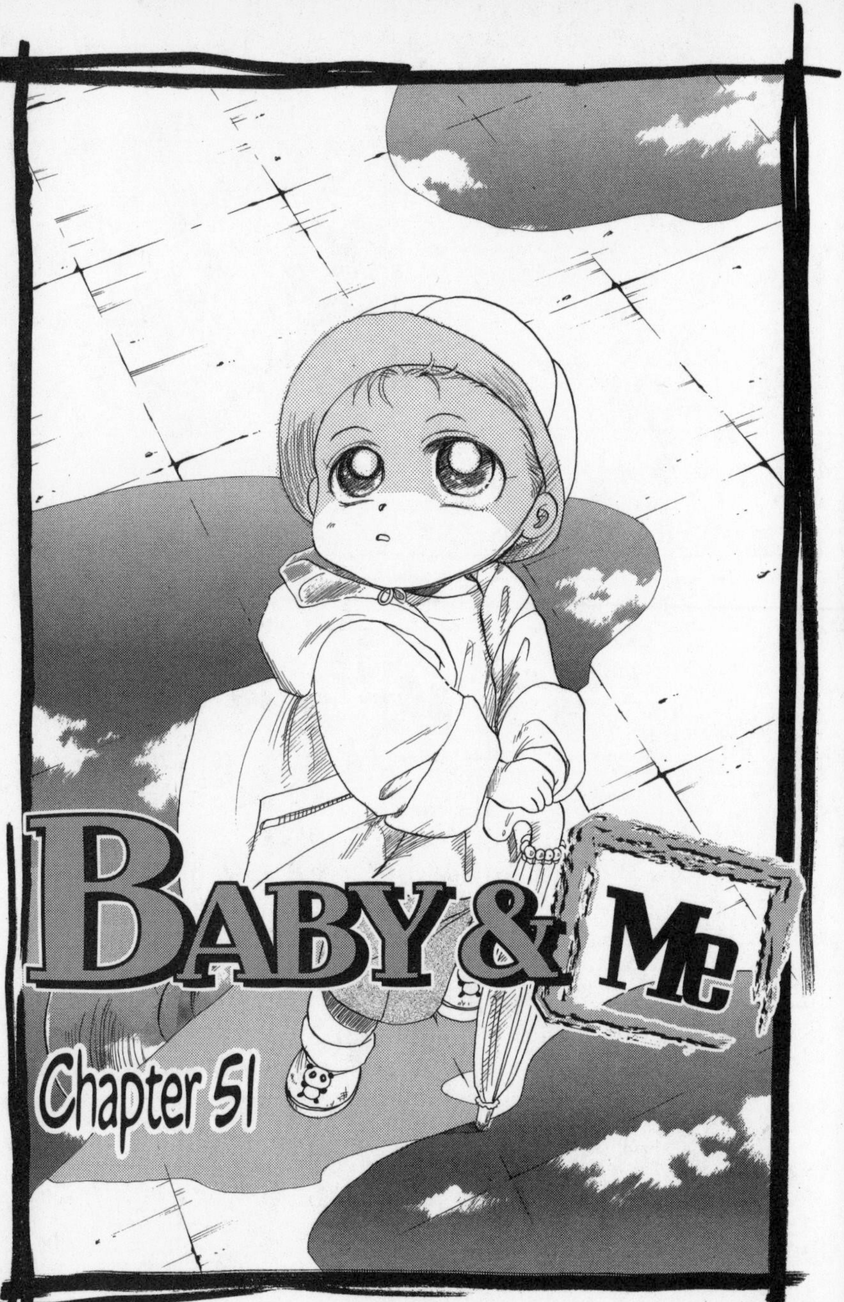
BABY & Me
Chapter 51

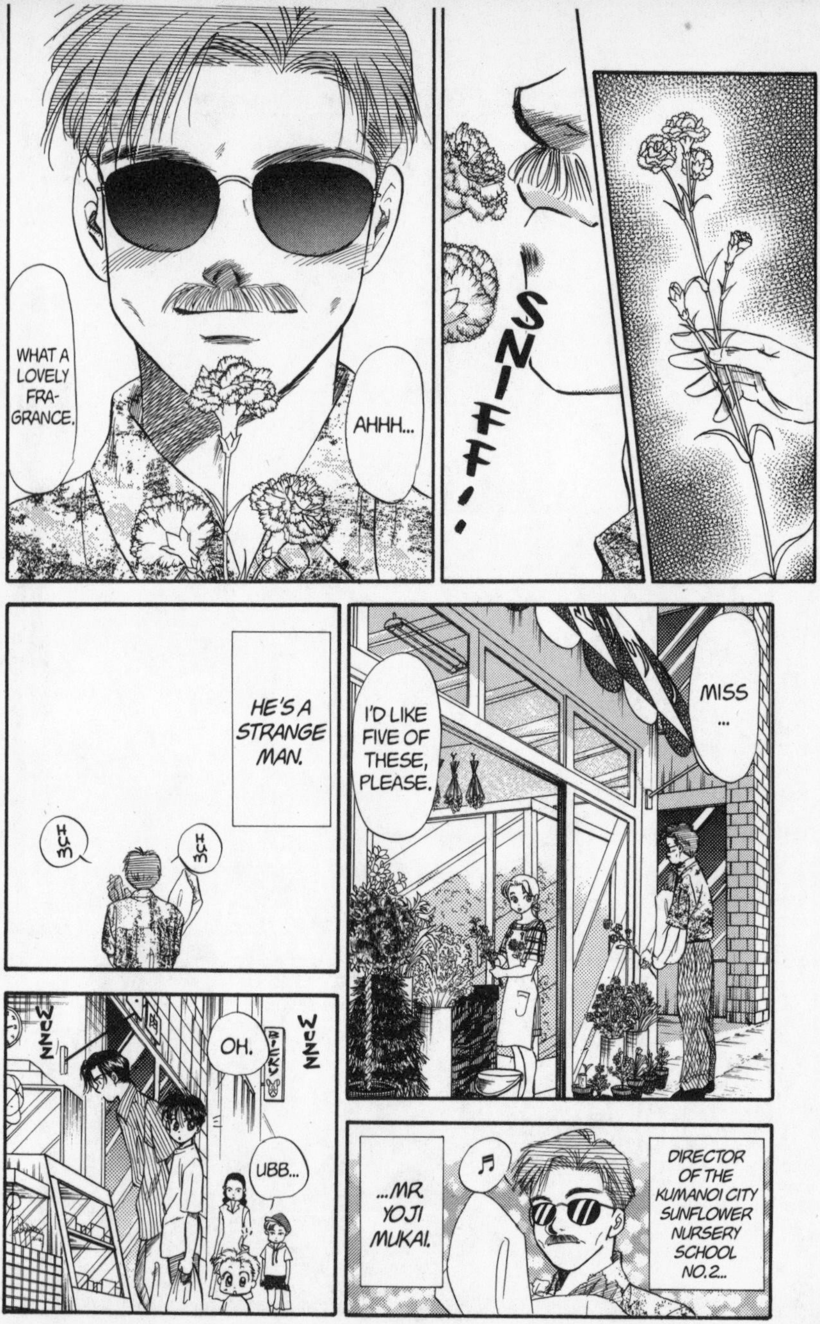
SNIFF!
AHHH...
WHAT A LOVELY FRA-GRANCE.
MISS ...
I'D LIKE FIVE OF THESE, PLEASE.
HE'S A STRANGE MAN.
HUM
HUM
DIRECTOR OF THE KUMANOI CITY SUNFLOWER NURSERY SCHOOL NO.2...
♪
...MR. YOJI MUKAI.
WUZZ
OH.
WUZZ
UBB...

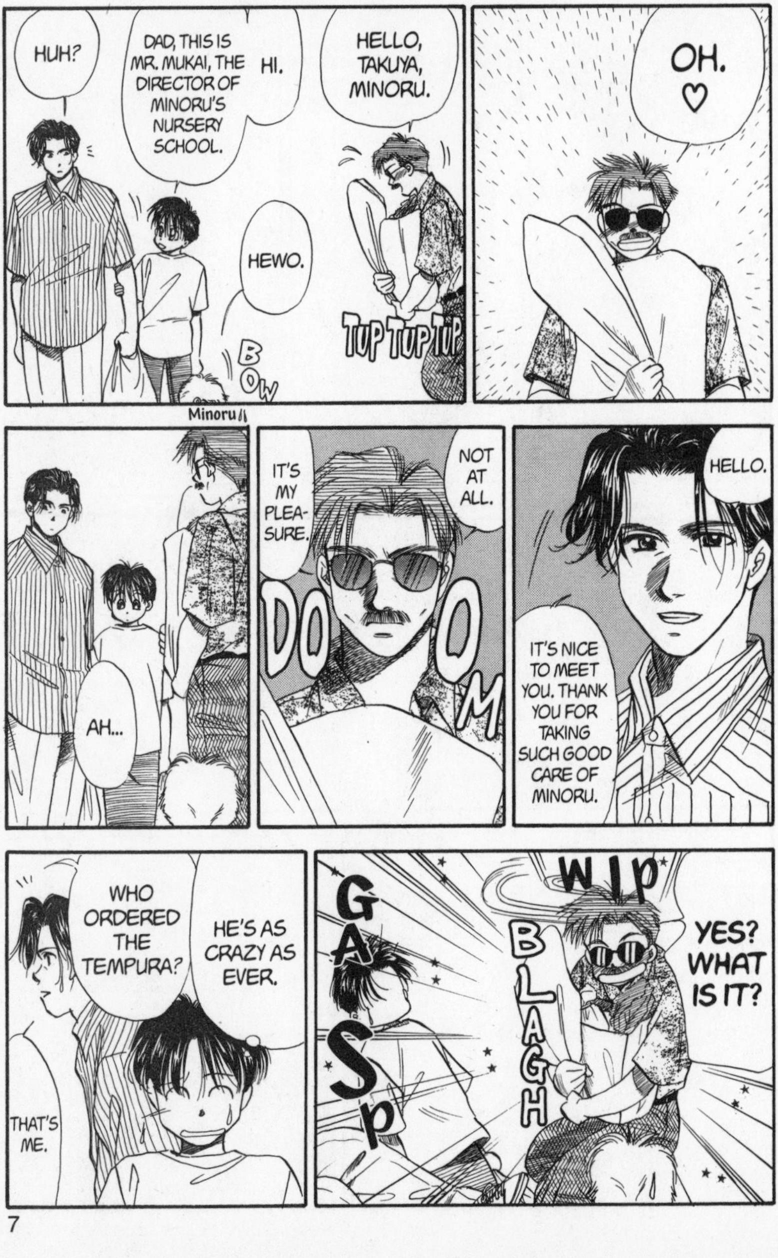
OH. ♡
HELLO, TAKUYA, MINORU.
TUP TUP TUP
HI.
DAD, THIS IS MR. MUKAI, THE DIRECTOR OF MINORU'S NURSERY SCHOOL.
HUH?
HEWO.
BOW
Minoru
HELLO.
IT'S NICE TO MEET YOU. THANK YOU FOR TAKING SUCH GOOD CARE OF MINORU.
NOT AT ALL.
IT'S MY PLEASURE.
DOOM
AH...
WIP
YES? WHAT IS IT?
BLAGH
GASP
HE'S AS CRAZY AS EVER.
WHO ORDERED THE TEMPURA?
THAT'S ME.

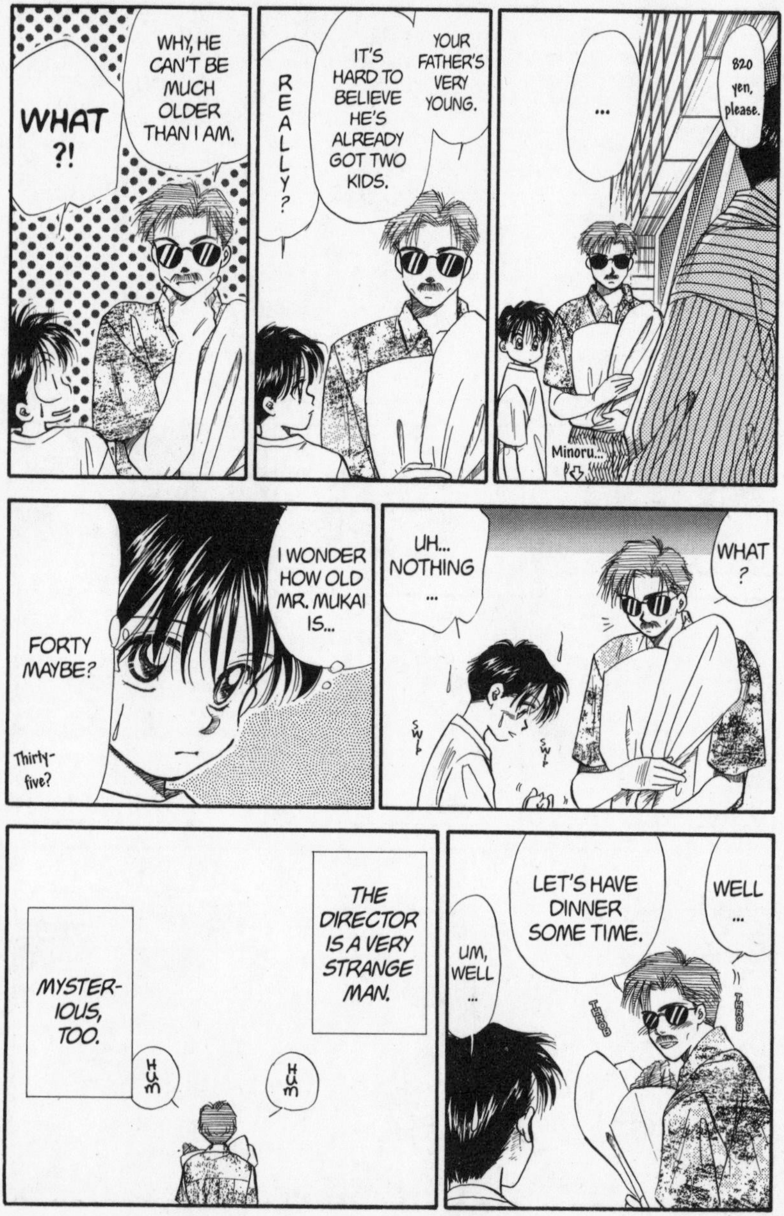
820 yen, please.
...
Minoru...
YOUR FATHER'S VERY YOUNG.
IT'S HARD TO BELIEVE HE'S ALREADY GOT TWO KIDS.
REALLY?
WHY, HE CAN'T BE MUCH OLDER THAN I AM.
WHAT?!
WHAT?
UH... NOTHING...
I WONDER HOW OLD MR. MUKAI IS...
FORTY MAYBE?
Thirty-five?
WELL...
LET'S HAVE DINNER SOME TIME.
UM, WELL...
THROB
THROB
THE DIRECTOR IS A VERY STRANGE MAN.
MYSTERIOUS, TOO.
HUM
HUM

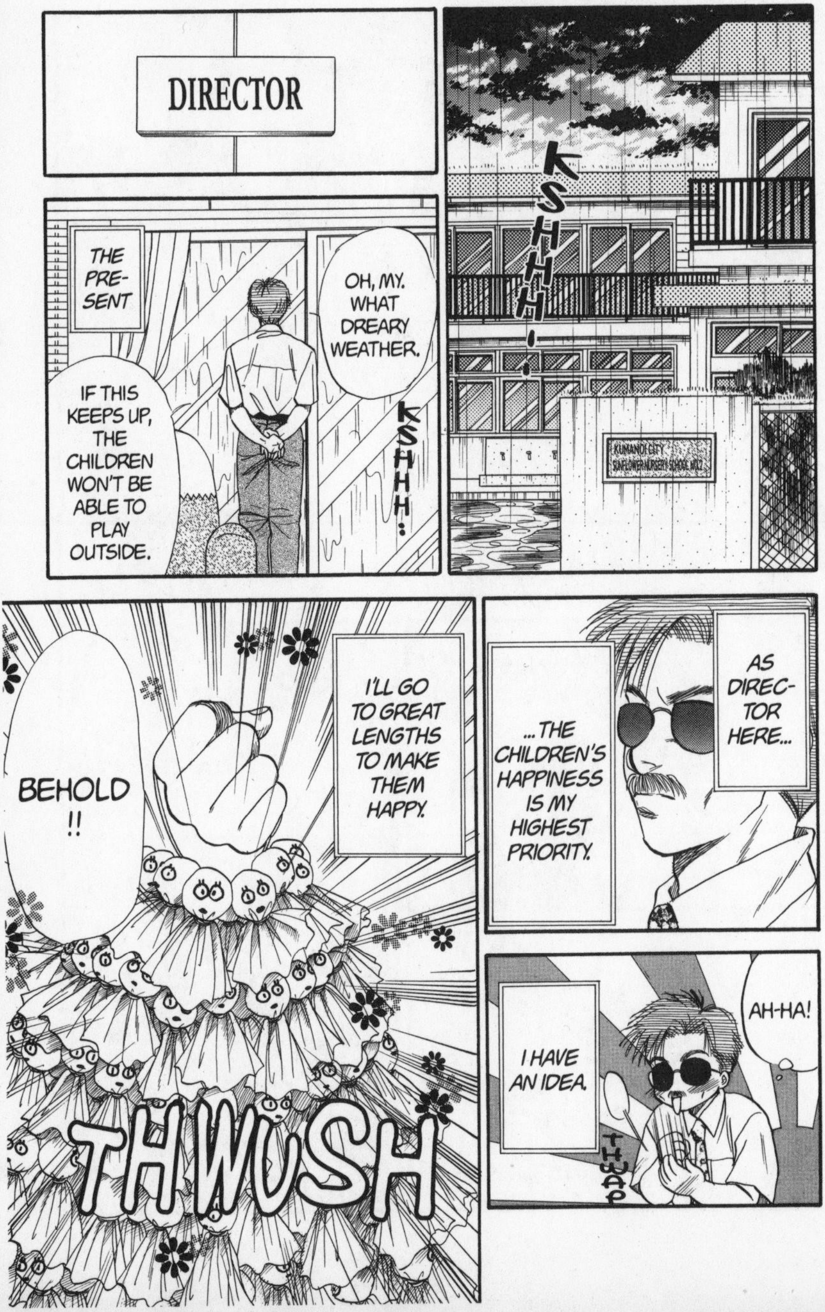
KSHHHH!!
KUMANOI CITY
SUNFLOWER NURSERY SCHOOL NO.2
DIRECTOR
THE PRESENT
OH, MY. WHAT DREARY WEATHER.
IF THIS KEEPS UP, THE CHILDREN WON'T BE ABLE TO PLAY OUTSIDE.
KSHHH..
AS DIRECTOR HERE...
...THE CHILDREN'S HAPPINESS IS MY HIGHEST PRIORITY.
AH-HA!
I HAVE AN IDEA.
THWAP
I'LL GO TO GREAT LENGTHS TO MAKE THEM HAPPY.
BEHOLD !!
THWUSH

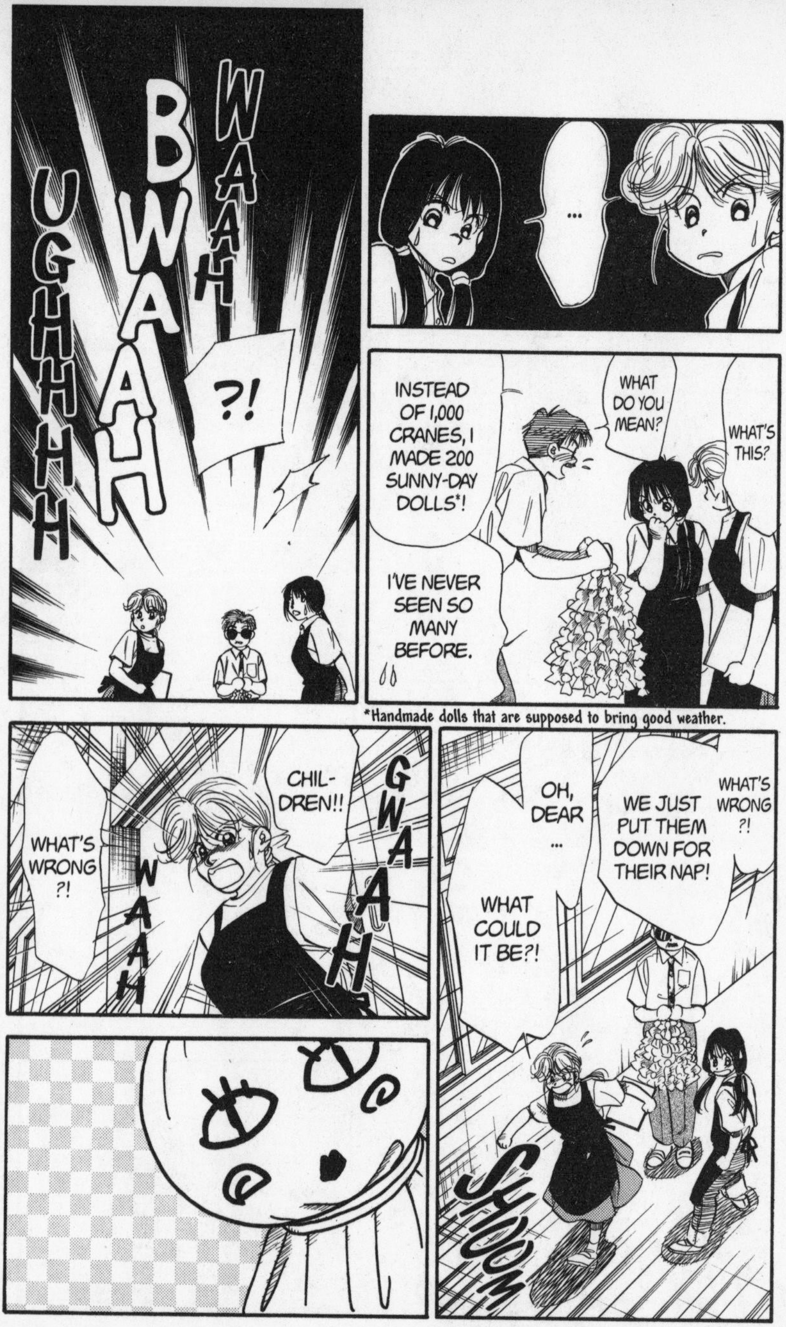
...
WHAT'S THIS?
WHAT DO YOU MEAN?
INSTEAD OF 1,000 CRANES, I MADE 200 SUNNY-DAY DOLLS*!
I'VE NEVER SEEN SO MANY BEFORE.
WAAAH!
BWAAH
?!
UGHHHHHH
WHAT'S WRONG?!
WE JUST PUT THEM DOWN FOR THEIR NAP!
OH, DEAR ...
WHAT COULD IT BE?!
SHOOM
GWAAH
CHIL-DREN!!
WAAH
WHAT'S WRONG?!

*Handmade dolls that are supposed to bring good weather.

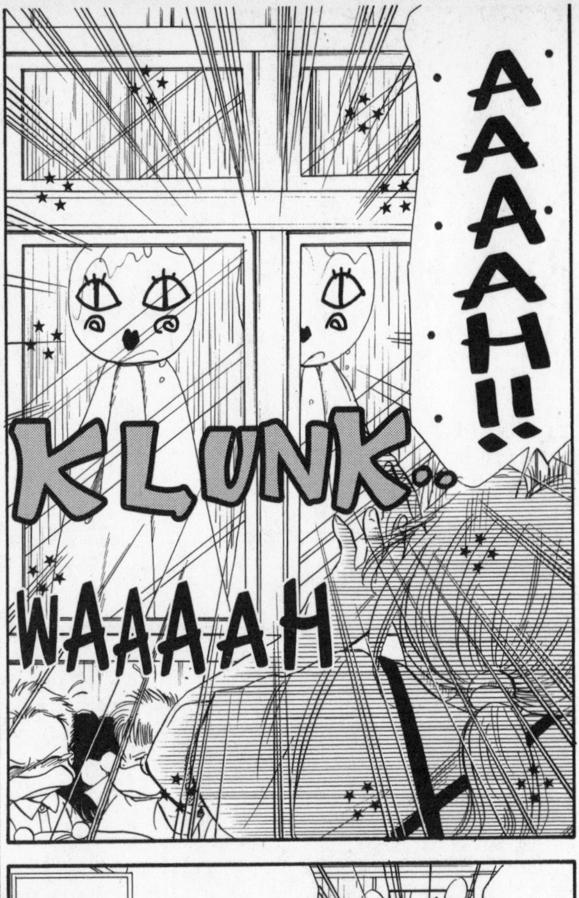
AAAAAH!!
KLUNK..
WAAAAH
MR. MUKAI!! WHAT HAVE YOU DONE?
I-I JUST THOUGHT THAT MAYBE...BIGGER SUNNY-DAY DOLLS WOULD BE MORE EFFECTIVE...
BUT IT SEEMS THAT MY FEELINGS ARE UNREQUITED!
SOB
SOB
SOB
SOB

Author's Note: Part 1

Hello, Marimo Ragawa here. Baby and Me has reached ten volumes!

Some people have commented sarcastically that this series has turned into Co-Stars and Me. But what's wrong with that? I can't help it if the supporting cast is popular. "Do more with Fujii!!" "I want more of Director Mukai!!" "I love the Kimura family!!" Or do you just want to read about Takuya and Minoru chapter after chapter? Readers would think I was in a rut if I did that. And no one would buy my manga then! It was rude of that person to write me and say, "Get your act together!" So this is my question for this year: What's wrong with Co-Stars and Me? Absolutely nothing. The End.

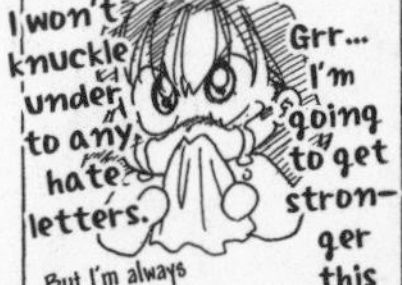
I won't knuckle under to any hate letters.
Grr... I'm going to get stronger this year.
But I'm always knuckling under...

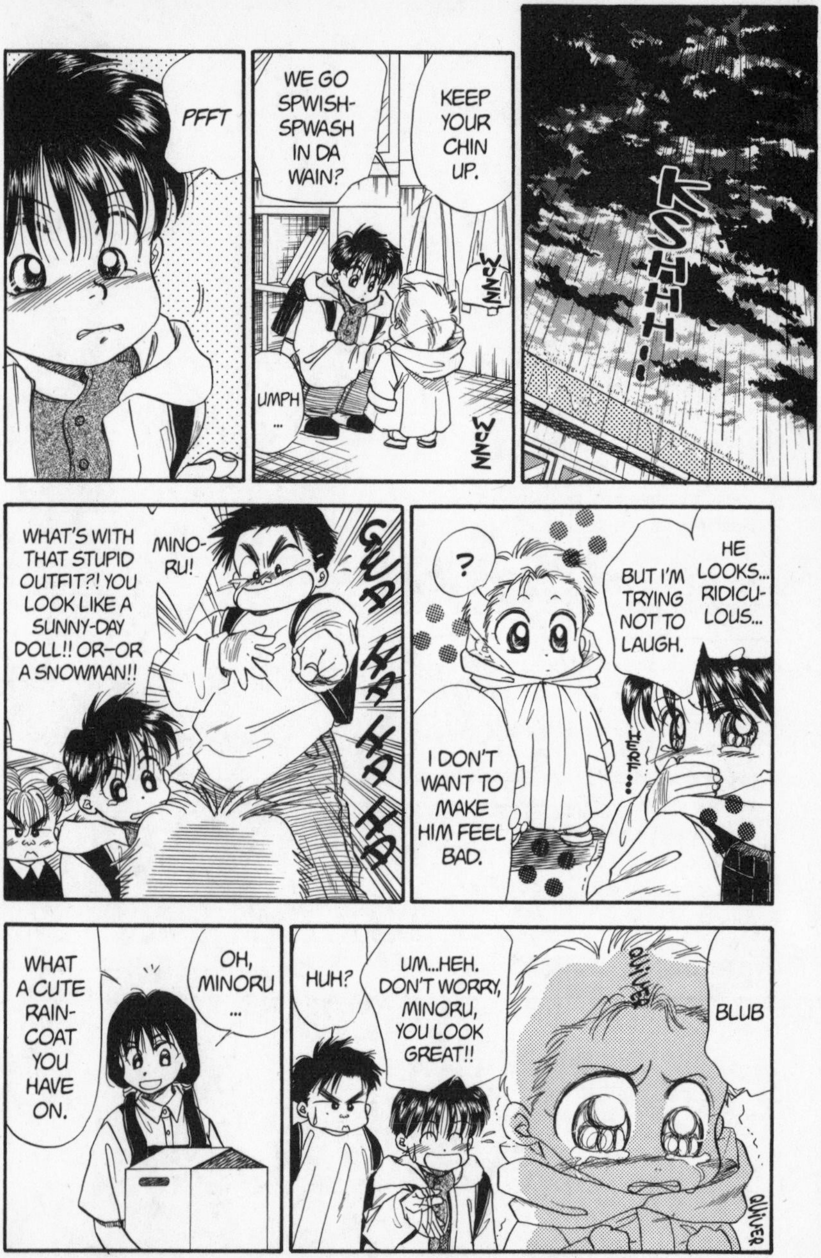
KSHHH...
KEEP YOUR CHIN UP.
WE GO SPWISH-SPWASH IN DA WAIN?
WUZN
UMPH ...
WUZN
PFFT
HE LOOKS... RIDICU-LOUS...
BUT I'M TRYING NOT TO LAUGH.
?
HERF...
I DON'T WANT TO MAKE HIM FEEL BAD.
GWA HA HA HA HA
MINO-RU!
WHAT'S WITH THAT STUPID OUTFIT?! YOU LOOK LIKE A SUNNY-DAY DOLL!! OR–OR A SNOWMAN!!
QUIVER
BLUB
UM...HEH. DON'T WORRY, MINORU, YOU LOOK GREAT!!
HUH?
QUIVER
OH, MINORU ...
WHAT A CUTE RAIN-COAT YOU HAVE ON.

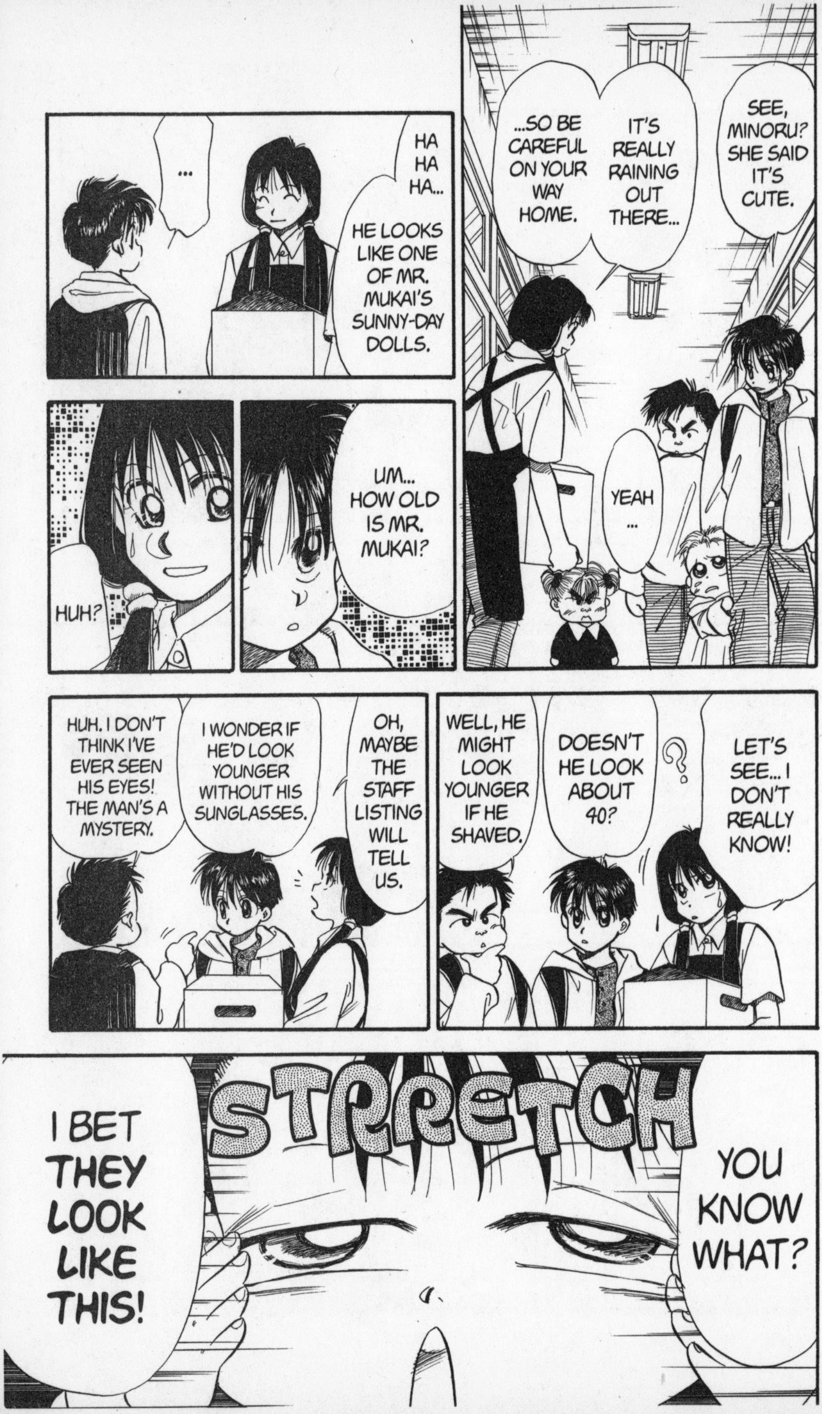
SEE, MINORU? SHE SAID IT'S CUTE.
IT'S REALLY RAINING OUT THERE...
...SO BE CAREFUL ON YOUR WAY HOME.
YEAH ...
HA HA HA...
HE LOOKS LIKE ONE OF MR. MUKAI'S SUNNY-DAY DOLLS.
...
UM... HOW OLD IS MR. MUKAI?
HUH?
LET'S SEE... I DON'T REALLY KNOW!
?
DOESN'T HE LOOK ABOUT 40?
WELL, HE MIGHT LOOK YOUNGER IF HE SHAVED.
OH, MAYBE THE STAFF LISTING WILL TELL US.
I WONDER IF HE'D LOOK YOUNGER WITHOUT HIS SUNGLASSES.
HUH. I DON'T THINK I'VE EVER SEEN HIS EYES! THE MAN'S A MYSTERY.
YOU KNOW WHAT?
STRRETCH
I BET THEY LOOK LIKE THIS!

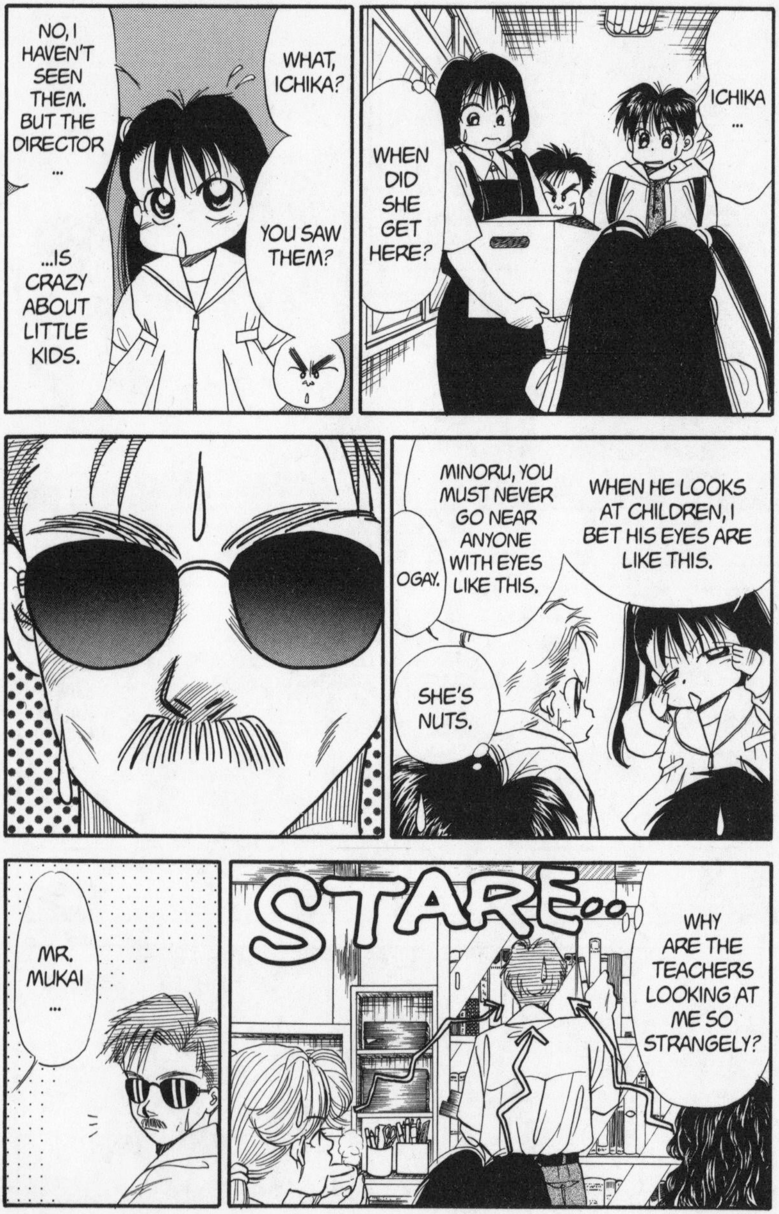
ICHIKA ...
WHEN DID SHE GET HERE?
WHAT, ICHIKA?
YOU SAW THEM?
NO, I HAVEN'T SEEN THEM. BUT THE DIRECTOR ...
...IS CRAZY ABOUT LITTLE KIDS.
WHEN HE LOOKS AT CHILDREN, I BET HIS EYES ARE LIKE THIS.
MINORU, YOU MUST NEVER GO NEAR ANYONE WITH EYES LIKE THIS.
OGAY.
SHE'S NUTS.
WHY ARE THE TEACHERS LOOKING AT ME SO STRANGELY?
STARE..
MR. MUKAI ...

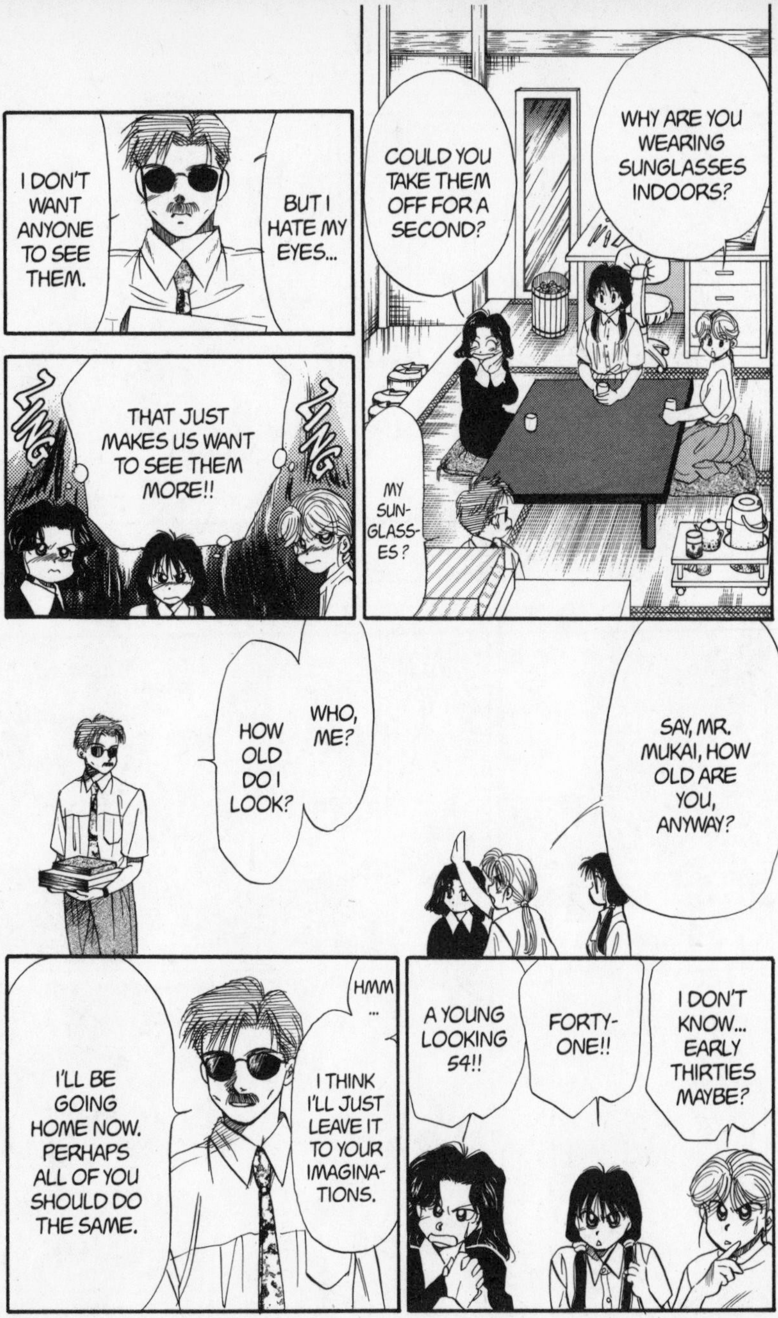
WHY ARE YOU WEARING SUNGLASSES INDOORS?
COULD YOU TAKE THEM OFF FOR A SECOND?
MY SUNGLASSES?
BUT I HATE MY EYES...
I DON'T WANT ANYONE TO SEE THEM.
ZING
ZING
THAT JUST MAKES US WANT TO SEE THEM MORE!!
SAY, MR. MUKAI, HOW OLD ARE YOU, ANYWAY?
WHO, ME?
HOW OLD DO I LOOK?
I DON'T KNOW... EARLY THIRTIES MAYBE?
FORTY-ONE!!
A YOUNG LOOKING 54!!
HMM ...
I THINK I'LL JUST LEAVE IT TO YOUR IMAGINATIONS.
I'LL BE GOING HOME NOW. PERHAPS ALL OF YOU SHOULD DO THE SAME.

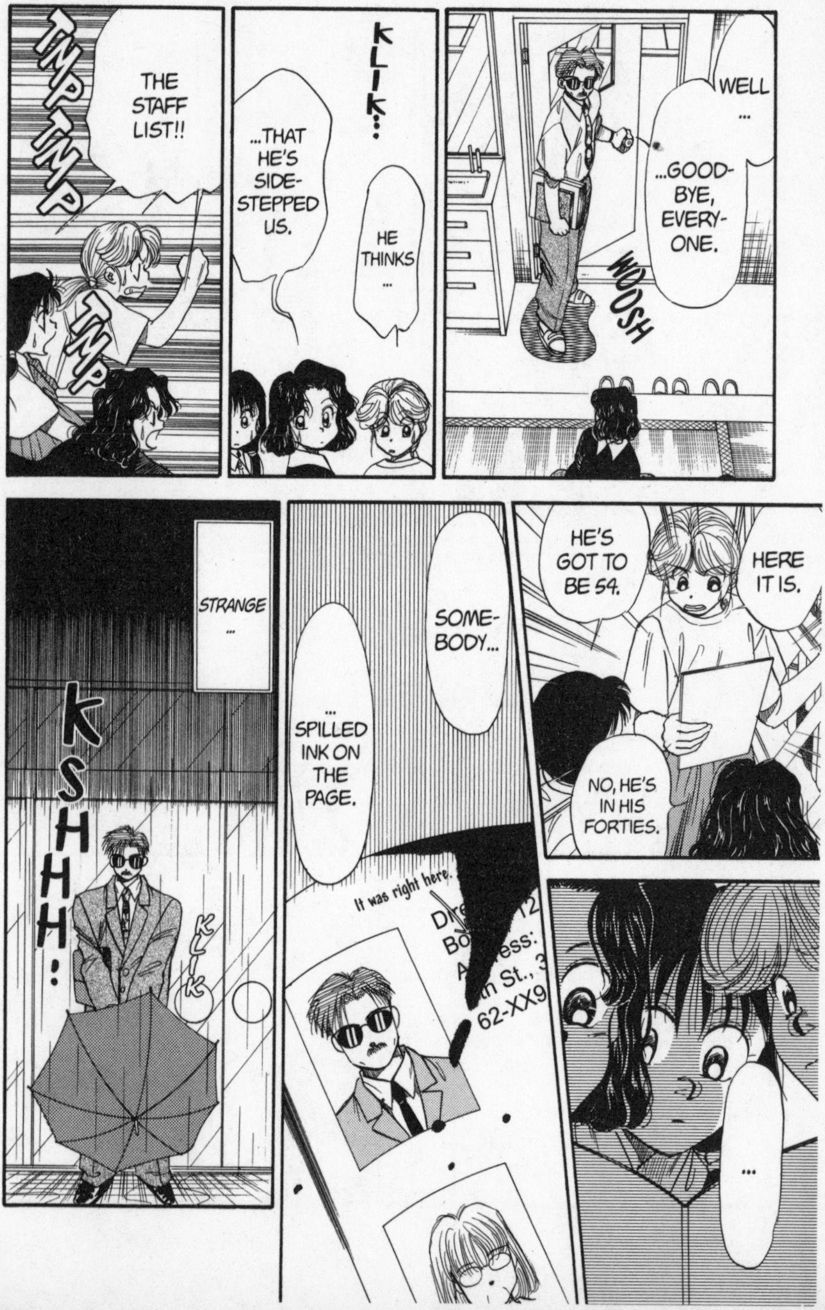

WELL ...
...GOOD-BYE, EVERY-ONE.
WOOSH
HE THINKS ...
...THAT HE'S SIDE-STEPPED US.
KLIK
THE STAFF LIST!!
TMP TMP
TMP
HERE IT IS.
HE'S GOT TO BE 54.
NO, HE'S IN HIS FORTIES.
...
SOMEBODY...
...SPILLED INK ON THE PAGE.
It was right here.
62-XX9
STRANGE ...
KSHHH
KLIK

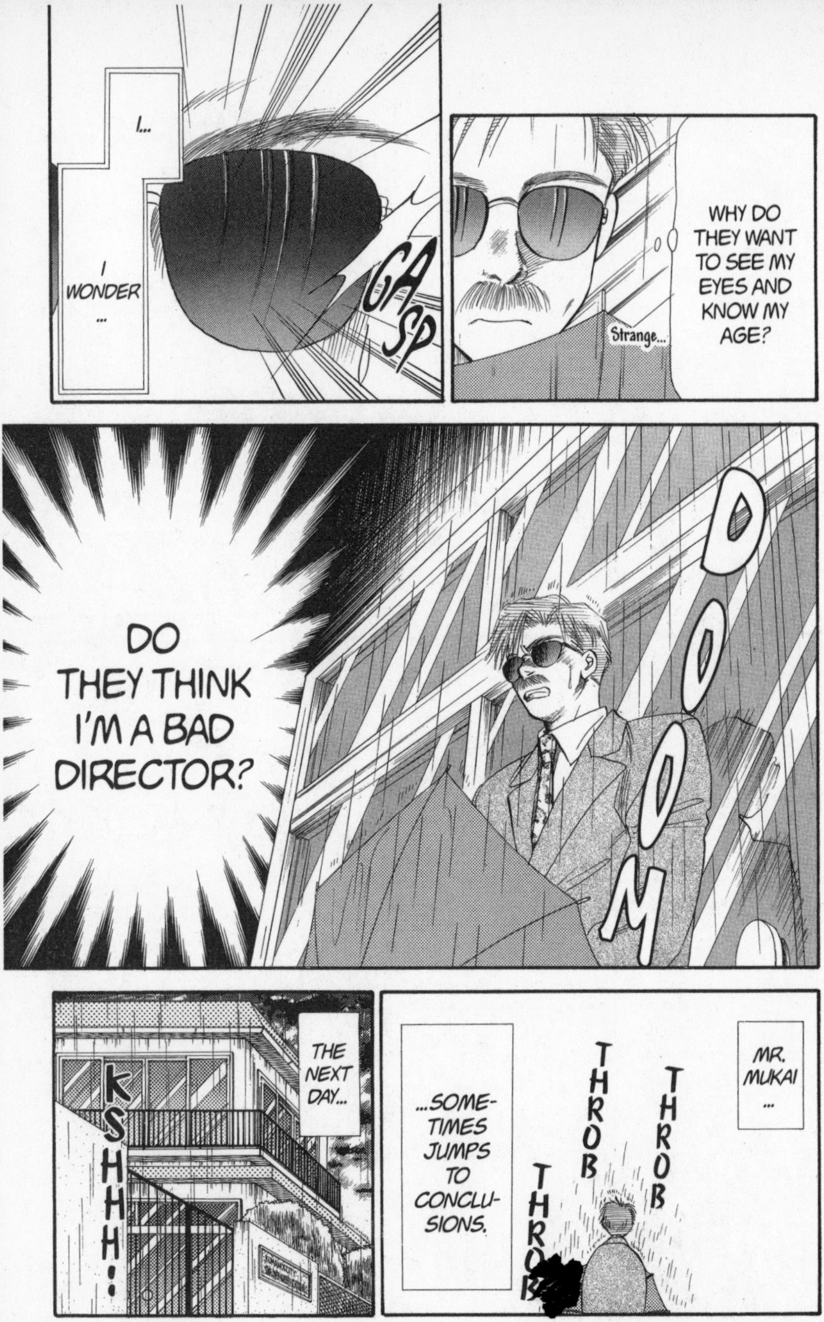
WHY DO THEY WANT TO SEE MY EYES AND KNOW MY AGE?
Strange...
I...
I WONDER...
GASP
DO THEY THINK I'M A BAD DIRECTOR?
DOOOM
MR. MUKAI...
...SOMETIMES JUMPS TO CONCLUSIONS.
THROB
THROB
THROB
THE NEXT DAY...
KSHHH!

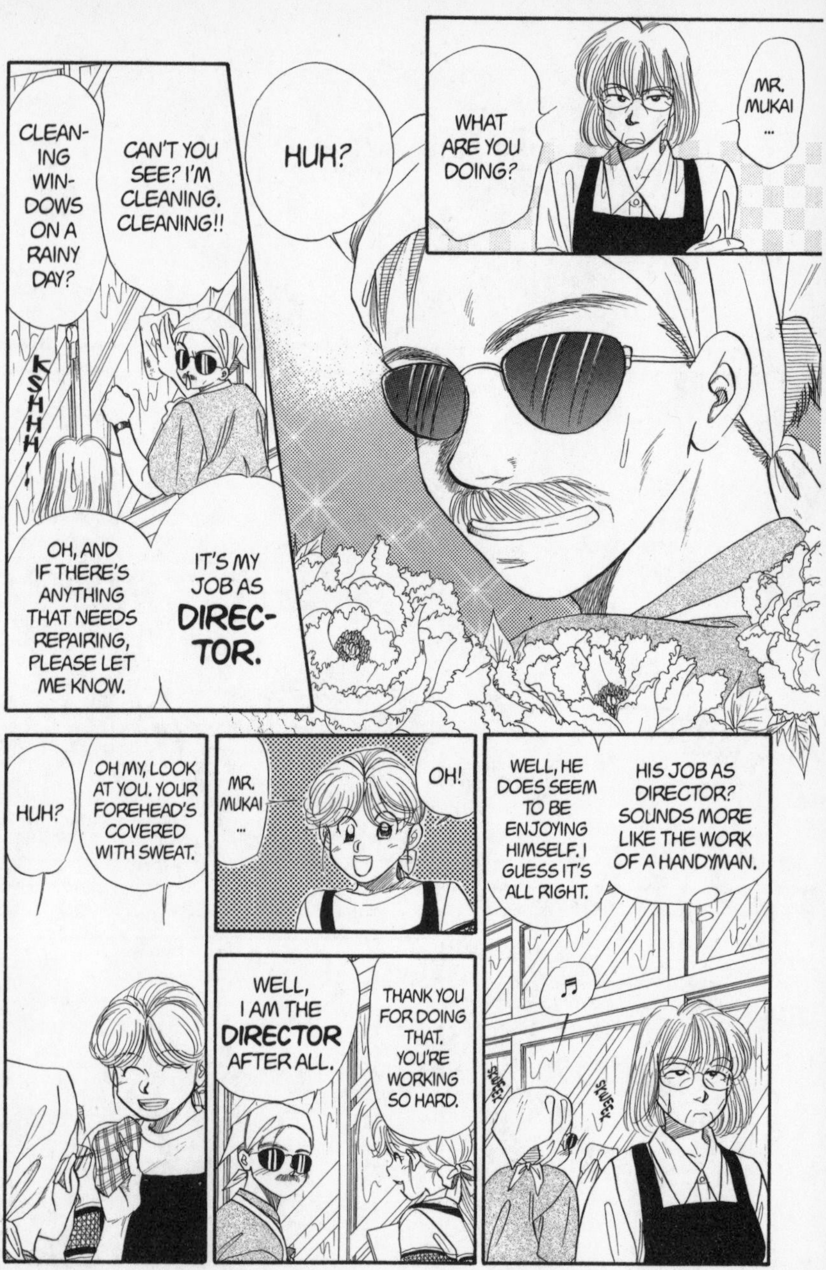
MR. MUKAI ...
WHAT ARE YOU DOING?
HUH?
CAN'T YOU SEE? I'M CLEANING. CLEANING!!
CLEAN-ING WIN-DOWS ON A RAINY DAY?
KSHHH!
IT'S MY JOB AS DIRECTOR.
OH, AND IF THERE'S ANYTHING THAT NEEDS REPAIRING, PLEASE LET ME KNOW.
HIS JOB AS DIRECTOR? SOUNDS MORE LIKE THE WORK OF A HANDYMAN.
WELL, HE DOES SEEM TO BE ENJOYING HIMSELF. I GUESS IT'S ALL RIGHT.
♬
OH!
MR. MUKAI ...
THANK YOU FOR DOING THAT. YOU'RE WORKING SO HARD.
WELL, I AM THE DIRECTOR AFTER ALL.
OH MY, LOOK AT YOU. YOUR FOREHEAD'S COVERED WITH SWEAT.
HUH?

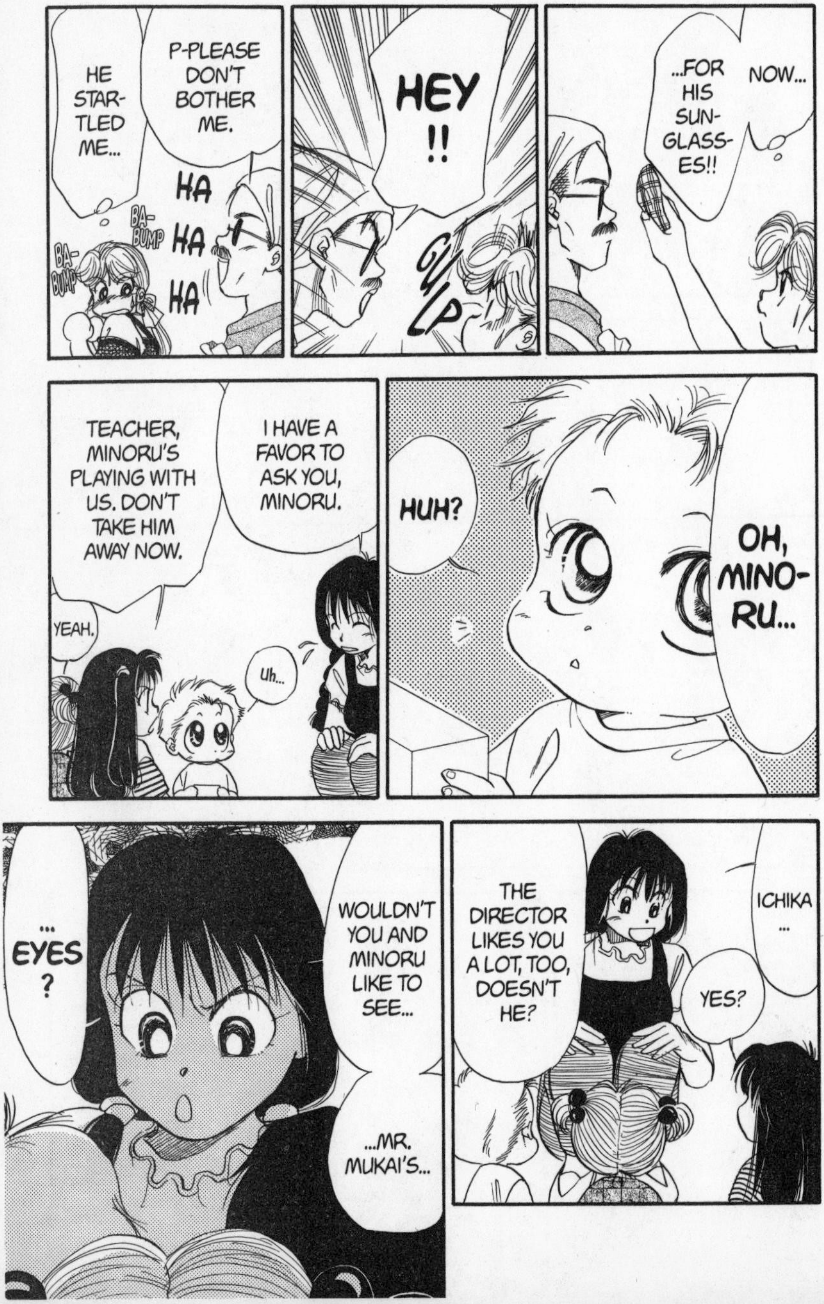
NOW...
...FOR HIS SUN-GLASS-ES!!
HEY!!
GULP
P-PLEASE DON'T BOTHER ME.
HE STAR-TLED ME...
HA HA HA
BA-BUMP
BA-BUMP
OH, MINO-RU...
HUH?
I HAVE A FAVOR TO ASK YOU, MINORU.
TEACHER, MINORU'S PLAYING WITH US. DON'T TAKE HIM AWAY NOW.
Uh...
YEAH.
ICHIKA...
YES?
THE DIRECTOR LIKES YOU A LOT, TOO, DOESN'T HE?
WOULDN'T YOU AND MINORU LIKE TO SEE...
...MR. MUKAI'S...
...EYES?

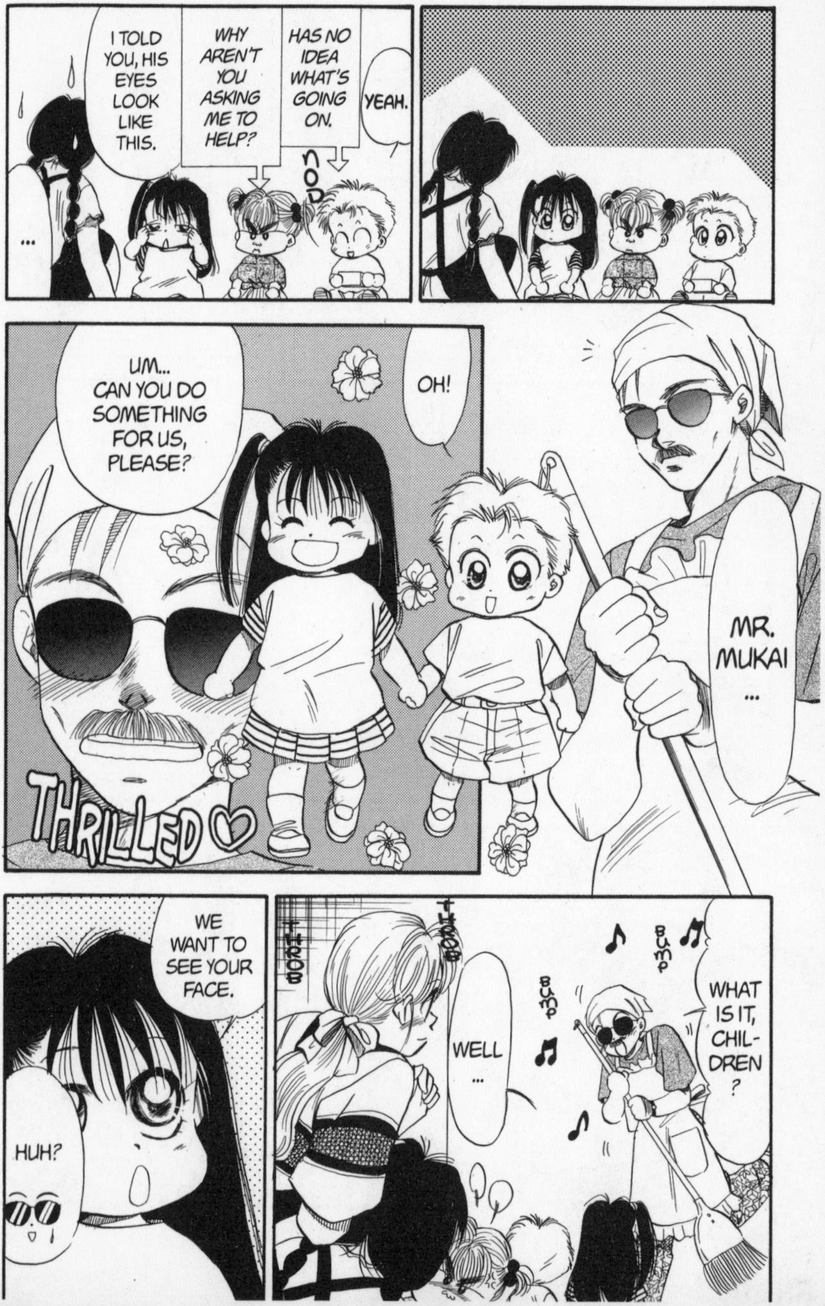
YEAH.
HAS NO IDEA WHAT'S GOING ON.
NOD
WHY AREN'T YOU ASKING ME TO HELP?
I TOLD YOU, HIS EYES LOOK LIKE THIS.
...
MR. MUKAI ...
OH!
UM... CAN YOU DO SOMETHING FOR US, PLEASE?
THRILLED
WHAT IS IT, CHIL-DREN?
BUMP
BUMP
THROB
THROB
WELL ...
WE WANT TO SEE YOUR FACE.
HUH?

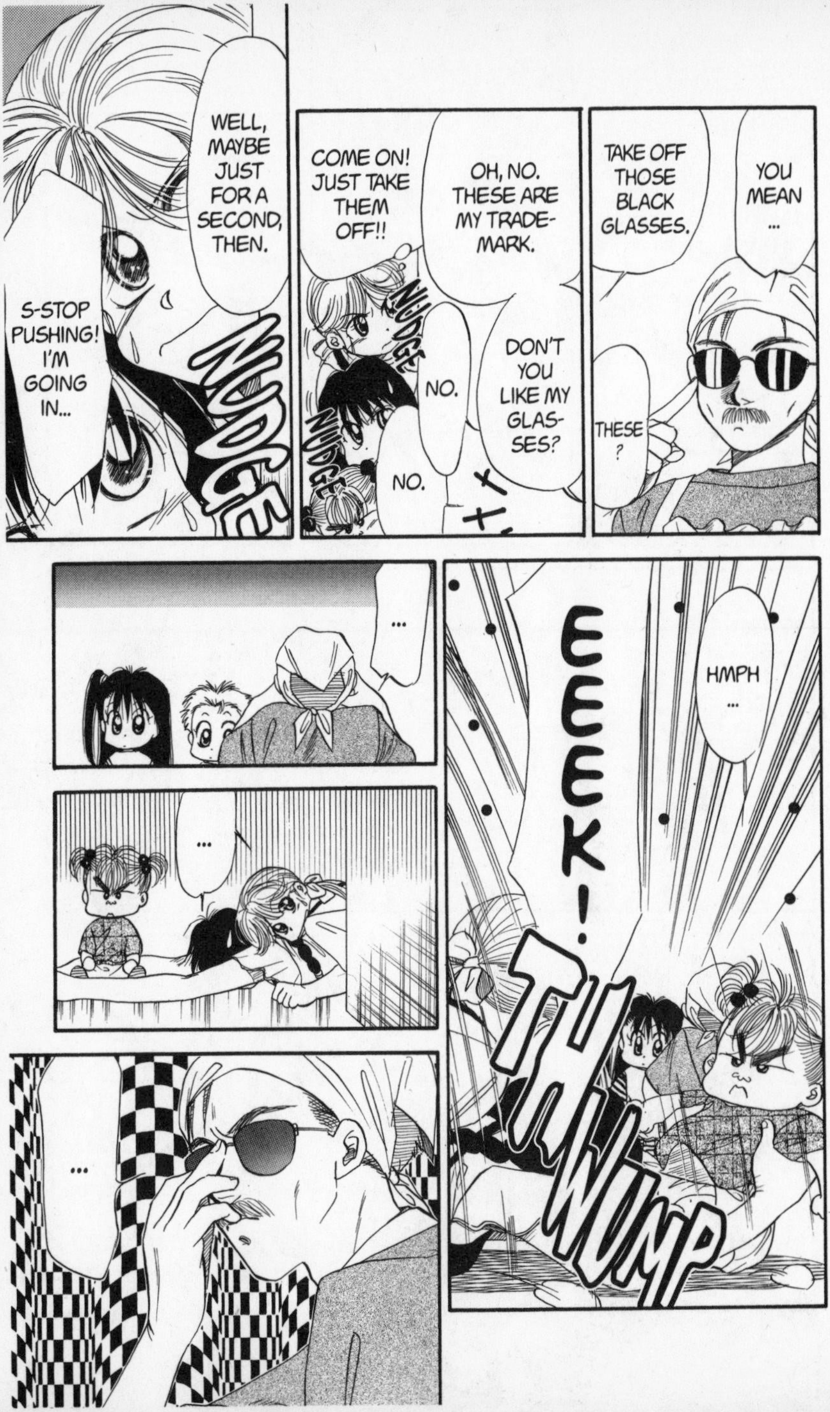
YOU MEAN ...
TAKE OFF THOSE BLACK GLASSES.
THESE ?
OH, NO. THESE ARE MY TRADE-MARK.
COME ON! JUST TAKE THEM OFF!!
NUDGE
DON'T YOU LIKE MY GLAS-SES?
NO.
NUDGE
NO.
WELL, MAYBE JUST FOR A SECOND, THEN.
NUDGE
S-STOP PUSHING! I'M GOING IN...
HMPH ...
EEEK!
THWUMP
...
...
...

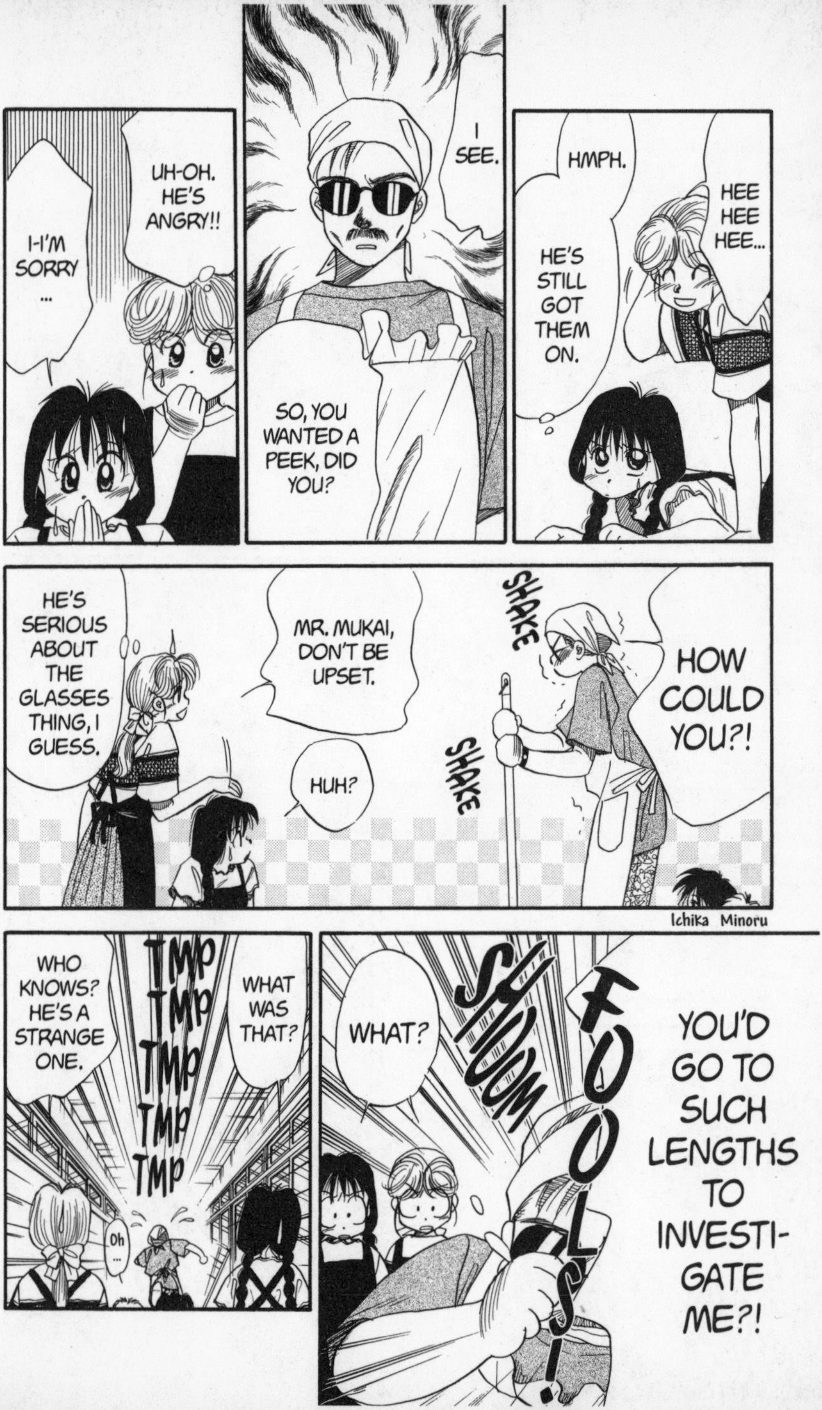
HMPH.
HEE HEE HEE...
HE'S STILL GOT THEM ON.
I SEE.
SO, YOU WANTED A PEEK, DID YOU?
UH-OH. HE'S ANGRY!!
I-I'M SORRY ...
HOW COULD YOU?!
SHAKE
SHAKE
MR. MUKAI, DON'T BE UPSET.
HUH?
HE'S SERIOUS ABOUT THE GLASSES THING, I GUESS.
Ichika Minoru
YOU'D GO TO SUCH LENGTHS TO INVESTI-GATE ME?!
FOOLS!
SHWOOM
WHAT?
WHAT WAS THAT?
TMP TMP TMP TMP TMP TMP
WHO KNOWS? HE'S A STRANGE ONE.
Oh ...

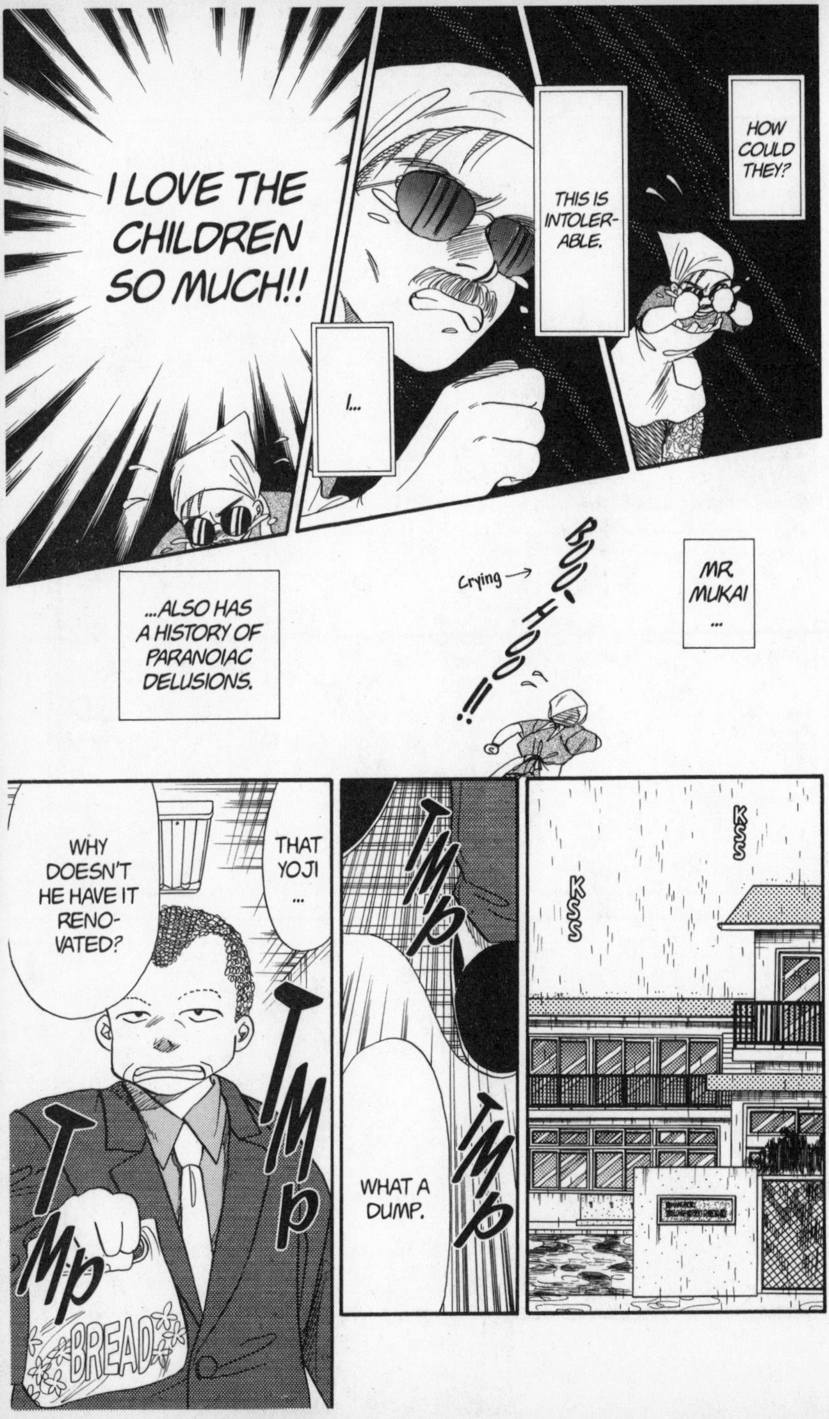
HOW COULD THEY?
THIS IS INTOLER-ABLE.
I...
I LOVE THE CHILDREN SO MUCH!!
MR. MUKAI ...
Crying →
BOO HOO!!
...ALSO HAS A HISTORY OF PARANOIAC DELUSIONS.
KSS
KSS
TMP
TMP
WHAT A DUMP.
THAT YOJI ...
WHY DOESN'T HE HAVE IT RENO-VATED?
TMP
TMP
BREAD

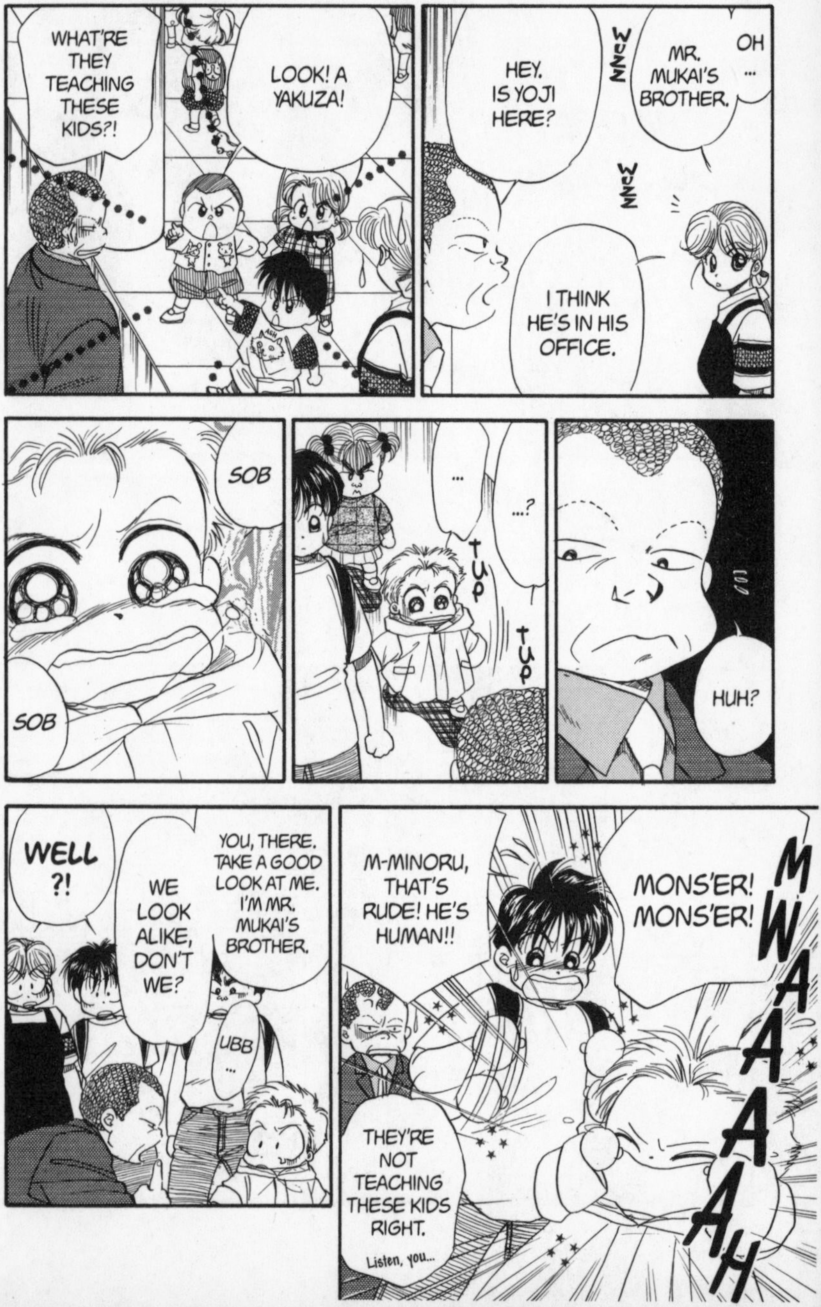
OH ...
MR. MUKAI'S BROTHER.
WUZZ
HEY. IS YOJI HERE?
WUZZ
I THINK HE'S IN HIS OFFICE.
LOOK! A YAKUZA!
WHAT'RE THEY TEACHING THESE KIDS?!
HUH?
...?
...
TUP
TUP
SOB
SOB
MONS'ER! MONS'ER!
MWAAAAAH
M-MINORU, THAT'S RUDE! HE'S HUMAN!!
THEY'RE NOT TEACHING THESE KIDS RIGHT.
Listen, you...
YOU, THERE. TAKE A GOOD LOOK AT ME. I'M MR. MUKAI'S BROTHER.
WE LOOK ALIKE, DON'T WE?
WELL?!
UBB ...

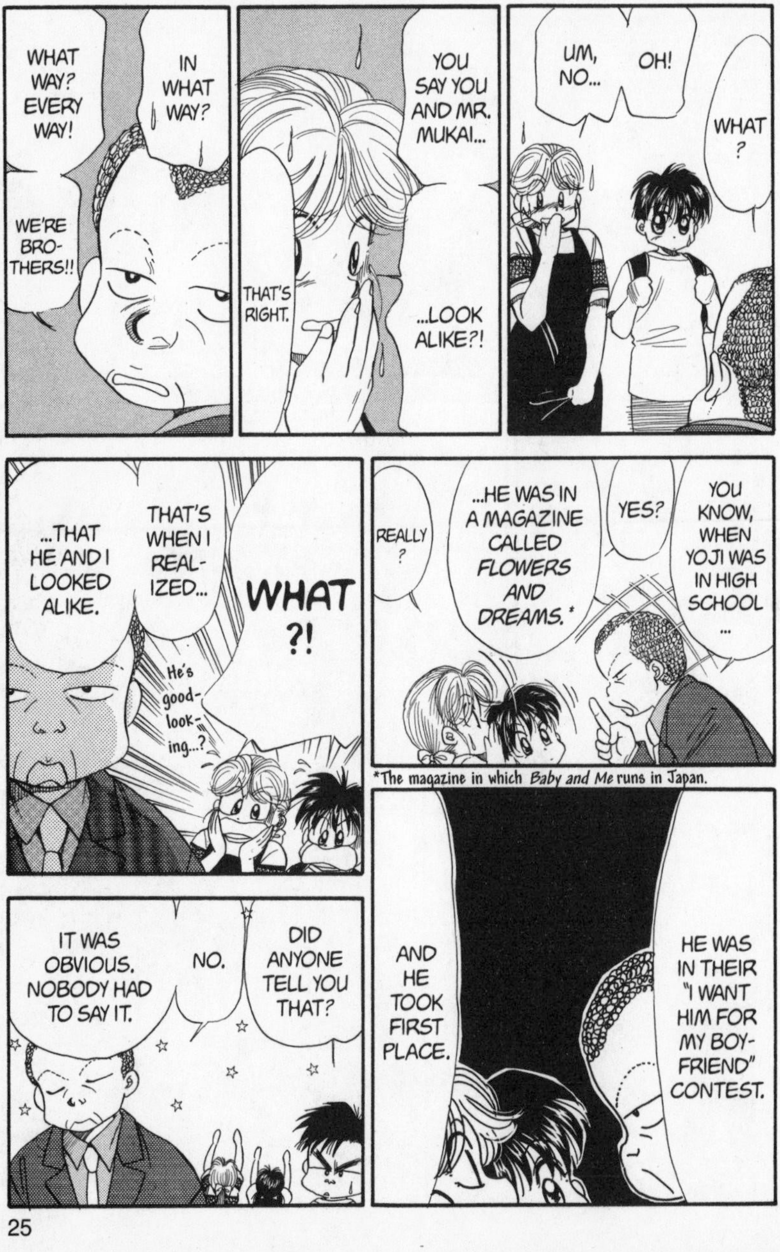
UM, NO...
OH!
WHAT?
YOU SAY YOU AND MR. MUKAI...
THAT'S RIGHT.
...LOOK ALIKE?!
IN WHAT WAY?
WHAT WAY? EVERY WAY!
WE'RE BRO-THERS!!
YOU KNOW, WHEN YOJI WAS IN HIGH SCHOOL...
YES?
...HE WAS IN A MAGAZINE CALLED *FLOWERS AND DREAMS.**
REALLY?
HE WAS IN THEIR "I WANT HIM FOR MY BOY-FRIEND" CONTEST.
AND HE TOOK FIRST PLACE.
WHAT?!
THAT'S WHEN I REAL-IZED...
...THAT HE AND I LOOKED ALIKE.
He's good-look-ing...?
DID ANYONE TELL YOU THAT?
NO.
IT WAS OBVIOUS. NOBODY HAD TO SAY IT.

*The magazine in which *Baby and Me* runs in Japan.

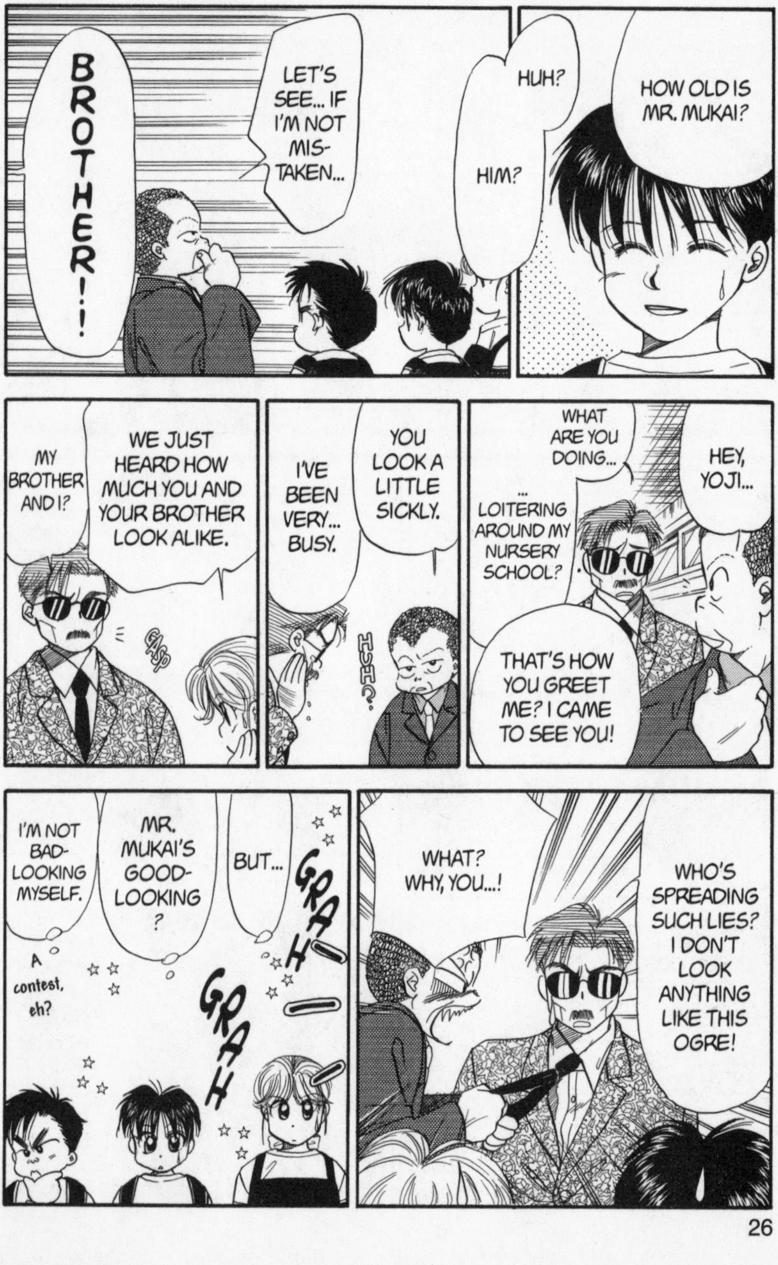
HOW OLD IS MR. MUKAI?
HUH?
HIM?
LET'S SEE... IF I'M NOT MIS-TAKEN...
BROTHER!!
HEY, YOJI...
WHAT ARE YOU DOING...
... LOITERING AROUND MY NURSERY SCHOOL?
THAT'S HOW YOU GREET ME? I CAME TO SEE YOU!
YOU LOOK A LITTLE SICKLY.
I'VE BEEN VERY... BUSY.
HUH?
WE JUST HEARD HOW MUCH YOU AND YOUR BROTHER LOOK ALIKE.
MY BROTHER AND I?
GASP
WHO'S SPREADING SUCH LIES? I DON'T LOOK ANYTHING LIKE THIS OGRE!
WHAT? WHY, YOU...!
GRAH
GRAH
BUT...
MR. MUKAI'S GOOD-LOOKING?
I'M NOT BAD-LOOKING MYSELF.
A contest, eh?

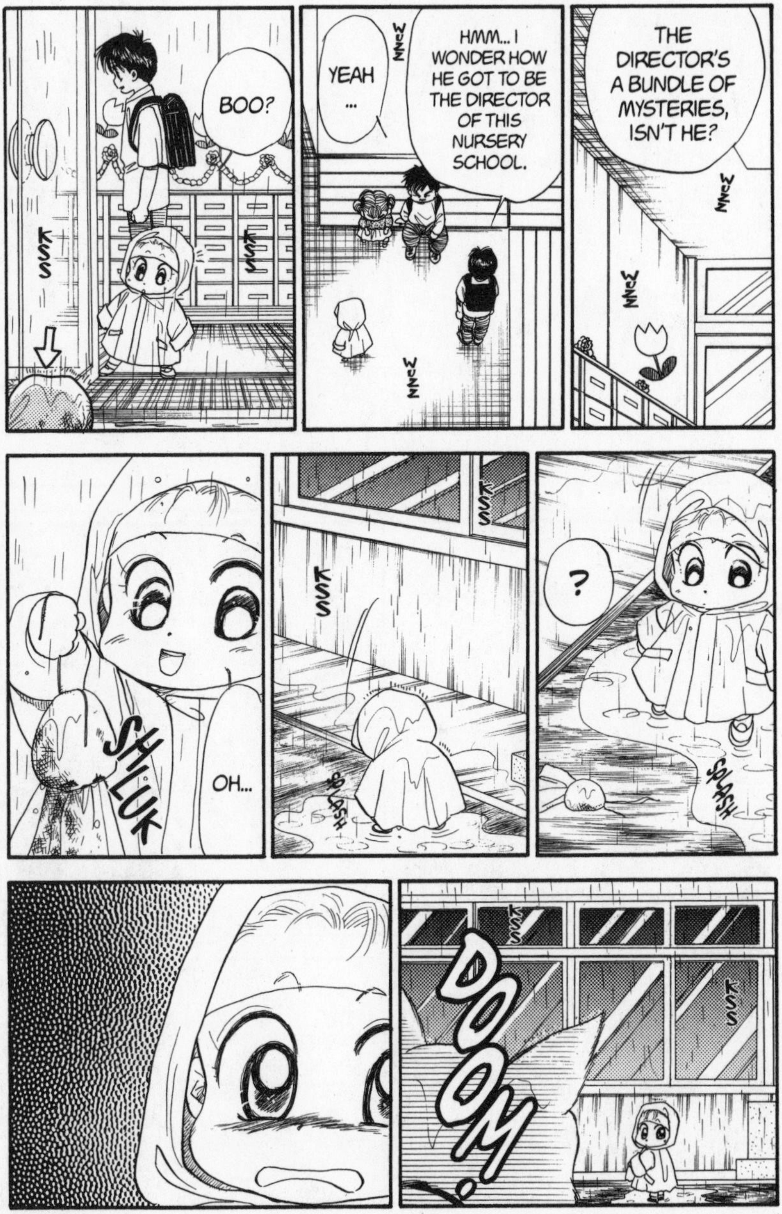
THE DIRECTOR'S A BUNDLE OF MYSTERIES, ISN'T HE?
WUZZ
WUZZ
HMM... I WONDER HOW HE GOT TO BE THE DIRECTOR OF THIS NURSERY SCHOOL.
WUZZ
YEAH ...
WUZZ
BOO?
KSS
KSS
?
SPLASH
KSS
KSS
SPLASH
SHLUK
OH...
KSS
KSS
DOOM!

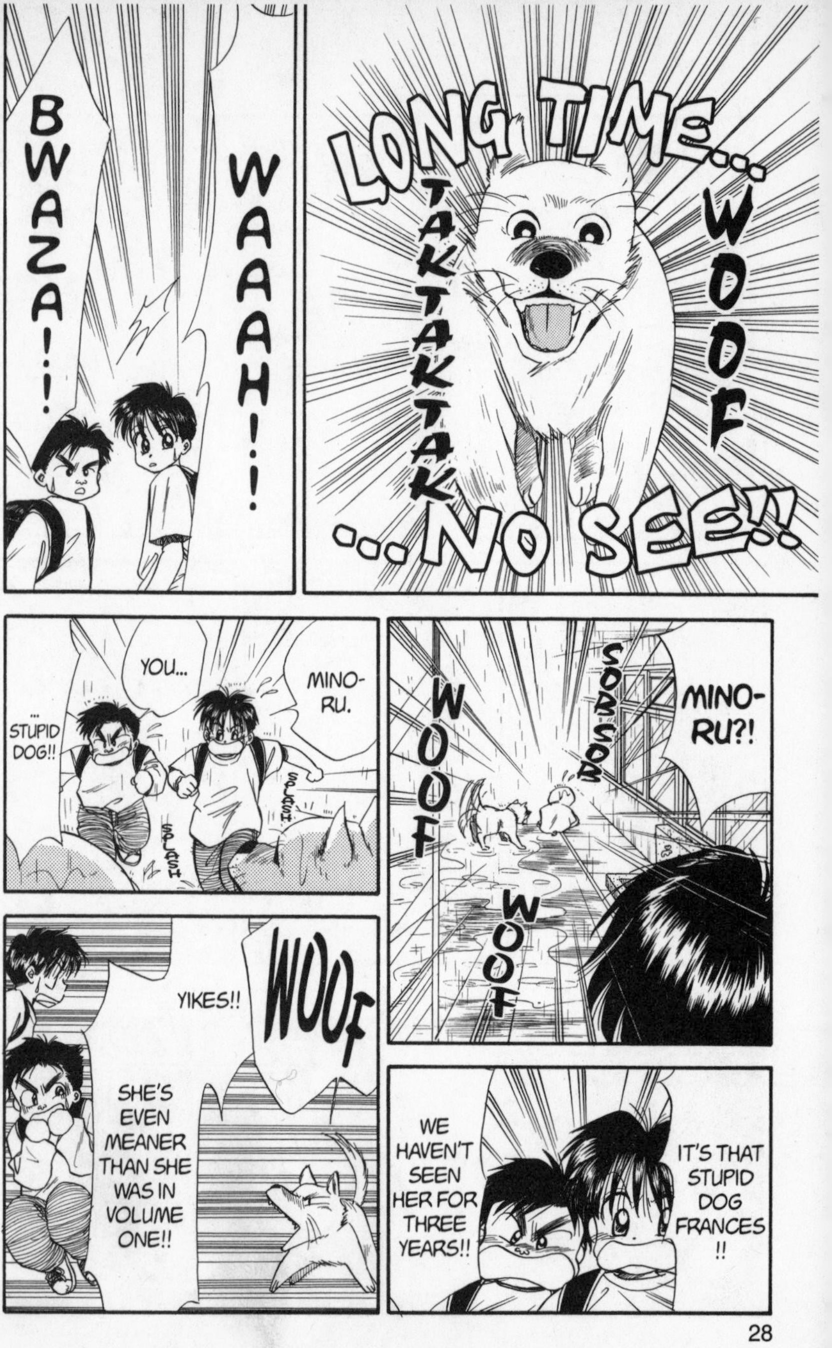
LONG TIME...
TAKTAKTAK
WOOF
...NO SEE!!
WAAAH!!
BWAZA!!
MINO-RU?!
SOBSOB
WOOF
WOOF
MINO-RU.
YOU...
...STUPID DOG!!
SPLASH
SPLASH
IT'S THAT STUPID DOG FRANCES!!
WE HAVEN'T SEEN HER FOR THREE YEARS!!
WOOF
YIKES!!
SHE'S EVEN MEANER THAN SHE WAS IN VOLUME ONE!!

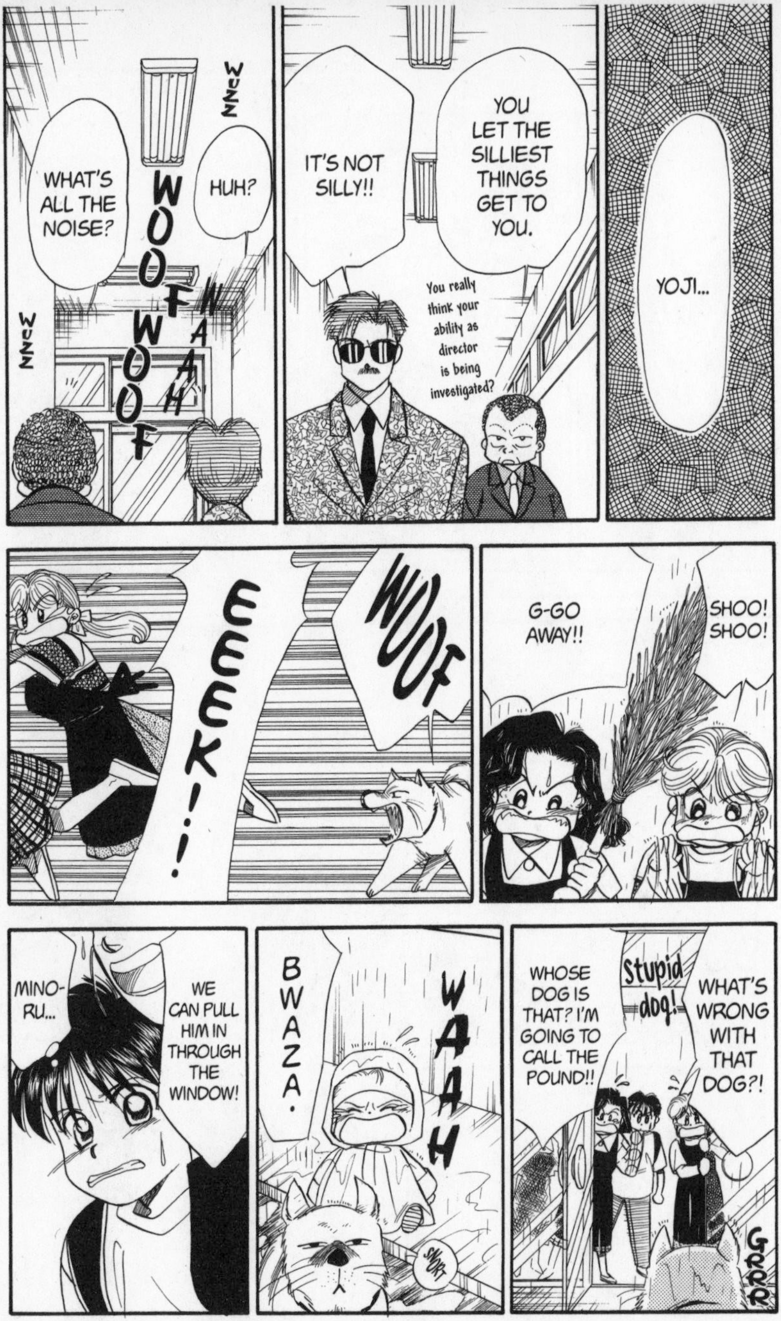
YOJI...
YOU LET THE SILLIEST THINGS GET TO YOU.
IT'S NOT SILLY!!
You really think your ability as director is being investigated?
WUZZ
HUH?
WAAH
WOOF WOOF WOOF
WHAT'S ALL THE NOISE?
WUZZ
SHOO! SHOO!
G-GO AWAY!!
WOOF
EEEEK!!
WHAT'S WRONG WITH THAT DOG?!
Stupid dog!
WHOSE DOG IS THAT? I'M GOING TO CALL THE POUND!!
GRRR
WAAAH
BWAZA.
SNORT
WE CAN PULL HIM IN THROUGH THE WINDOW!
MINO-RU...

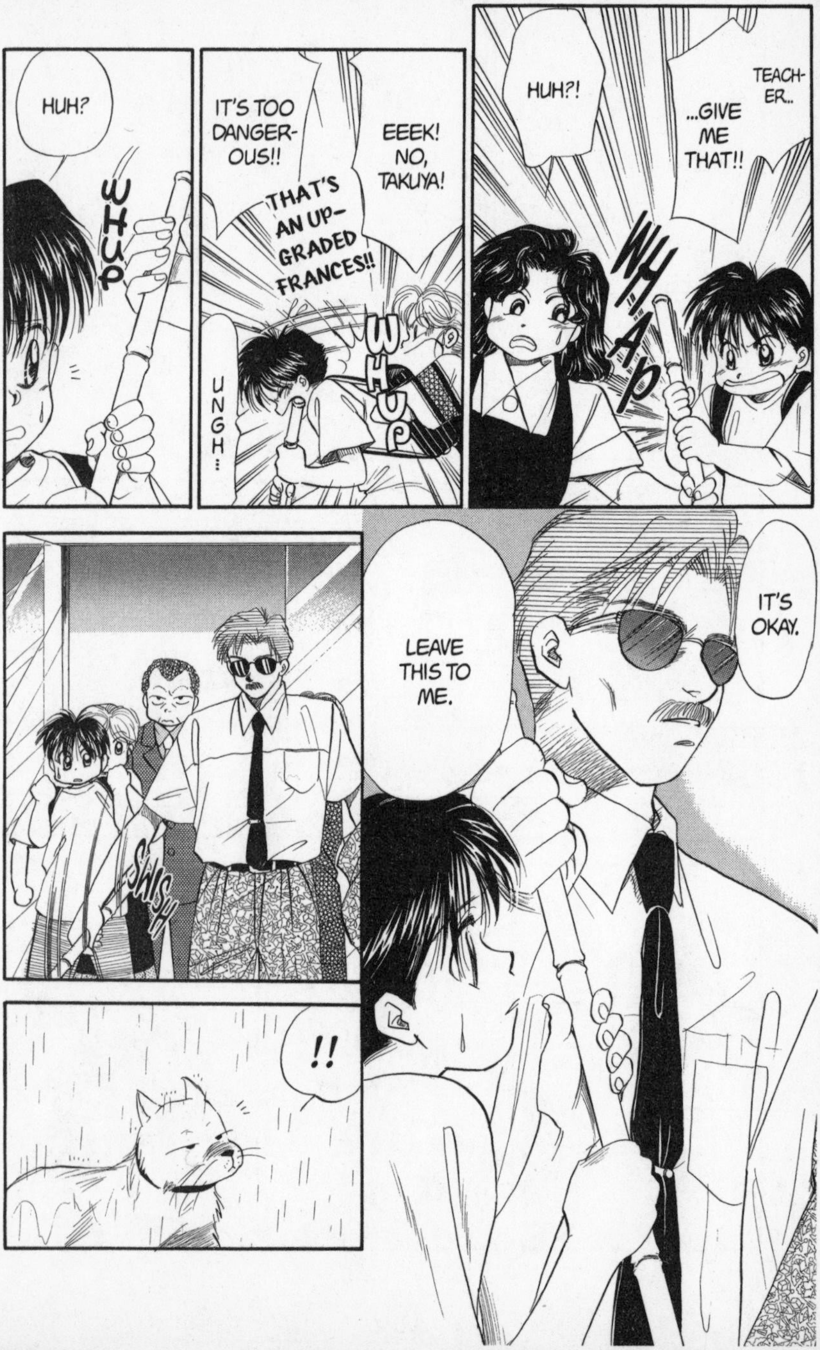
TEACHER..
...GIVE ME THAT!!
HUH?!
WHAP
EEEK! NO, TAKUYA!
IT'S TOO DANGEROUS!!
THAT'S AN UPGRADED FRANCES!!
WHUP
UNGH...
HUH?
WHUP
IT'S OKAY.
LEAVE THIS TO ME.
SWISH
!!

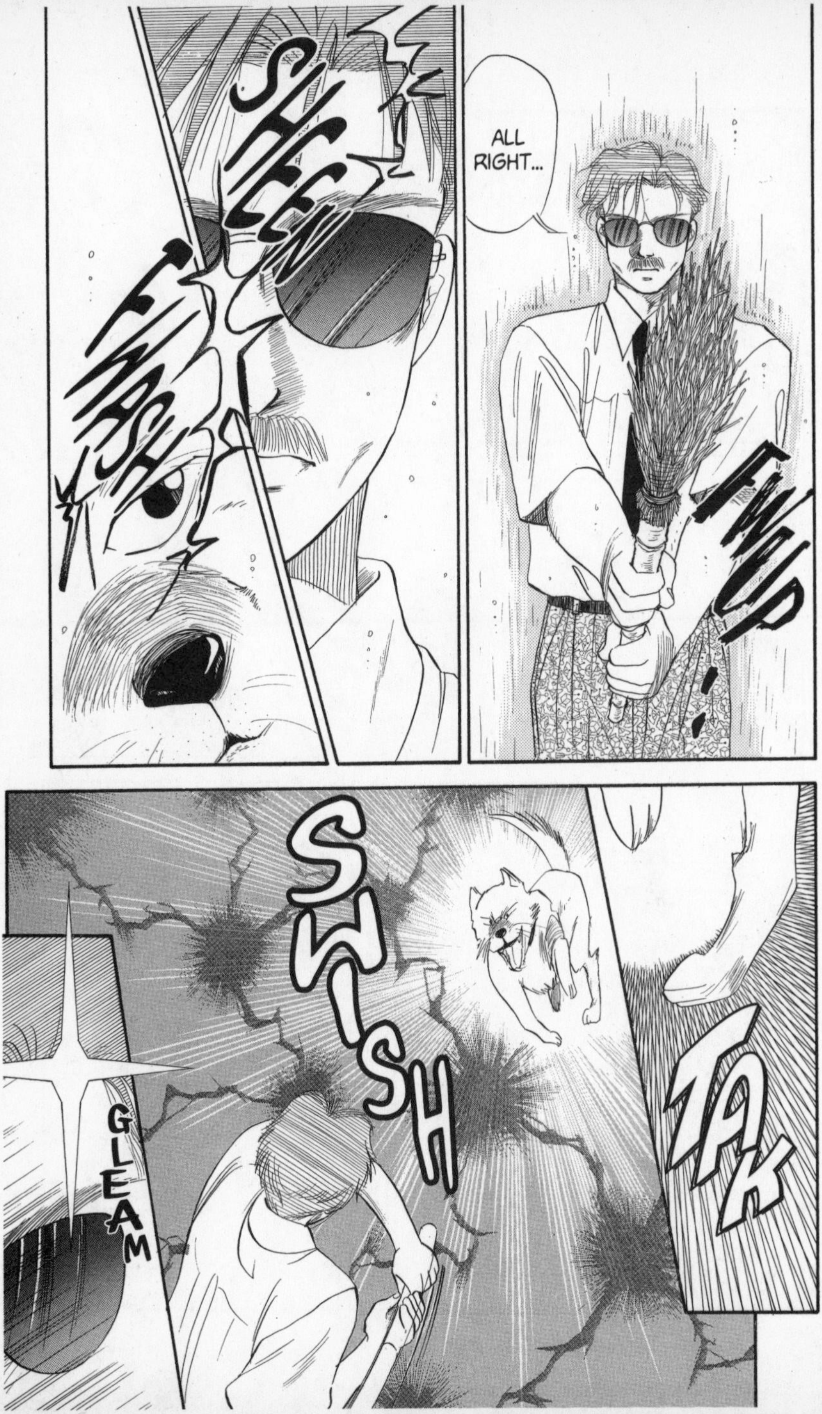
ALL RIGHT...
FWUP
SHEEN
FWASH
TAK
SWISH
GLEAM

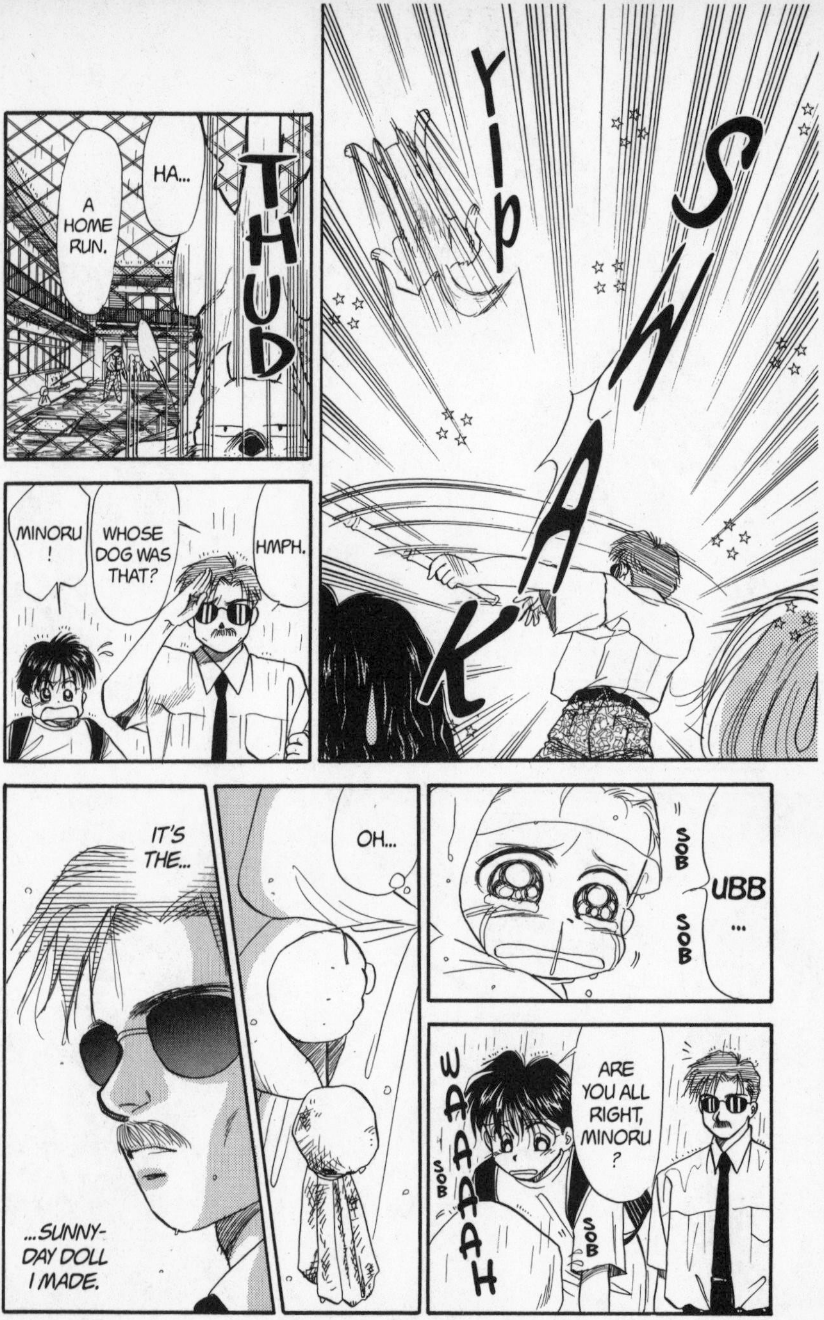
SWAK
Yip
THUD
HA...
A HOME RUN.
HMPH.
WHOSE DOG WAS THAT?
MINORU!
UBB...
SOB SOB
ARE YOU ALL RIGHT, MINORU?
WAAAAH
SOB
SOB
OH...
IT'S THE...
...SUNNY-DAY DOLL I MADE.

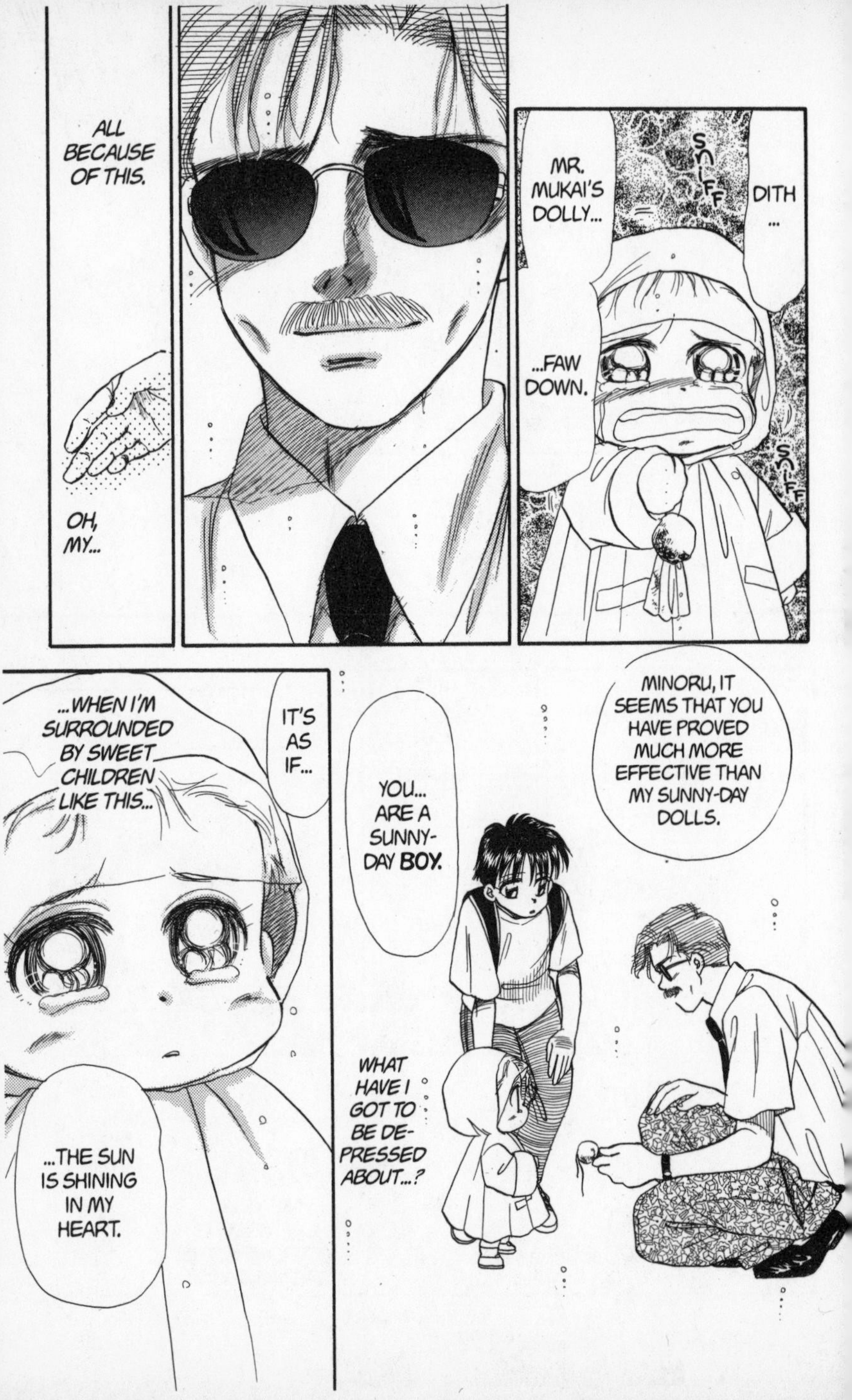
DITH ...
SNIFF
MR. MUKAI'S DOLLY...
...FAW DOWN.
SNIFF
ALL BECAUSE OF THIS.
OH, MY...
MINORU, IT SEEMS THAT YOU HAVE PROVED MUCH MORE EFFECTIVE THAN MY SUNNY-DAY DOLLS.
YOU... ARE A SUNNY-DAY BOY.
WHAT HAVE I GOT TO BE DE-PRESSED ABOUT...?
IT'S AS IF...
...WHEN I'M SURROUNDED BY SWEET CHILDREN LIKE THIS...
...THE SUN IS SHINING IN MY HEART.

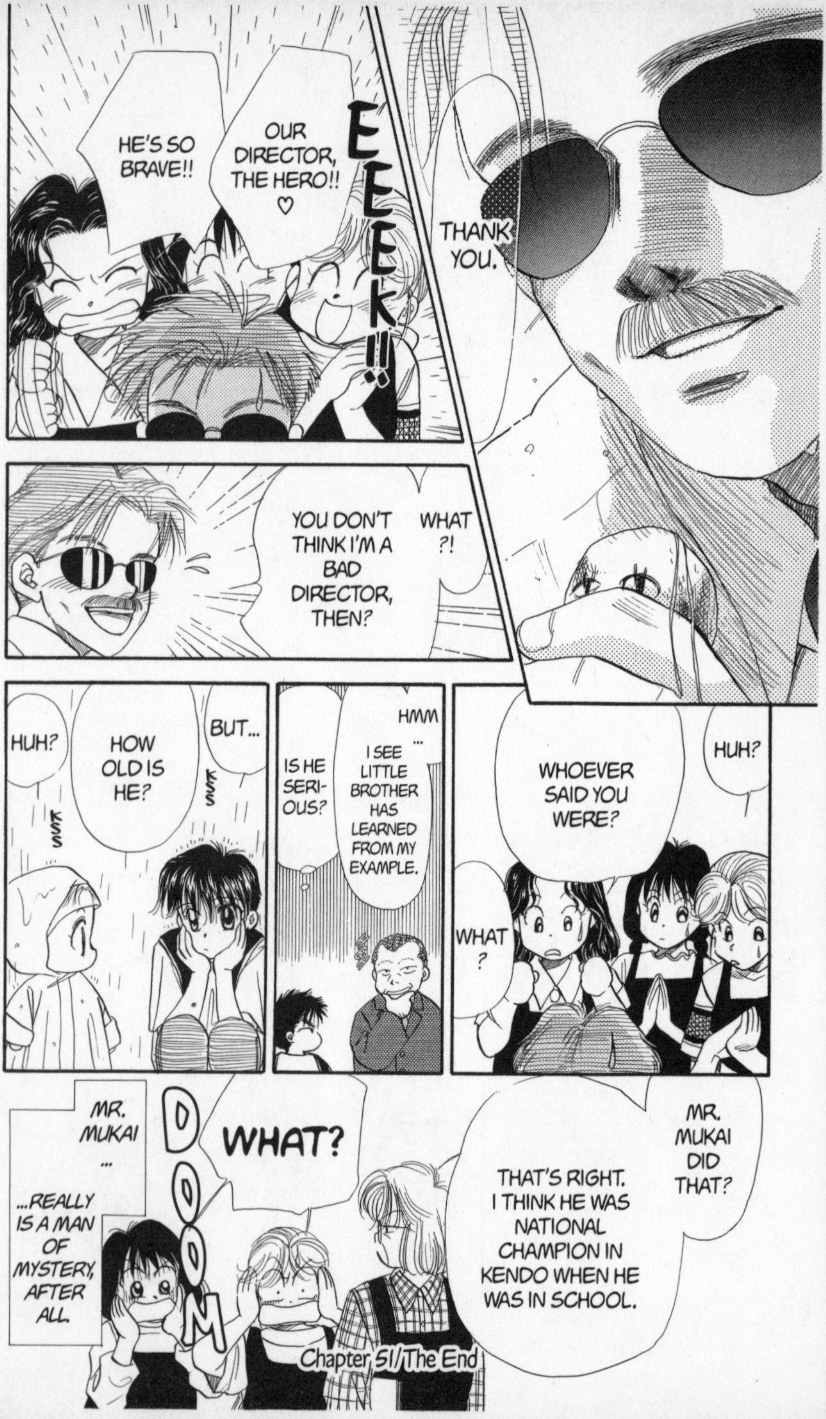
THANK YOU.
EEEK!!
OUR DIRECTOR, THE HERO!! ♡
HE'S SO BRAVE!!
WHAT ?!
YOU DON'T THINK I'M A BAD DIRECTOR, THEN?
HUH?
WHOEVER SAID YOU WERE?
WHAT ?
HMM ...
I SEE LITTLE BROTHER HAS LEARNED FROM MY EXAMPLE.
IS HE SERIOUS?
BUT...
KSS
HOW OLD IS HE?
HUH?
KSS
MR. MUKAI DID THAT?
THAT'S RIGHT. I THINK HE WAS NATIONAL CHAMPION IN KENDO WHEN HE WAS IN SCHOOL.
WHAT?
DOOOM
MR. MUKAI ...
...REALLY IS A MAN OF MYSTERY, AFTER ALL.
Chapter 51/The End

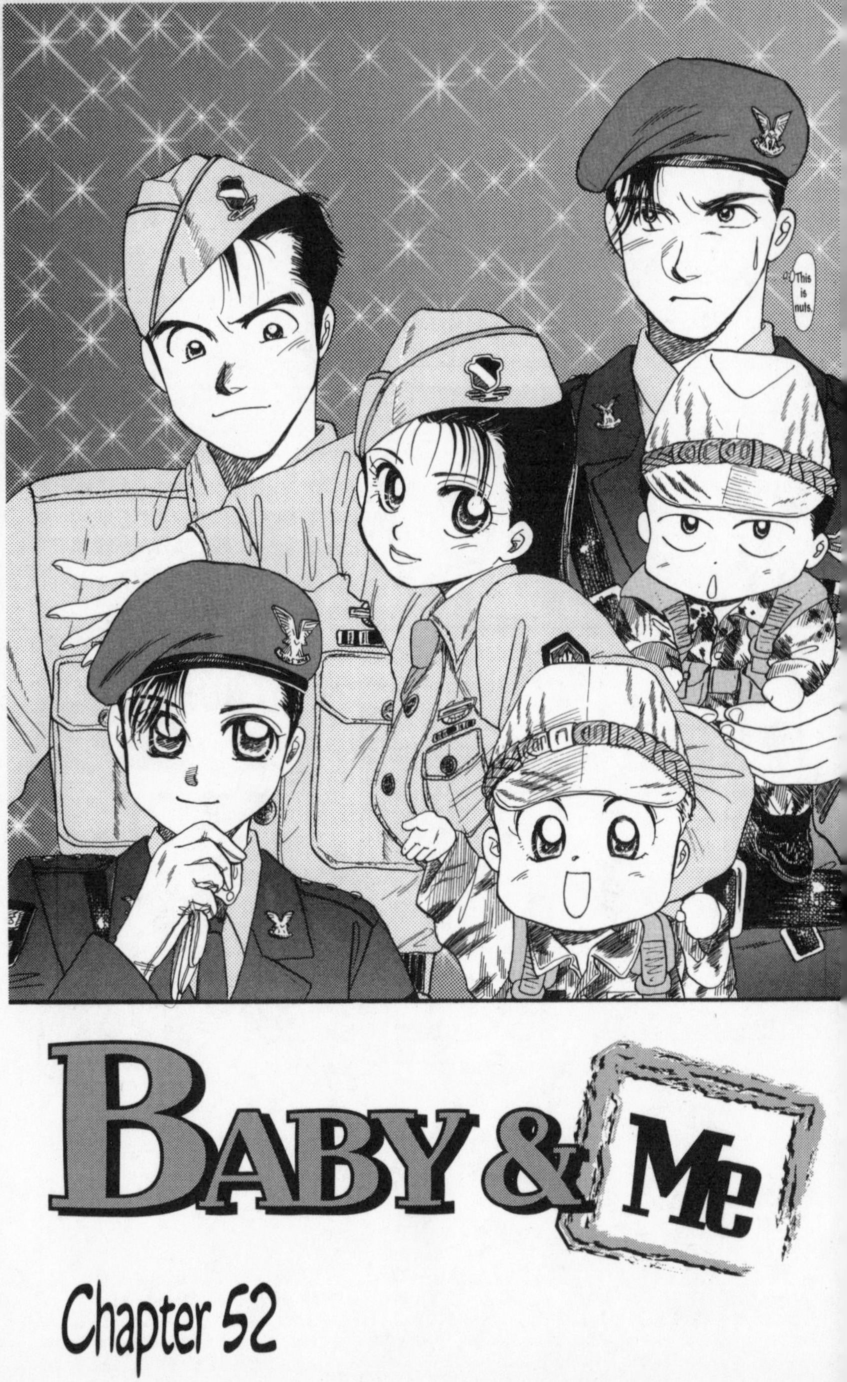
This is nuts.

Baby & Me

Chapter 52

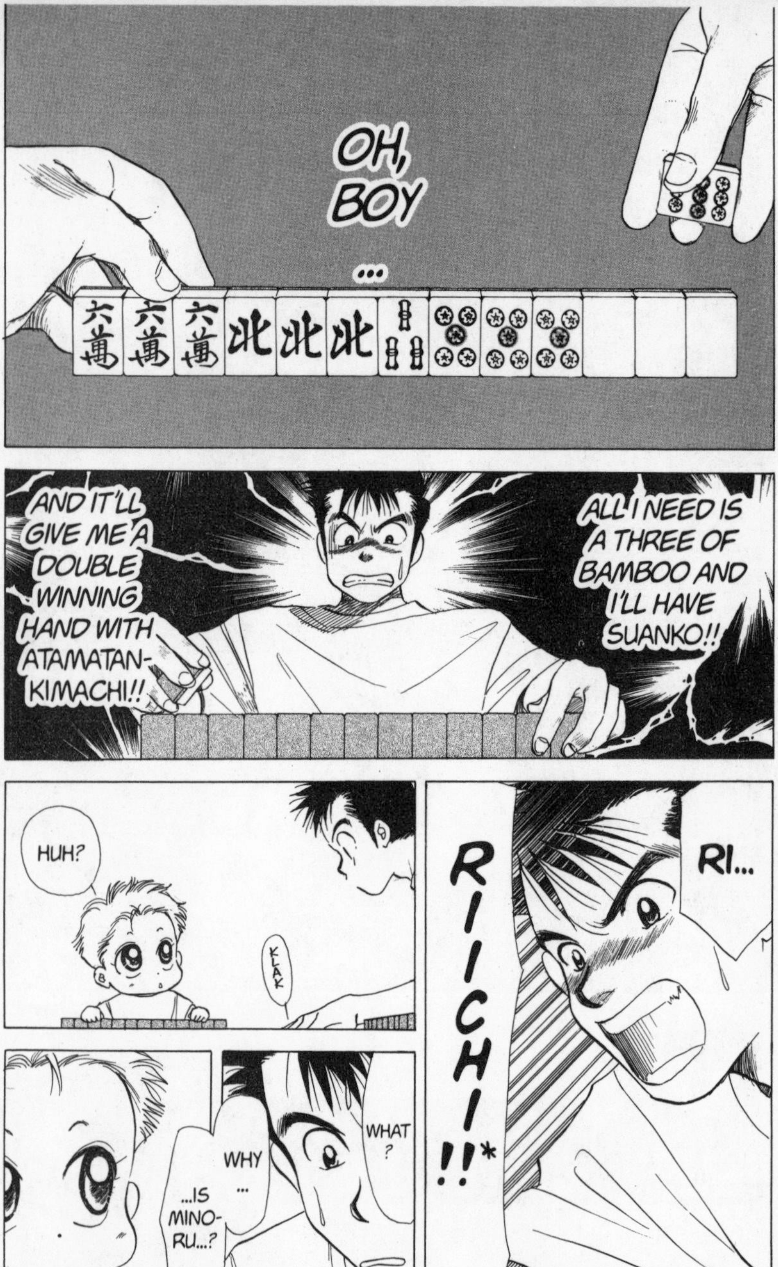
OH, BOY ...
ALL I NEED IS A THREE OF BAMBOO AND I'LL HAVE SUANKO!!
AND IT'LL GIVE ME A DOUBLE WINNING HAND WITH ATAMATAN-KIMACHI!!
RI...
RIICHI!!*
KLAK
HUH?
WHAT?
WHY...
...IS MINO-RU...?

*When you have a hand like this, it's better not to call *riichi*, but Seiichi is too excited.

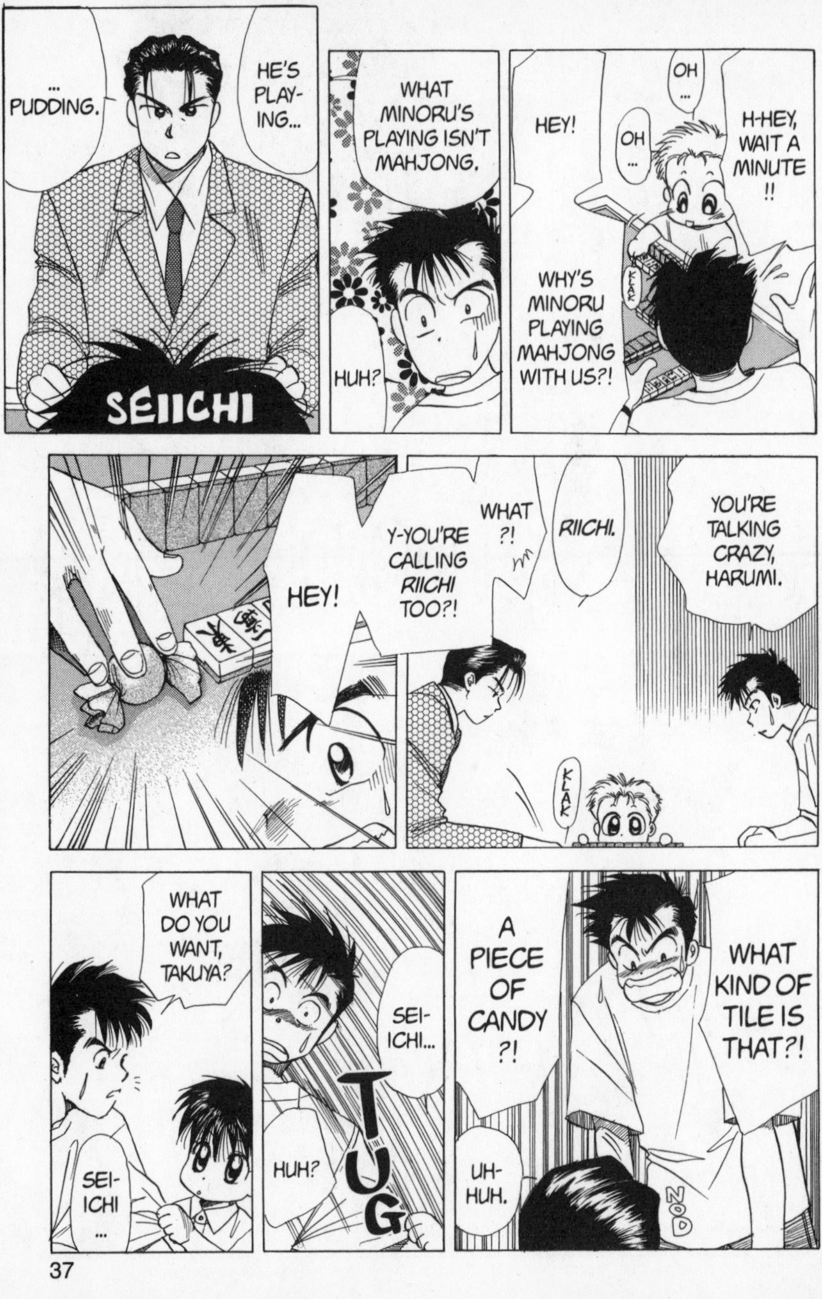
H-HEY, WAIT A MINUTE !!
OH ...
OH ...
HEY!
WHY'S MINORU PLAYING MAHJONG WITH US?!
KLAK
WHAT MINORU'S PLAYING ISN'T MAHJONG.
HUH?
HE'S PLAY-ING...
... PUDDING.
SEIICHI
YOU'RE TALKING CRAZY, HARUMI.
RIICHI.
WHAT ?!
KLAK
Y-YOU'RE CALLING RIICHI TOO?!
HEY!
WHAT KIND OF TILE IS THAT?!
A PIECE OF CANDY ?!
UH-HUH.
NOD
SEI-ICHI...
HUH?
TUG
WHAT DO YOU WANT, TAKUYA?
SEI-ICHI ...

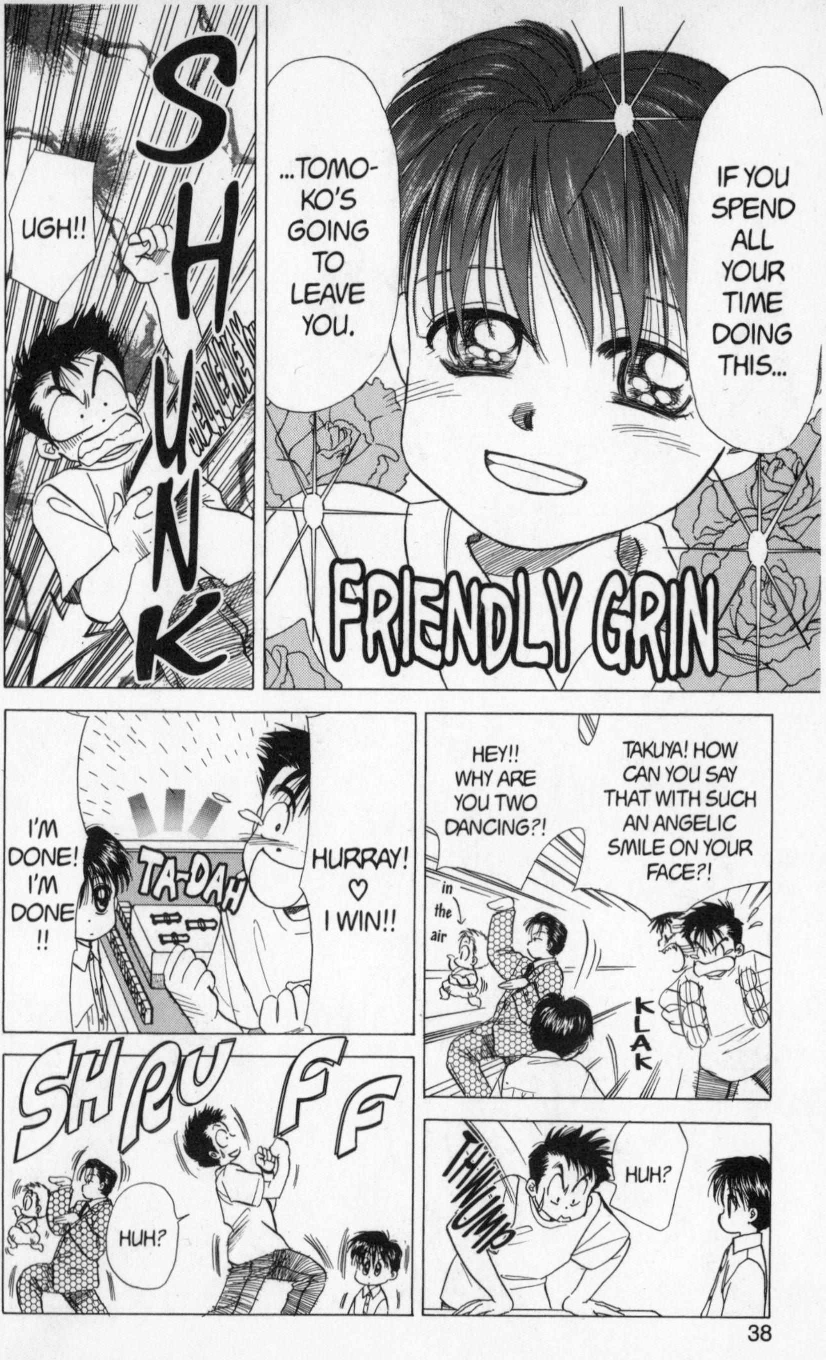
IF YOU SPEND ALL YOUR TIME DOING THIS...
...TOMO-KO'S GOING TO LEAVE YOU.
FRIENDLY GRIN
SHUNK
UGH!!
TAKUYA! HOW CAN YOU SAY THAT WITH SUCH AN ANGELIC SMILE ON YOUR FACE?!
HEY!! WHY ARE YOU TWO DANCING?!
in the air
KLAK
HURRAY! ♡ I WIN!!
TA-DAH
I'M DONE! I'M DONE!!
THWUMP
HUH?
SHRUFF
HUH?

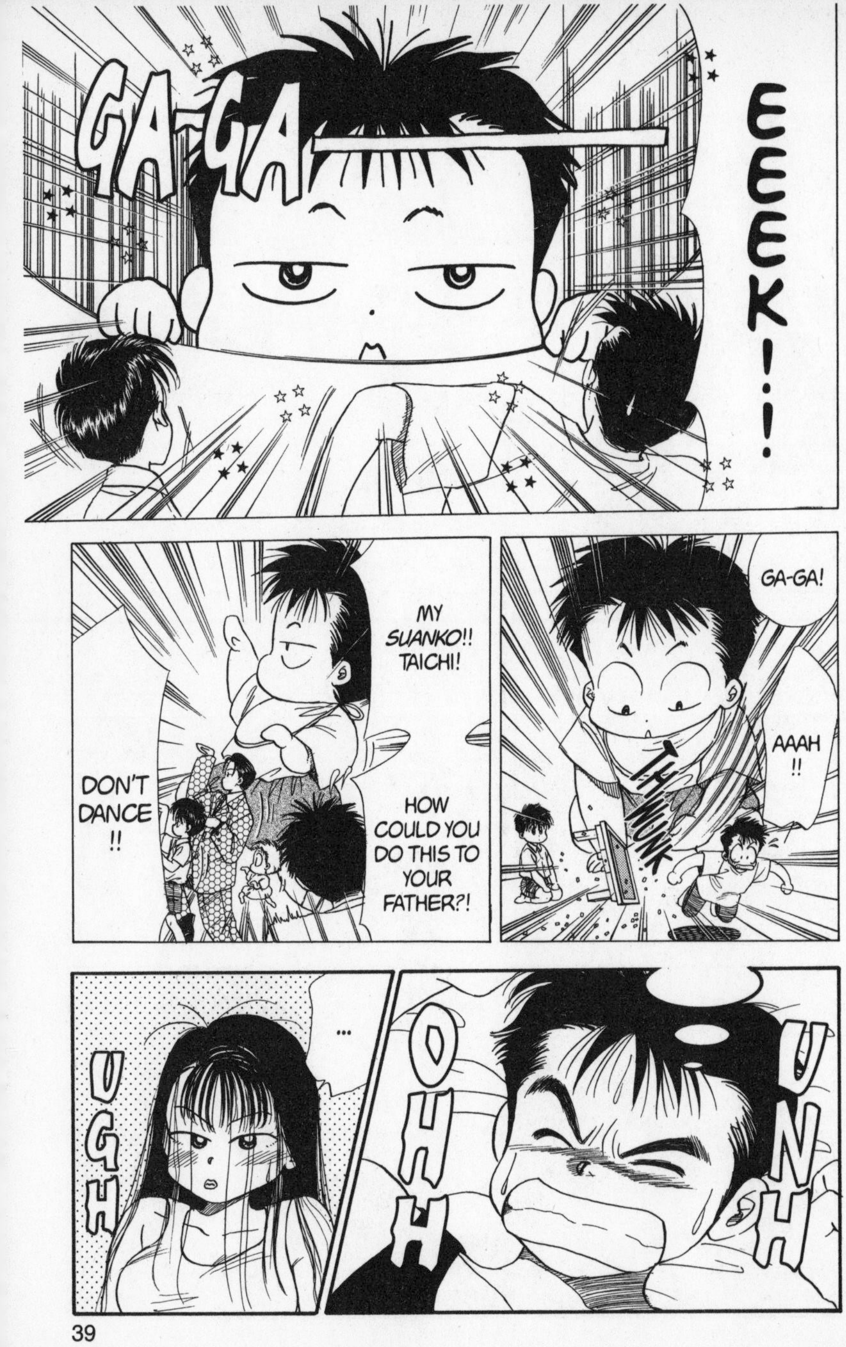
EEEK!!
GA-GA
GA-GA!
AAAH!!
THUNK
MY SUANKO!! TAICHI!
HOW COULD YOU DO THIS TO YOUR FATHER?!
DON'T DANCE!!
UNH
OHHH
...
UGH

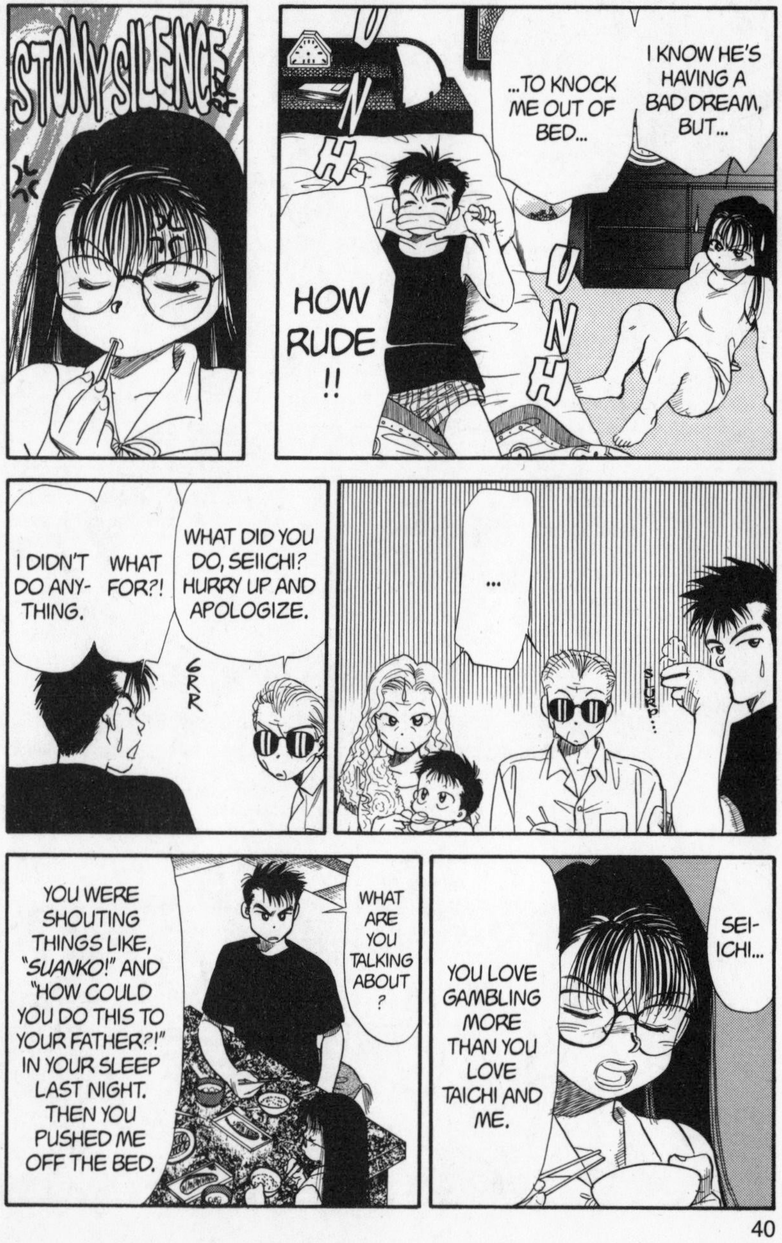
UNH
I KNOW HE'S HAVING A BAD DREAM, BUT...
...TO KNOCK ME OUT OF BED...
UNH
HOW RUDE !!
STONY SILENCE
...
SLURP...
WHAT DID YOU DO, SEIICHI? HURRY UP AND APOLOGIZE.
GRR
WHAT FOR?!
I DIDN'T DO ANY-THING.
SEI-ICHI...
YOU LOVE GAMBLING MORE THAN YOU LOVE TAICHI AND ME.
WHAT ARE YOU TALKING ABOUT ?
YOU WERE SHOUTING THINGS LIKE, "SUANKO!" AND "HOW COULD YOU DO THIS TO YOUR FATHER?!" IN YOUR SLEEP LAST NIGHT. THEN YOU PUSHED ME OFF THE BED.

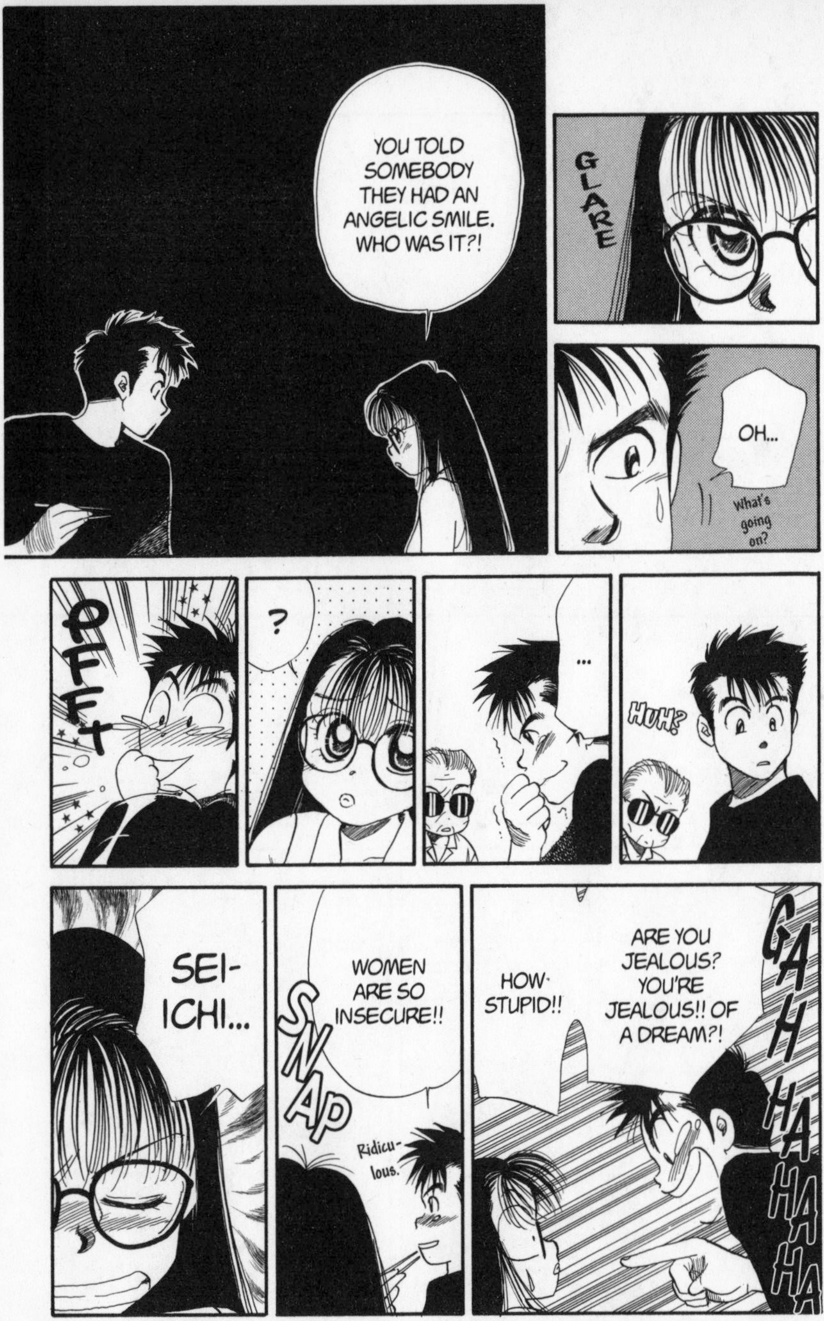
GLARE
OH...
What's going on?
YOU TOLD SOMEBODY THEY HAD AN ANGELIC SMILE. WHO WAS IT?!
HUH?
...
?
PFFFT
GAHAHAHAHA
ARE YOU JEALOUS? YOU'RE JEALOUS!! OF A DREAM?!
HOW· STUPID!!
WOMEN ARE SO INSECURE!!
SNAP
Ridicu-lous.
SEI-ICHI...

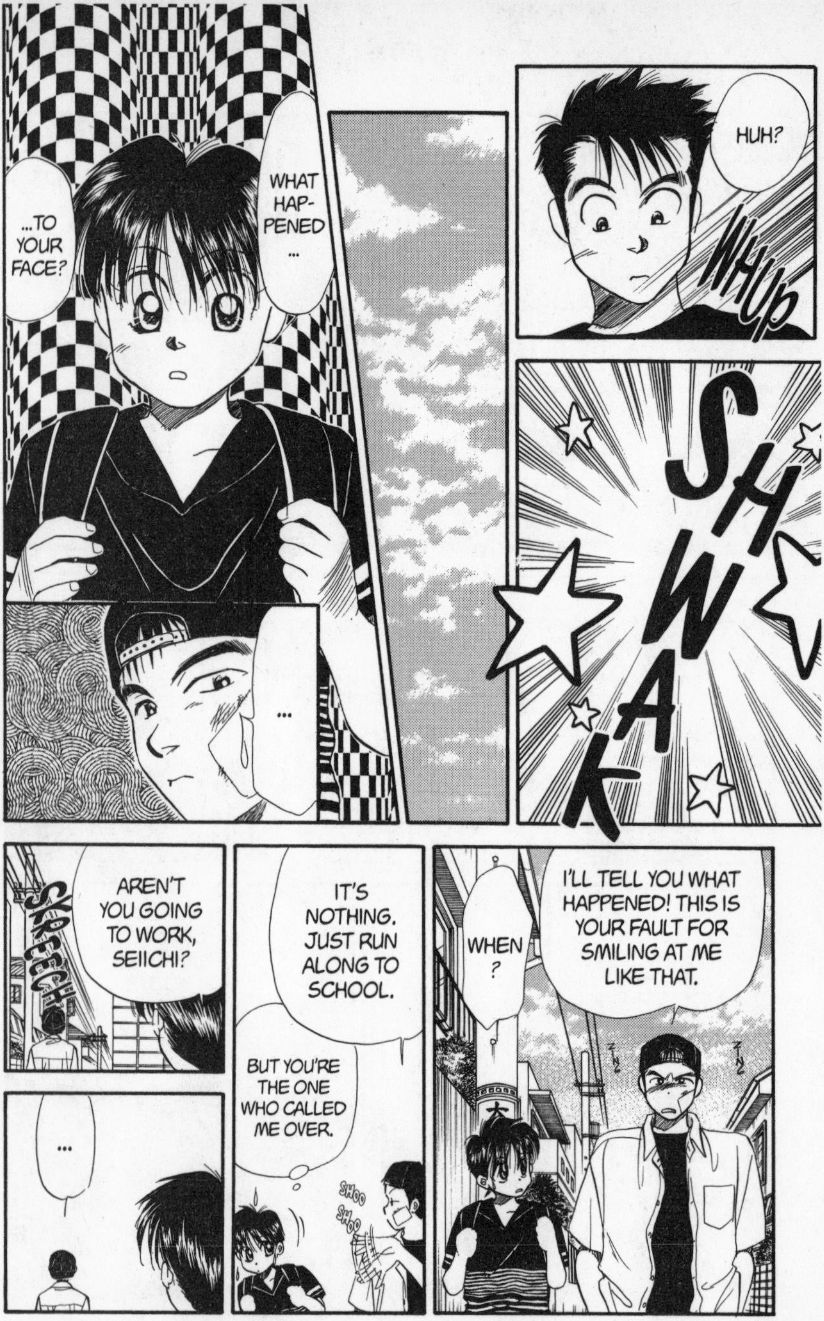
HUH?
WHUP
SHWAK
WHAT HAPPENED...
...TO YOUR FACE?
...
I'LL TELL YOU WHAT HAPPENED! THIS IS YOUR FAULT FOR SMILING AT ME LIKE THAT.
WHEN?
IT'S NOTHING. JUST RUN ALONG TO SCHOOL.
BUT YOU'RE THE ONE WHO CALLED ME OVER.
SHOO SHOO
AREN'T YOU GOING TO WORK, SEIICHI?
SKREECH
...

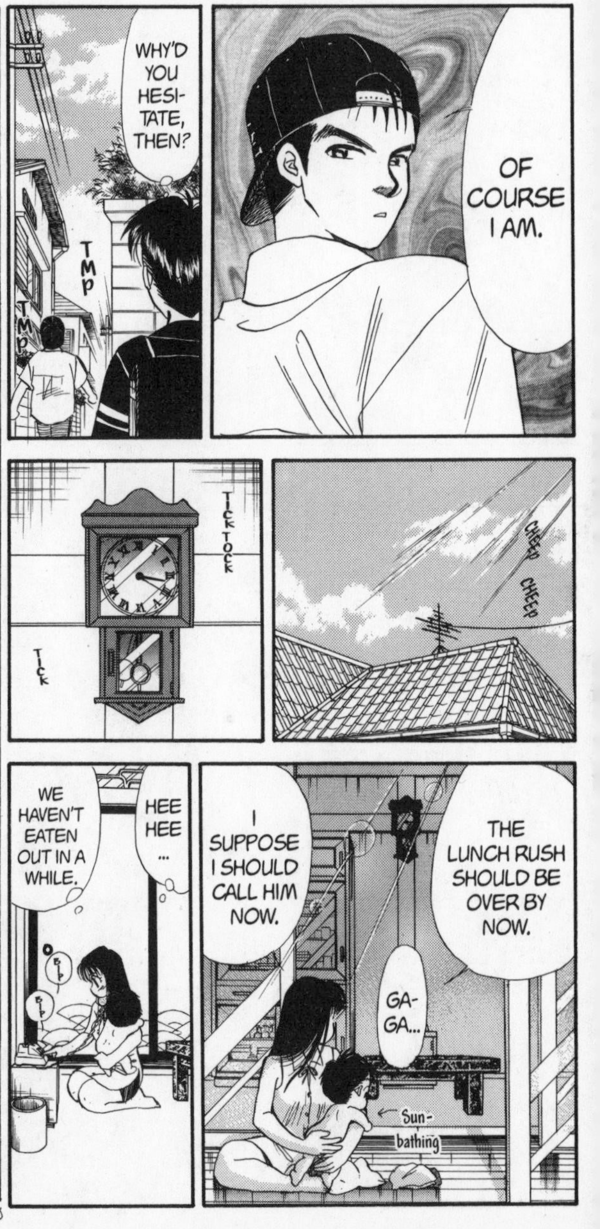
OF COURSE I AM.
WHY'D YOU HESI-TATE, THEN?
TMP
TMP
CHEEP
CHEEP
TICK TOCK
TICK
THE LUNCH RUSH SHOULD BE OVER BY NOW.
I SUPPOSE I SHOULD CALL HIM NOW.
GA-GA...
Sun-bathing
HEE HEE ...
WE HAVEN'T EATEN OUT IN A WHILE.
BLIP
BLIP

Author's Note: Part 2

In December of 1994, I went back to visit my parents. When I lived at home, we had a tomcat named Chihaya, but he disappeared.

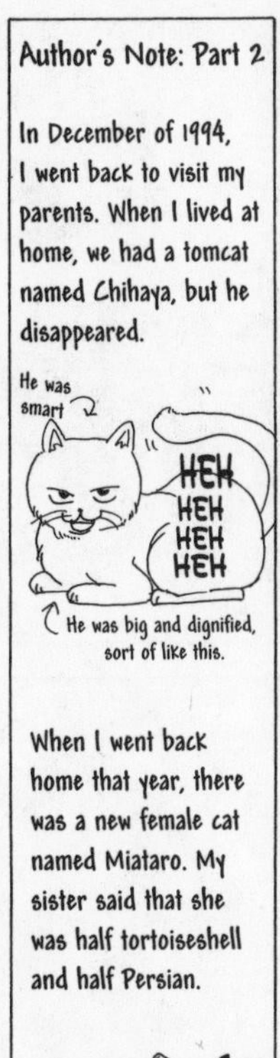
He was smart
HEH HEH HEH HEH

He was big and dignified, sort of like this.

When I went back home that year, there was a new female cat named Miataro. My sister said that she was half tortoiseshell and half Persian.

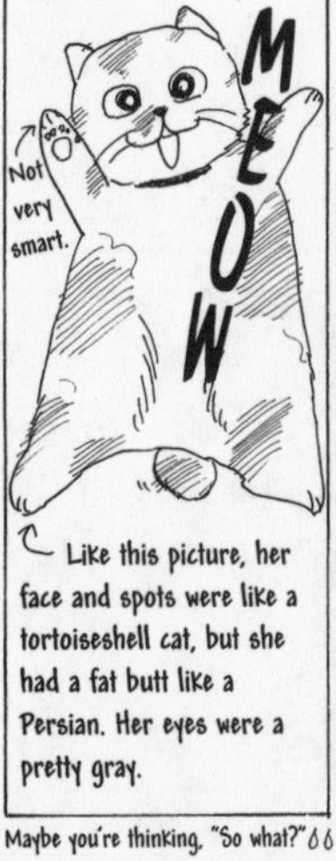
Not very smart.
MEOW

Like this picture, her face and spots were like a tortoiseshell cat, but she had a fat butt like a Persian. Her eyes were a pretty gray.

Maybe you're thinking, "So what?"

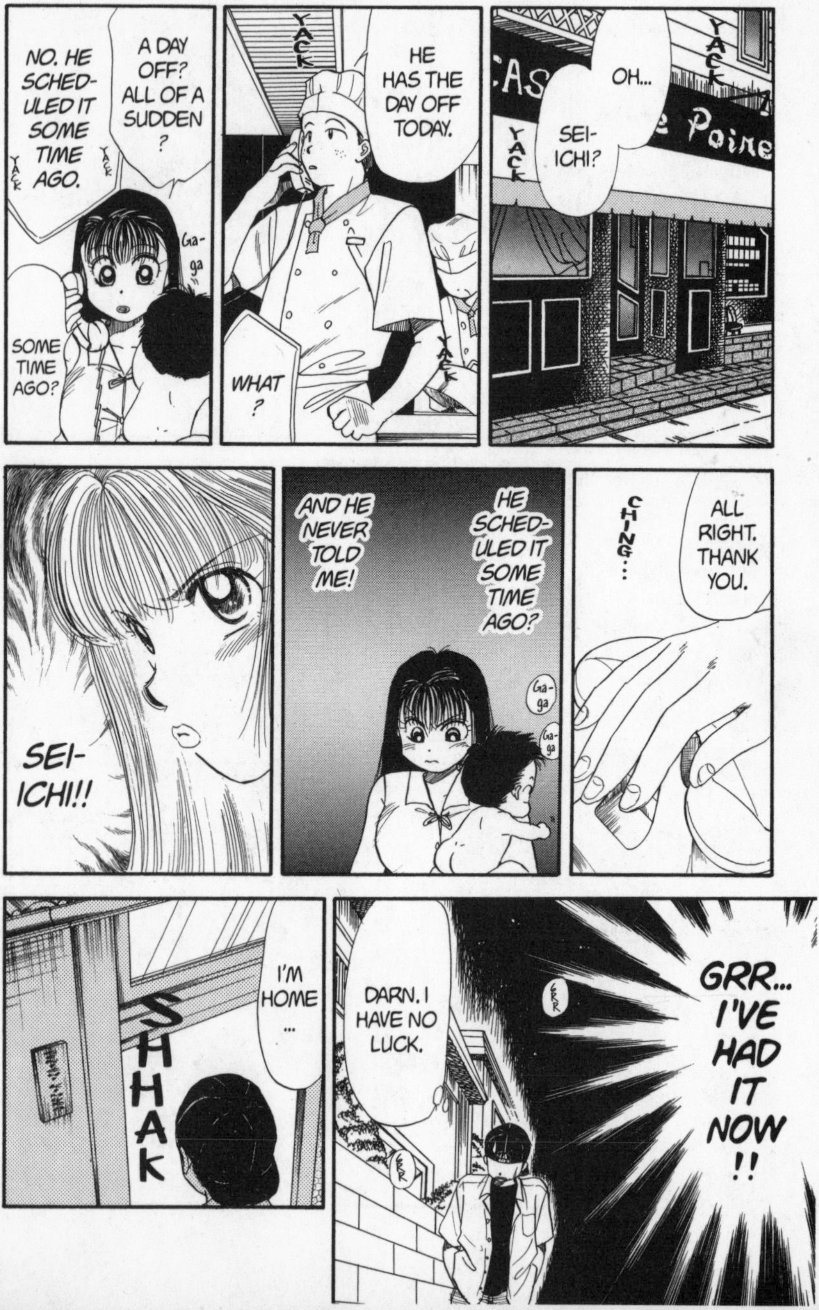
YACK
OH... SEI-ICHI?
YACK
YACK
HE HAS THE DAY OFF TODAY.
WHAT?
YACK
A DAY OFF? ALL OF A SUDDEN?
NO. HE SCHED-ULED IT SOME TIME AGO.
YACK
YACK
Ga-ga
SOME TIME AGO?
CHING...
ALL RIGHT. THANK YOU.
HE SCHED-ULED IT SOME TIME AGO?
AND HE NEVER TOLD ME!
Ga-ga
Ga-ga
SEI-ICHI!!
GRR... I'VE HAD IT NOW!!
GRR
DARN. I HAVE NO LUCK.
GRR
I'M HOME...
SHHAK

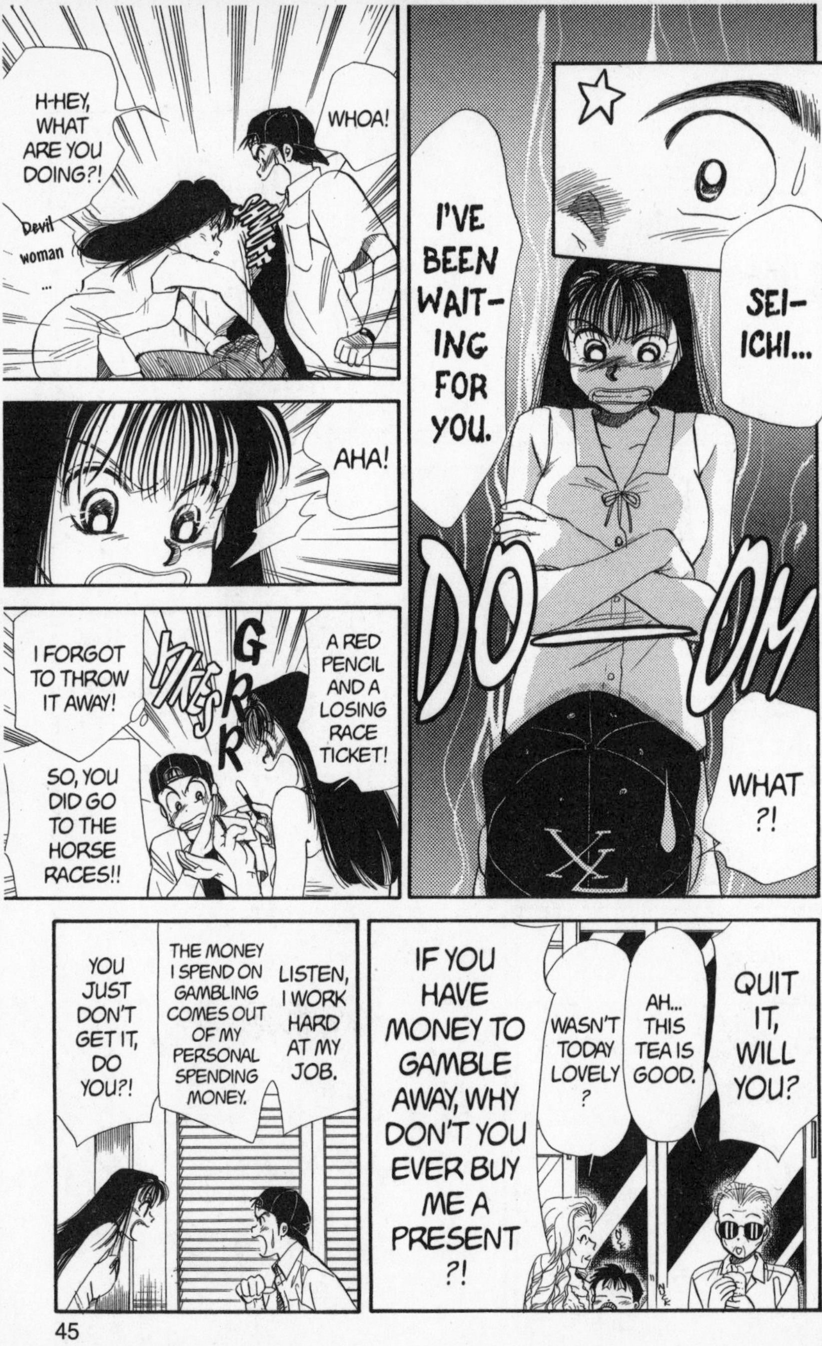
SEI-ICHI...
I'VE BEEN WAITING FOR YOU.
DO—OM
WHAT?!
WHOA!
H-HEY, WHAT ARE YOU DOING?!
Devil woman ...
AHA!
A RED PENCIL AND A LOSING RACE TICKET!
GRRR
YIKES
I FORGOT TO THROW IT AWAY!
SO, YOU DID GO TO THE HORSE RACES!!
QUIT IT, WILL YOU?
AH... THIS TEA IS GOOD.
WASN'T TODAY LOVELY?
IF YOU HAVE MONEY TO GAMBLE AWAY, WHY DON'T YOU EVER BUY ME A PRESENT?!
LISTEN, I WORK HARD AT MY JOB.
THE MONEY I SPEND ON GAMBLING COMES OUT OF MY PERSONAL SPENDING MONEY.
YOU JUST DON'T GET IT, DO YOU?!

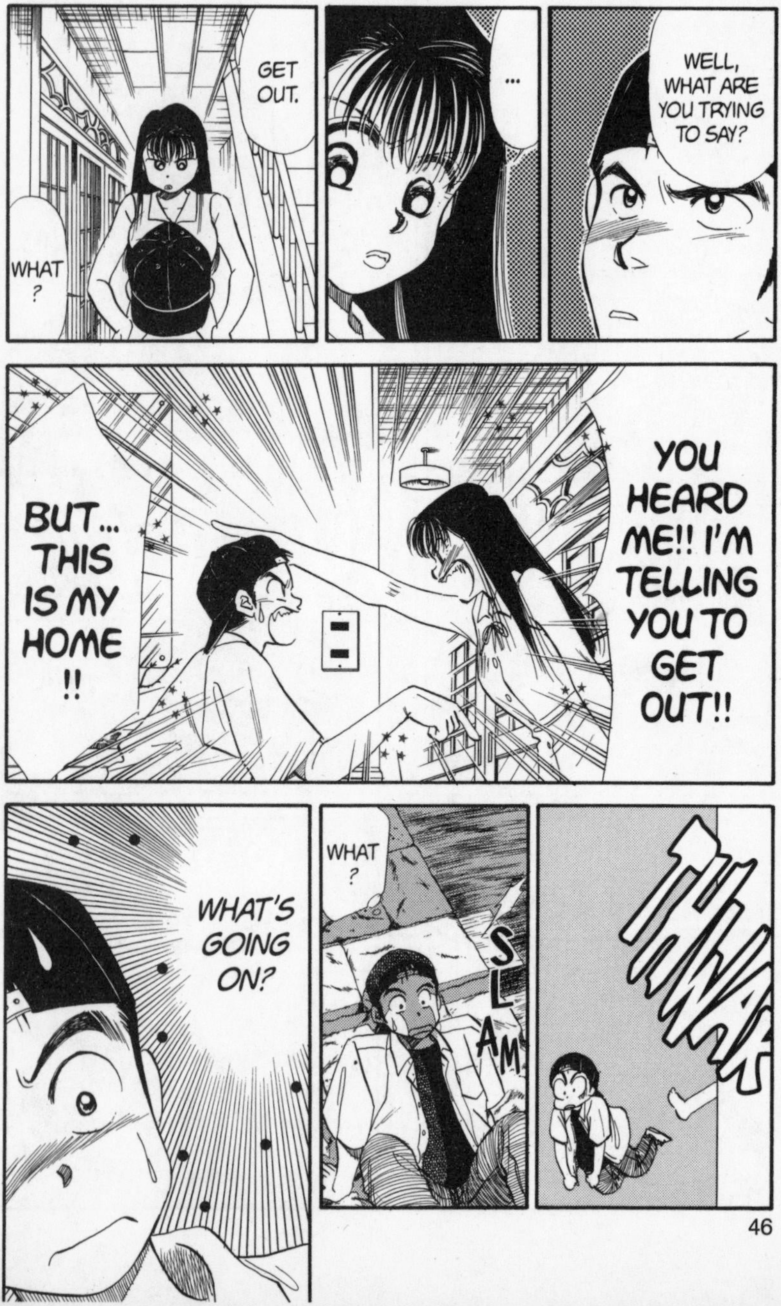
WELL, WHAT ARE YOU TRYING TO SAY?
...
GET OUT.
WHAT ?
YOU HEARD ME!! I'M TELLING YOU TO GET OUT!!
BUT... THIS IS MY HOME !!
THWAK
WHAT ?
SLAM
WHAT'S GOING ON?

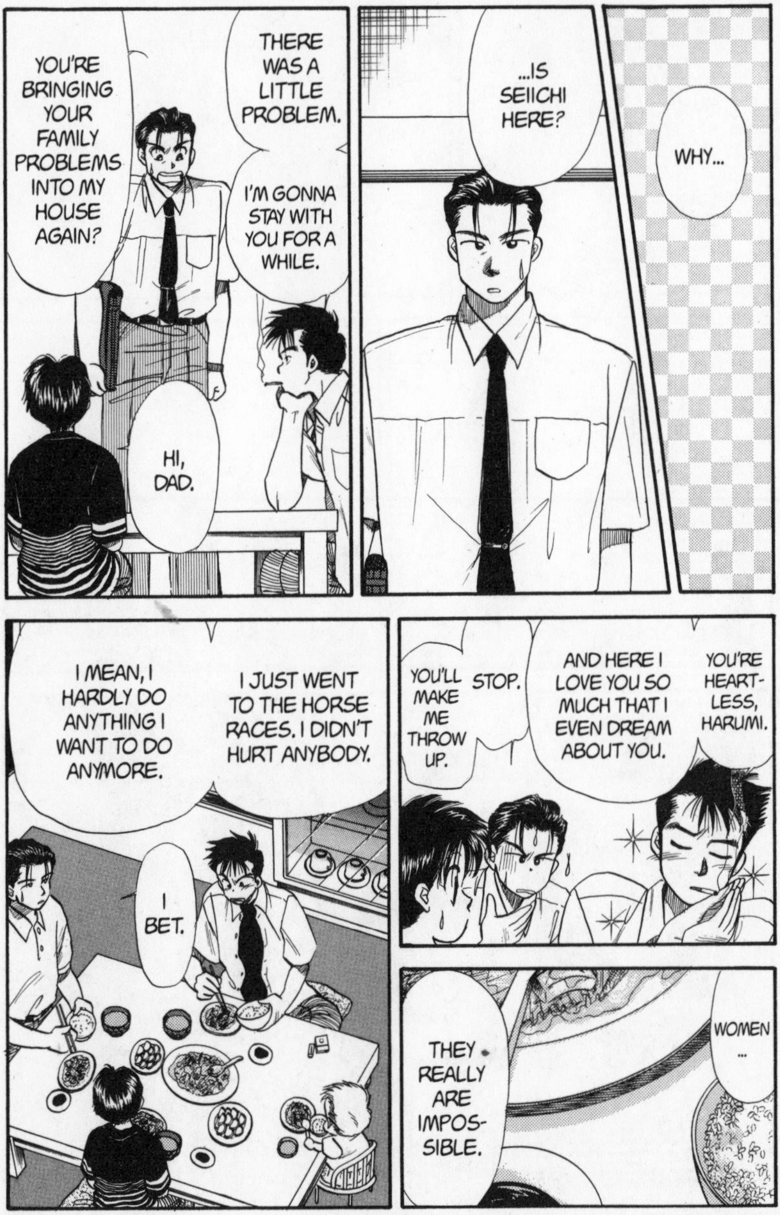
WHY...
...IS SEIICHI HERE?
THERE WAS A LITTLE PROBLEM.
I'M GONNA STAY WITH YOU FOR A WHILE.
YOU'RE BRINGING YOUR FAMILY PROBLEMS INTO MY HOUSE AGAIN?
HI, DAD.
YOU'RE HEARTLESS, HARUMI.
AND HERE I LOVE YOU SO MUCH THAT I EVEN DREAM ABOUT YOU.
STOP.
YOU'LL MAKE ME THROW UP.
WOMEN...
THEY REALLY ARE IMPOSSIBLE.
I JUST WENT TO THE HORSE RACES. I DIDN'T HURT ANYBODY.
I MEAN, I HARDLY DO ANYTHING I WANT TO DO ANYMORE.
I BET.

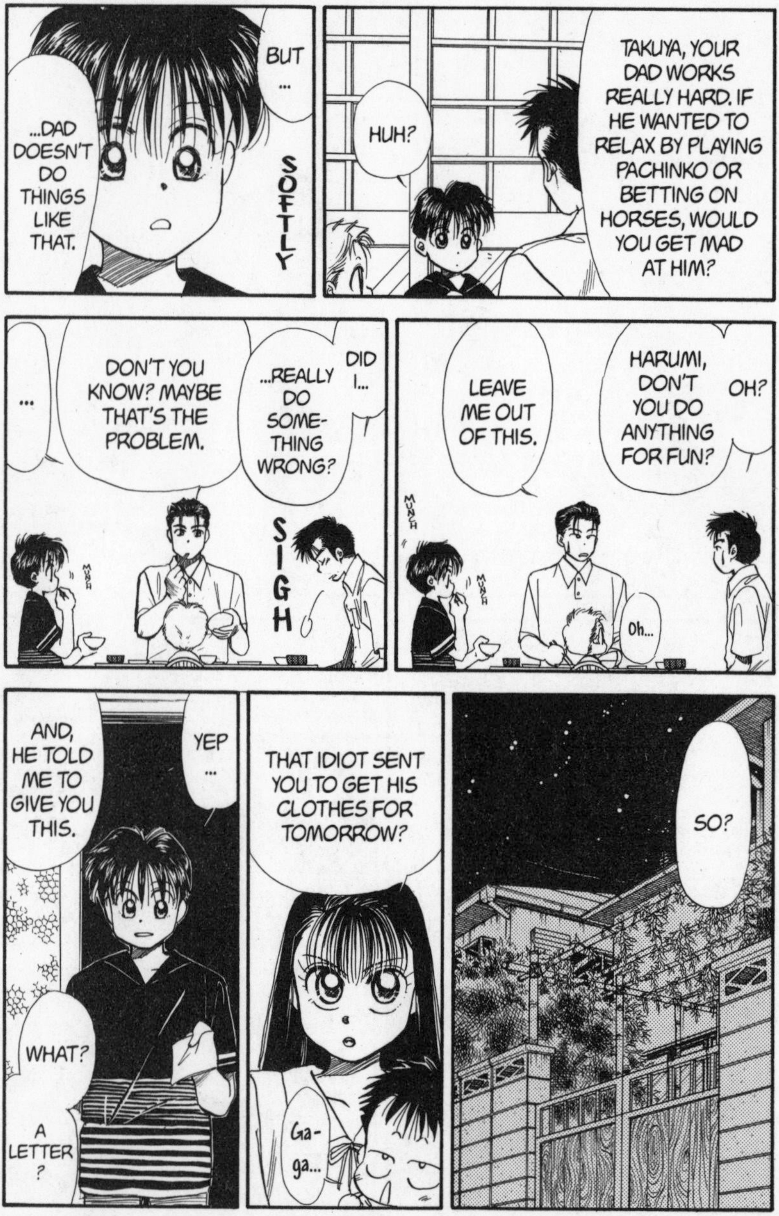
TAKUYA, YOUR DAD WORKS REALLY HARD. IF HE WANTED TO RELAX BY PLAYING PACHINKO OR BETTING ON HORSES, WOULD YOU GET MAD AT HIM?
HUH?
BUT ...
SOFTLY
...DAD DOESN'T DO THINGS LIKE THAT.
OH?
HARUMI, DON'T YOU DO ANYTHING FOR FUN?
LEAVE ME OUT OF THIS.
MUNCH
MUNCH
Oh...
DID I...
...REALLY DO SOMETHING WRONG?
SIGH
DON'T YOU KNOW? MAYBE THAT'S THE PROBLEM.
...
SO?
THAT IDIOT SENT YOU TO GET HIS CLOTHES FOR TOMORROW?
Ga-ga...
YEP ...
AND, HE TOLD ME TO GIVE YOU THIS.
WHAT?
A LETTER?

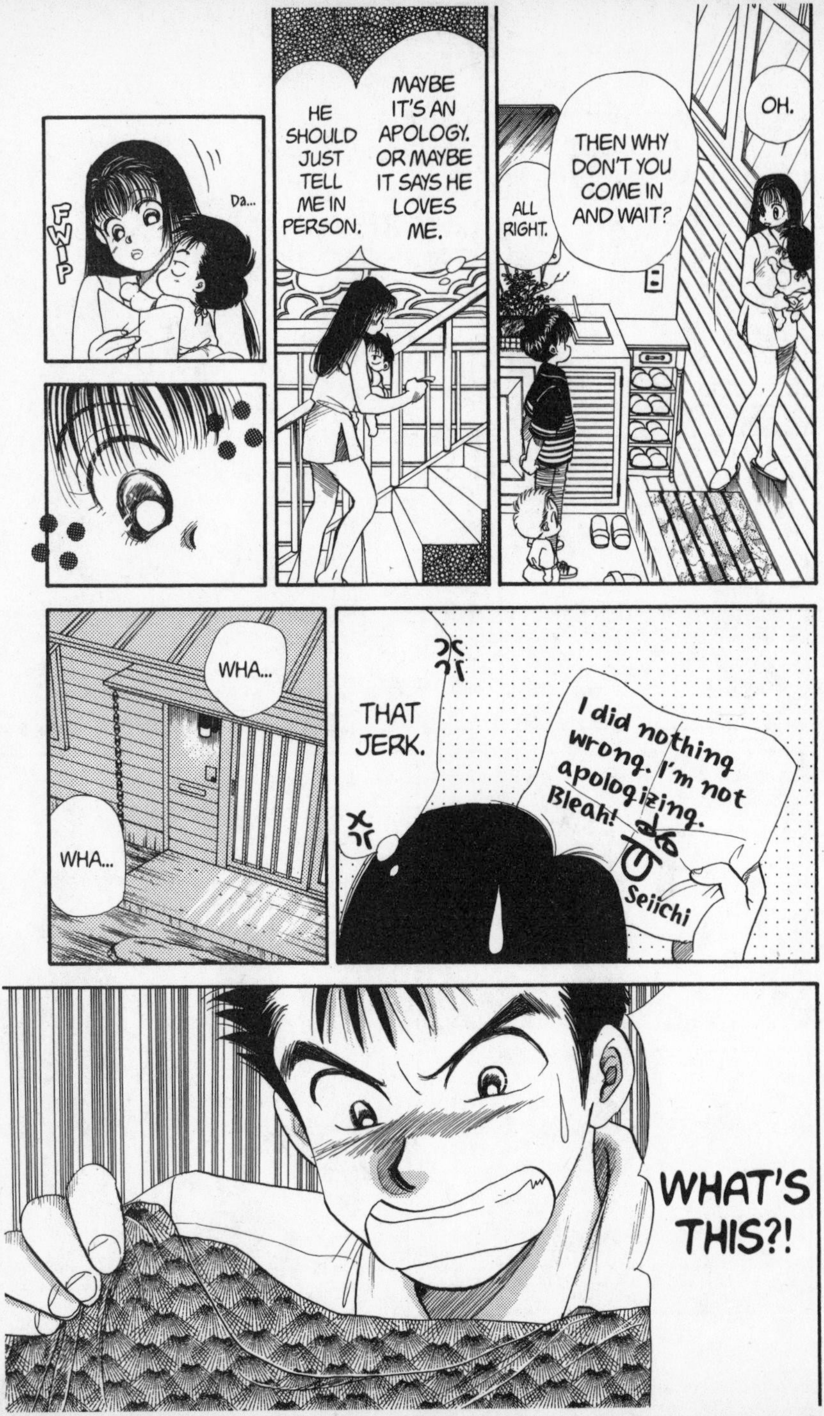
OH.
THEN WHY DON'T YOU COME IN AND WAIT?
ALL RIGHT.
MAYBE IT'S AN APOLOGY. OR MAYBE IT SAYS HE LOVES ME.
HE SHOULD JUST TELL ME IN PERSON.
Da...
FWIP
I did nothing wrong. I'm not apologizing. Bleah!
Seiichi
THAT JERK.
WHA...
WHA...
WHAT'S THIS?!

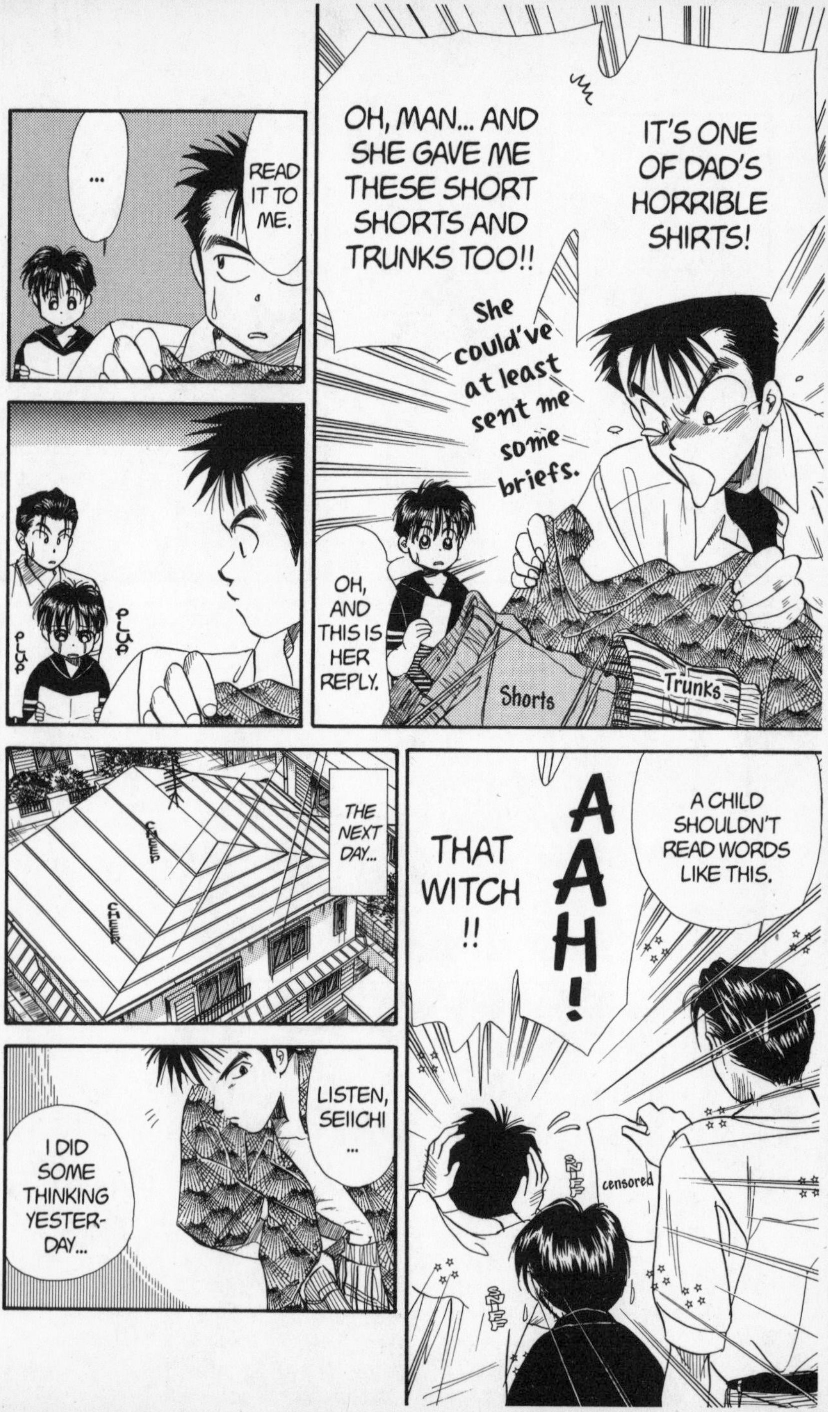
IT'S ONE OF DAD'S HORRIBLE SHIRTS!
OH, MAN... AND SHE GAVE ME THESE SHORT SHORTS AND TRUNKS TOO!!
She could've at least sent me some briefs.
OH, AND THIS IS HER REPLY.
Trunks
Shorts
READ IT TO ME.
...
PLUP
PLUP
A CHILD SHOULDN'T READ WORDS LIKE THIS.
AAH!
THAT WITCH !!
censored
SNIFF
SNIFF
THE NEXT DAY...
CHEEP
CHEEP
LISTEN, SEIICHI ...
I DID SOME THINKING YESTER-DAY...

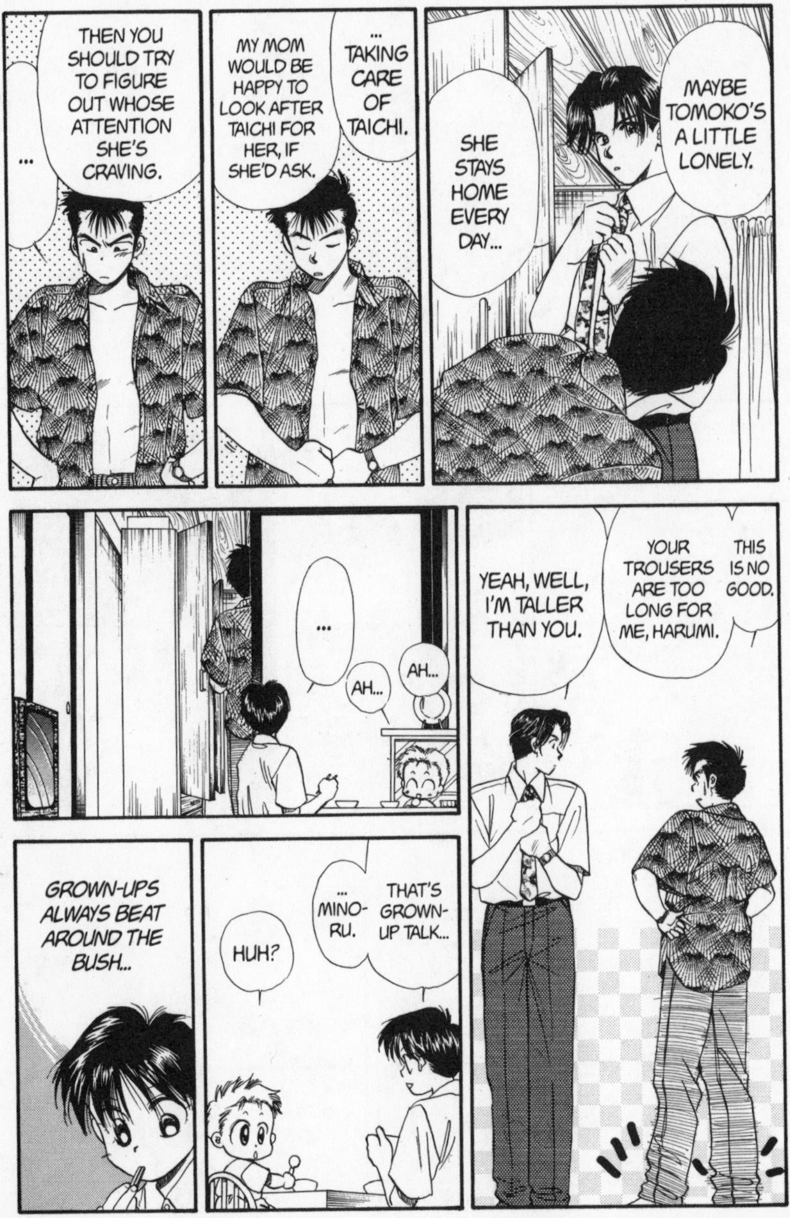
MAYBE TOMOKO'S A LITTLE LONELY.
SHE STAYS HOME EVERY DAY...
... TAKING CARE OF TAICHI.
MY MOM WOULD BE HAPPY TO LOOK AFTER TAICHI FOR HER, IF SHE'D ASK.
THEN YOU SHOULD TRY TO FIGURE OUT WHOSE ATTENTION SHE'S CRAVING.
...
THIS IS NO GOOD.
YOUR TROUSERS ARE TOO LONG FOR ME, HARUMI.
YEAH, WELL, I'M TALLER THAN YOU.
AH...
AH...
...
THAT'S GROWN-UP TALK...
... MINO-RU.
HUH?
GROWN-UPS ALWAYS BEAT AROUND THE BUSH...

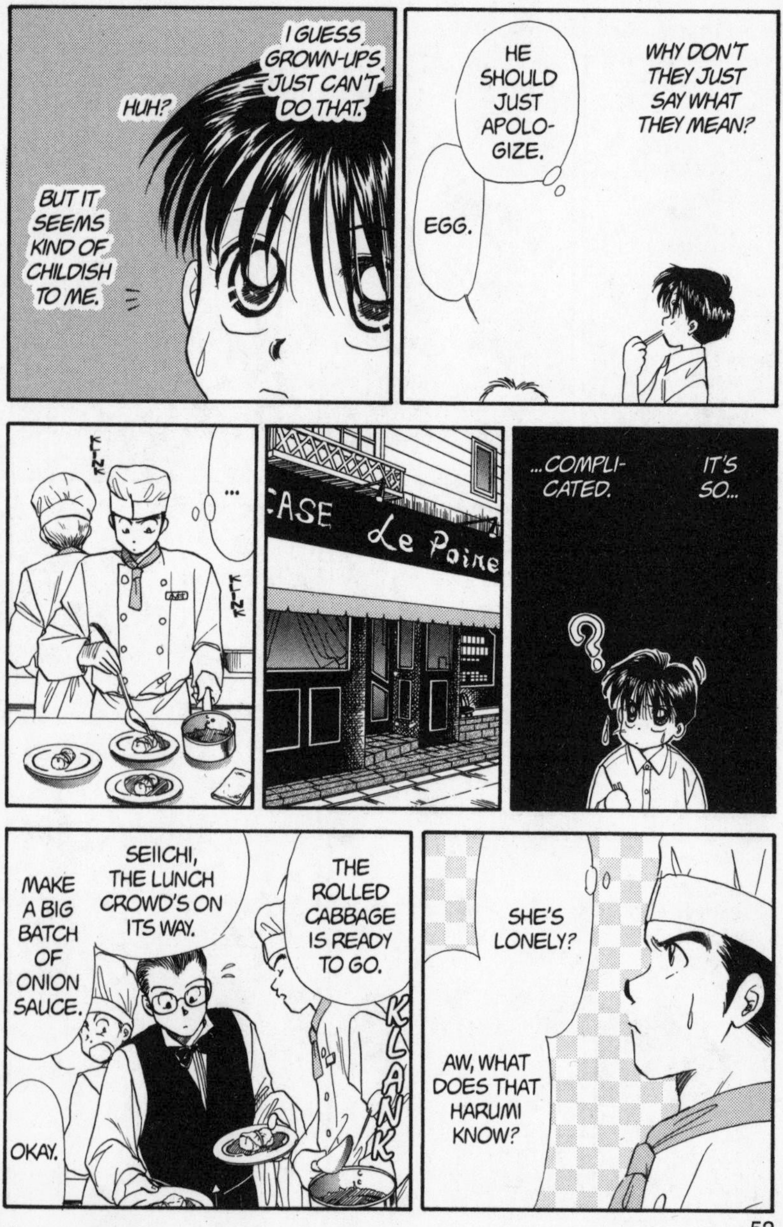
WHY DON'T THEY JUST SAY WHAT THEY MEAN?
HE SHOULD JUST APOLOGIZE.
EGG.
I GUESS GROWN-UPS JUST CAN'T DO THAT.
HUH?
BUT IT SEEMS KIND OF CHILDISH TO ME.
IT'S SO...
...COMPLICATED.
...
KLINK
KLINK
SHE'S LONELY?
AW, WHAT DOES THAT HARUMI KNOW?
THE ROLLED CABBAGE IS READY TO GO.
SEIICHI, THE LUNCH CROWD'S ON ITS WAY.
MAKE A BIG BATCH OF ONION SAUCE.
OKAY.
KLANK

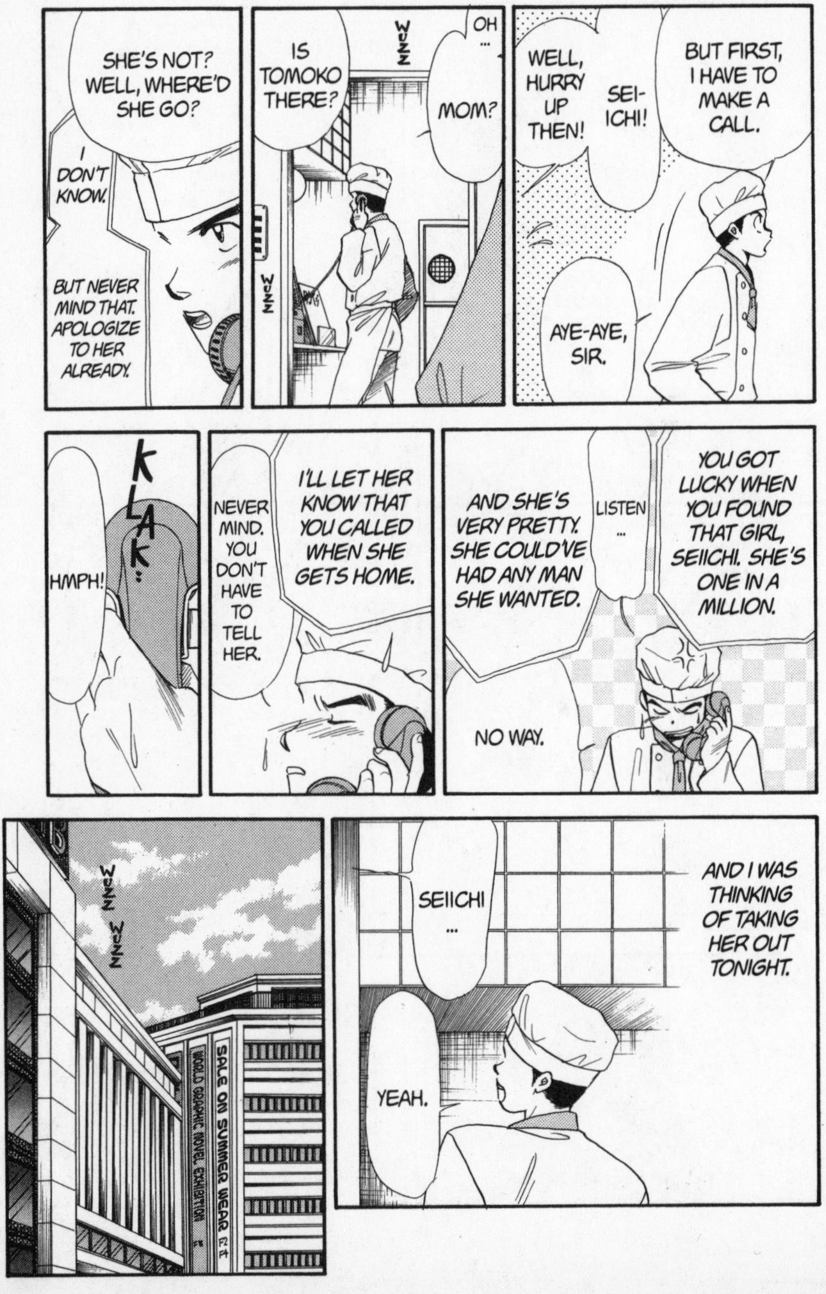
BUT FIRST, I HAVE TO MAKE A CALL.
SEI-ICHI!
WELL, HURRY UP THEN!
AYE-AYE, SIR.
OH ... MOM?
WUZZ
IS TOMOKO THERE?
WUZZ
SHE'S NOT? WELL, WHERE'D SHE GO?
I DON'T KNOW.
BUT NEVER MIND THAT. APOLOGIZE TO HER ALREADY.
YOU GOT LUCKY WHEN YOU FOUND THAT GIRL, SEIICHI. SHE'S ONE IN A MILLION.
LISTEN ...
AND SHE'S VERY PRETTY. SHE COULD'VE HAD ANY MAN SHE WANTED.
NO WAY.
I'LL LET HER KNOW THAT YOU CALLED WHEN SHE GETS HOME.
NEVER MIND. YOU DON'T HAVE TO TELL HER.
KLAK!
HMPH!
AND I WAS THINKING OF TAKING HER OUT TONIGHT.
SEIICHI ...
YEAH.
WUZZ WUZZ
SALE ON SUMMER WEAR
WORLD GRAPHIC NOVEL EXHIBITION

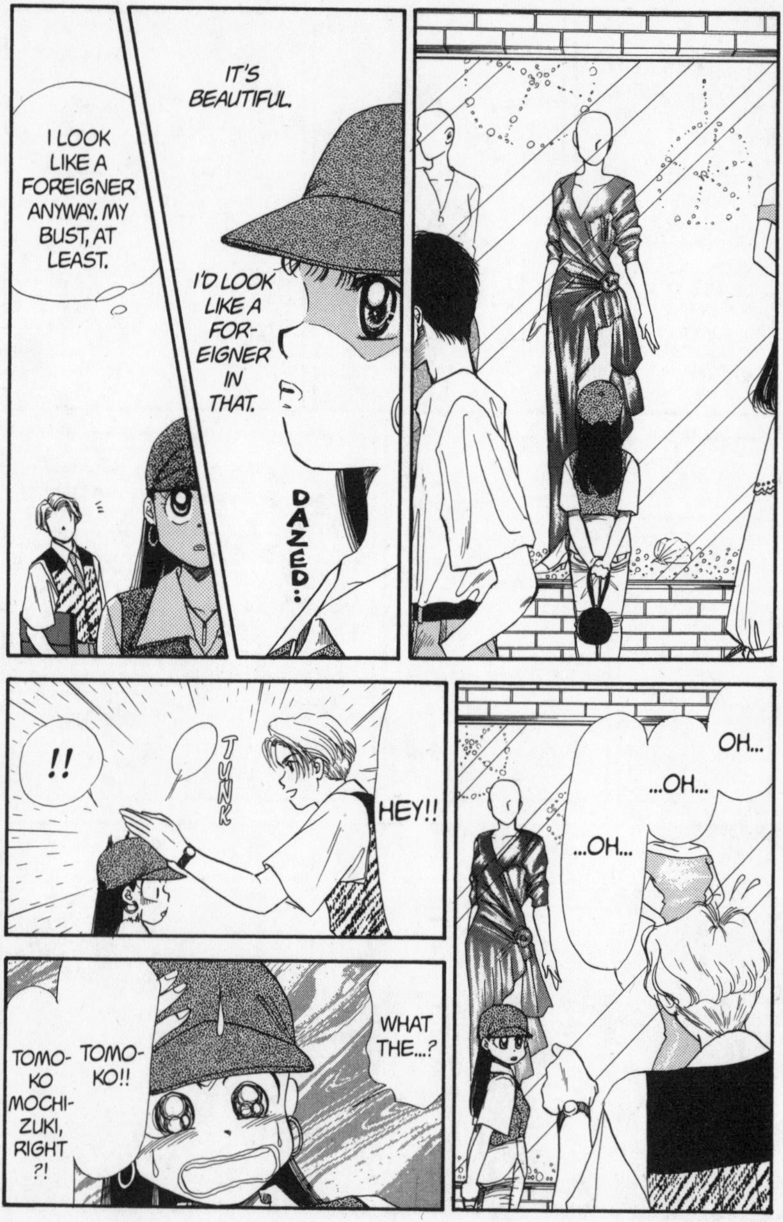
IT'S BEAUTIFUL.
I'D LOOK LIKE A FOR-EIGNER IN THAT.
DAZED..
I LOOK LIKE A FOREIGNER ANYWAY. MY BUST, AT LEAST.
OH...
...OH...
...OH...
HEY!!
TUNK
!!
WHAT THE...?
TOMO-KO!!
TOMO-KO MOCHI-ZUKI, RIGHT?!

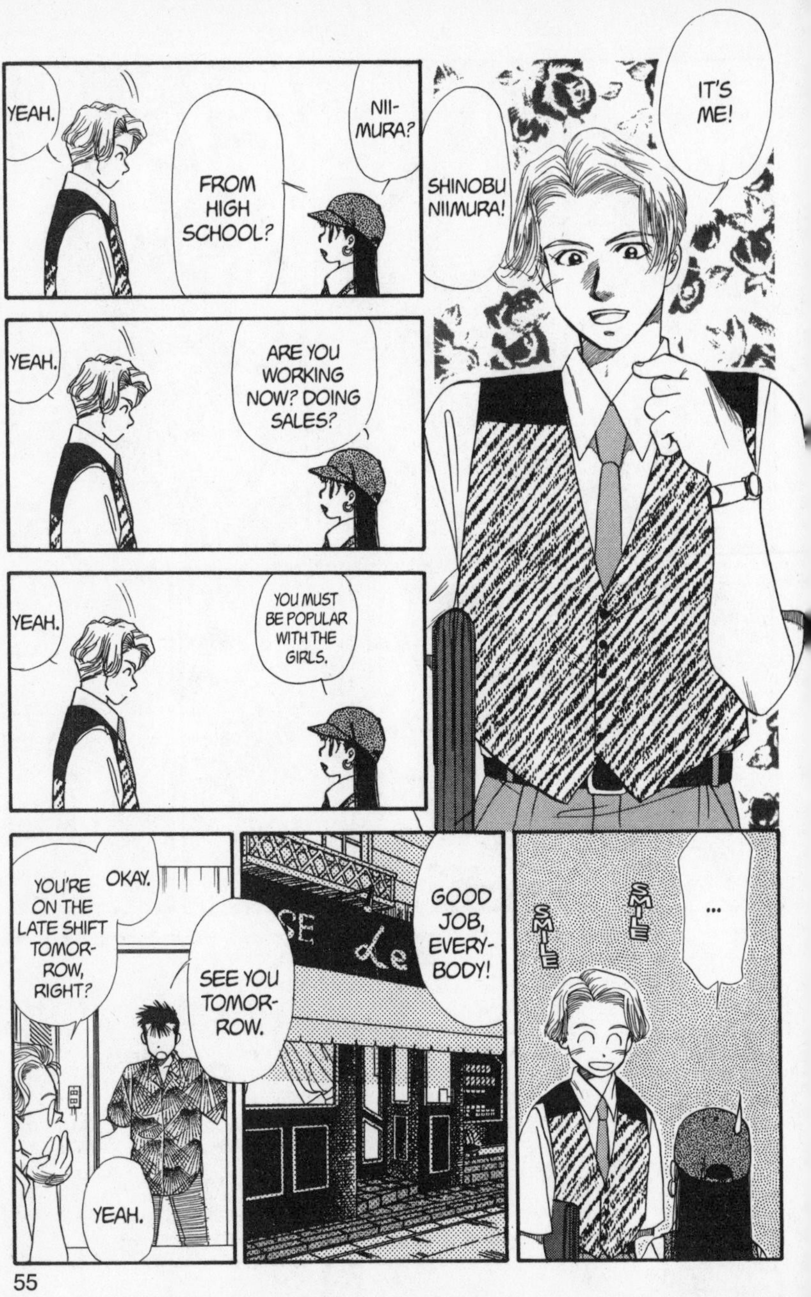
IT'S ME!
SHINOBU NIIMURA!
NII-MURA?
FROM HIGH SCHOOL?
YEAH.
ARE YOU WORKING NOW? DOING SALES?
YEAH.
YOU MUST BE POPULAR WITH THE GIRLS.
YEAH.
SMILE
SMILE
...
GOOD JOB, EVERY-BODY!
OKAY.
YOU'RE ON THE LATE SHIFT TOMOR-ROW, RIGHT?
SEE YOU TOMOR-ROW.
YEAH.

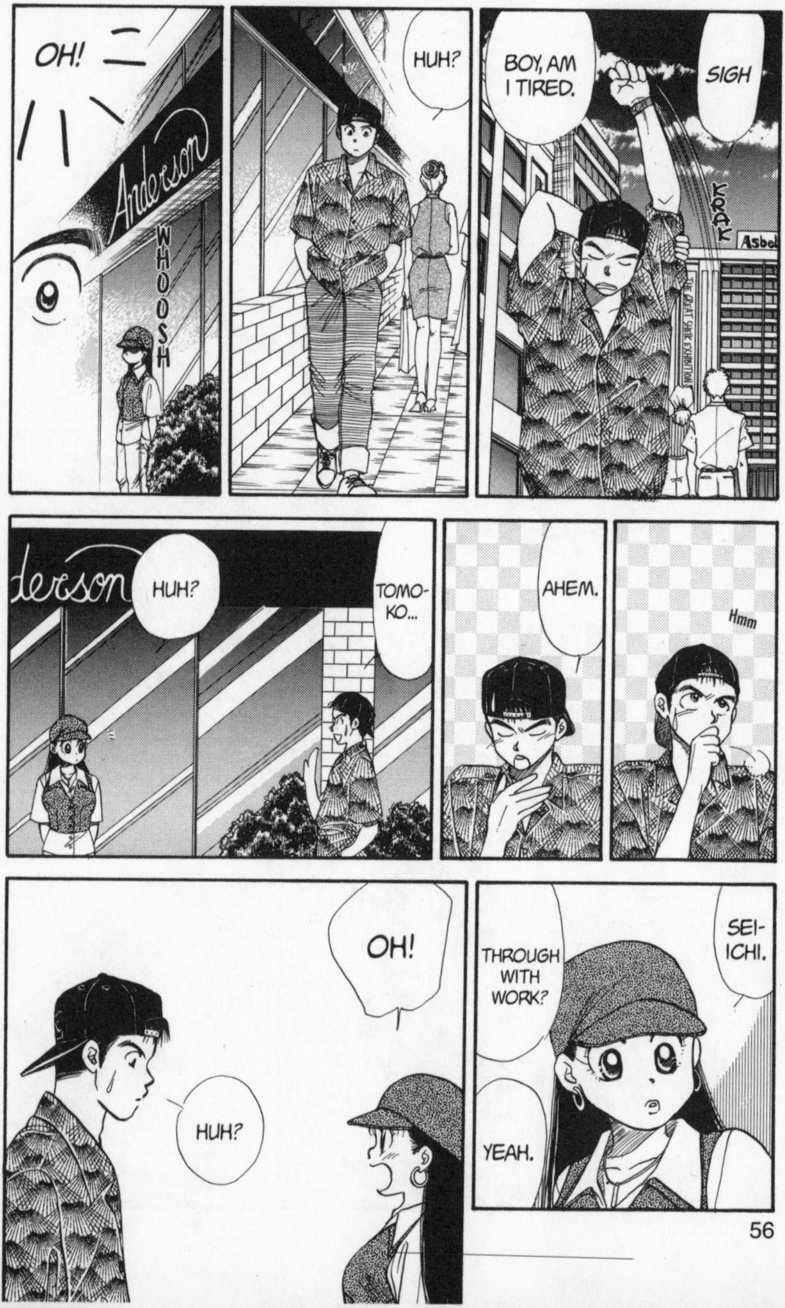
SIGH
BOY, AM I TIRED.
KRAK
Asbel
HUH?
OH!
Anderson
WHOOSH
Hmm
AHEM.
TOMO-KO...
HUH?
derson
SEI-ICHI.
THROUGH WITH WORK?
YEAH.
OH!
HUH?

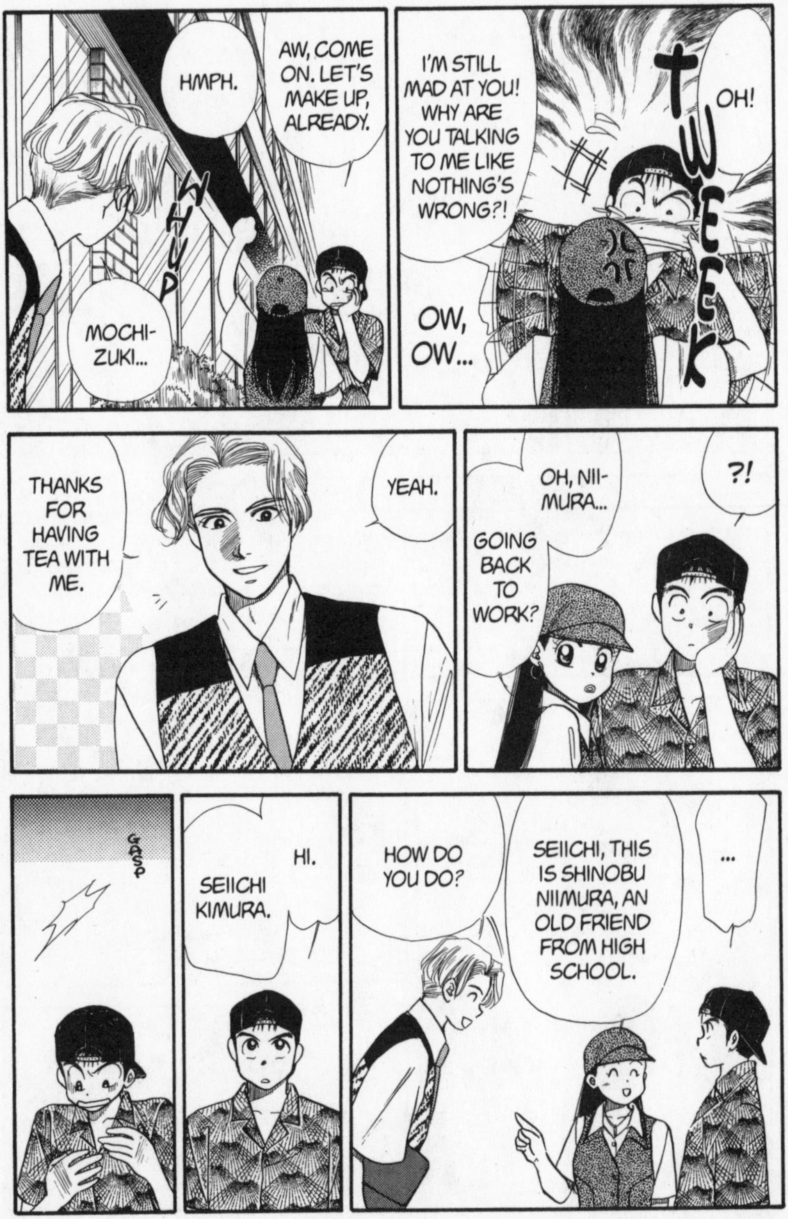
OH!
TWEEK
I'M STILL MAD AT YOU! WHY ARE YOU TALKING TO ME LIKE NOTHING'S WRONG?!
OW, OW...
AW, COME ON. LET'S MAKE UP, ALREADY.
HMPH.
WHUP
MOCHIZUKI...
?!
OH, NIIMURA...
GOING BACK TO WORK?
YEAH.
THANKS FOR HAVING TEA WITH ME.
...
SEIICHI, THIS IS SHINOBU NIIMURA, AN OLD FRIEND FROM HIGH SCHOOL.
HOW DO YOU DO?
HI.
SEIICHI KIMURA.
GASP

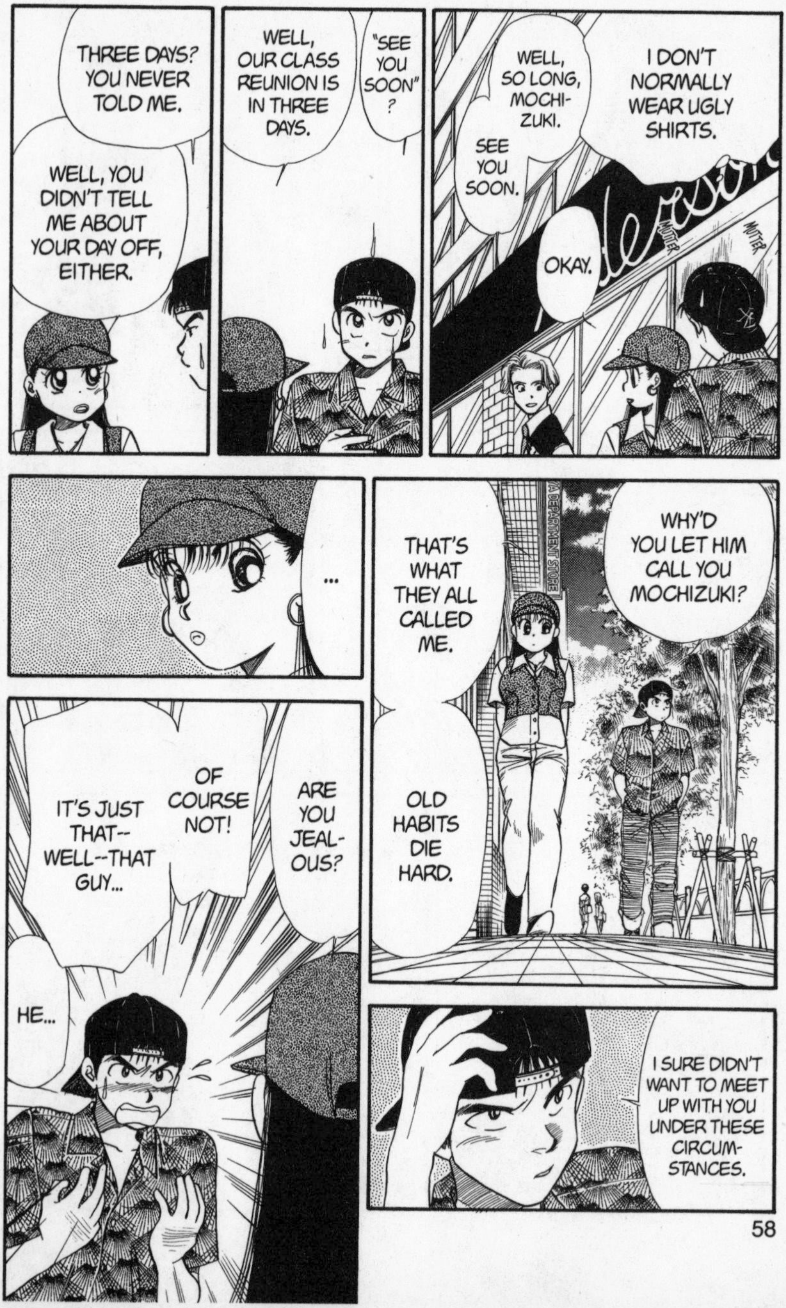
I DON'T NORMALLY WEAR UGLY SHIRTS.
WELL, SO LONG, MOCHIZUKI.
SEE YOU SOON.
OKAY.
MUTTER
MUTTER
"SEE YOU SOON"?
WELL, OUR CLASS REUNION IS IN THREE DAYS.
THREE DAYS? YOU NEVER TOLD ME.
WELL, YOU DIDN'T TELL ME ABOUT YOUR DAY OFF, EITHER.
WHY'D YOU LET HIM CALL YOU MOCHIZUKI?
DEPARTMENT STORE
THAT'S WHAT THEY ALL CALLED ME.
OLD HABITS DIE HARD.
...
ARE YOU JEALOUS?
OF COURSE NOT!
IT'S JUST THAT--WELL--THAT GUY...
HE...
I SURE DIDN'T WANT TO MEET UP WITH YOU UNDER THESE CIRCUMSTANCES.

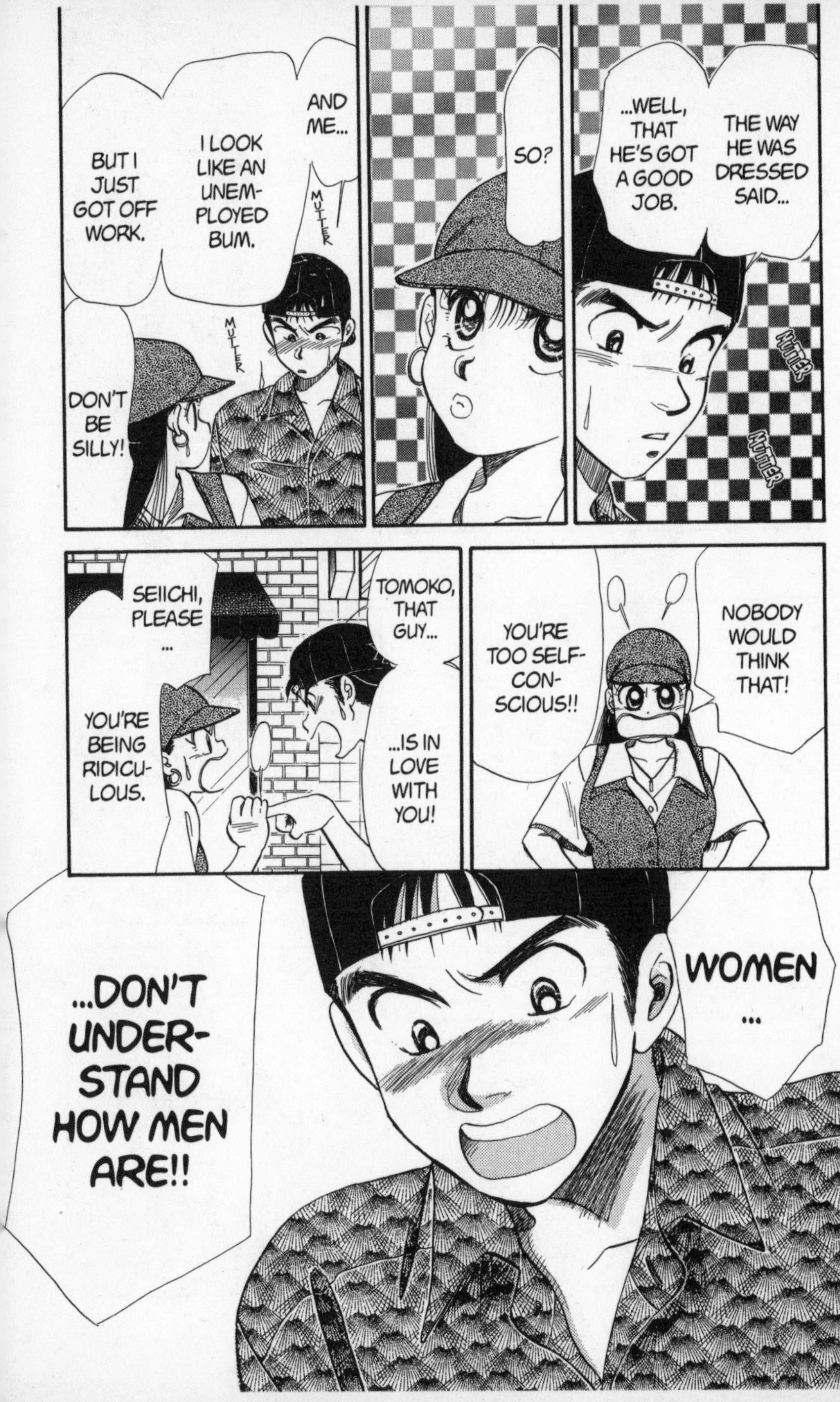
THE WAY HE WAS DRESSED SAID...
...WELL, THAT HE'S GOT A GOOD JOB.
MUTTER
MUTTER
SO?
AND ME...
I LOOK LIKE AN UNEMPLOYED BUM.
BUT I JUST GOT OFF WORK.
MUTTER
MUTTER
DON'T BE SILLY!
NOBODY WOULD THINK THAT!
YOU'RE TOO SELF-CONSCIOUS!!
TOMOKO, THAT GUY...
...IS IN LOVE WITH YOU!
SEIICHI, PLEASE...
YOU'RE BEING RIDICULOUS.
WOMEN...
...DON'T UNDERSTAND HOW MEN ARE!!

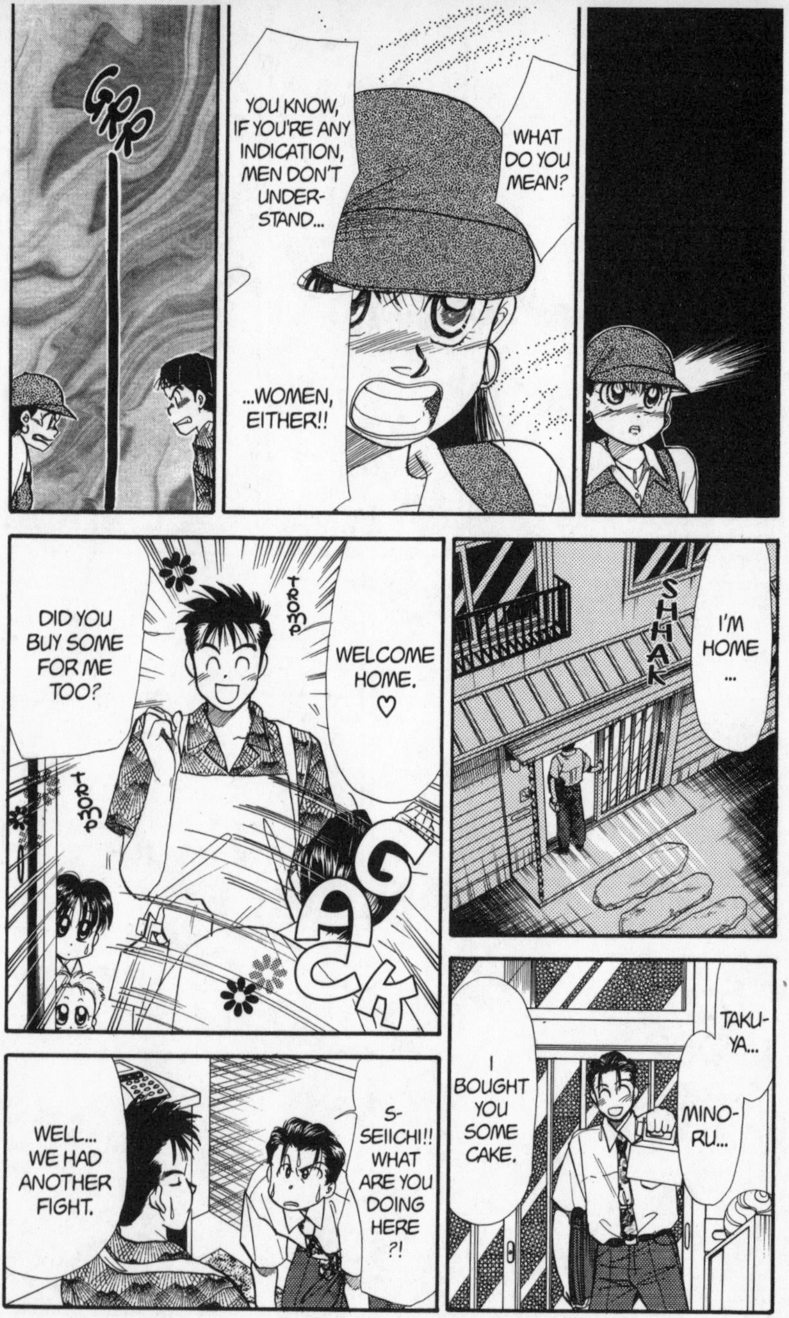
WHAT DO YOU MEAN?
YOU KNOW, IF YOU'RE ANY INDICATION, MEN DON'T UNDER-STAND...
...WOMEN, EITHER!!
GRR
SHHAK
I'M HOME ...
WELCOME HOME. ♡
TROMP
DID YOU BUY SOME FOR ME TOO?
TROMP
GACK
TAKU-YA...
MINO-RU...
I BOUGHT YOU SOME CAKE.
S-SEIICHI!! WHAT ARE YOU DOING HERE ?!
WELL... WE HAD ANOTHER FIGHT.

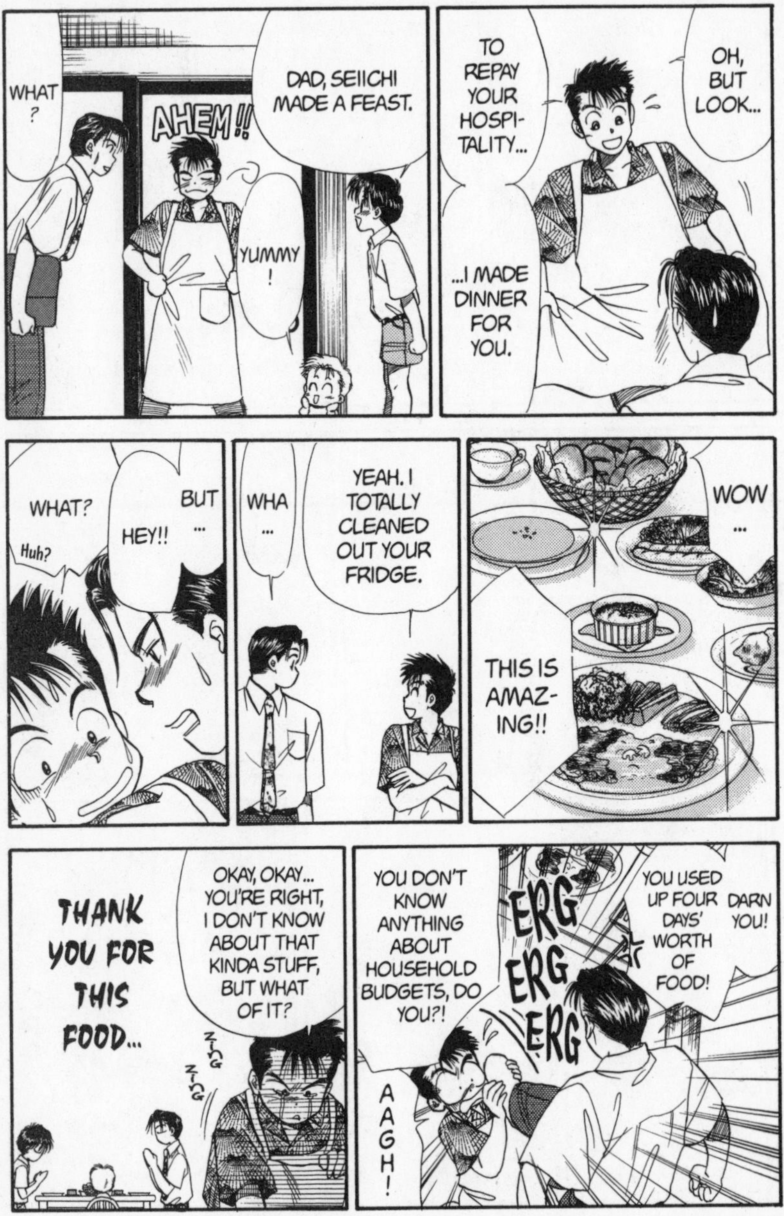
OH, BUT LOOK...
TO REPAY YOUR HOSPITALITY...
...I MADE DINNER FOR YOU.
DAD, SEIICHI MADE A FEAST.
YUMMY!
AHEM!!
WHAT?
WOW...
THIS IS AMAZING!!
YEAH. I TOTALLY CLEANED OUT YOUR FRIDGE.
WHA...
BUT...
HEY!!
WHAT?
Huh?
DARN YOU!
YOU USED UP FOUR DAYS' WORTH OF FOOD!
ERG ERG ERG
YOU DON'T KNOW ANYTHING ABOUT HOUSEHOLD BUDGETS, DO YOU?!
AAGH!
OKAY, OKAY... YOU'RE RIGHT, I DON'T KNOW ABOUT THAT KINDA STUFF, BUT WHAT OF IT?
ZING ZING
THANK YOU FOR THIS FOOD...

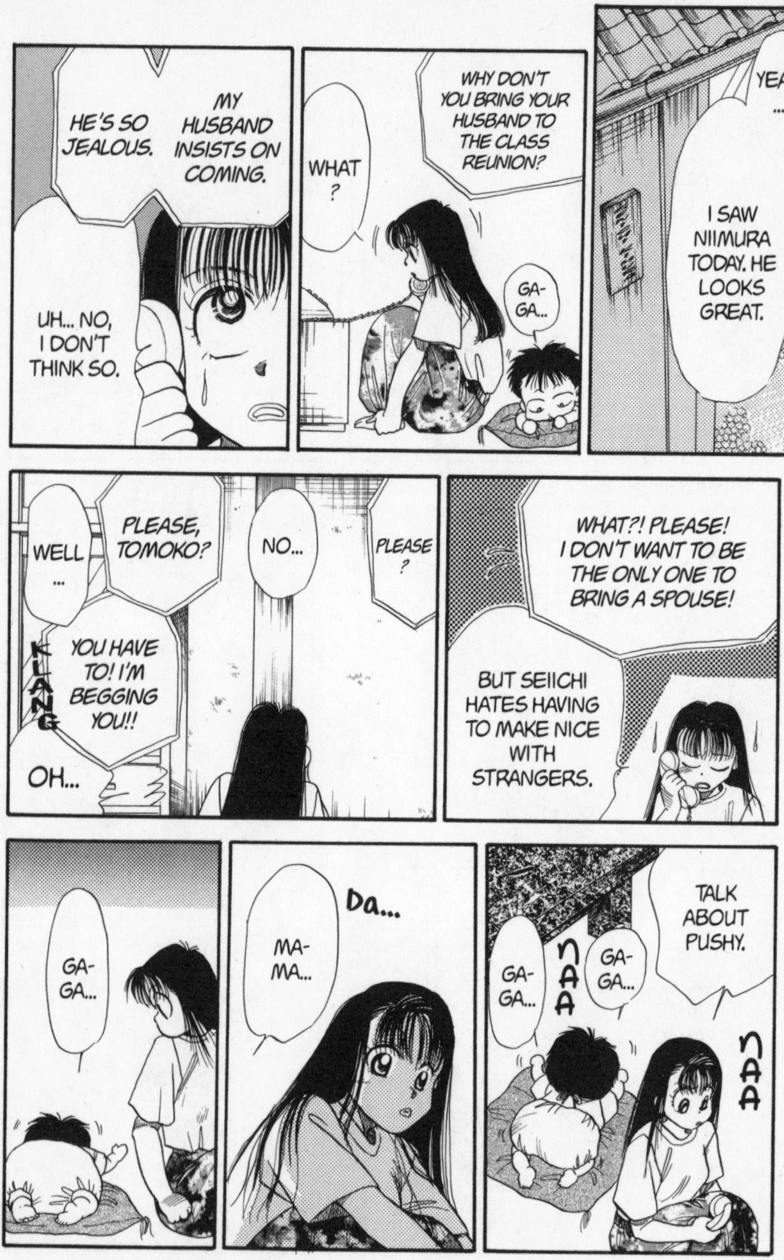
YEAH ...
I SAW NIIMURA TODAY. HE LOOKS GREAT.
WHY DON'T YOU BRING YOUR HUSBAND TO THE CLASS REUNION?
WHAT ?
GA-GA...
MY HUSBAND INSISTS ON COMING.
HE'S SO JEALOUS.
UH... NO, I DON'T THINK SO.
WHAT?! PLEASE! I DON'T WANT TO BE THE ONLY ONE TO BRING A SPOUSE!
BUT SEIICHI HATES HAVING TO MAKE NICE WITH STRANGERS.
PLEASE ?
NO...
PLEASE, TOMOKO?
WELL ...
YOU HAVE TO! I'M BEGGING YOU!!
KLANG
OH...
TALK ABOUT PUSHY.
GA-GA...
NAA
GA-GA...
NAA
Da...
MA-MA...
GA-GA...

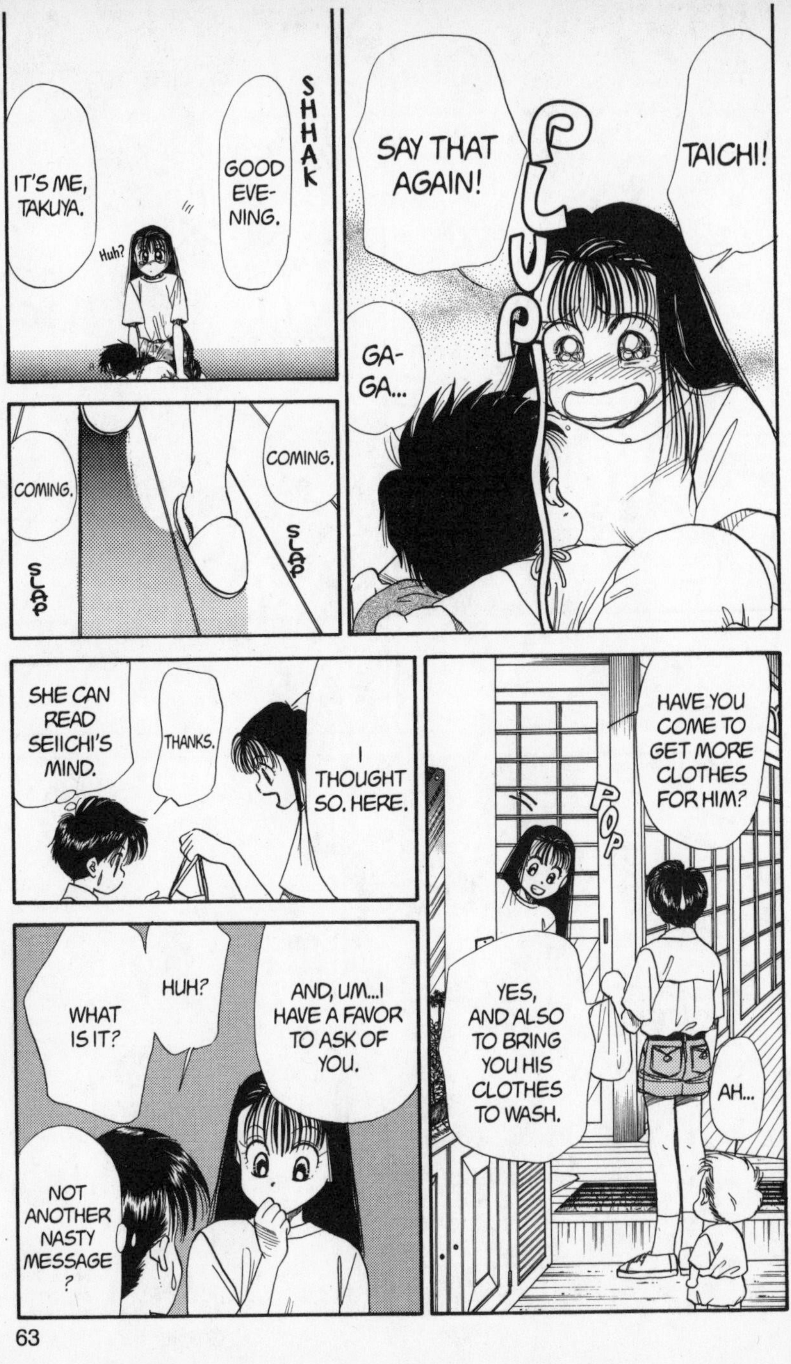
TAICHI!
SAY THAT AGAIN!
PLUP
GA-GA...
SHHHAK
GOOD EVE-NING.
IT'S ME, TAKUYA.
Huh?
COMING.
SLAP
COMING.
SLAP
HAVE YOU COME TO GET MORE CLOTHES FOR HIM?
POP
YES, AND ALSO TO BRING YOU HIS CLOTHES TO WASH.
AH...
I THOUGHT SO. HERE.
THANKS.
SHE CAN READ SEIICHI'S MIND.
AND, UM...I HAVE A FAVOR TO ASK OF YOU.
HUH?
WHAT IS IT?
NOT ANOTHER NASTY MESSAGE?

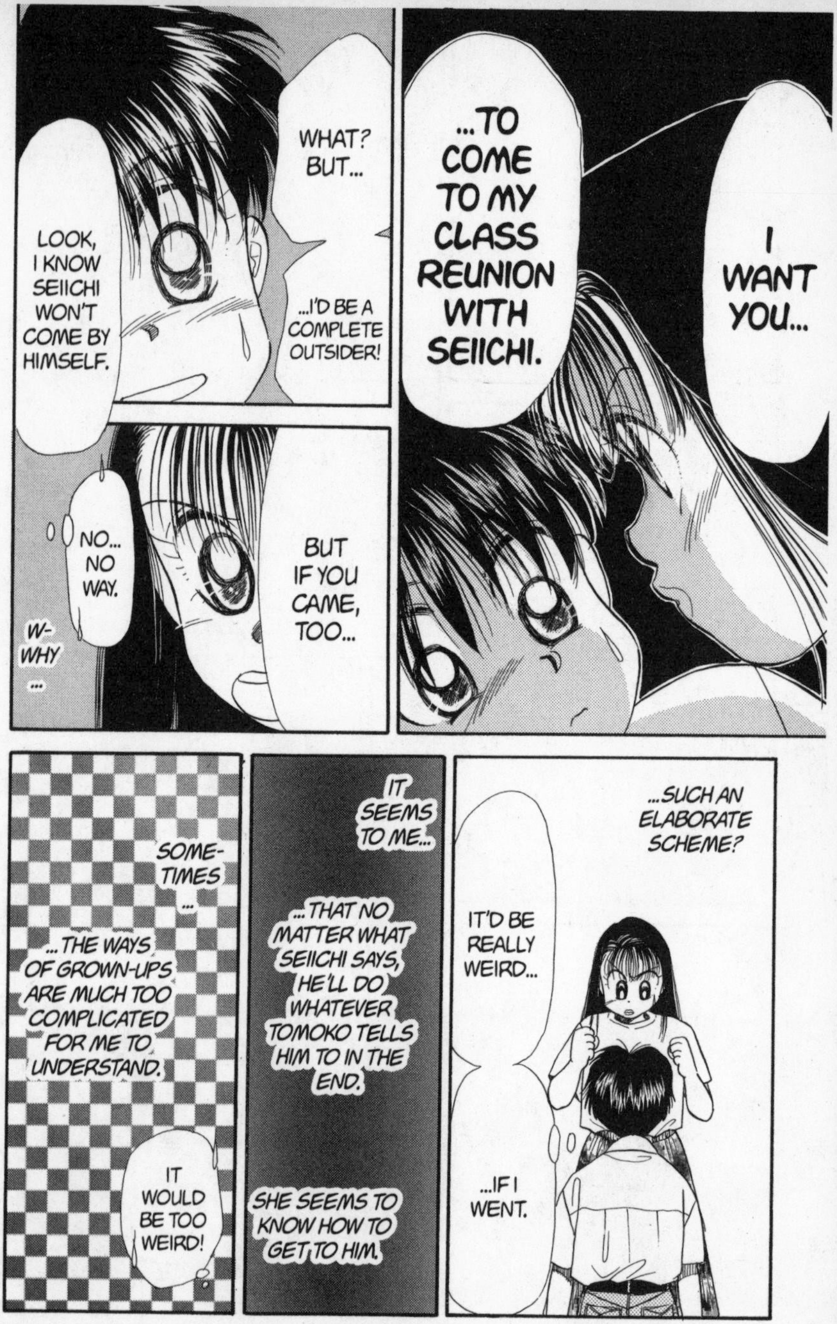
I WANT YOU...
...TO COME TO MY CLASS REUNION WITH SEIICHI.
WHAT? BUT...
...I'D BE A COMPLETE OUTSIDER!
LOOK, I KNOW SEIICHI WON'T COME BY HIMSELF.
BUT IF YOU CAME, TOO...
NO... NO WAY.
W- WHY ...
...SUCH AN ELABORATE SCHEME?
IT'D BE REALLY WEIRD...
...IF I WENT.
IT SEEMS TO ME...
...THAT NO MATTER WHAT SEIICHI SAYS, HE'LL DO WHATEVER TOMOKO TELLS HIM TO IN THE END.
SHE SEEMS TO KNOW HOW TO GET TO HIM.
SOME-TIMES ...
...THE WAYS OF GROWN-UPS ARE MUCH TOO COMPLICATED FOR ME TO UNDERSTAND.
IT WOULD BE TOO WEIRD!

Chapter 52 / The End

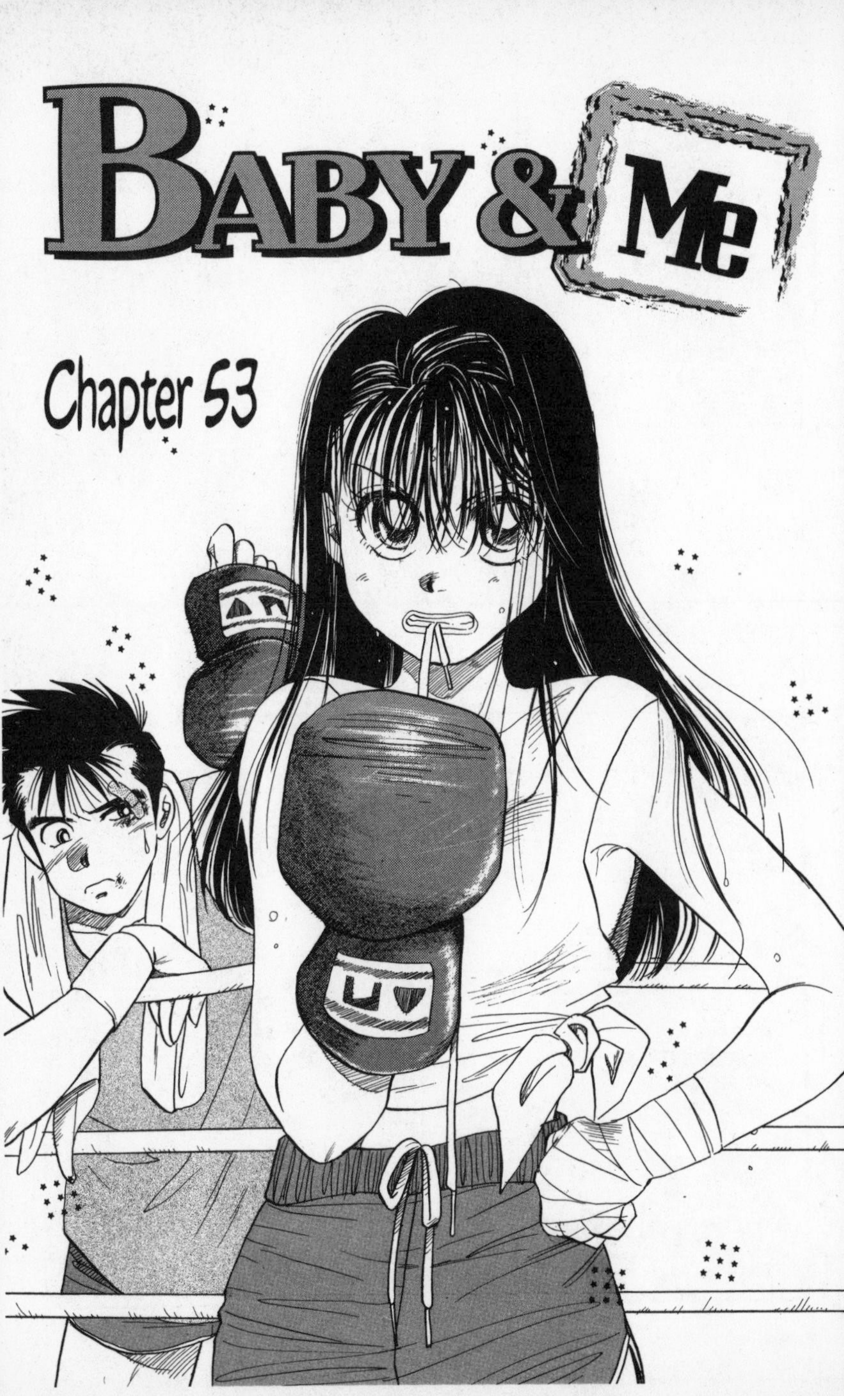
BABY & ME
Chapter 53

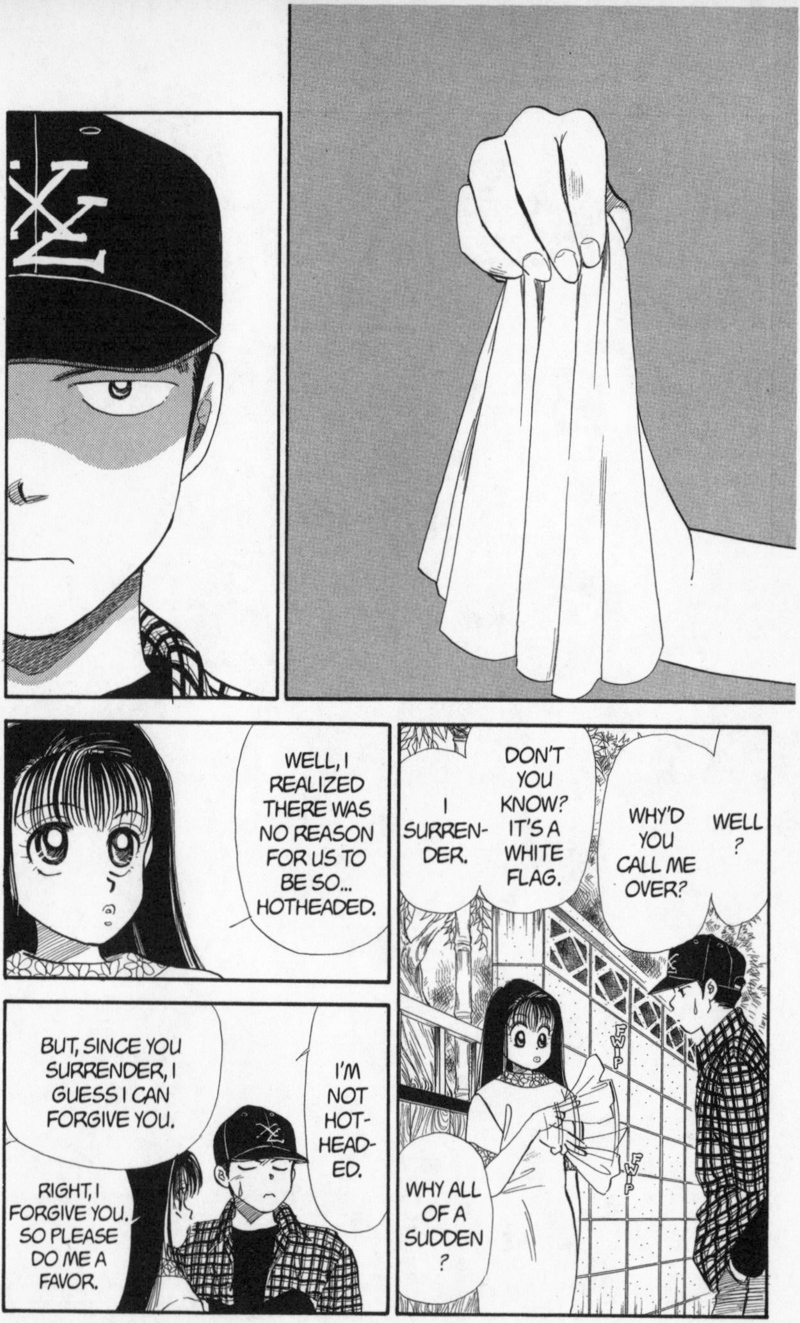

WELL?
WHY'D YOU CALL ME OVER?
DON'T YOU KNOW? IT'S A WHITE FLAG.
I SURREN-DER.
FWIP
FWIP
WHY ALL OF A SUDDEN?
WELL, I REALIZED THERE WAS NO REASON FOR US TO BE SO... HOTHEADED.
I'M NOT HOT-HEAD-ED.
BUT, SINCE YOU SURRENDER, I GUESS I CAN FORGIVE YOU.
RIGHT, I FORGIVE YOU. SO PLEASE DO ME A FAVOR.

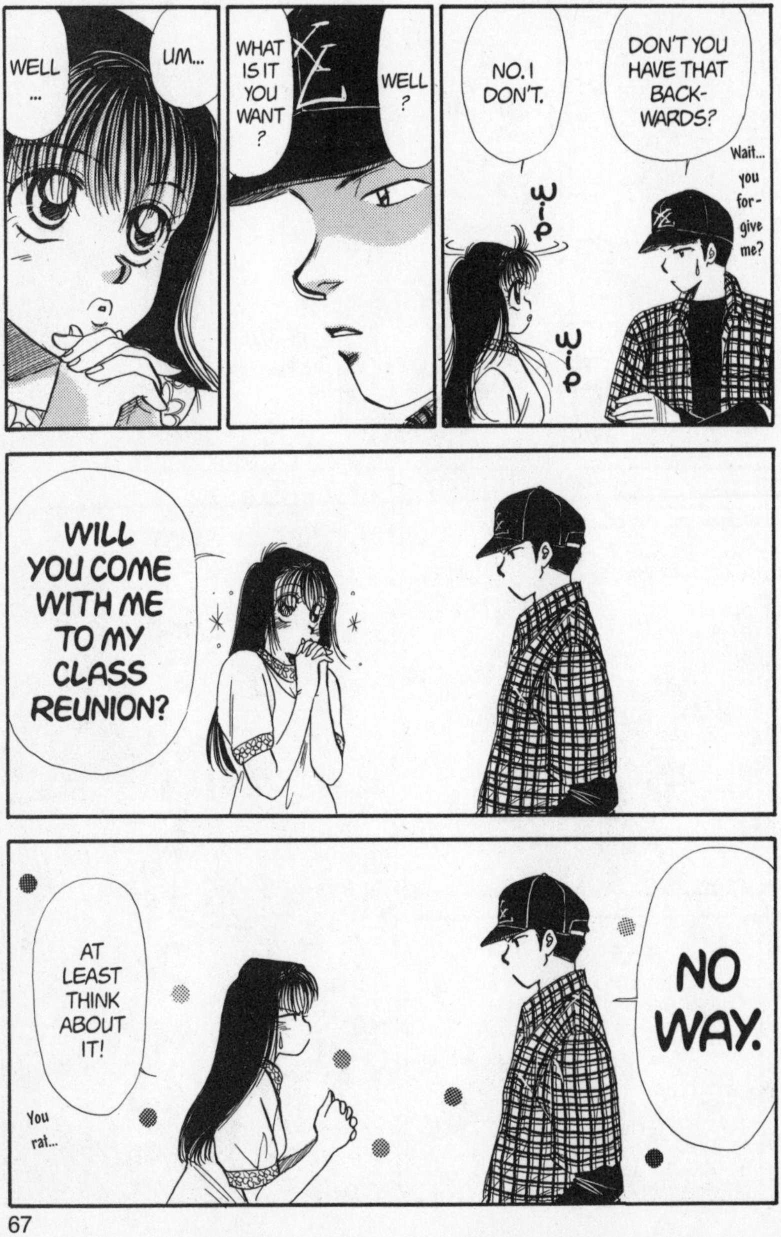

DON'T YOU HAVE THAT BACK- WARDS?
Wait... you for- give me?
NO. I DON'T.
WIP
WIP
WELL ?
WHAT IS IT YOU WANT ?
UM...
WELL ...
WILL YOU COME WITH ME TO MY CLASS REUNION?
NO WAY.
AT LEAST THINK ABOUT IT!
You rat...

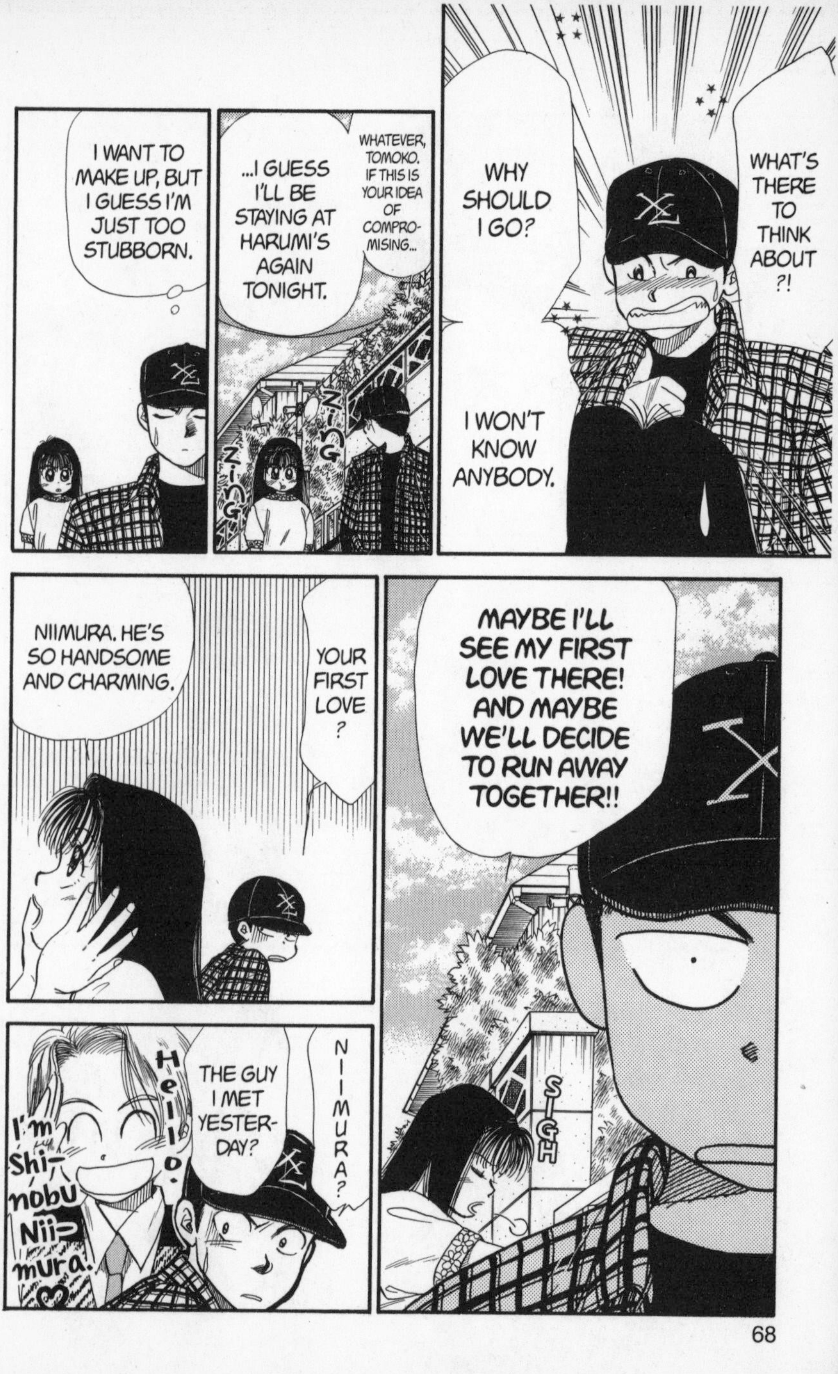
WHAT'S THERE TO THINK ABOUT?!
WHY SHOULD I GO?
I WON'T KNOW ANYBODY.
WHATEVER, TOMOKO. IF THIS IS YOUR IDEA OF COMPRO-MISING...
...I GUESS I'LL BE STAYING AT HARUMI'S AGAIN TONIGHT.
ZING
ZING
I WANT TO MAKE UP, BUT I GUESS I'M JUST TOO STUBBORN.
MAYBE I'LL SEE MY FIRST LOVE THERE! AND MAYBE WE'LL DECIDE TO RUN AWAY TOGETHER!!
SIGH
YOUR FIRST LOVE?
NIIMURA. HE'S SO HANDSOME AND CHARMING.
NIIMURA?
THE GUY I MET YESTER-DAY?
Hello.
I'm Shi-nobu Nii-mura.

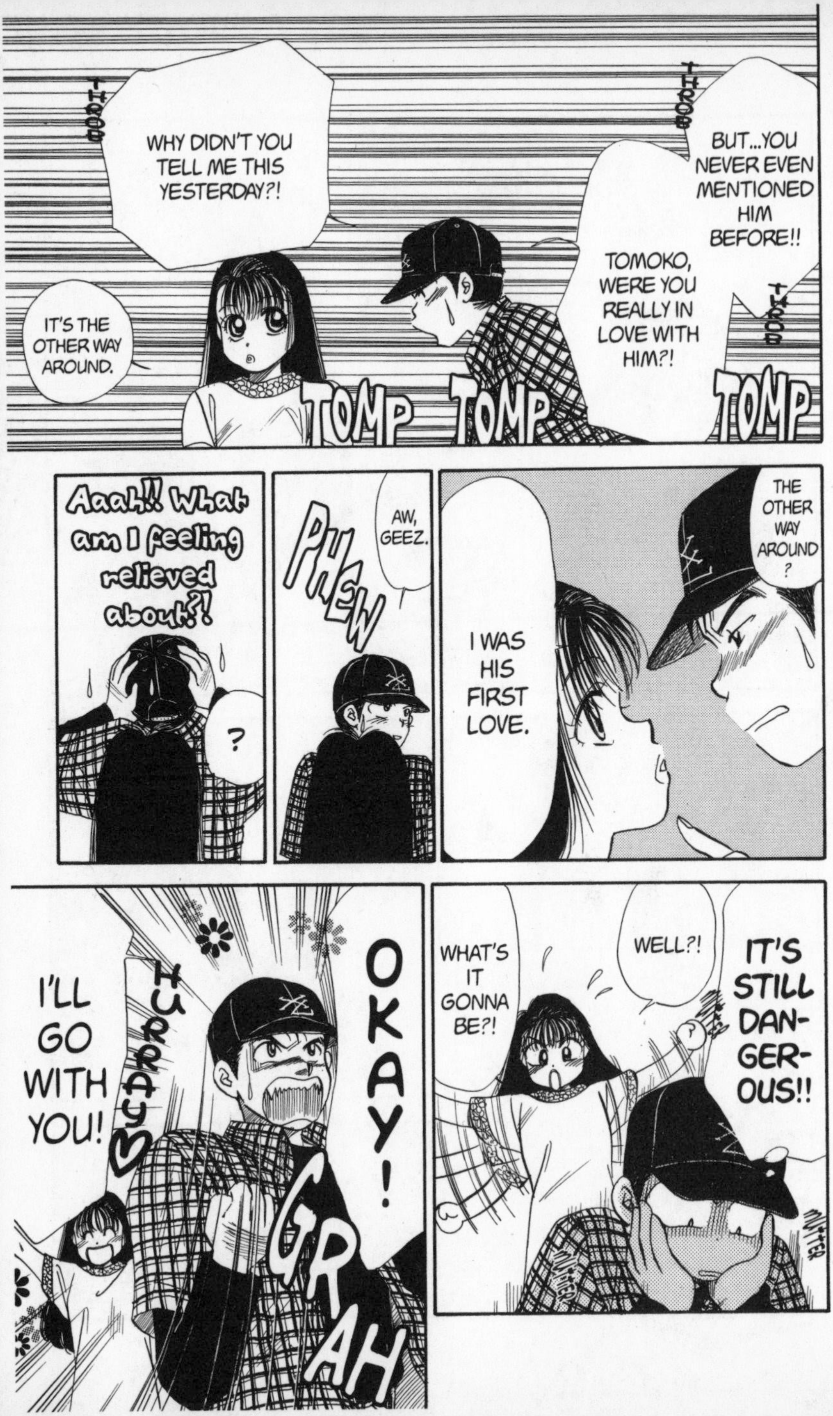
THROB
BUT...YOU NEVER EVEN MENTIONED HIM BEFORE!!
THROB
TOMOKO, WERE YOU REALLY IN LOVE WITH HIM?!
THROB
WHY DIDN'T YOU TELL ME THIS YESTERDAY?!
IT'S THE OTHER WAY AROUND.
TOMP TOMP TOMP
THE OTHER WAY AROUND?
I WAS HIS FIRST LOVE.
AW, GEEZ.
PHEW
Aaah!! What am I feeling relieved about?!
?
IT'S STILL DAN-GER-OUS!!
WELL?!
WHAT'S IT GONNA BE?!
MUTTER
MUTTER
OKAY!
HURRAY♥
I'LL GO WITH YOU!
GRAAH

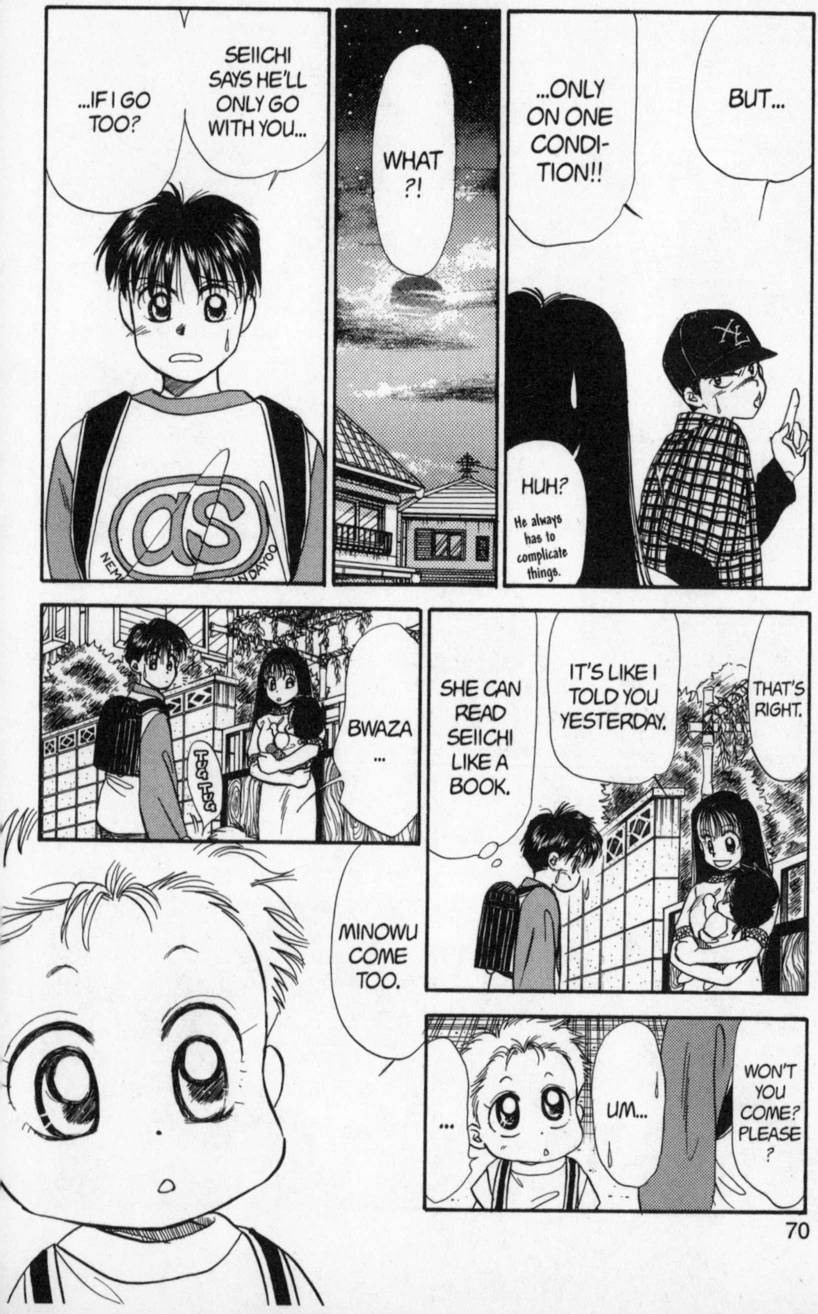
BUT...
...ONLY ON ONE CONDITION!!
HUH?
He always has to complicate things.
WHAT ?!
SEIICHI SAYS HE'LL ONLY GO WITH YOU...
...IF I GO TOO?
THAT'S RIGHT.
IT'S LIKE I TOLD YOU YESTERDAY.
SHE CAN READ SEIICHI LIKE A BOOK.
BWAZA ...
Tug Tug
WON'T YOU COME? PLEASE ?
UM...
...
MINOWU COME TOO.

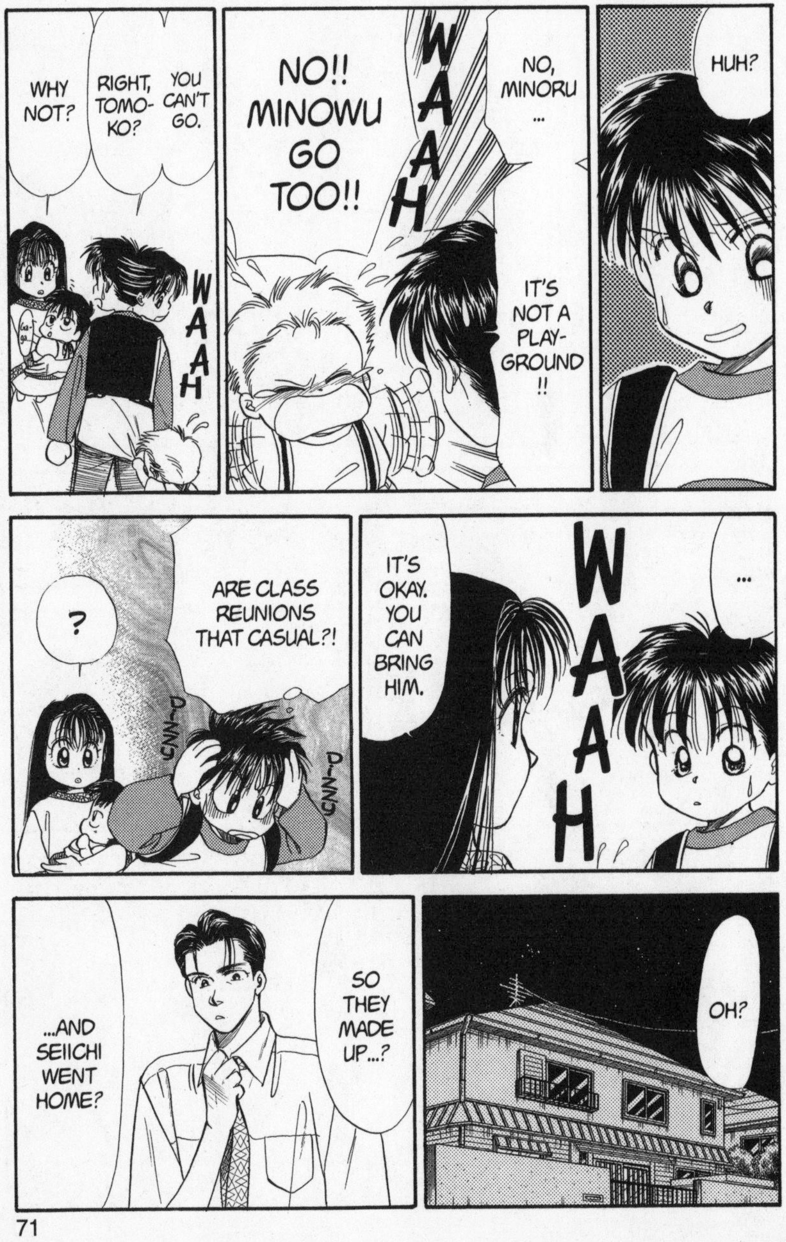
HUH?
NO, MINORU ...
IT'S NOT A PLAY-GROUND !!
WAAH
NO!! MINOWU GO TOO!!
YOU CAN'T GO.
RIGHT, TOMO-KO?
WHY NOT?
WAAH
...
WAAH
IT'S OKAY. YOU CAN BRING HIM.
ARE CLASS REUNIONS THAT CASUAL?!
DIZZY
DIZZY
?
OH?
SO THEY MADE UP...?
...AND SEIICHI WENT HOME?

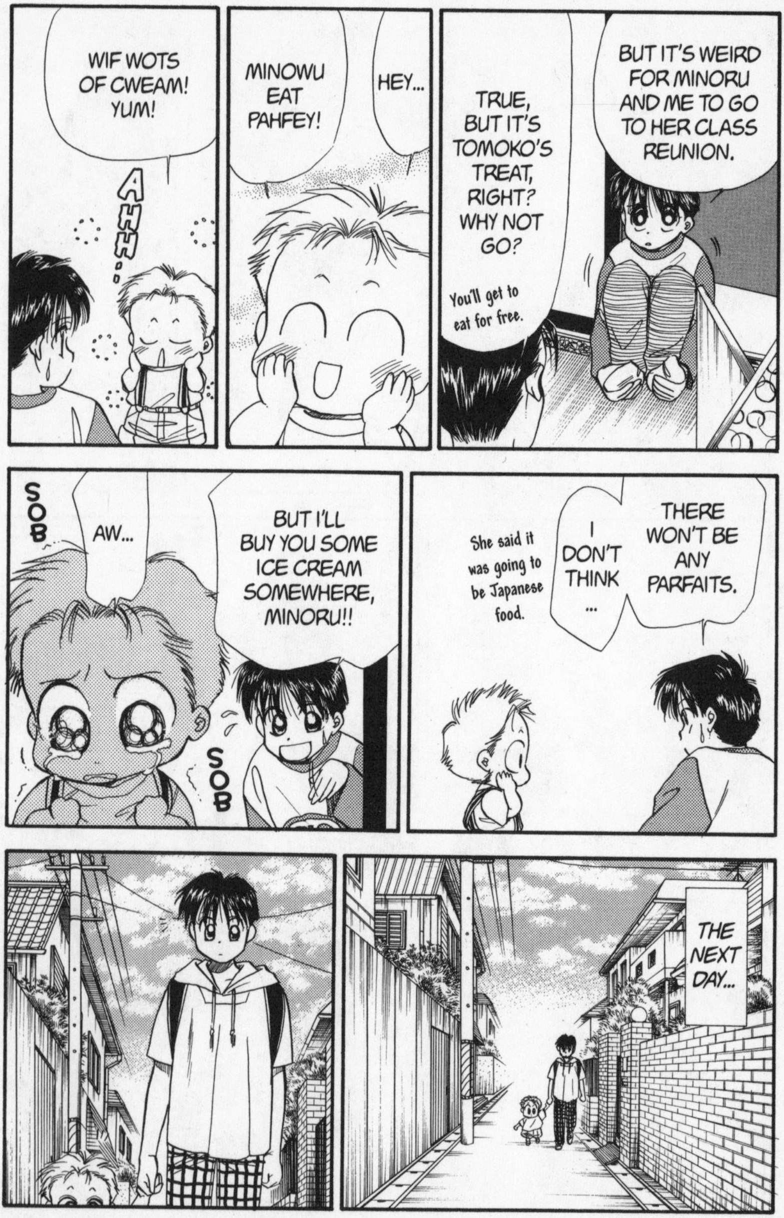

BUT IT'S WEIRD FOR MINORU AND ME TO GO TO HER CLASS REUNION.
TRUE, BUT IT'S TOMOKO'S TREAT, RIGHT? WHY NOT GO?
You'll get to eat for free.
HEY...
MINOWU EAT PAHFEY!
WIF WOTS OF CWEAM! YUM!
AHHH..
THERE WON'T BE ANY PARFAITS.
I DON'T THINK ...
She said it was going to be Japanese food.
BUT I'LL BUY YOU SOME ICE CREAM SOMEWHERE, MINORU!!
AW...
SOB
SOB
THE NEXT DAY...

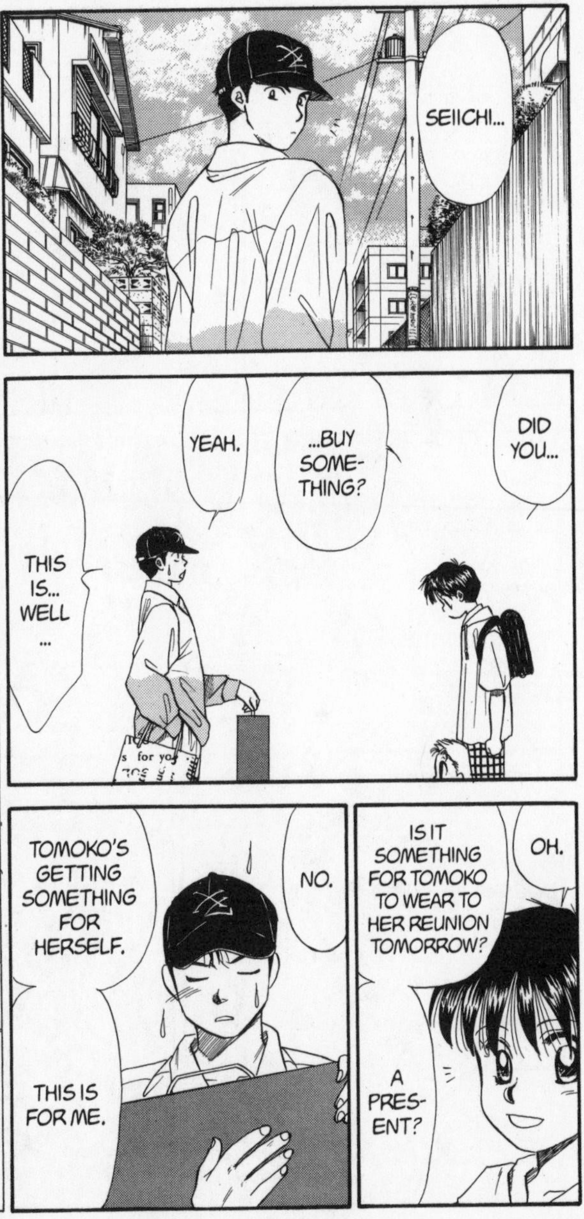
SEIICHI...
DID YOU...
...BUY SOMETHING?
YEAH.
THIS IS... WELL ...
OH.
IS IT SOMETHING FOR TOMOKO TO WEAR TO HER REUNION TOMORROW?
A PRESENT?
NO.
TOMOKO'S GETTING SOMETHING FOR HERSELF.
THIS IS FOR ME.

Author's Note: Part 3

One day, I noticed my brother hadn't shaved, so I told him to just let it grow. I was hoping he'd grow a big thick beard like you see in foreign movies, but my brother's beard was very sparse. It looked like a worm-eaten lawn. Then our sister said, "That looks disgusting. Shave it off!!" I wonder if my brother was hurt by her words. Being a woman, I don't know.

A quick lesson in Minoru-Speak.

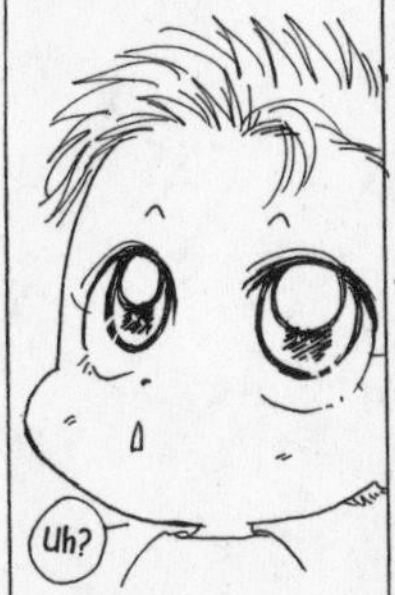
Uh?

"Th" becomes either "d," "z," or sometimes "f." Oddly, "s" sometimes becomes "th." "R" becomes "w." Leave out articles as desired.

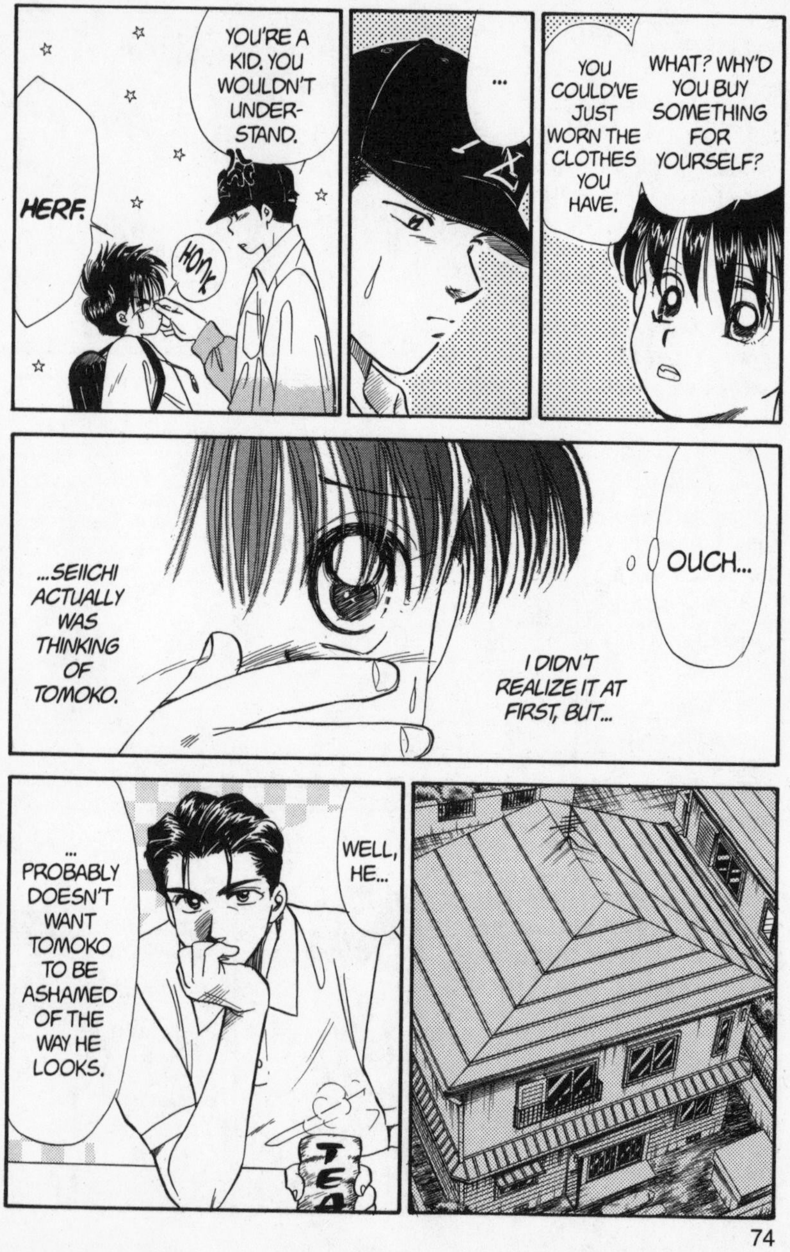
WHAT? WHY'D YOU BUY SOMETHING FOR YOURSELF?
YOU COULD'VE JUST WORN THE CLOTHES YOU HAVE.
...
YOU'RE A KID. YOU WOULDN'T UNDER-STAND.
HONK
HERF.
OUCH...
I DIDN'T REALIZE IT AT FIRST, BUT...
...SEIICHI ACTUALLY WAS THINKING OF TOMOKO.
WELL, HE...
...PROBABLY DOESN'T WANT TOMOKO TO BE ASHAMED OF THE WAY HE LOOKS.
TEA

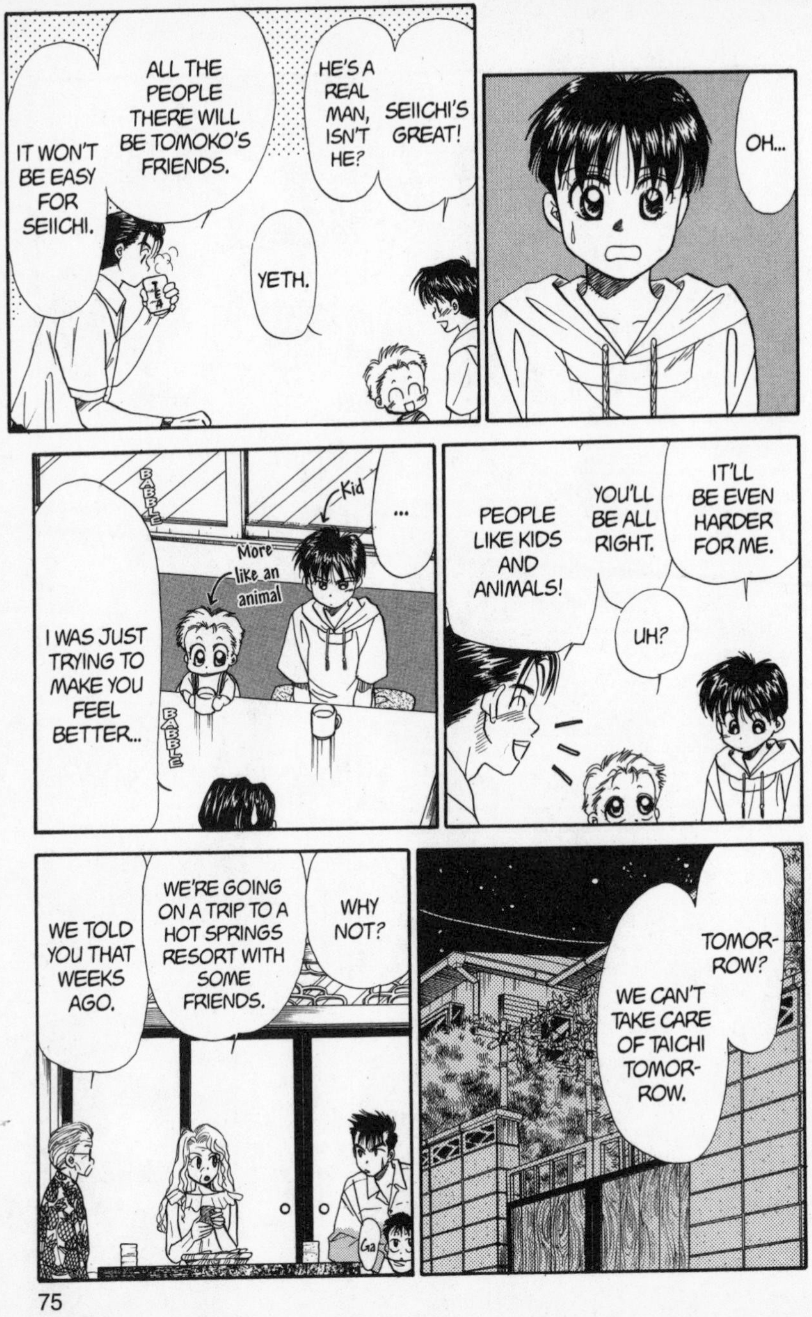
OH...
SEIICHI'S GREAT!
HE'S A REAL MAN, ISN'T HE?
YETH.
ALL THE PEOPLE THERE WILL BE TOMOKO'S FRIENDS.
IT WON'T BE EASY FOR SEIICHI.
IT'LL BE EVEN HARDER FOR ME.
YOU'LL BE ALL RIGHT.
UH?
PEOPLE LIKE KIDS AND ANIMALS!
...
Kid
BABBLE
More like an animal
I WAS JUST TRYING TO MAKE YOU FEEL BETTER...
BABBLE
TOMORROW?
WE CAN'T TAKE CARE OF TAICHI TOMORROW.
WHY NOT?
WE'RE GOING ON A TRIP TO A HOT SPRINGS RESORT WITH SOME FRIENDS.
WE TOLD YOU THAT WEEKS AGO.
Ga

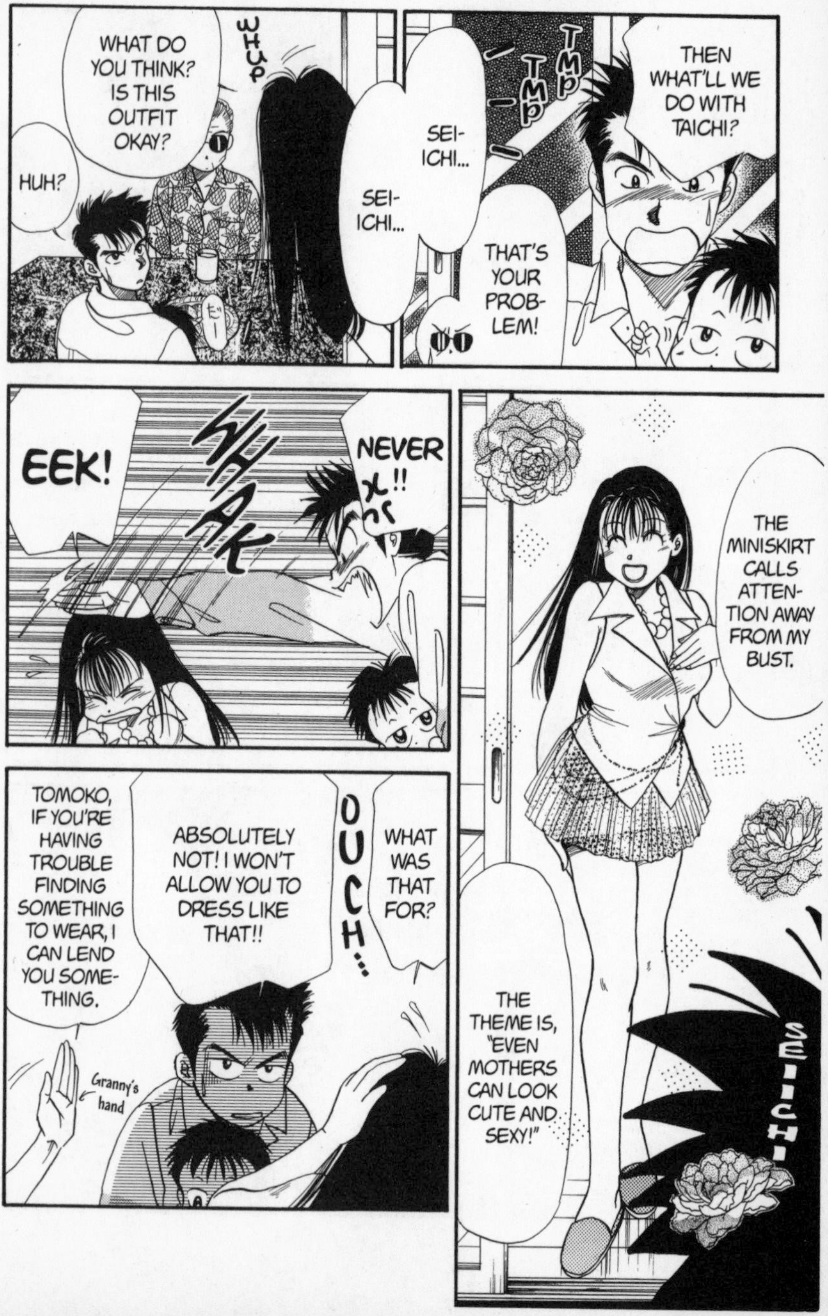
THEN WHAT'LL WE DO WITH TAICHI?
TMP TMP
SEI-ICHI...
SEI-ICHI...
THAT'S YOUR PROB-LEM!
WHUP
WHAT DO YOU THINK? IS THIS OUTFIT OKAY?
HUH?
THE MINISKIRT CALLS ATTEN-TION AWAY FROM MY BUST.
THE THEME IS, "EVEN MOTHERS CAN LOOK CUTE AND SEXY!"
SEIICHI
NEVER!!
WHAK
EEK!
WHAT WAS THAT FOR?
OUCH...
ABSOLUTELY NOT! I WON'T ALLOW YOU TO DRESS LIKE THAT!!
TOMOKO, IF YOU'RE HAVING TROUBLE FINDING SOMETHING TO WEAR, I CAN LEND YOU SOME-THING.
Granny's hand

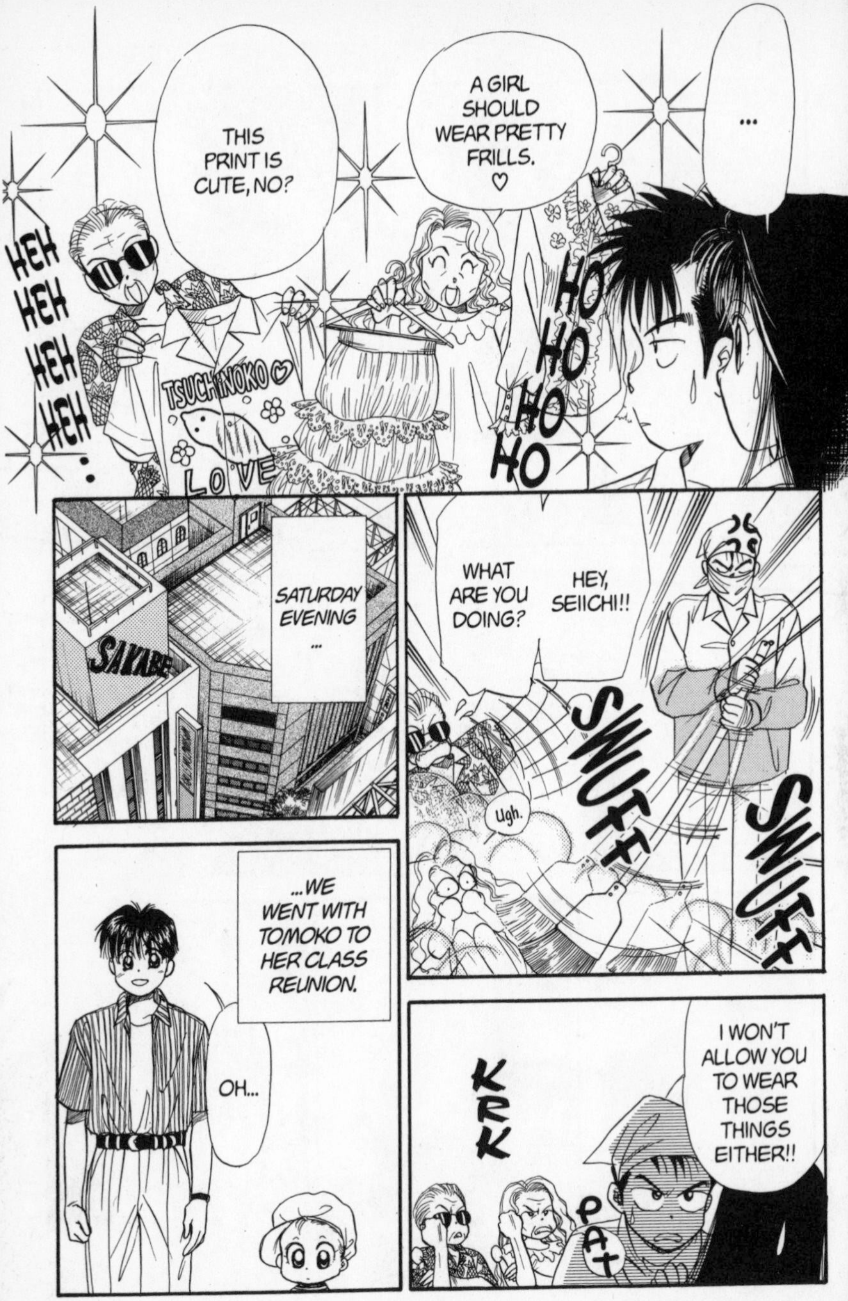
...
A GIRL SHOULD WEAR PRETTY FRILLS. ♡
HO HO HO HO
THIS PRINT IS CUTE, NO?
HEH HEH HEH HEH
TSUCHINOKO ♡
LOVE
HEY, SEIICHI!!
WHAT ARE YOU DOING?
SWUFF
SWUFF
Ugh.
I WON'T ALLOW YOU TO WEAR THOSE THINGS EITHER!!
KRK
PAT
SATURDAY EVENING ...
SAKABE
...WE WENT WITH TOMOKO TO HER CLASS REUNION.
OH...

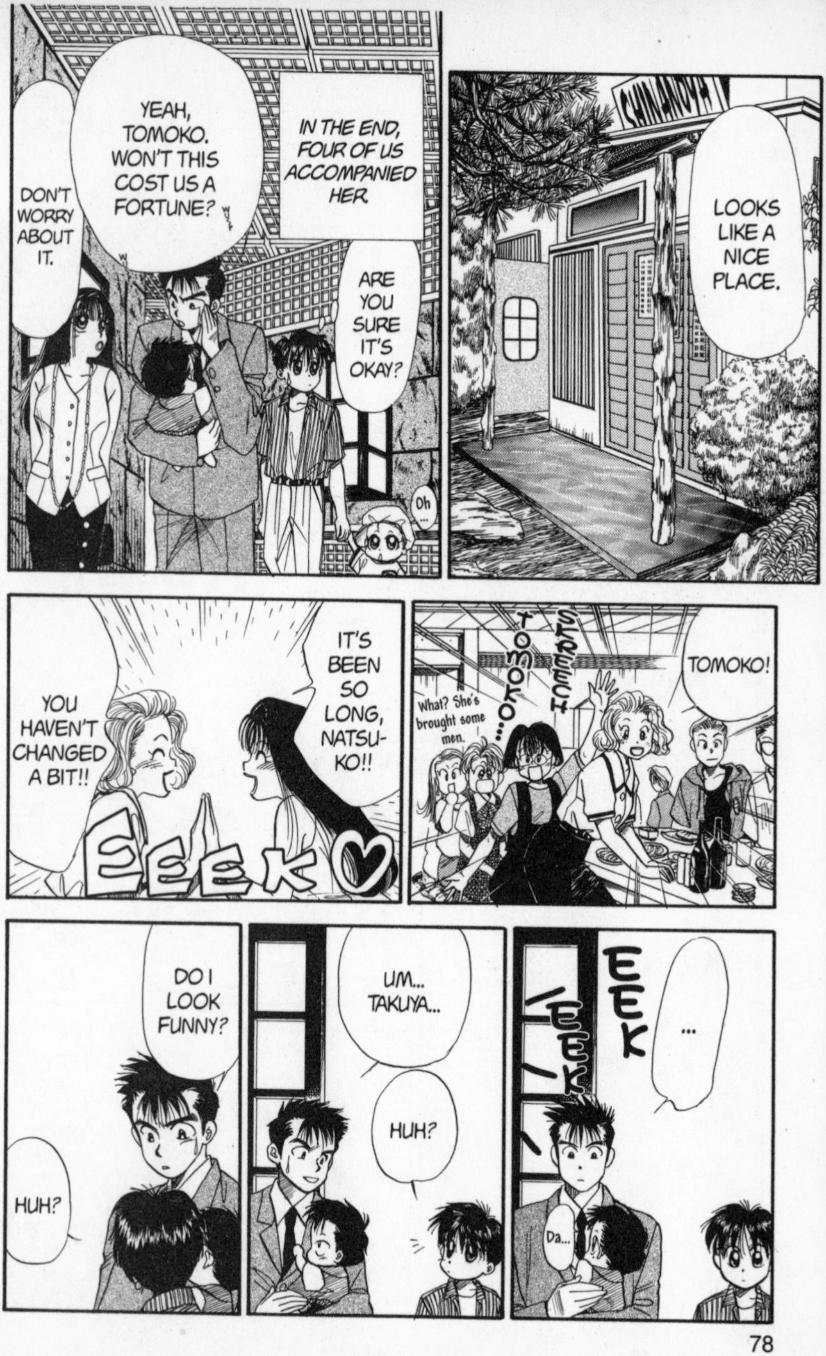
CHINANDYA
LOOKS LIKE A NICE PLACE.
IN THE END, FOUR OF US ACCOMPANIED HER.
YEAH, TOMOKO. WON'T THIS COST US A FORTUNE?
DON'T WORRY ABOUT IT.
ARE YOU SURE IT'S OKAY?
Oh ...
TOMOKO!
SKREECH
TOMOKO...
What? She's brought some men.
IT'S BEEN SO LONG, NATSUKO!!
YOU HAVEN'T CHANGED A BIT!!
EEEK♡
EEK
EEEK
...
Da...
UM... TAKUYA...
HUH?
DO I LOOK FUNNY?
HUH?

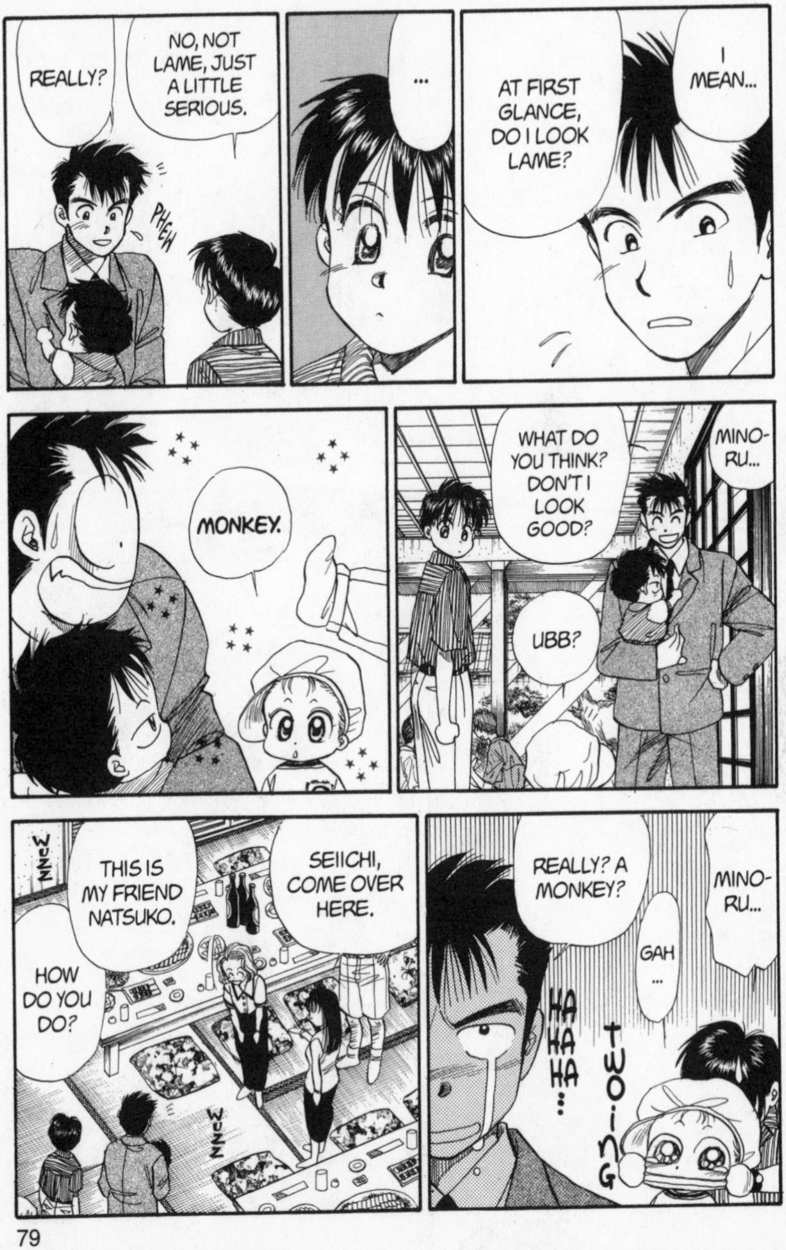
I MEAN...
AT FIRST GLANCE, DO I LOOK LAME?
...
NO, NOT LAME, JUST A LITTLE SERIOUS.
REALLY?
PHEW
MINO-RU...
WHAT DO YOU THINK? DON'T I LOOK GOOD?
UBB?
MONKEY.
MINO-RU...
REALLY? A MONKEY?
GAH...
TWOING
HA HA HA...
SEIICHI, COME OVER HERE.
THIS IS MY FRIEND NATSUKO.
WUZZ
HOW DO YOU DO?
WUZZ

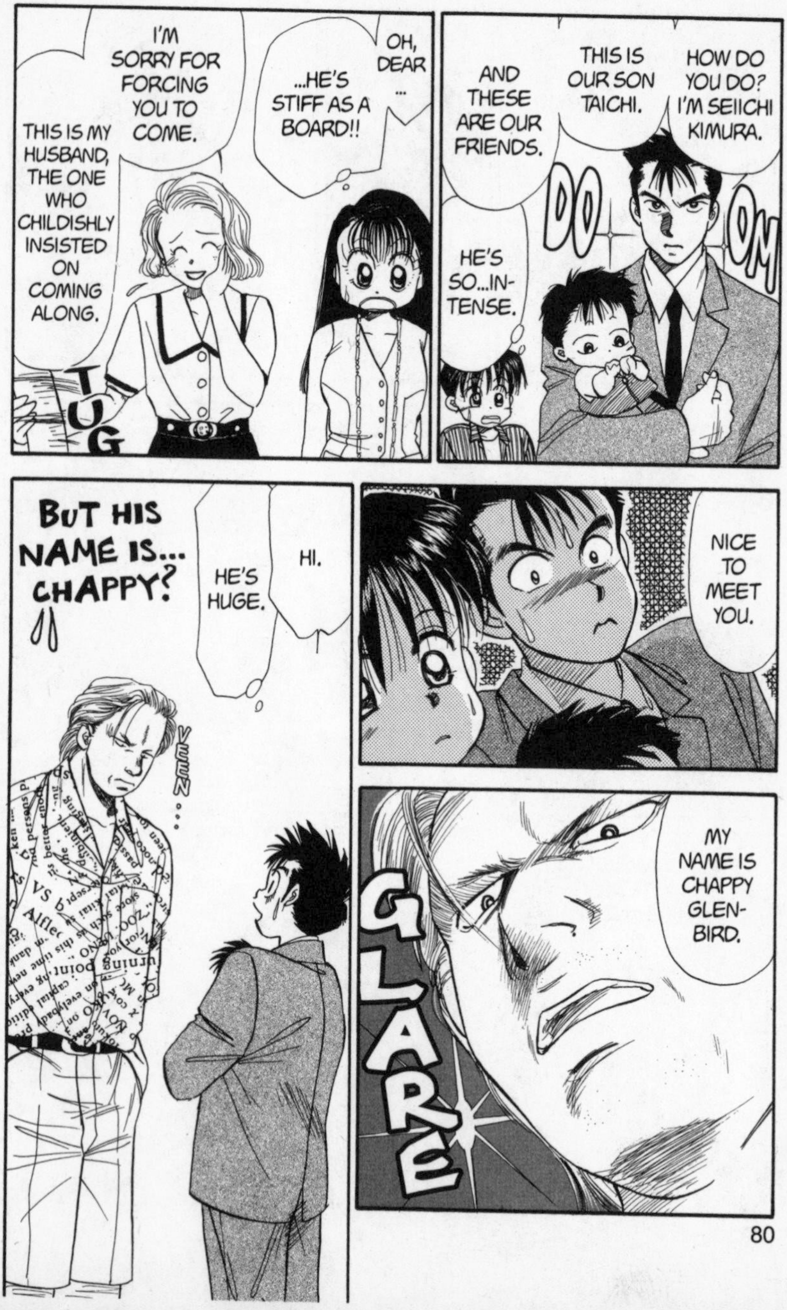
HOW DO YOU DO? I'M SEIICHI KIMURA.
THIS IS OUR SON TAICHI.
AND THESE ARE OUR FRIENDS.
DO
OM
HE'S SO...IN-TENSE.
OH, DEAR ...
...HE'S STIFF AS A BOARD!!
I'M SORRY FOR FORCING YOU TO COME.
THIS IS MY HUSBAND, THE ONE WHO CHILDISHLY INSISTED ON COMING ALONG.
TUG
NICE TO MEET YOU.
MY NAME IS CHAPPY GLEN-BIRD.
GLARE
HI.
HE'S HUGE.
BUT HIS NAME IS... CHAPPY?
VEEN...

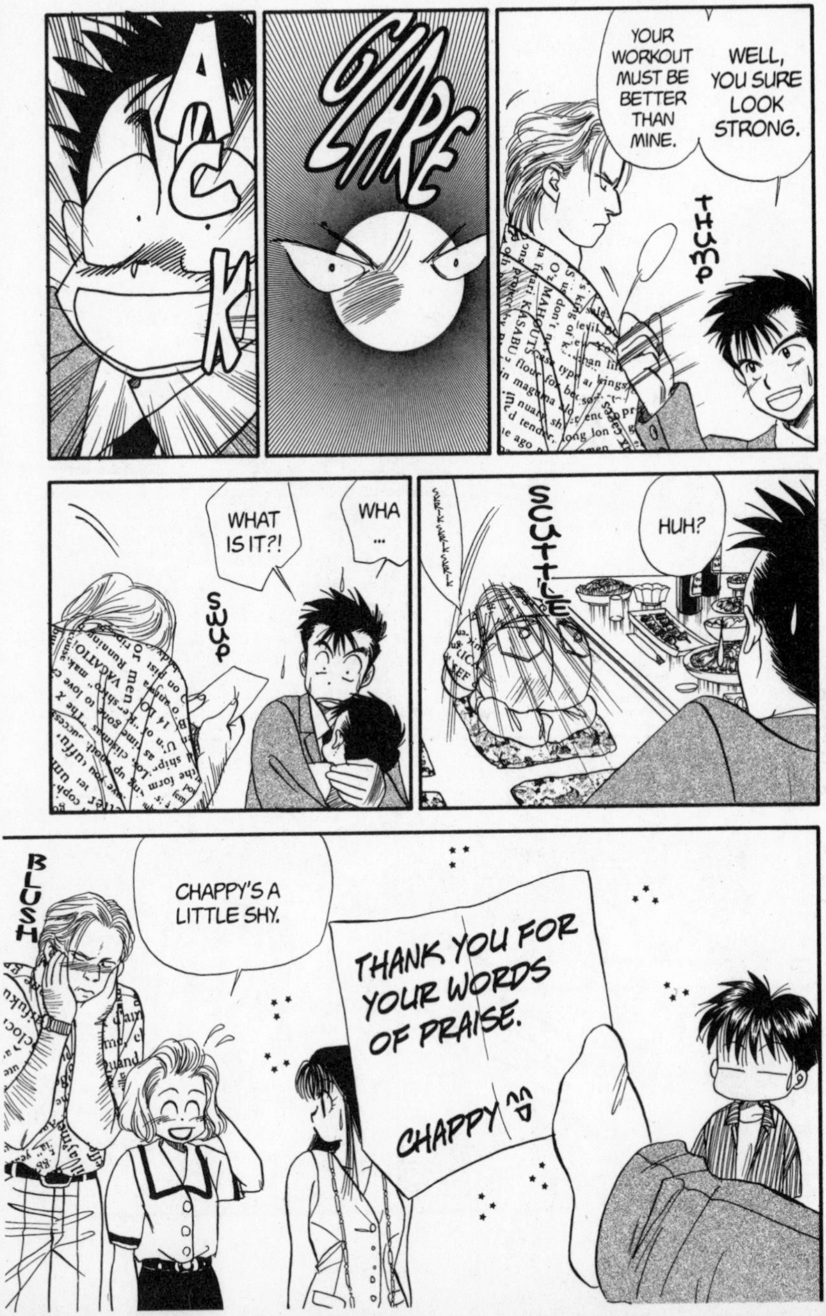
WELL, YOU SURE LOOK STRONG.
YOUR WORKOUT MUST BE BETTER THAN MINE.
THUMP
GLARE
ACK
HUH?
SCUTTLE
WHA...
WHAT IS IT?!
SWUP
THANK YOU FOR YOUR WORDS OF PRAISE.
CHAPPY
CHAPPY'S A LITTLE SHY.
BLUSH

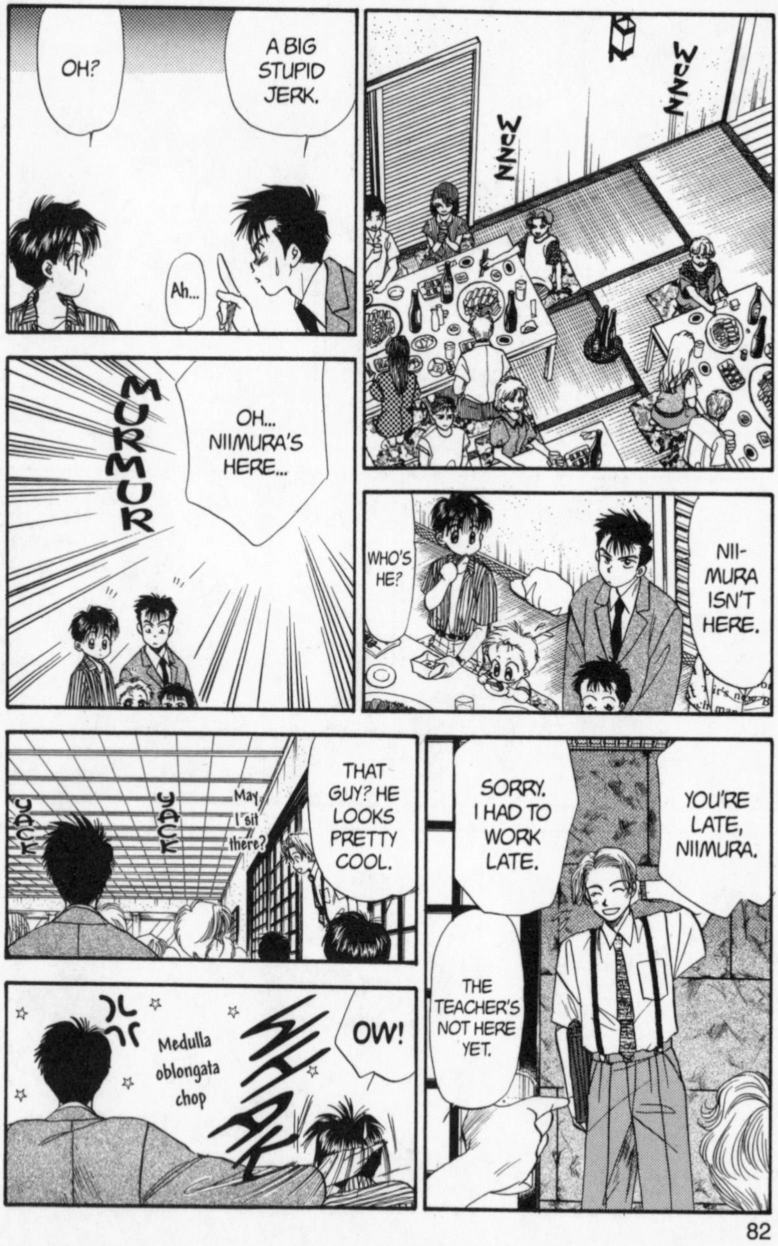
WUZZ
WUZZ
A BIG STUPID JERK.
OH?
Ah...
NII-MURA ISN'T HERE.
WHO'S HE?
OH... NIIMURA'S HERE...
MURMUR
YOU'RE LATE, NIIMURA.
SORRY. I HAD TO WORK LATE.
THE TEACHER'S NOT HERE YET.
THAT GUY? HE LOOKS PRETTY COOL.
May I sit there?
YACK
YACK
OW!
WHAK
Medulla oblongata chop

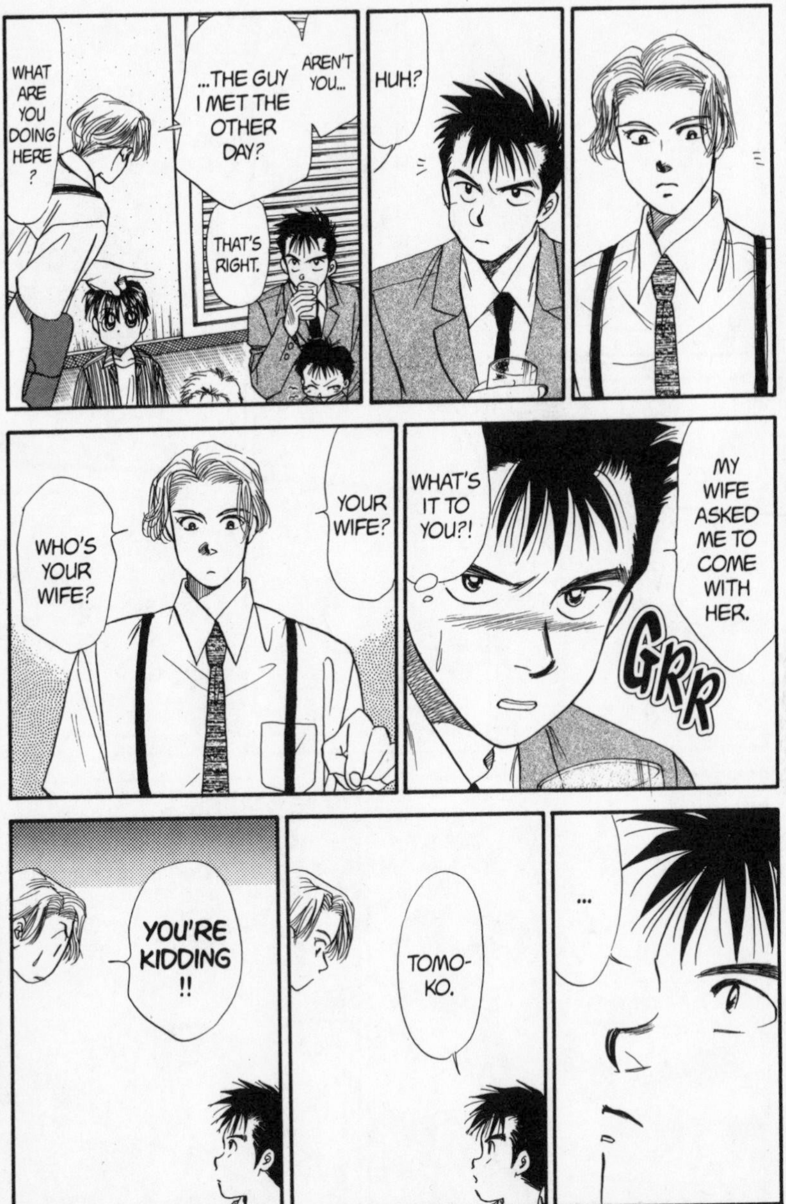
HUH?
AREN'T YOU...
...THE GUY I MET THE OTHER DAY?
THAT'S RIGHT.
WHAT ARE YOU DOING HERE?
MY WIFE ASKED ME TO COME WITH HER.
GRR
WHAT'S IT TO YOU?!
YOUR WIFE?
WHO'S YOUR WIFE?
...
TOMO-KO.
YOU'RE KIDDING!!

WHAT'S THAT SUP-POSED TO MEAN?
I-IT'S JUST THAT... I THOUGHT YOU TWO WERE JUST FRIENDS.
IS THAT YOUR KID?
YES.
OH.
WOW...
SIGH
HEE HEE
WHAT A LAUGH.
I CAME TO SEE THE GIRL SHINOBU LIKED, AND SHE'S MARRIED.
AND THERE ARE LOTS OF RANDOM PEOPLE HERE.
BUT YOU MADE SUCH A FUSS WHEN I INSISTED ON COMING.
YOUR GIRL-FRIEND ?
KAK KAK KAK
NO, I DIDN'T ...

Looks catty

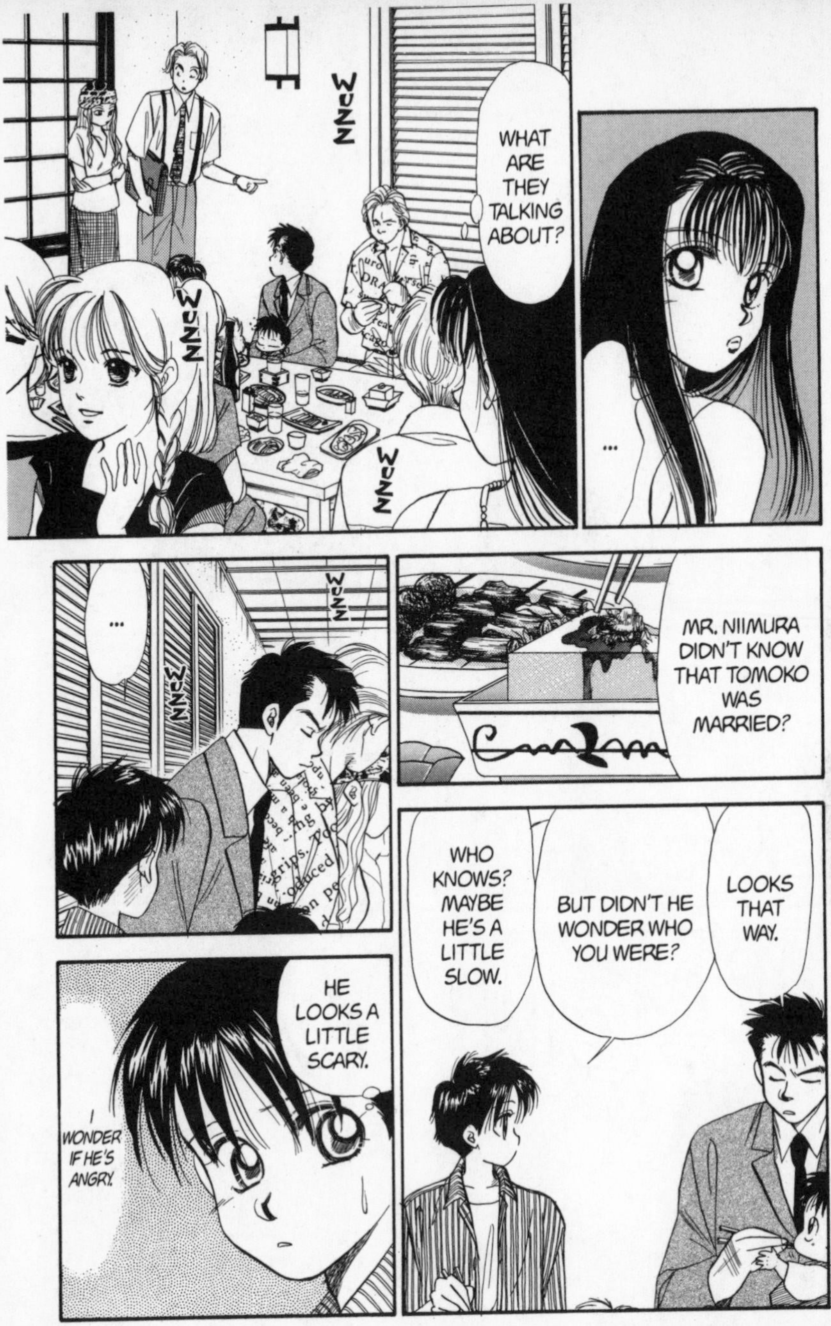
...
WUZZ
WHAT ARE THEY TALKING ABOUT?
WUZZ
WUZZ
MR. NIIMURA DIDN'T KNOW THAT TOMOKO WAS MARRIED?
WUZZ
...
WUZZ
LOOKS THAT WAY.
BUT DIDN'T HE WONDER WHO YOU WERE?
WHO KNOWS? MAYBE HE'S A LITTLE SLOW.
HE LOOKS A LITTLE SCARY.
I WONDER IF HE'S ANGRY.

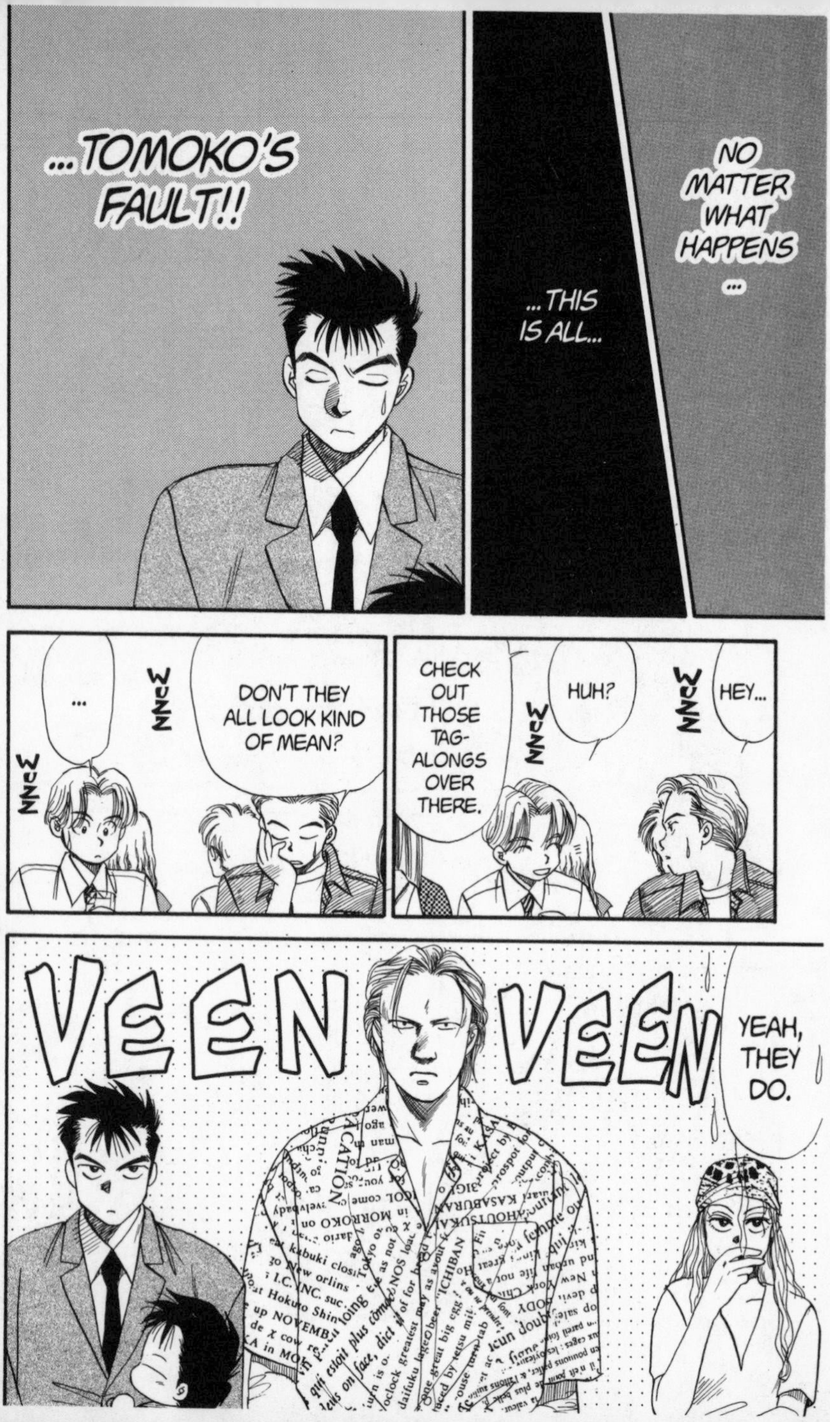
NO MATTER WHAT HAPPENS ...
...THIS IS ALL...
...TOMOKO'S FAULT!!
HEY...
WUZZ
HUH?
WUZZ
CHECK OUT THOSE TAG-ALONGS OVER THERE.
DON'T THEY ALL LOOK KIND OF MEAN?
WUZZ
...
WUZZ
YEAH, THEY DO.
VEEN
VEEN

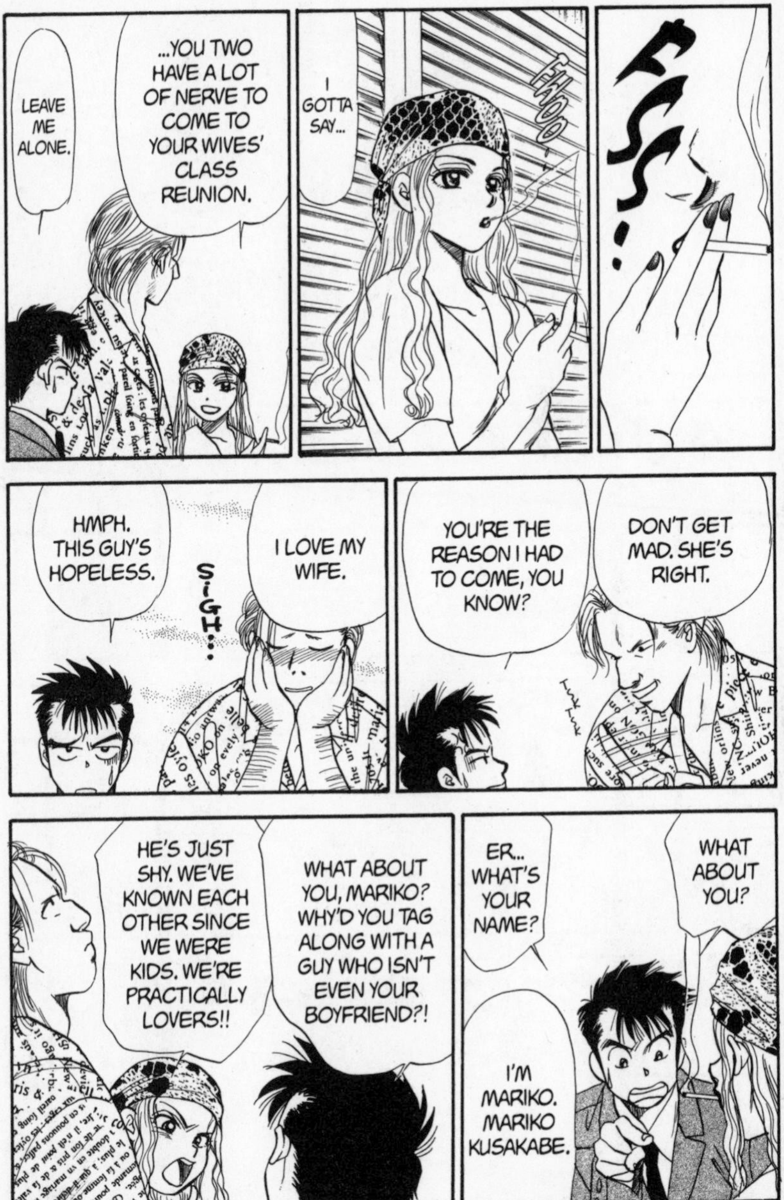
I GOTTA SAY...
...YOU TWO HAVE A LOT OF NERVE TO COME TO YOUR WIVES' CLASS REUNION.
LEAVE ME ALONE.
DON'T GET MAD. SHE'S RIGHT.
YOU'RE THE REASON I HAD TO COME, YOU KNOW?
I LOVE MY WIFE.
SIGH...
HMPH. THIS GUY'S HOPELESS.
WHAT ABOUT YOU?
ER... WHAT'S YOUR NAME?
I'M MARIKO. MARIKO KUSAKABE.
WHAT ABOUT YOU, MARIKO? WHY'D YOU TAG ALONG WITH A GUY WHO ISN'T EVEN YOUR BOYFRIEND?!
HE'S JUST SHY. WE'VE KNOWN EACH OTHER SINCE WE WERE KIDS. WE'RE PRACTICALLY LOVERS!!

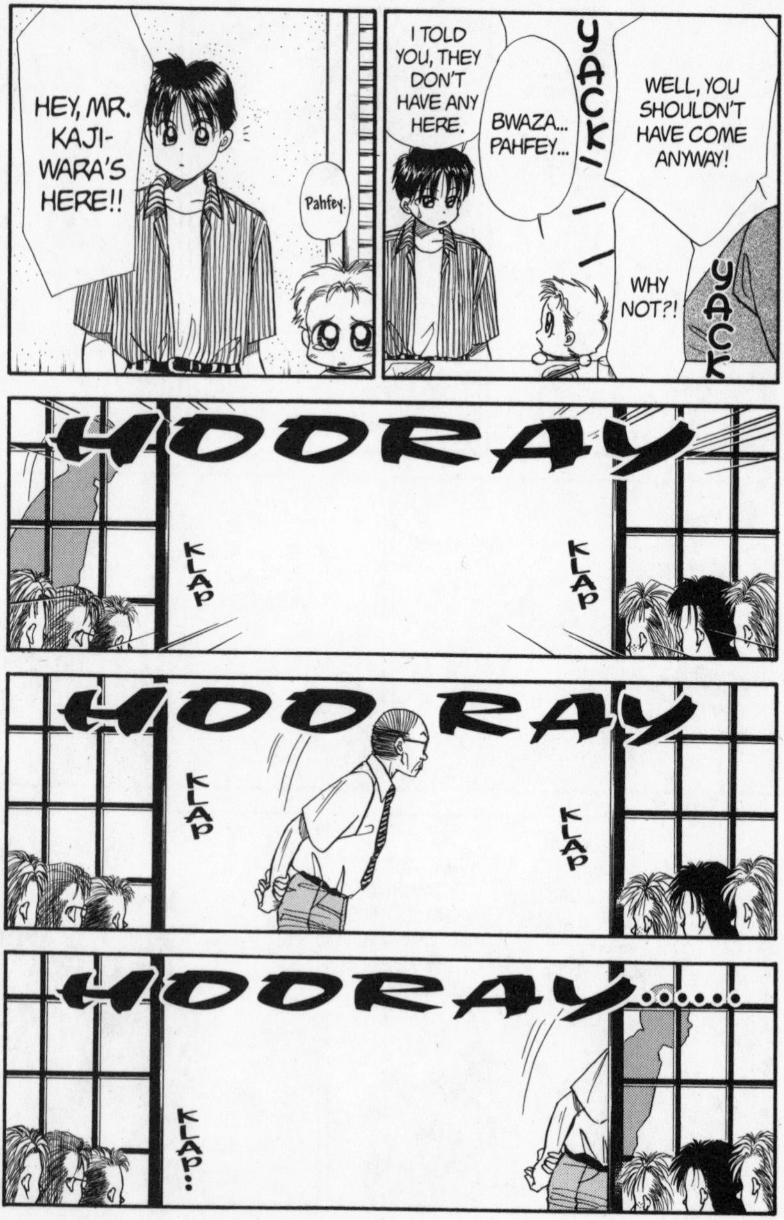
WELL, YOU SHOULDN'T HAVE COME ANYWAY!
YACK YACK
YACK
WHY NOT?!
I TOLD YOU, THEY DON'T HAVE ANY HERE.
BWAZA... PAHFEY...
Pahfey.
HEY, MR. KAJI-WARA'S HERE!!
HOORAY
KLAP
KLAP
HOO RAY
KLAP
KLAP
HOORAY......
KLAP..

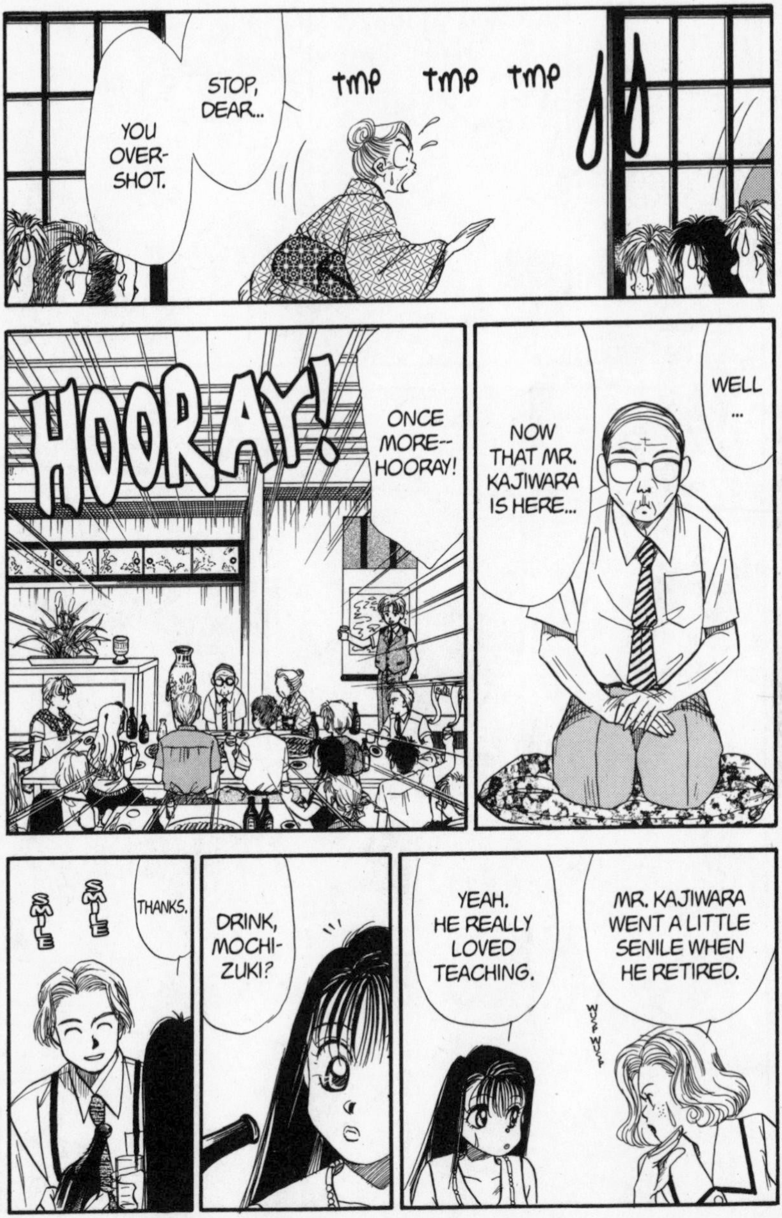
TMP TMP TMP
STOP, DEAR...
YOU OVER-SHOT.
WELL ...
NOW THAT MR. KAJIWARA IS HERE...
ONCE MORE--HOORAY!
HOORAY!
MR. KAJIWARA WENT A LITTLE SENILE WHEN HE RETIRED.
WUSP WUSP
YEAH. HE REALLY LOVED TEACHING.
DRINK, MOCHI-ZUKI?
THANKS.
SMILE SMILE

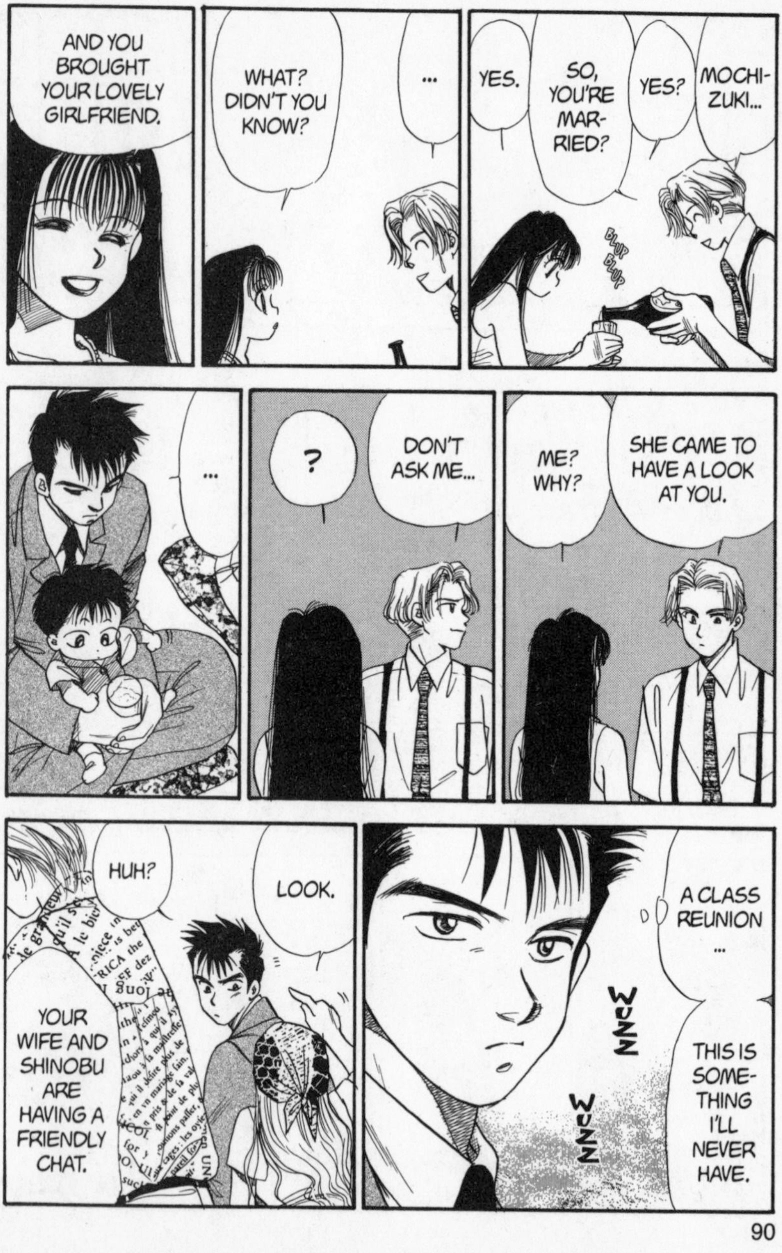
MOCHI-ZUKI...
YES?
SO, YOU'RE MAR-RIED?
YES.
BLUP BLUP
...
WHAT? DIDN'T YOU KNOW?
AND YOU BROUGHT YOUR LOVELY GIRLFRIEND.
SHE CAME TO HAVE A LOOK AT YOU.
ME? WHY?
DON'T ASK ME...
?
...
A CLASS REUNION ...
WUZZ
WUZZ
THIS IS SOME-THING I'LL NEVER HAVE.
LOOK.
HUH?
YOUR WIFE AND SHINOBU ARE HAVING A FRIENDLY CHAT.

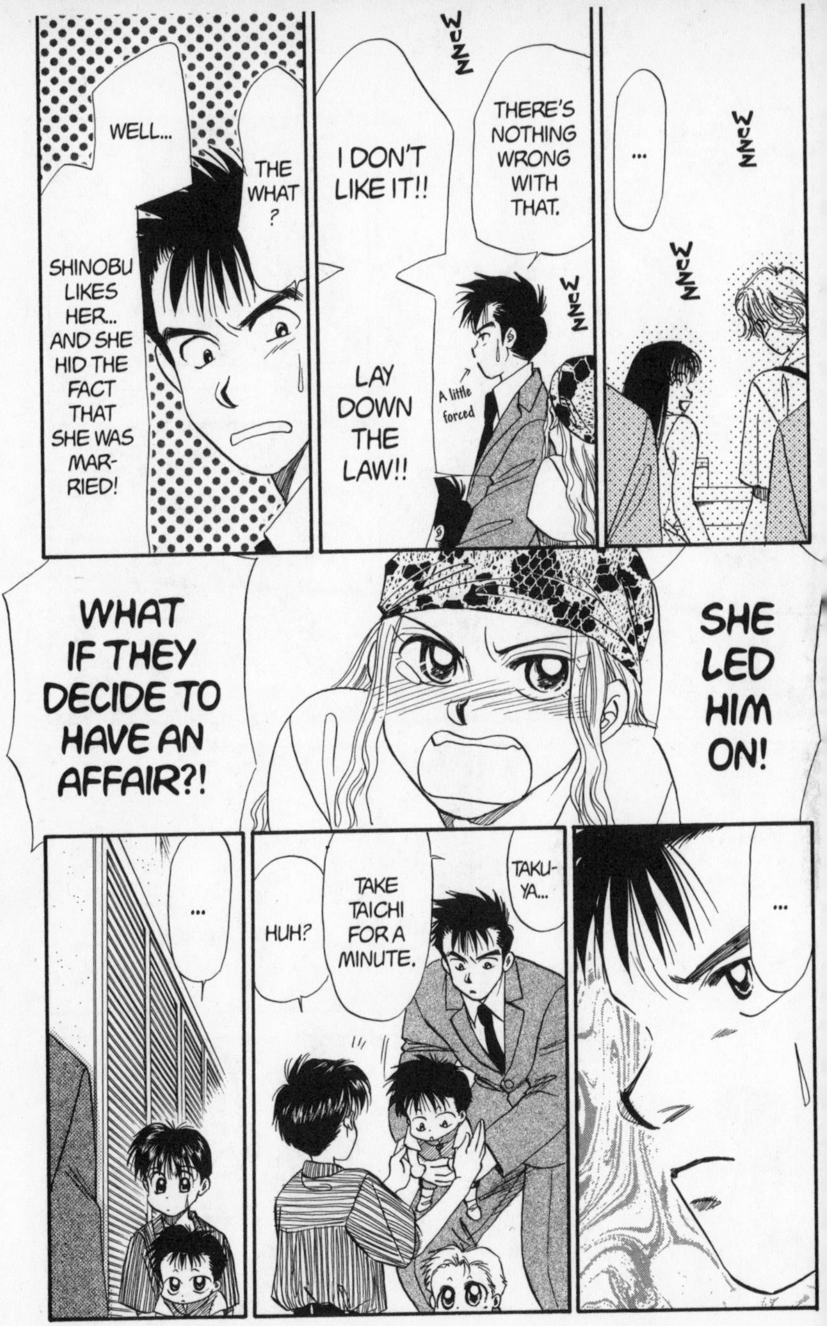
WUZZ
...
WUZZ
WUZZ
THERE'S NOTHING WRONG WITH THAT.
I DON'T LIKE IT!!
WUZZ
A little forced
LAY DOWN THE LAW!!
THE WHAT?
WELL...
SHINOBU LIKES HER... AND SHE HID THE FACT THAT SHE WAS MAR-RIED!
SHE LED HIM ON!
WHAT IF THEY DECIDE TO HAVE AN AFFAIR?!
...
TAKU-YA...
TAKE TAICHI FOR A MINUTE.
HUH?
...

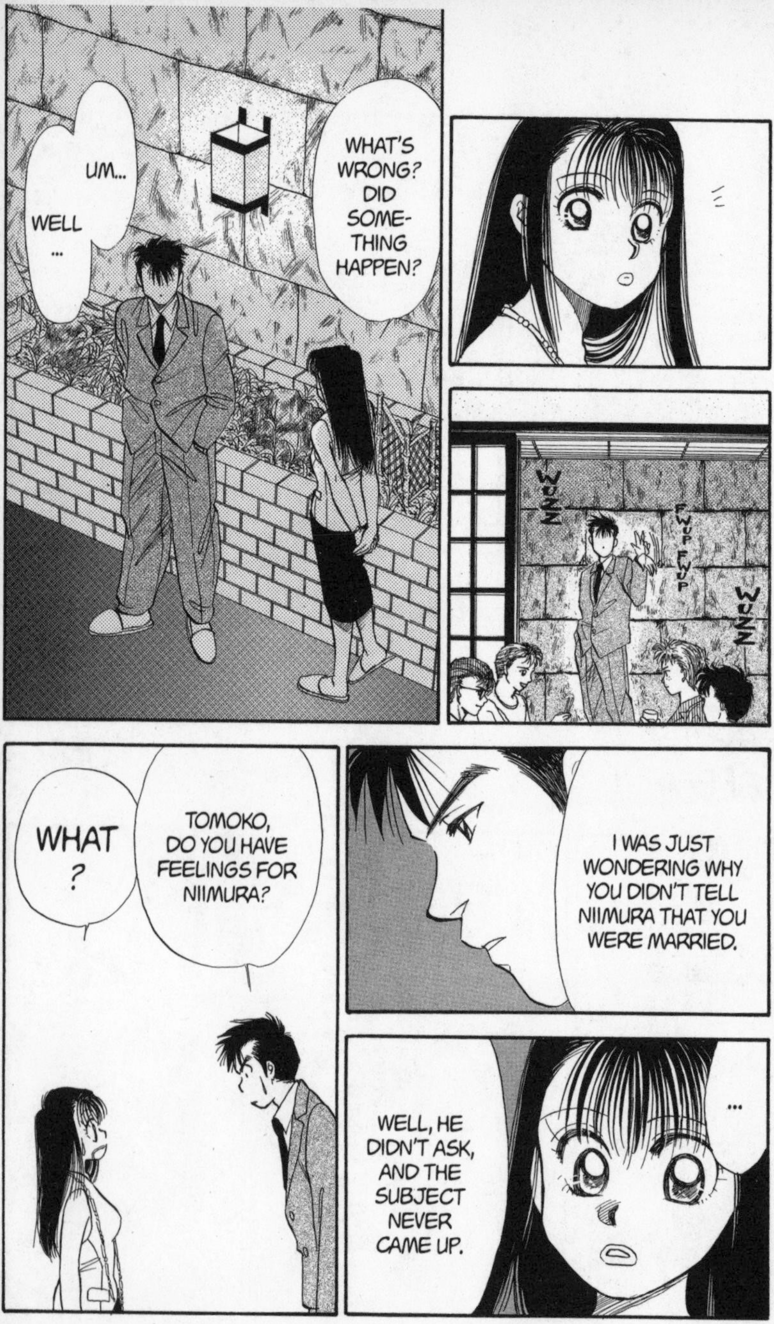
WUZZ
FWUP FWUP
WUZZ
WHAT'S WRONG? DID SOMETHING HAPPEN?
UM... WELL ...
I WAS JUST WONDERING WHY YOU DIDN'T TELL NIIMURA THAT YOU WERE MARRIED.
...
WELL, HE DIDN'T ASK, AND THE SUBJECT NEVER CAME UP.
TOMOKO, DO YOU HAVE FEELINGS FOR NIIMURA?
WHAT ?

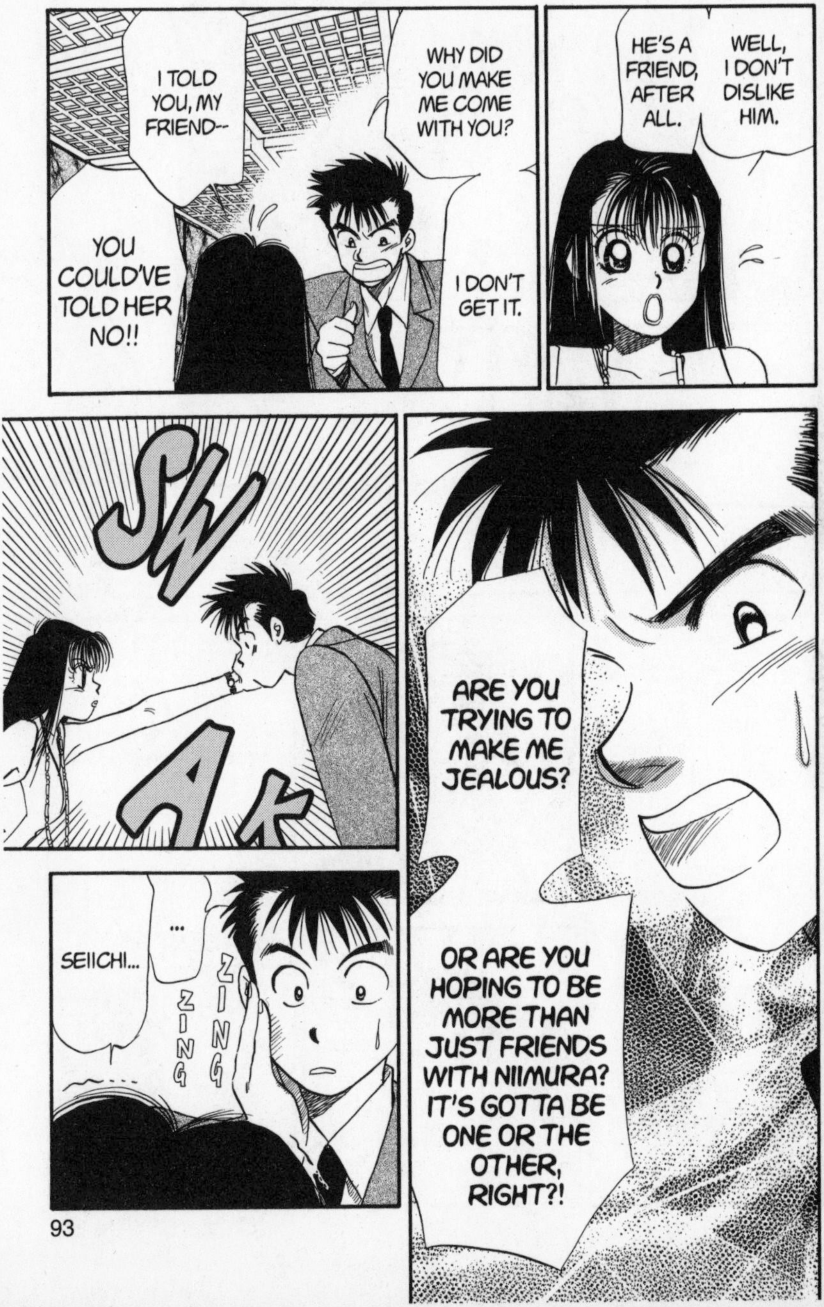
WELL, I DON'T DISLIKE HIM.
HE'S A FRIEND, AFTER ALL.
WHY DID YOU MAKE ME COME WITH YOU?
I TOLD YOU, MY FRIEND--
I DON'T GET IT.
YOU COULD'VE TOLD HER NO!!
ARE YOU TRYING TO MAKE ME JEALOUS?
OR ARE YOU HOPING TO BE MORE THAN JUST FRIENDS WITH NIIMURA? IT'S GOTTA BE ONE OR THE OTHER, RIGHT?!
SWAK
...
SEIICHI...
ZING
ZING

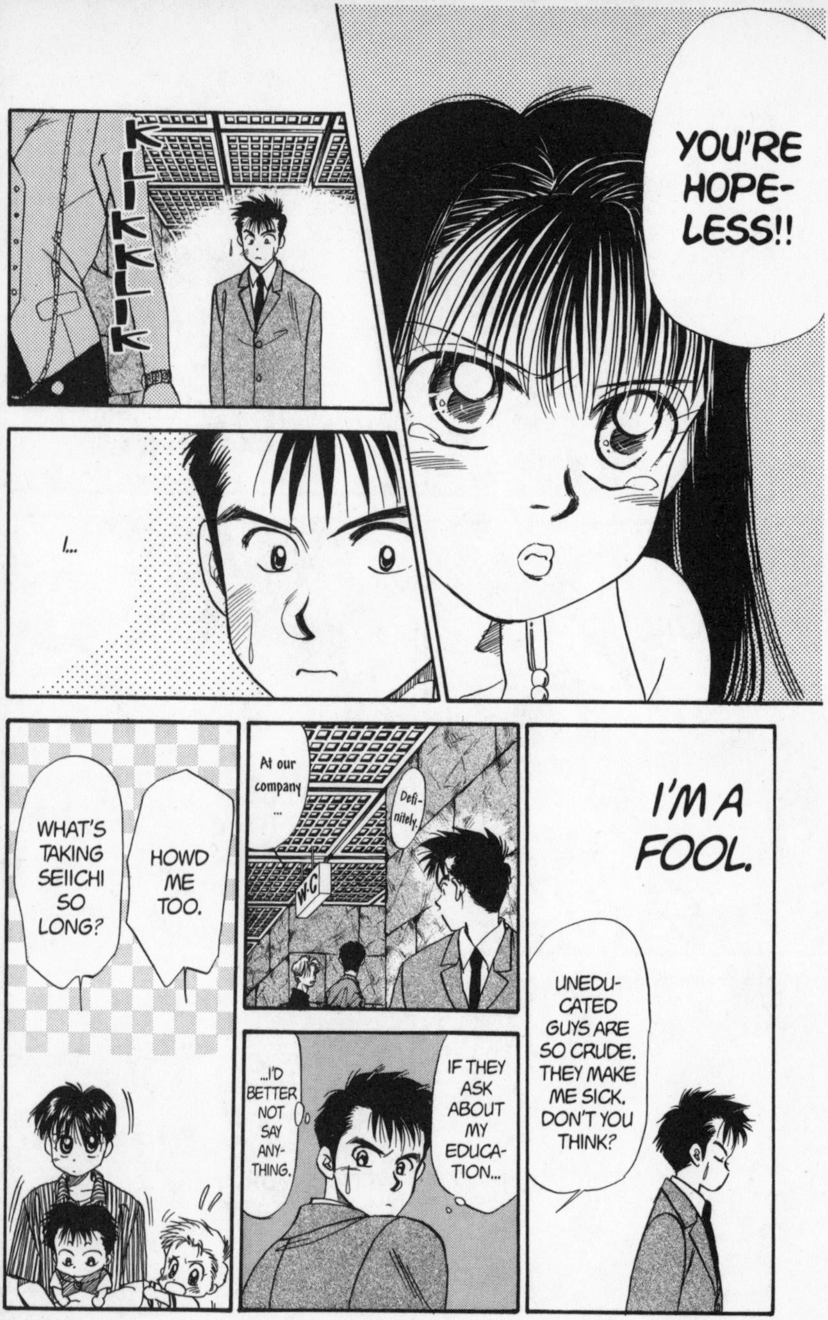
YOU'RE HOPE-LESS!!
KLIKKLIK
I...
I'M A FOOL.
UNEDU-CATED GUYS ARE SO CRUDE. THEY MAKE ME SICK. DON'T YOU THINK?
At our company...
Defi-nitely.
W-C
IF THEY ASK ABOUT MY EDUCA-TION...
...I'D BETTER NOT SAY ANY-THING.
WHAT'S TAKING SEIICHI SO LONG?
HOWD ME TOO.

Chapter 53 / The End

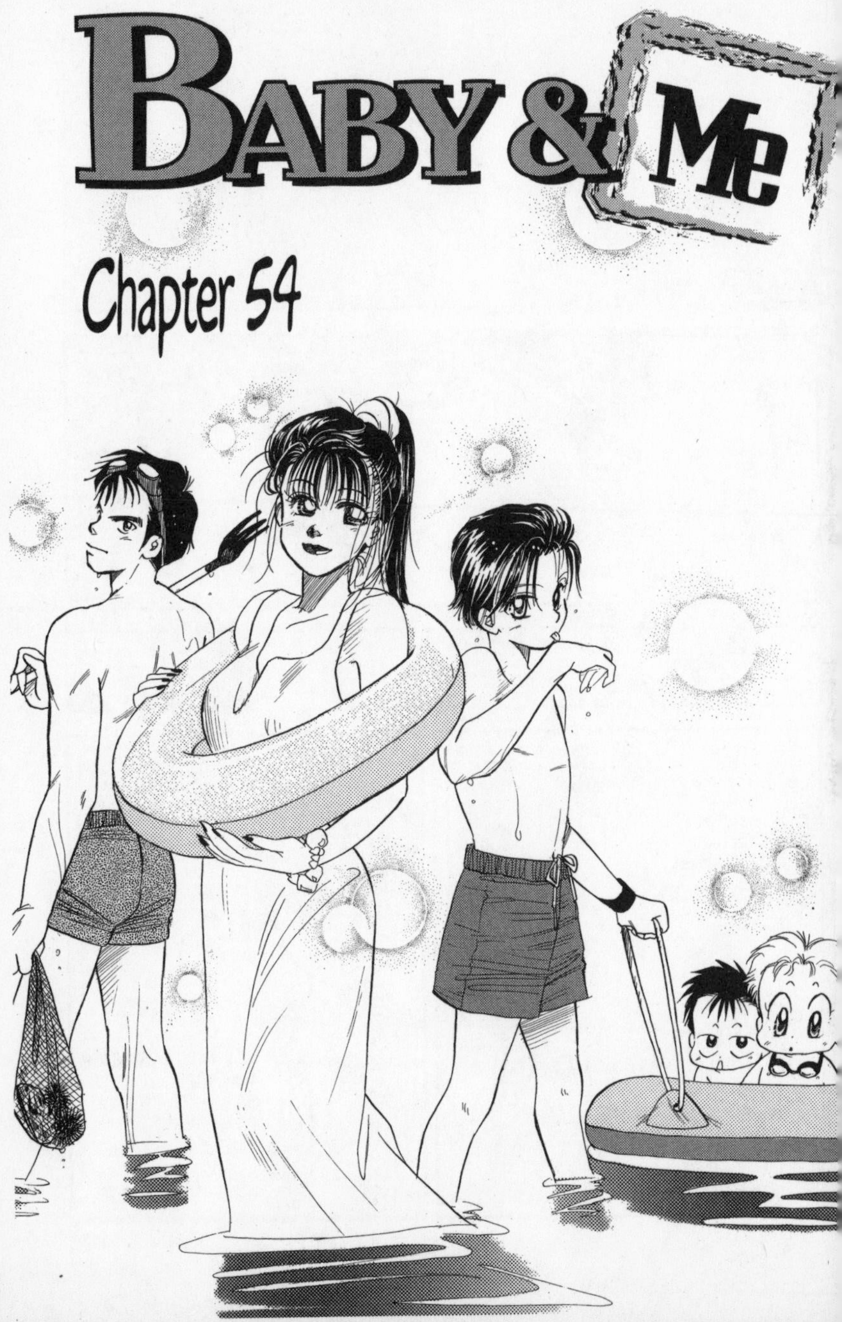
BABY & ME
Chapter 54

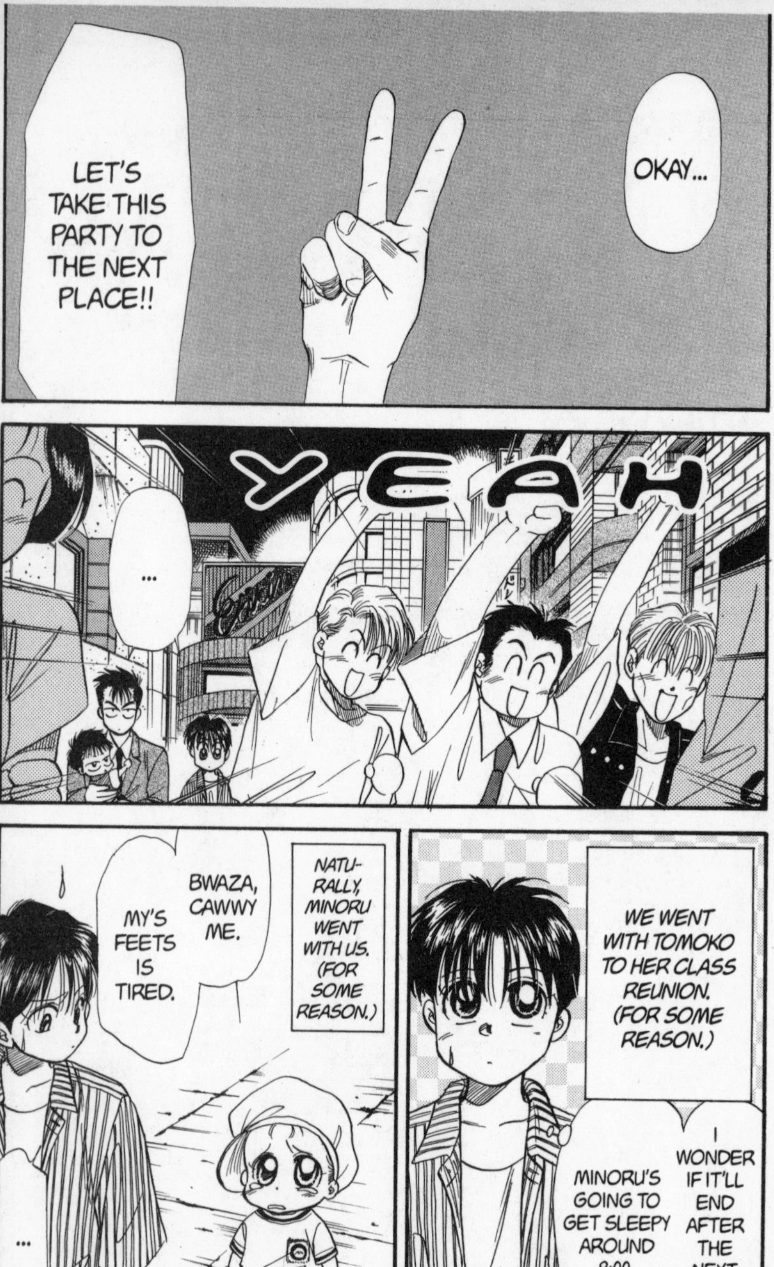
OKAY...
LET'S TAKE THIS PARTY TO THE NEXT PLACE!!
YEAH
...
WE WENT WITH TOMOKO TO HER CLASS REUNION. (FOR SOME REASON.)
I WONDER IF IT'LL END AFTER THE NEXT PLACE...
MINORU'S GOING TO GET SLEEPY AROUND 9:00.
NATU-RALLY, MINORU WENT WITH US. (FOR SOME REASON.)
BWAZA, CAWWY ME.
MY'S FEETS IS TIRED.
...

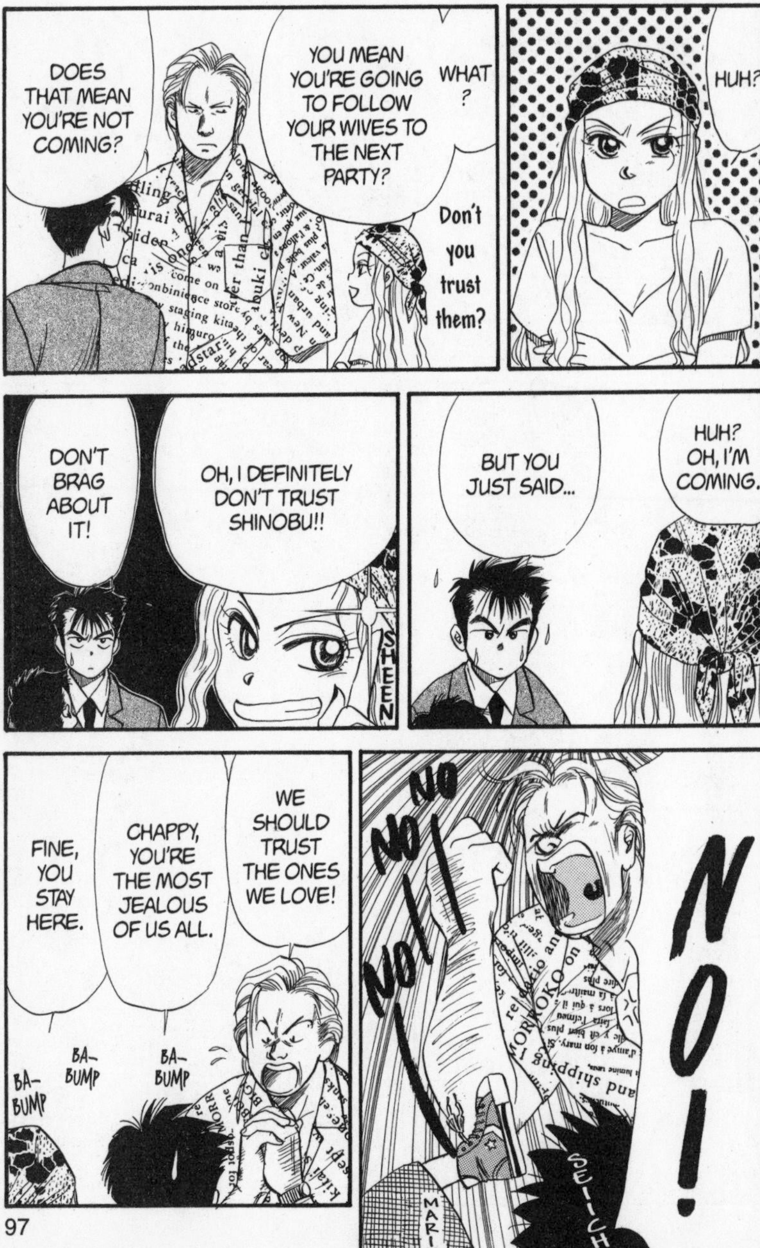
HUH?
WHAT?
YOU MEAN YOU'RE GOING TO FOLLOW YOUR WIVES TO THE NEXT PARTY?
Don't you trust them?
DOES THAT MEAN YOU'RE NOT COMING?
HUH? OH, I'M COMING.
BUT YOU JUST SAID...
OH, I DEFINITELY DON'T TRUST SHINOBU!!
SHEEN
DON'T BRAG ABOUT IT!
NO!
NO NO NO!!
SEIICHI
MARIKO
WE SHOULD TRUST THE ONES WE LOVE!
CHAPPY, YOU'RE THE MOST JEALOUS OF US ALL.
FINE, YOU STAY HERE.
BA-BUMP
BA-BUMP
BA-BUMP

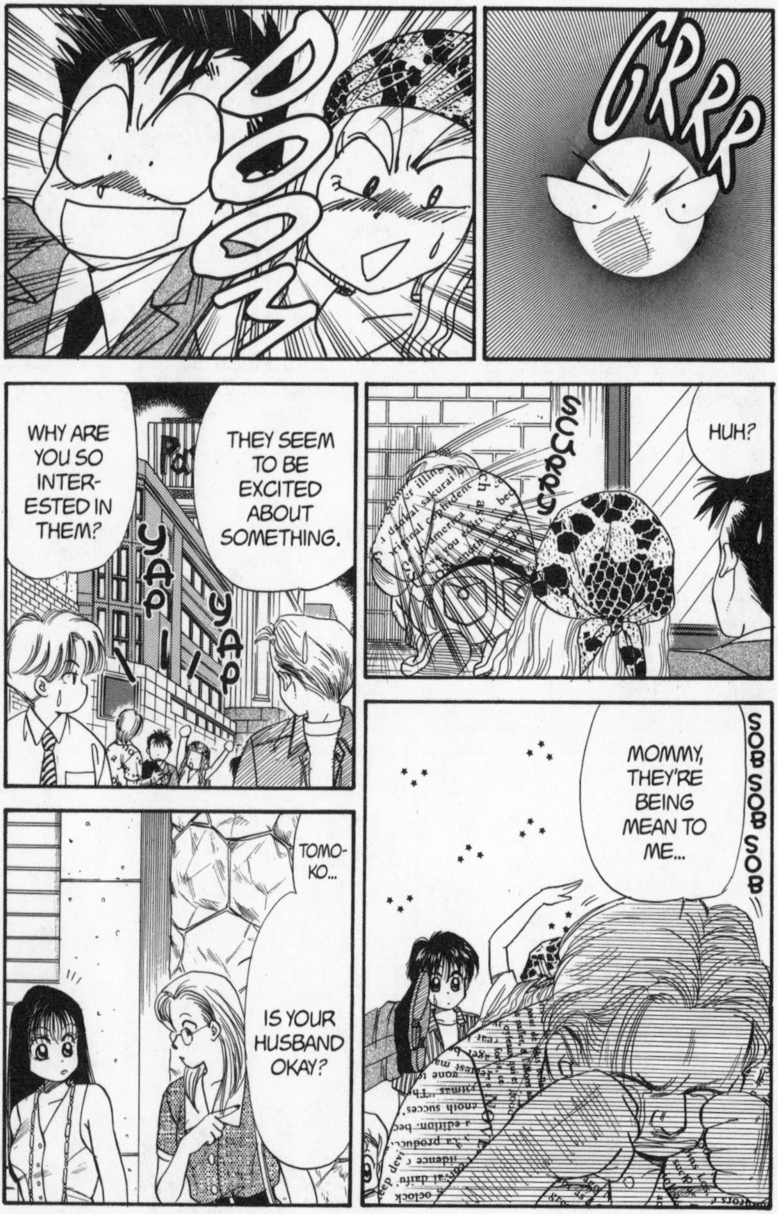
GRRR
DOOM
HUH?
SCURRY
THEY SEEM TO BE EXCITED ABOUT SOMETHING.
WHY ARE YOU SO INTER-ESTED IN THEM?
YAP YAP!
YAP YAP!
SOB SOB SOB
MOMMY, THEY'RE BEING MEAN TO ME...
TOMO-KO...
IS YOUR HUSBAND OKAY?

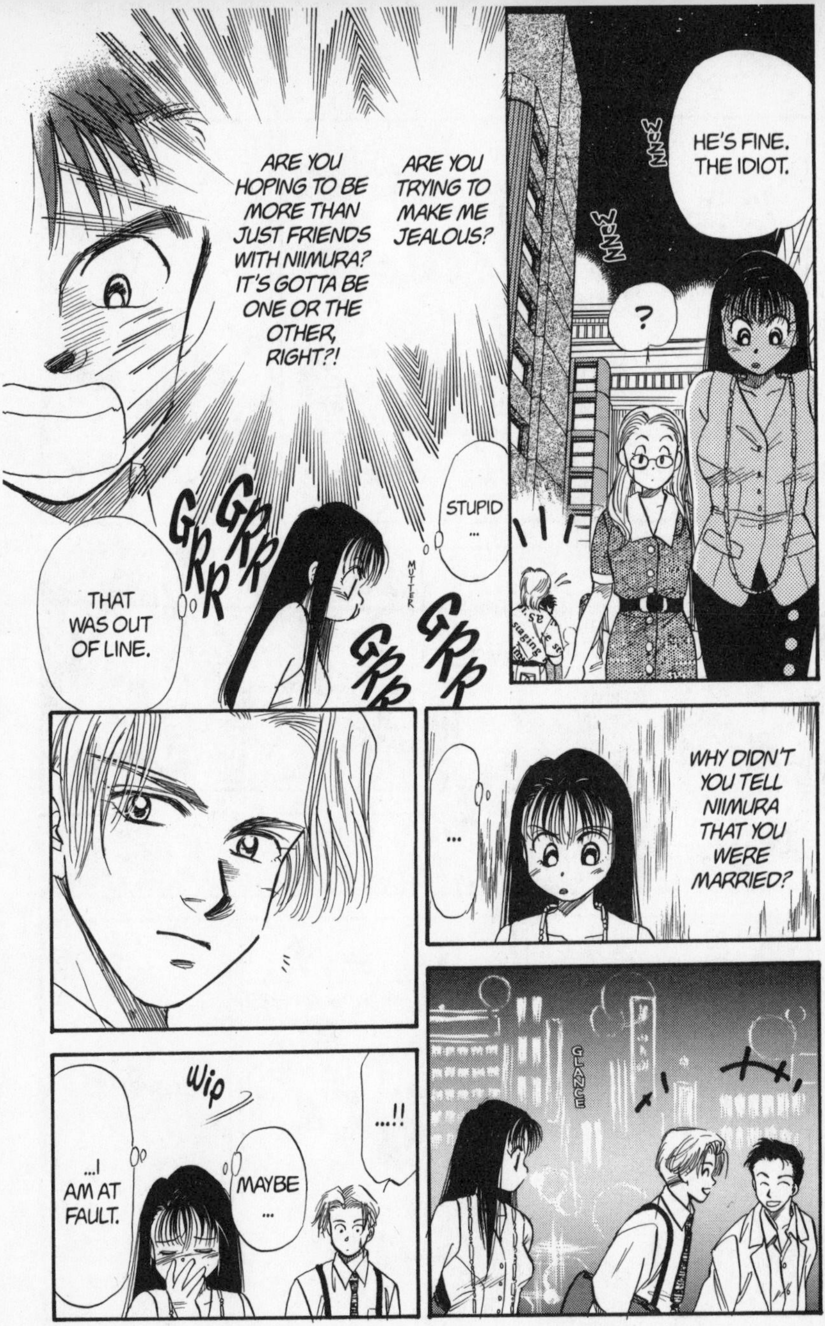
WUZZ
WUZZ
HE'S FINE. THE IDIOT.
?
ARE YOU TRYING TO MAKE ME JEALOUS?
ARE YOU HOPING TO BE MORE THAN JUST FRIENDS WITH NIIMURA? IT'S GOTTA BE ONE OR THE OTHER, RIGHT?!
STUPID ...
MUTTER
GRR
GRRR
GRR
GRRR
THAT WAS OUT OF LINE.
WHY DIDN'T YOU TELL NIIMURA THAT YOU WERE MARRIED?
...
GLANCE
...!!
wip
MAYBE ...
...I AM AT FAULT.

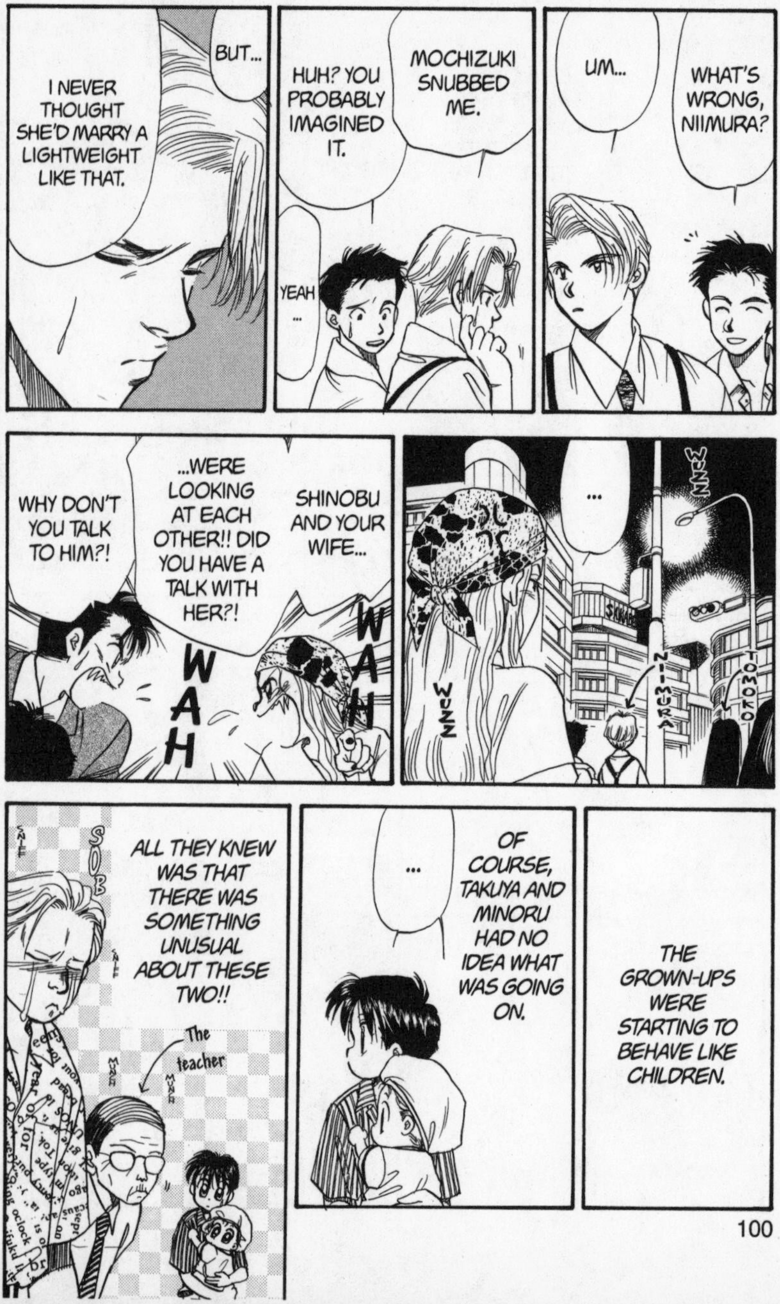
WHAT'S WRONG, NIIMURA?
UM...
MOCHIZUKI SNUBBED ME.
HUH? YOU PROBABLY IMAGINED IT.
YEAH ...
BUT...
I NEVER THOUGHT SHE'D MARRY A LIGHTWEIGHT LIKE THAT.
WUZZ
...
NIIMURA
TOMOKO
WUZZ
SHINOBU AND YOUR WIFE...
...WERE LOOKING AT EACH OTHER!! DID YOU HAVE A TALK WITH HER?!
WHY DON'T YOU TALK TO HIM?!
WAH
WAH
THE GROWN-UPS WERE STARTING TO BEHAVE LIKE CHILDREN.
OF COURSE, TAKUYA AND MINORU HAD NO IDEA WHAT WAS GOING ON.
...
SOB
SNIF
ALL THEY KNEW WAS THAT THERE WAS SOMETHING UNUSUAL ABOUT THESE TWO!!
SNIF
The teacher

Author's Note: Part 4

Hmm...

I like the paintings of the American artist Wyeth. They have great clarity, but they're heavy...no, they have a lot of depth. He has one called "Ghost." There's a man bathed in light, looking hazy, and he really does look like a ghost. I'd like to have one of his paintings, but I'm sure they cost millions of yen...or tens of millions. Oh... I want one! I want one! I want one for my treasure! Yeah...

My favorite illustrator is Peter Sato. I would always sigh when I look at his book of illustrations. I was stunned when I heard that he passed away last year. It can't be true. Someone please tell me it's a lie. And so Peter Sato's book of illustrations, *Pastel Works*, is now my treasure.

You know who Peter Sato is, don't you? One of his famous illustrations is the Mister Donut ad.

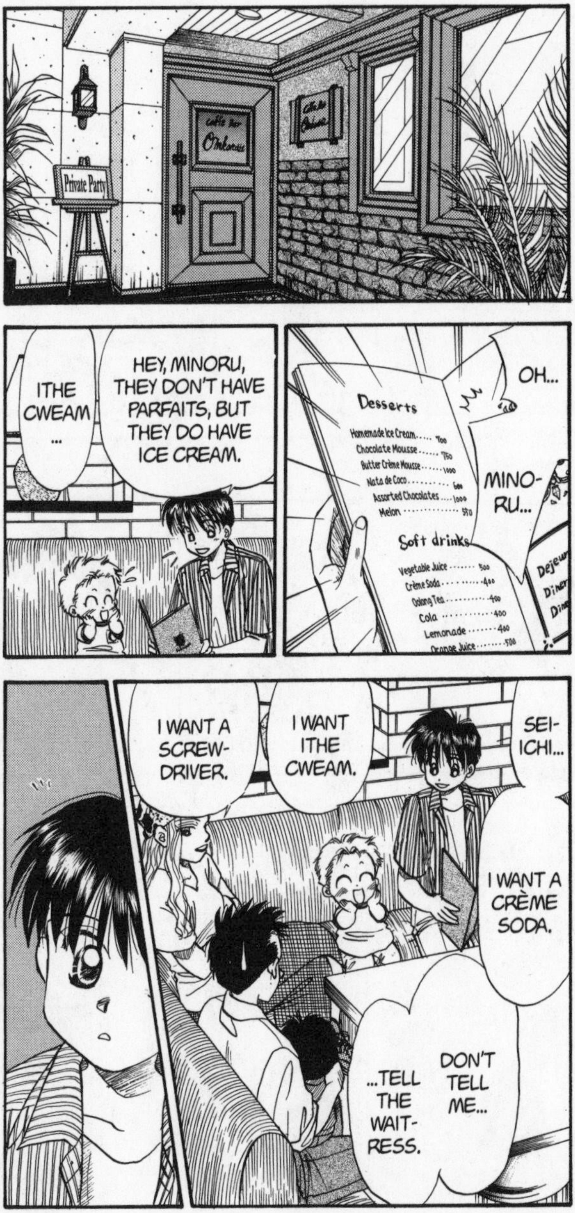

Private Party
OH...
MINO-RU...
Desserts
Homemade Ice Cream..... 700
Chocolate Mousse..... 750
Butter Crème Mousse..... 1000
Nata de Coco..... 600
Assorted Chocolates..... 1000
Melon..... 550
Soft drinks
Vegetable Juice..... 500
Crème Soda..... 400
Oolong Tea..... 400
Cola..... 400
Lemonade..... 400
Orange Juice..... 500
HEY, MINORU, THEY DON'T HAVE PARFAITS, BUT THEY DO HAVE ICE CREAM.
ITHE CWEAM...
SEI-ICHI...
I WANT ITHE CWEAM.
I WANT A SCREW-DRIVER.
I WANT A CRÈME SODA.
DON'T TELL ME...
...TELL THE WAIT-RESS.

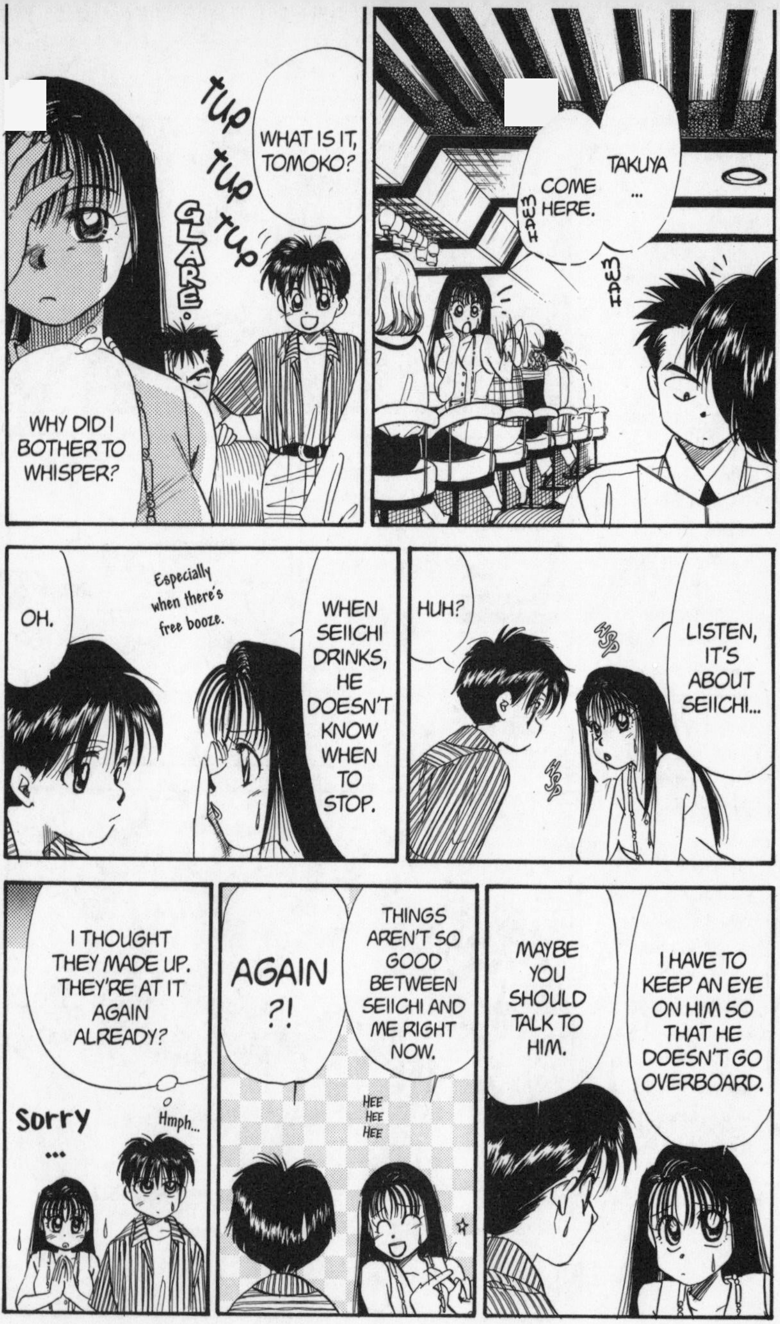
TAKUYA ... COME HERE.
WAH
WAH
WHAT IS IT, TOMOKO?
tup tup tup
GLARE.
WHY DID I BOTHER TO WHISPER?
LISTEN, IT'S ABOUT SEIICHI...
WSP
WSP
HUH?
WHEN SEIICHI DRINKS, HE DOESN'T KNOW WHEN TO STOP.
Especially when there's free booze.
OH.
I HAVE TO KEEP AN EYE ON HIM SO THAT HE DOESN'T GO OVERBOARD.
MAYBE YOU SHOULD TALK TO HIM.
THINGS AREN'T SO GOOD BETWEEN SEIICHI AND ME RIGHT NOW.
AGAIN ?!
HEE HEE HEE
I THOUGHT THEY MADE UP. THEY'RE AT IT AGAIN ALREADY?
Sorry ...
Hmph...

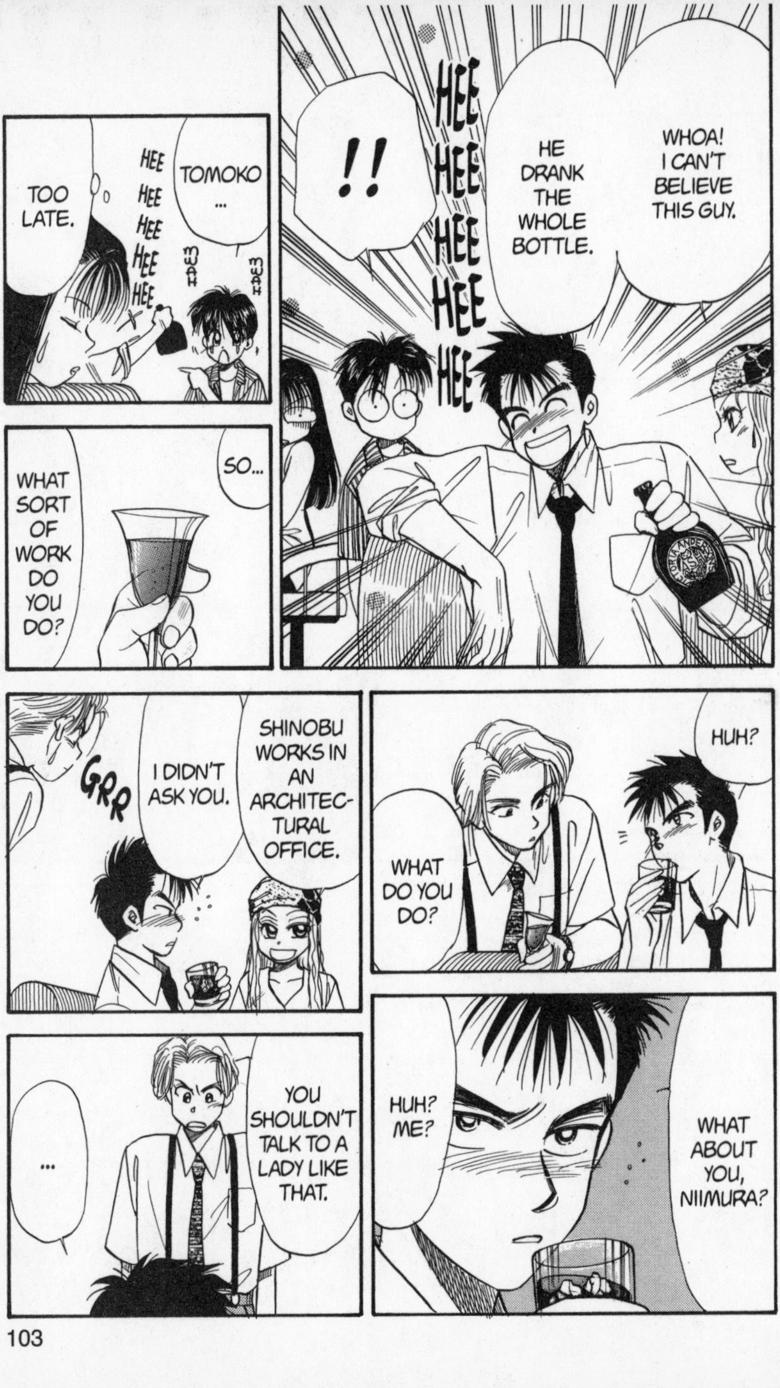
WHOA! I CAN'T BELIEVE THIS GUY.
HE DRANK THE WHOLE BOTTLE.
HEE HEE HEE HEE HEE
!!
TOMOKO ...
WAH WAH
HEE HEE HEE HEE HEE
TOO LATE.
SO...
WHAT SORT OF WORK DO YOU DO?
HUH?
WHAT DO YOU DO?
SHINOBU WORKS IN AN ARCHITEC-TURAL OFFICE.
I DIDN'T ASK YOU.
GRR
WHAT ABOUT YOU, NIIMURA?
HUH? ME?
YOU SHOULDN'T TALK TO A LADY LIKE THAT.
...

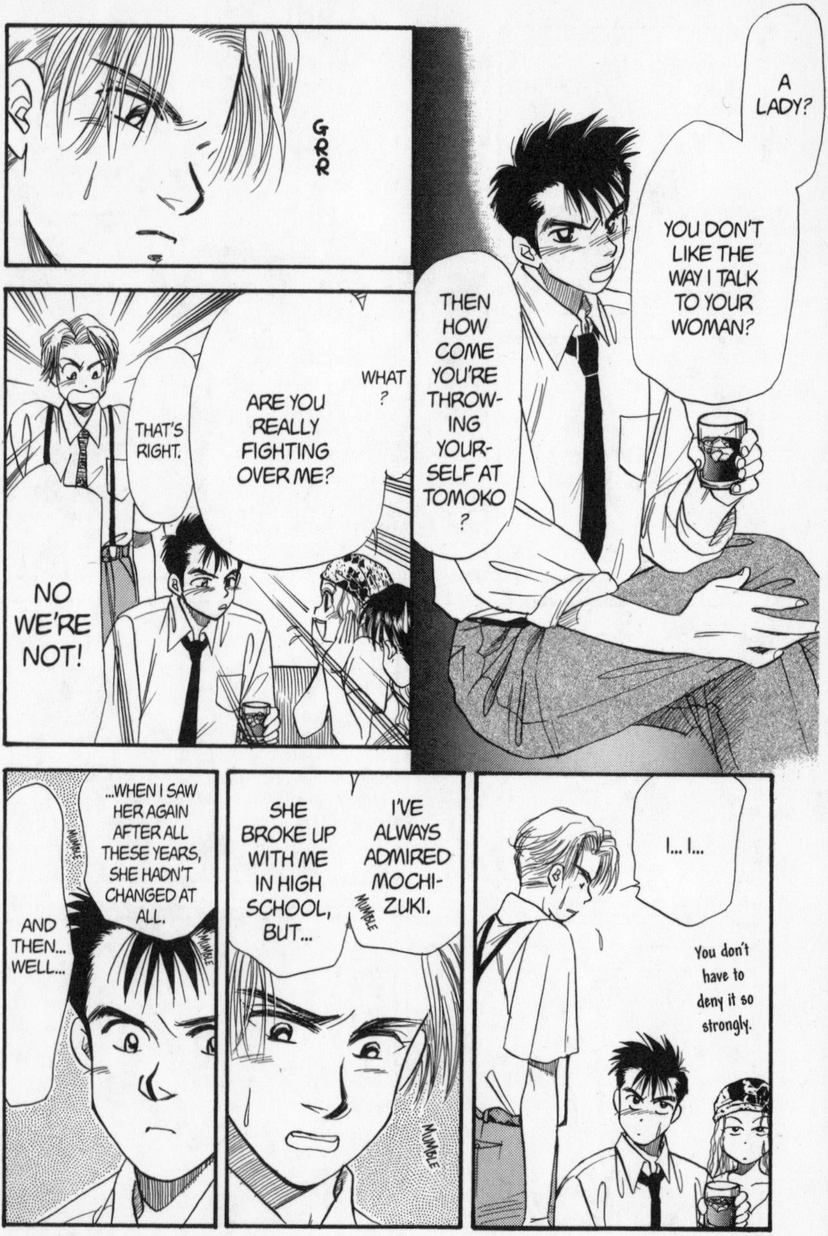
A LADY?
YOU DON'T LIKE THE WAY I TALK TO YOUR WOMAN?
THEN HOW COME YOU'RE THROWING YOURSELF AT TOMOKO?
GRR
WHAT?
ARE YOU REALLY FIGHTING OVER ME?
THAT'S RIGHT.
NO WE'RE NOT!
I... I...
You don't have to deny it so strongly.
I'VE ALWAYS ADMIRED MOCHIZUKI.
SHE BROKE UP WITH ME IN HIGH SCHOOL, BUT...
MUMBLE
MUMBLE
...WHEN I SAW HER AGAIN AFTER ALL THESE YEARS, SHE HADN'T CHANGED AT ALL.
AND THEN... WELL...
MUMBLE
MUMBLE

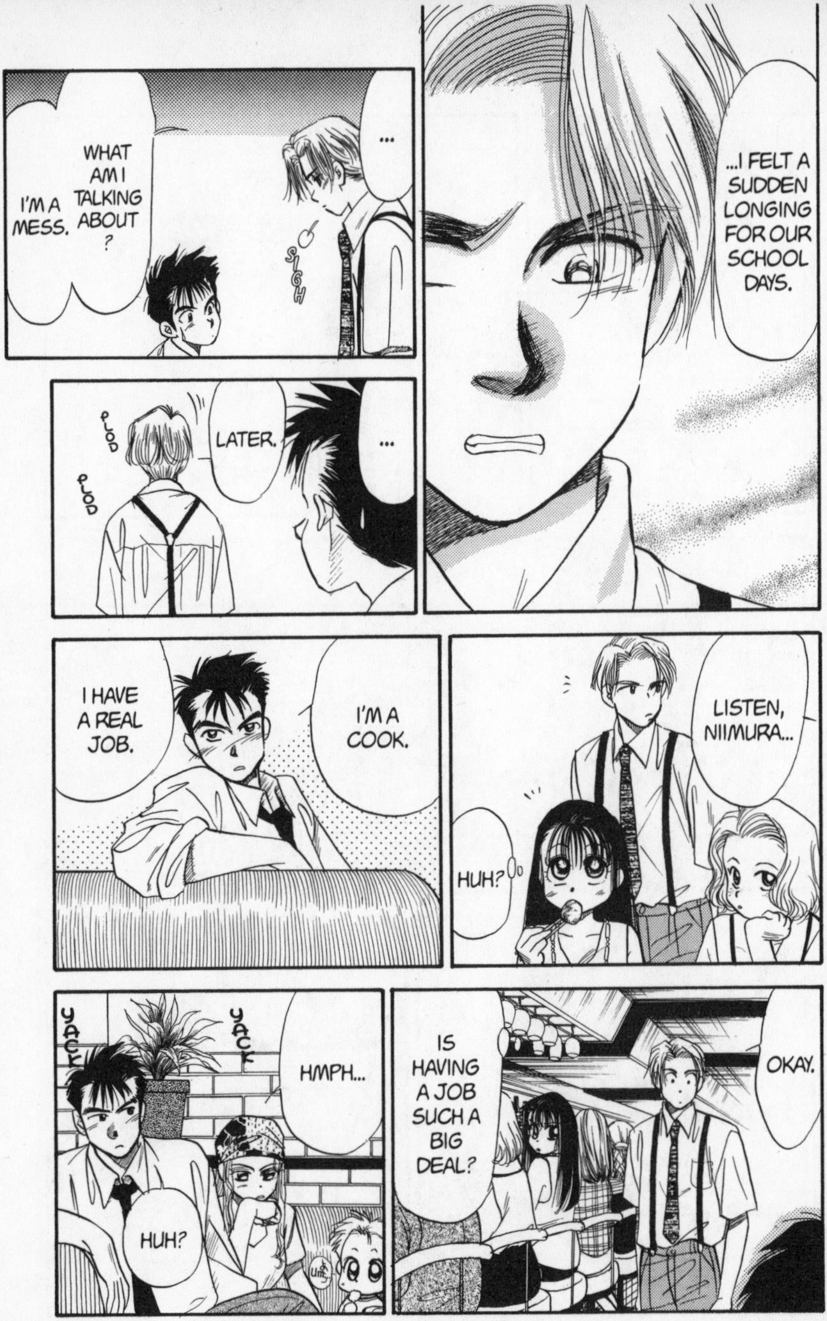
...I FELT A SUDDEN LONGING FOR OUR SCHOOL DAYS.
...
WHAT AM I TALKING ABOUT?
I'M A MESS.
SIGH
...
LATER.
PLOD
PLOD
LISTEN, NIIMURA...
HUH?
I'M A COOK.
I HAVE A REAL JOB.
OKAY.
IS HAVING A JOB SUCH A BIG DEAL?
HMPH...
YACK
YACK
HUH?

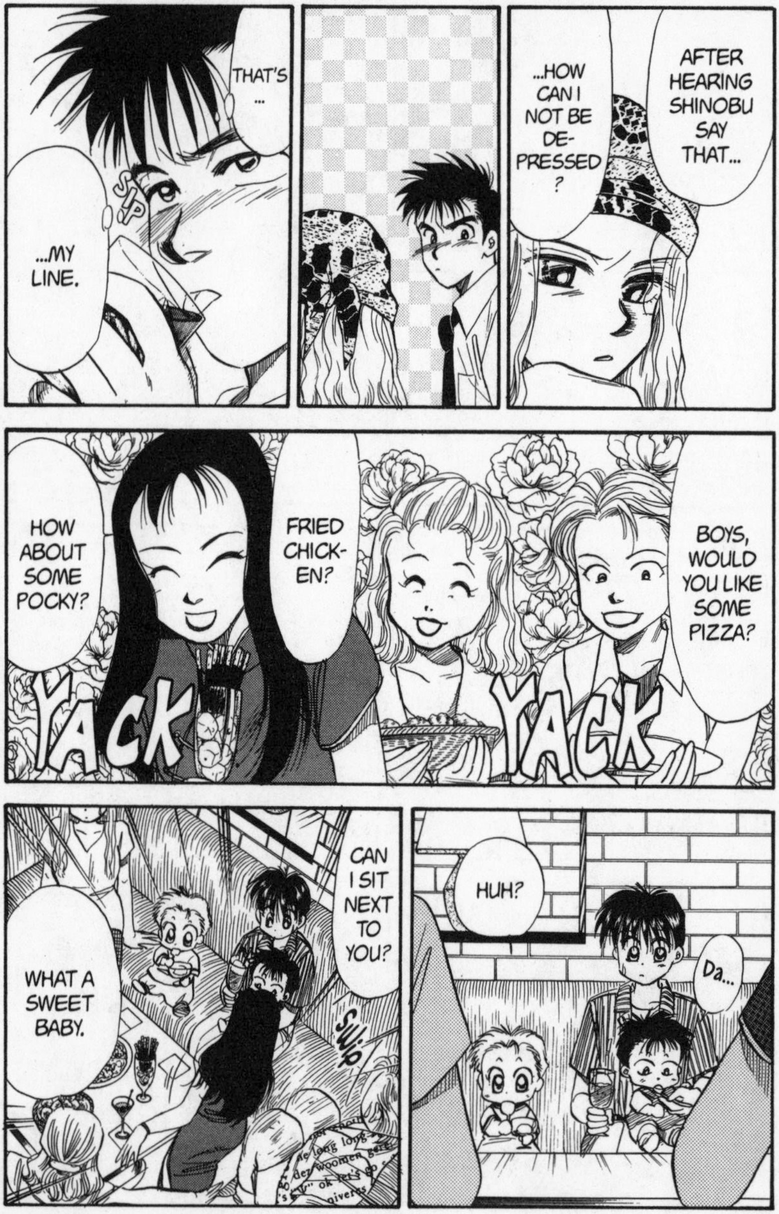
AFTER HEARING SHINOBU SAY THAT...
...HOW CAN I NOT BE DE-PRESSED?
THAT'S ...
SIP
...MY LINE.
BOYS, WOULD YOU LIKE SOME PIZZA?
YACK
FRIED CHICK-EN?
HOW ABOUT SOME POCKY?
YACK
HUH?
Da...
CAN I SIT NEXT TO YOU?
SWIP
WHAT A SWEET BABY.

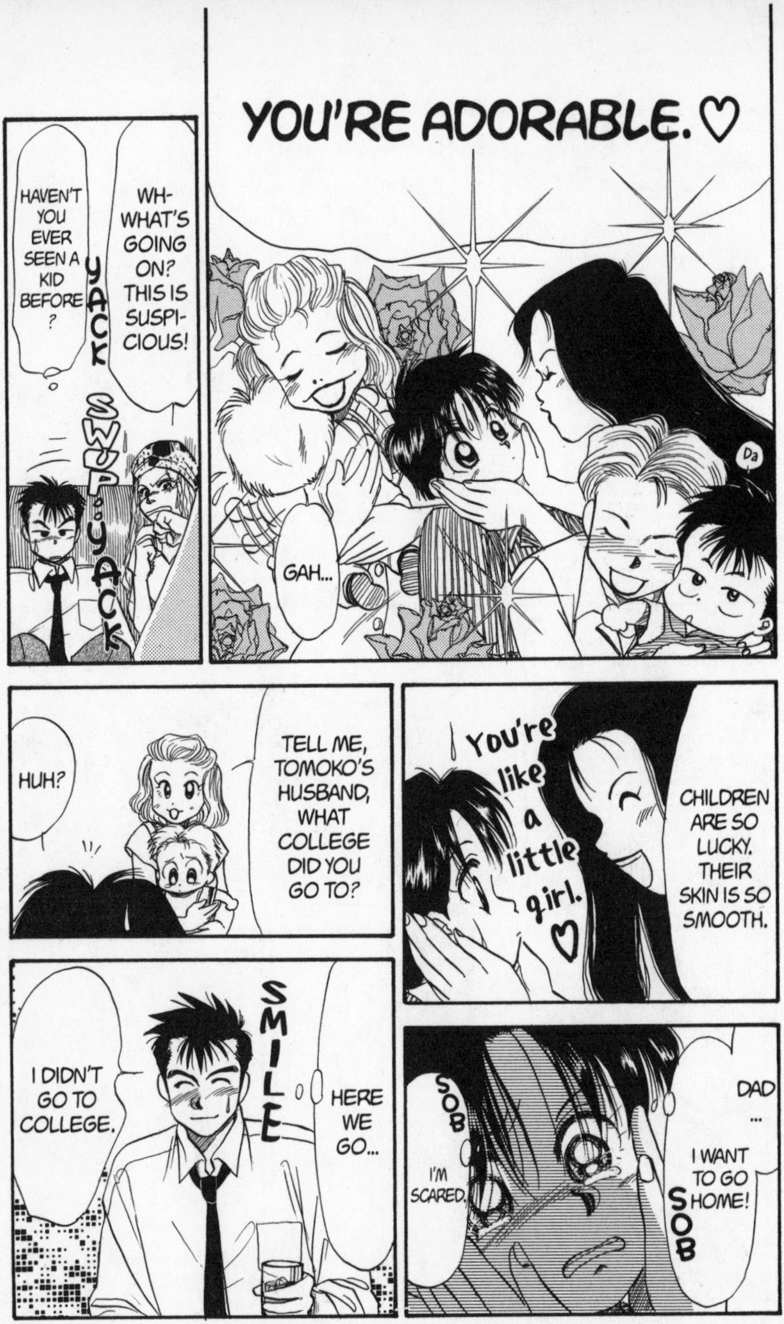
YOU'RE ADORABLE. ♡
Da
GAH...
WH- WHAT'S GOING ON? THIS IS SUSPICIOUS!
HAVEN'T YOU EVER SEEN A KID BEFORE?
YACK
SWUP
YACK
CHILDREN ARE SO LUCKY. THEIR SKIN IS SO SMOOTH.
You're like a little girl. ♡
DAD ... I WANT TO GO HOME!
SOB
I'M SCARED.
SOB
TELL ME, TOMOKO'S HUSBAND, WHAT COLLEGE DID YOU GO TO?
HUH?
SMILE
HERE WE GO...
I DIDN'T GO TO COLLEGE.

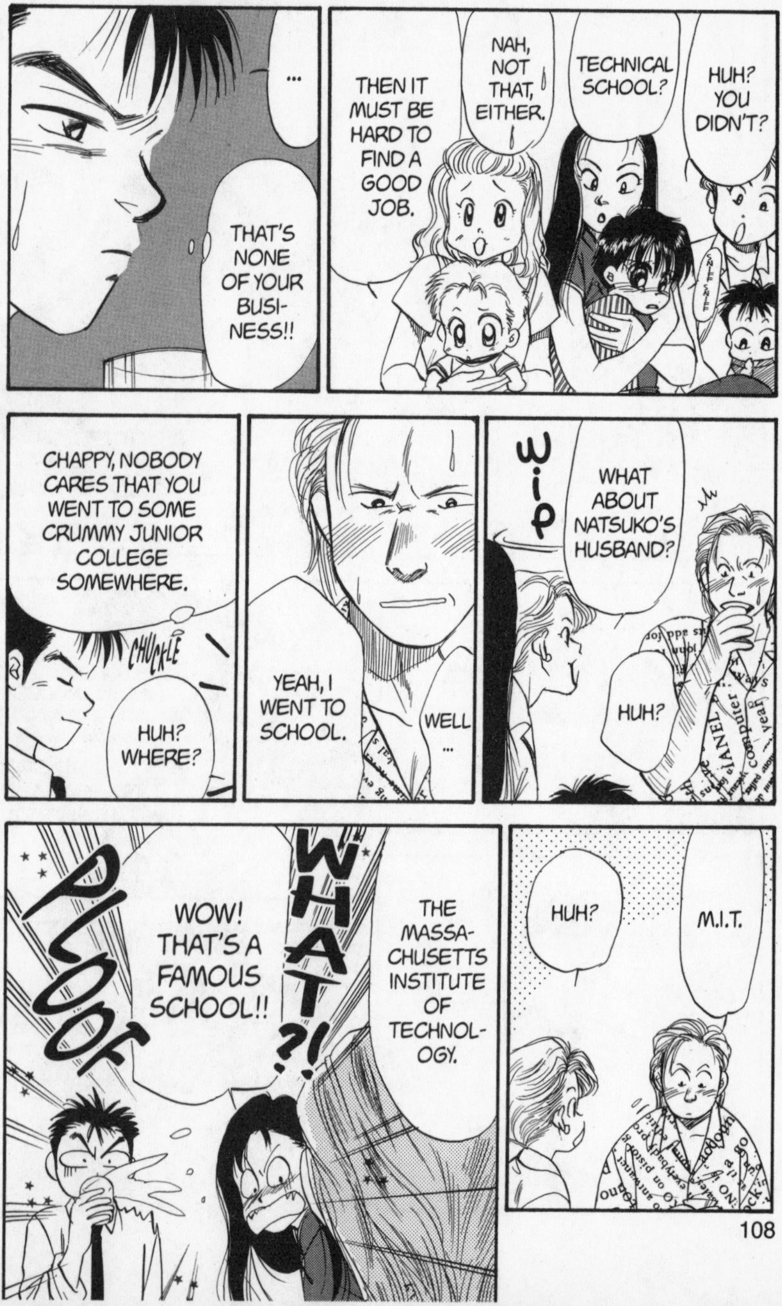
HUH? YOU DIDN'T?
TECHNICAL SCHOOL?
NAH, NOT THAT, EITHER.
THEN IT MUST BE HARD TO FIND A GOOD JOB.
SNIFF SNIFF
...
THAT'S NONE OF YOUR BUSINESS!!
WIP
WHAT ABOUT NATSUKO'S HUSBAND?
HUH?
WELL ...
YEAH, I WENT TO SCHOOL.
CHAPPY, NOBODY CARES THAT YOU WENT TO SOME CRUMMY JUNIOR COLLEGE SOMEWHERE.
CHUCKLE
HUH? WHERE?
M.I.T.
HUH?
THE MASSACHUSETTS INSTITUTE OF TECHNOLOGY.
WHAT?!
WOW! THAT'S A FAMOUS SCHOOL!!
PLOOF

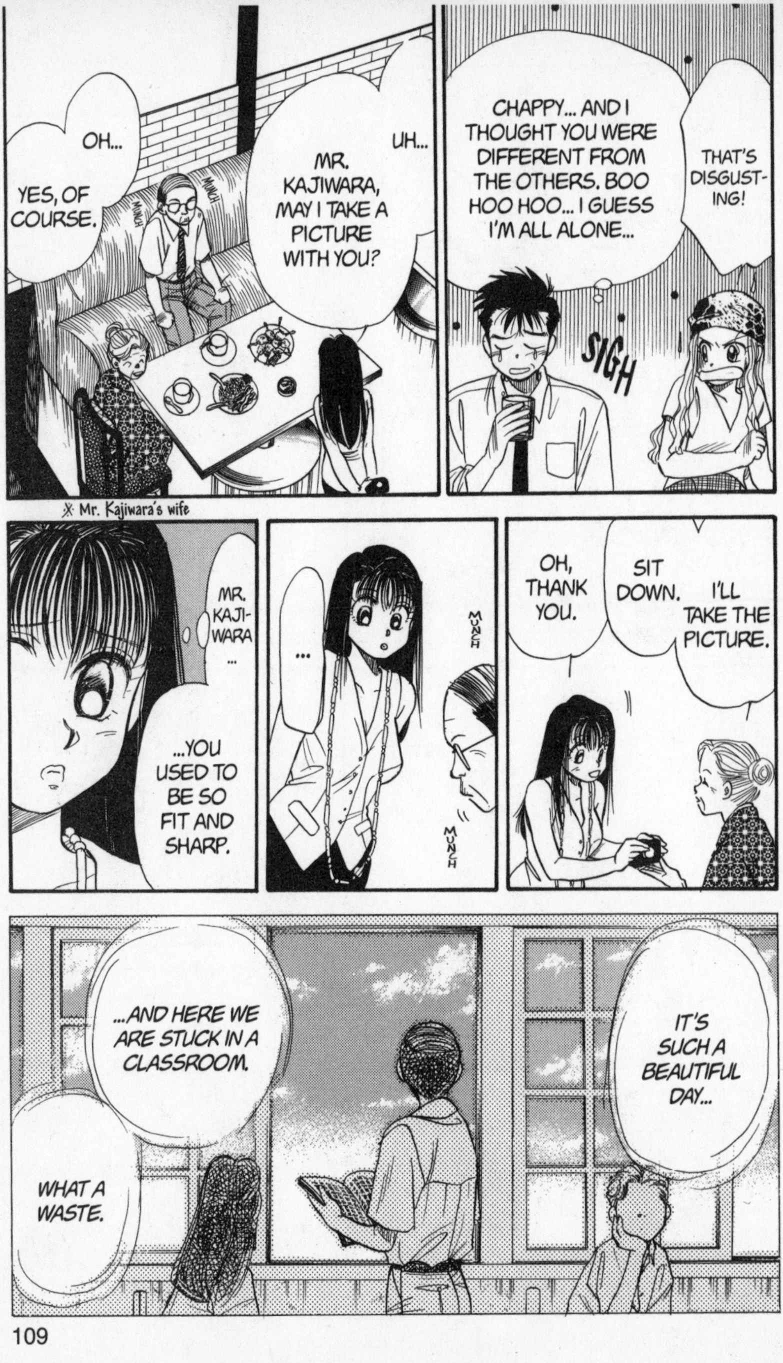
THAT'S DISGUSTING!
CHAPPY... AND I THOUGHT YOU WERE DIFFERENT FROM THE OTHERS. BOO HOO HOO... I GUESS I'M ALL ALONE...
SIGH
UH...
MR. KAJIWARA, MAY I TAKE A PICTURE WITH YOU?
OH...
YES, OF COURSE.
MUNCH
MUNCH
I'LL TAKE THE PICTURE.
SIT DOWN.
OH, THANK YOU.
MUNCH
...
MUNCH
MR. KAJIWARA...
...YOU USED TO BE SO FIT AND SHARP.
IT'S SUCH A BEAUTIFUL DAY...
...AND HERE WE ARE STUCK IN A CLASSROOM.
WHAT A WASTE.
※ Mr. Kajiwara's wife

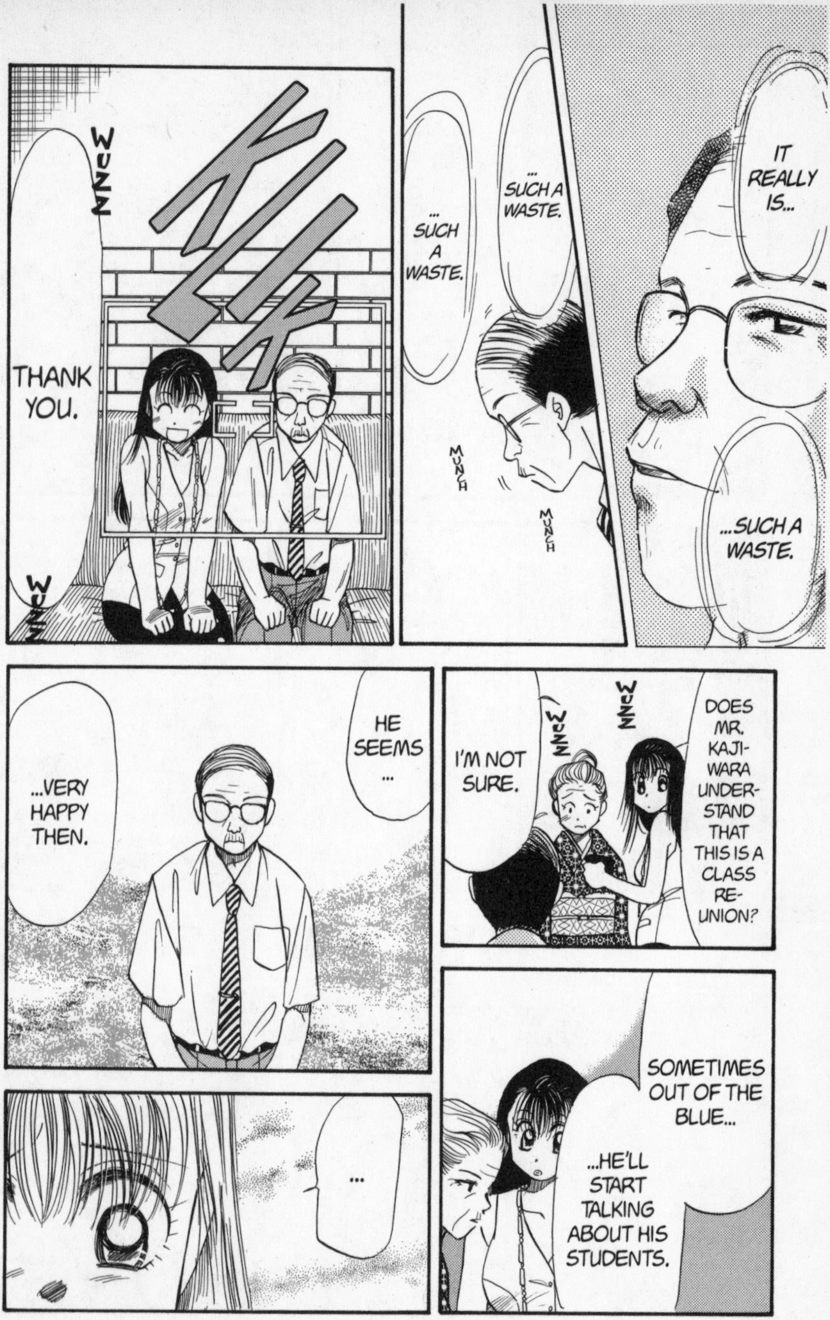
IT REALLY IS...
...SUCH A WASTE.
... SUCH A WASTE.
... SUCH A WASTE.
MUNCH
MUNCH
KLIK
WUZZ
THANK YOU.
WUZZ
DOES MR. KAJIWARA UNDERSTAND THAT THIS IS A CLASS REUNION?
WUZZ
WUZZ
I'M NOT SURE.
HE SEEMS ...
...VERY HAPPY THEN.
SOMETIMES OUT OF THE BLUE...
...HE'LL START TALKING ABOUT HIS STUDENTS.
...

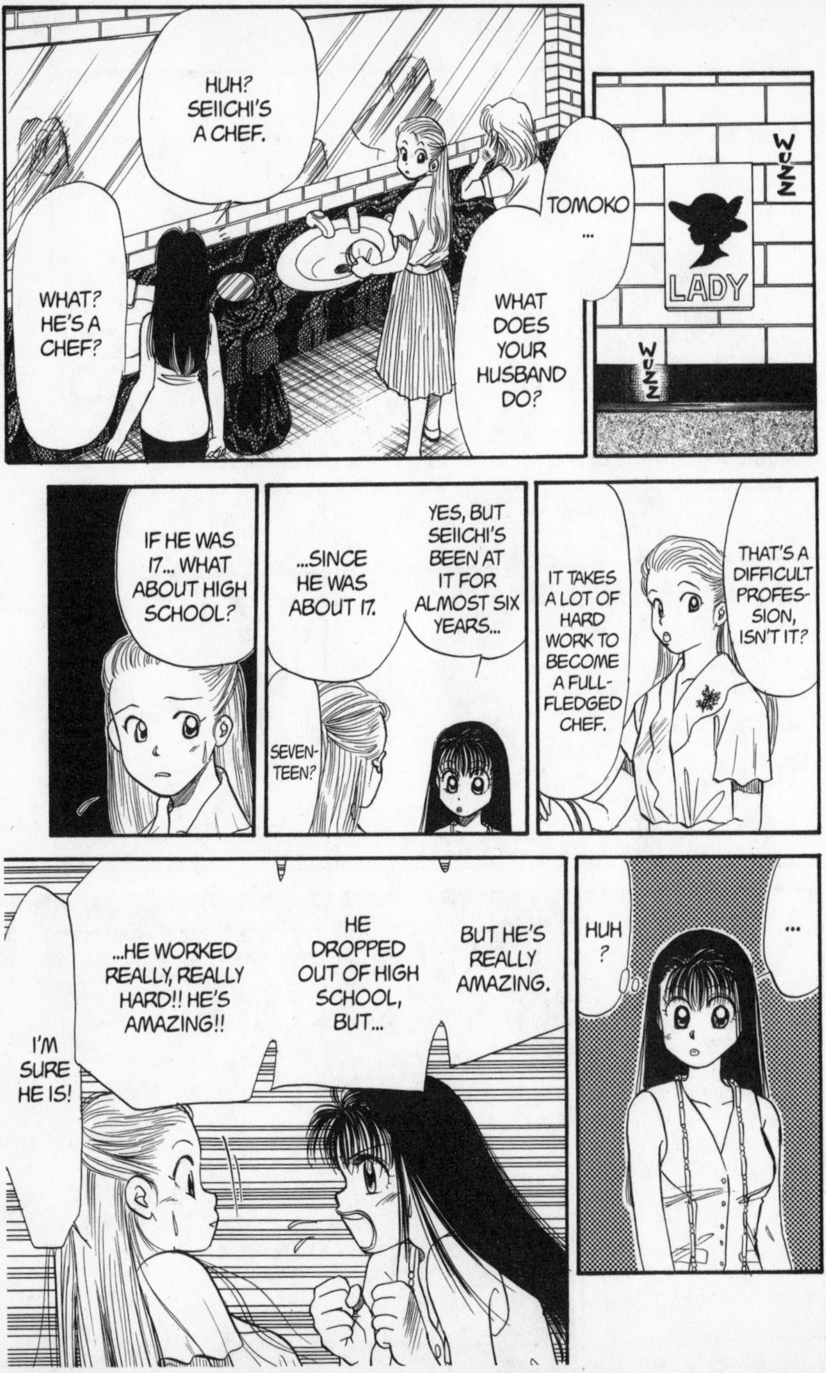
WUZZ
LADY
WUZZ
TOMOKO ...
WHAT DOES YOUR HUSBAND DO?
HUH? SEIICHI'S A CHEF.
WHAT? HE'S A CHEF?
THAT'S A DIFFICULT PROFESSION, ISN'T IT?
IT TAKES A LOT OF HARD WORK TO BECOME A FULL-FLEDGED CHEF.
YES, BUT SEIICHI'S BEEN AT IT FOR ALMOST SIX YEARS...
...SINCE HE WAS ABOUT 17.
SEVENTEEN?
IF HE WAS 17... WHAT ABOUT HIGH SCHOOL?
...
HUH?
BUT HE'S REALLY AMAZING.
HE DROPPED OUT OF HIGH SCHOOL, BUT...
...HE WORKED REALLY, REALLY HARD!! HE'S AMAZING!!
I'M SURE HE IS!

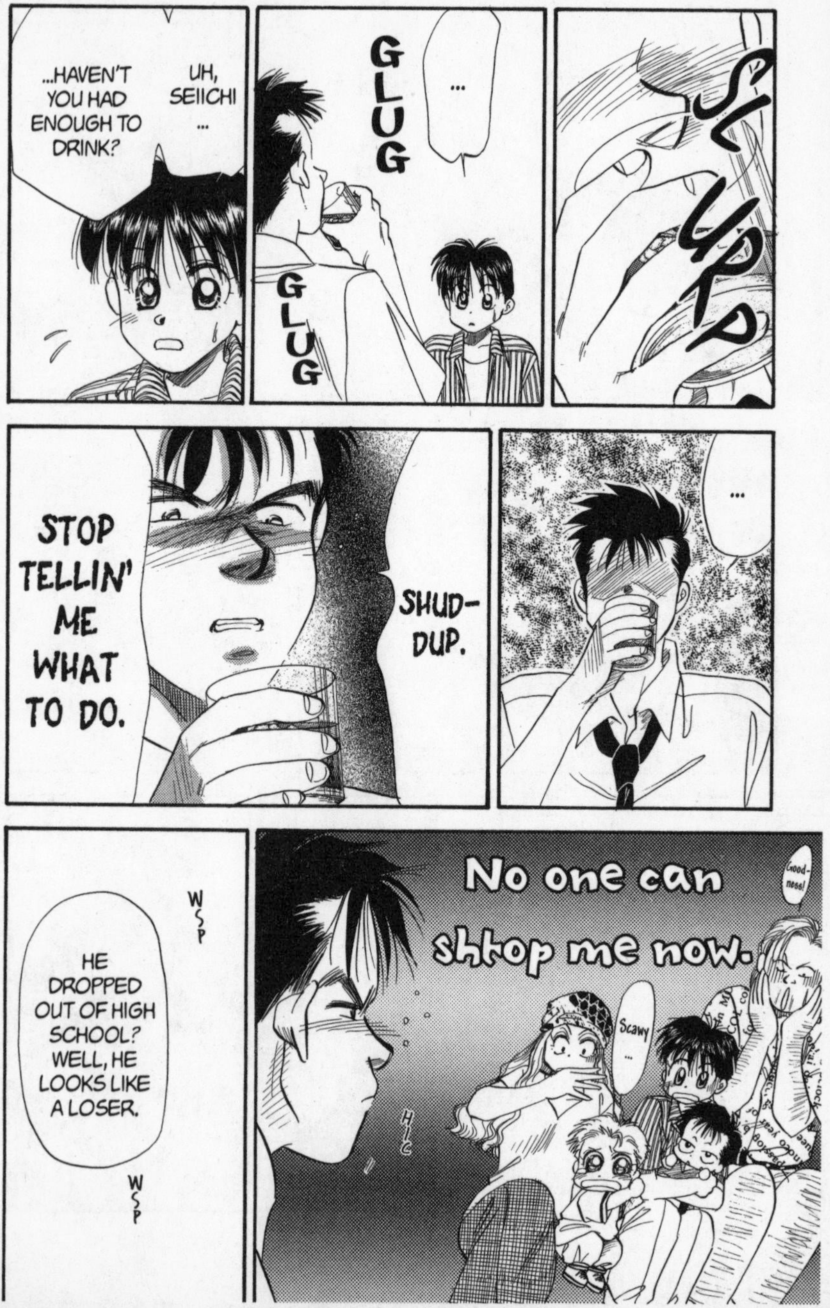
SLURP
GLUG
GLUG
...
UH, SEIICHI ...
...HAVEN'T YOU HAD ENOUGH TO DRINK?
...
SHUD-DUP.
STOP TELLIN' ME WHAT TO DO.
Good-ness!
No one can shtop me now.
Scawy ...
HIC
WSP
HE DROPPED OUT OF HIGH SCHOOL? WELL, HE LOOKS LIKE A LOSER.
WSP

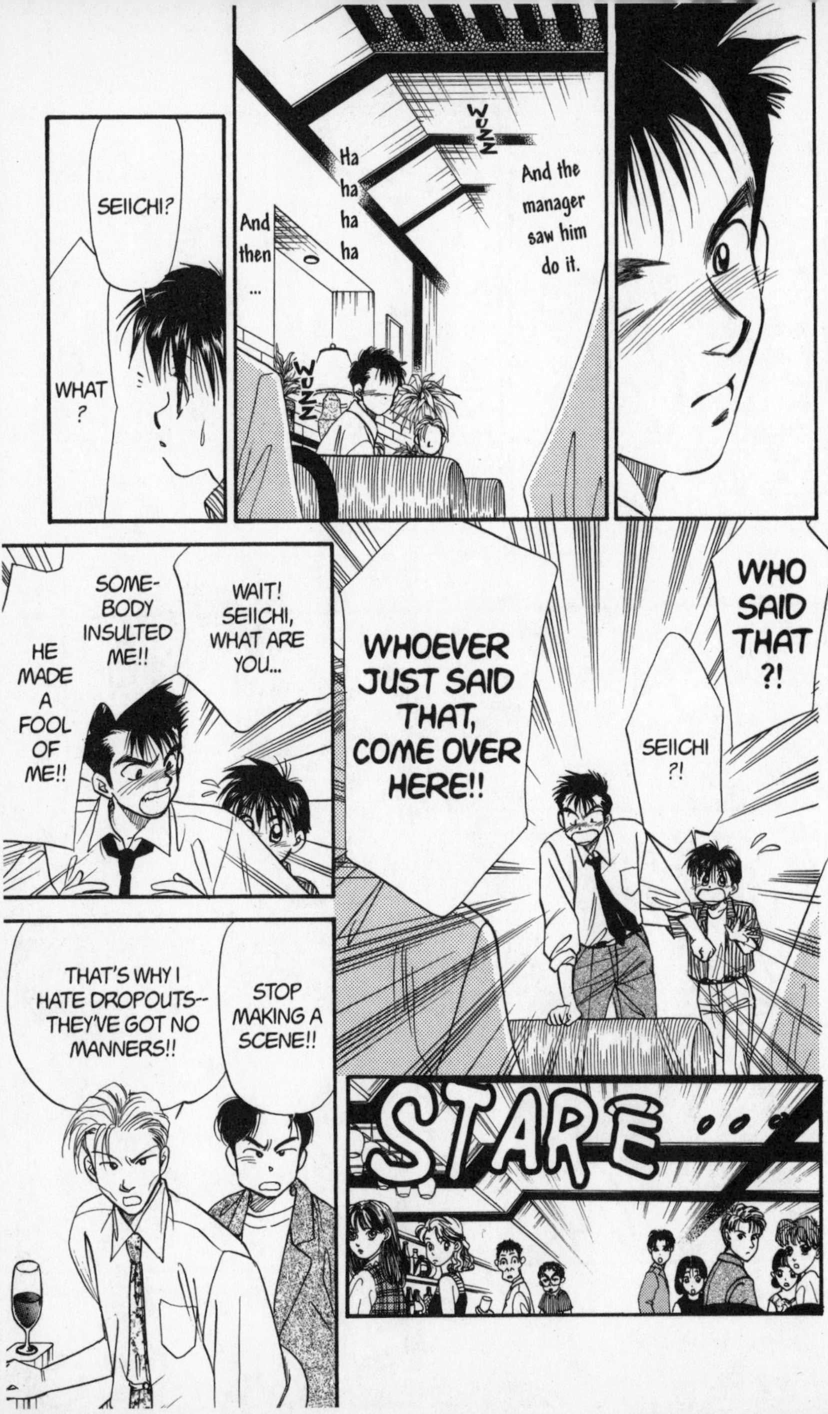
And the manager saw him do it.
WUZZ
Ha ha ha ha
And then ...
WUZZ
SEIICHI?
WHAT?
WHO SAID THAT?!
SEIICHI?!
WHOEVER JUST SAID THAT, COME OVER HERE!!
WAIT! SEIICHI, WHAT ARE YOU...
SOME-BODY INSULTED ME!!
HE MADE A FOOL OF ME!!
STOP MAKING A SCENE!!
THAT'S WHY I HATE DROPOUTS-- THEY'VE GOT NO MANNERS!!
STARE...

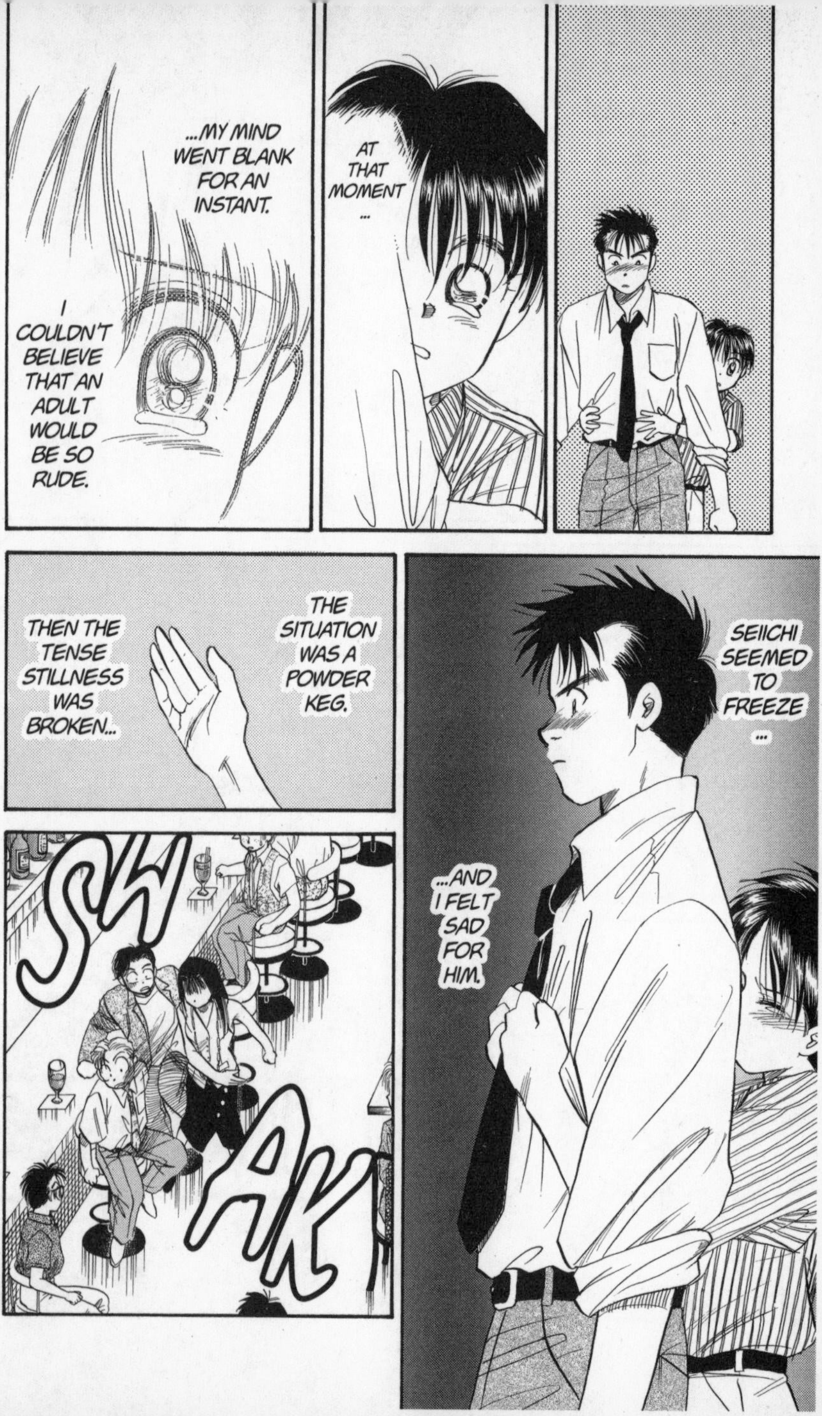
AT THAT MOMENT ...
...MY MIND WENT BLANK FOR AN INSTANT.
I COULDN'T BELIEVE THAT AN ADULT WOULD BE SO RUDE.
SEIICHI SEEMED TO FREEZE ...
...AND I FELT SAD FOR HIM.
THE SITUATION WAS A POWDER KEG.
THEN THE TENSE STILLNESS WAS BROKEN...
SW
AK

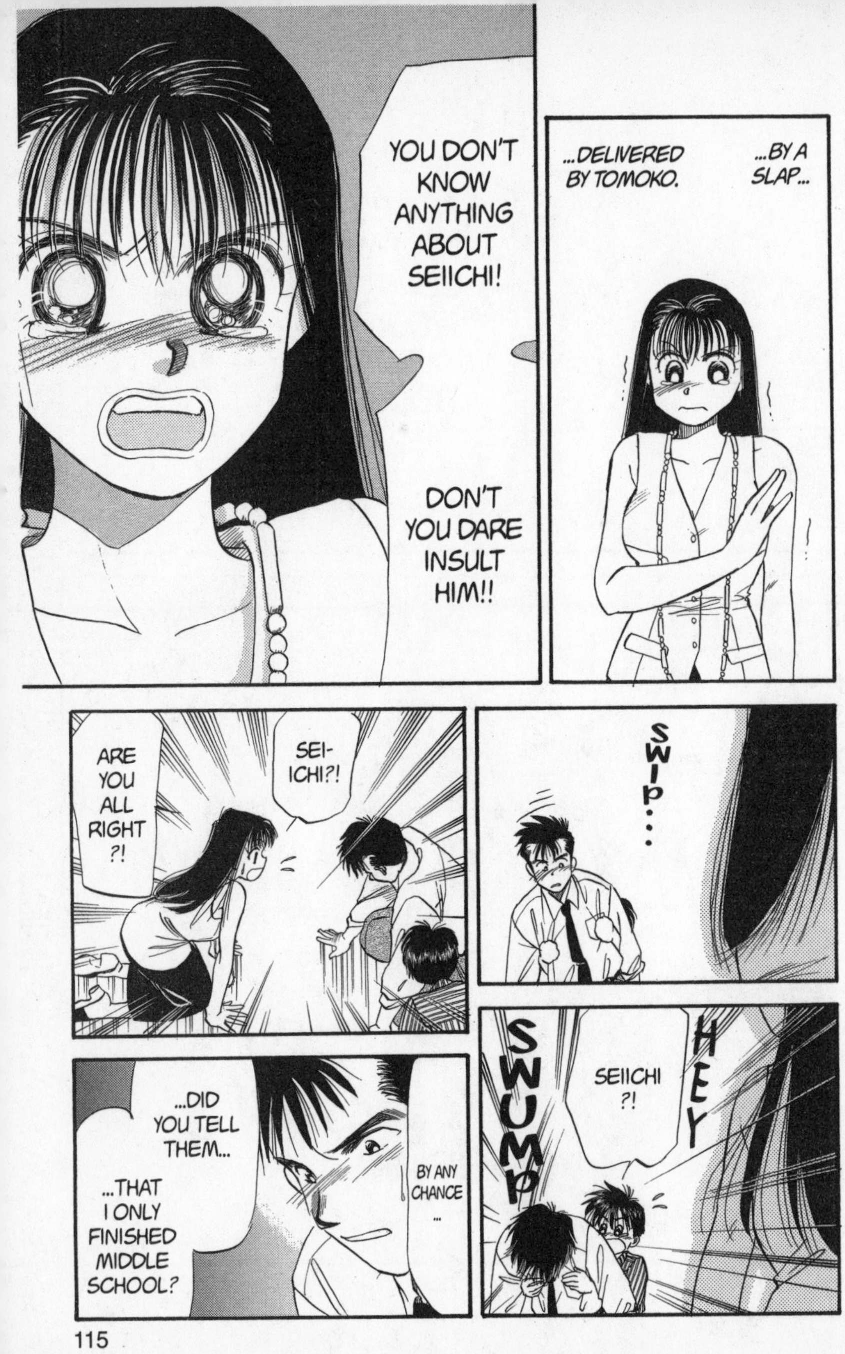
...BY A SLAP...
...DELIVERED BY TOMOKO.
YOU DON'T KNOW ANYTHING ABOUT SEIICHI!
DON'T YOU DARE INSULT HIM!!
SWIP...
SEI-ICHI?!
ARE YOU ALL RIGHT?!
HEY
SEIICHI ?!
SWUMP
BY ANY CHANCE ...
...DID YOU TELL THEM...
...THAT I ONLY FINISHED MIDDLE SCHOOL?

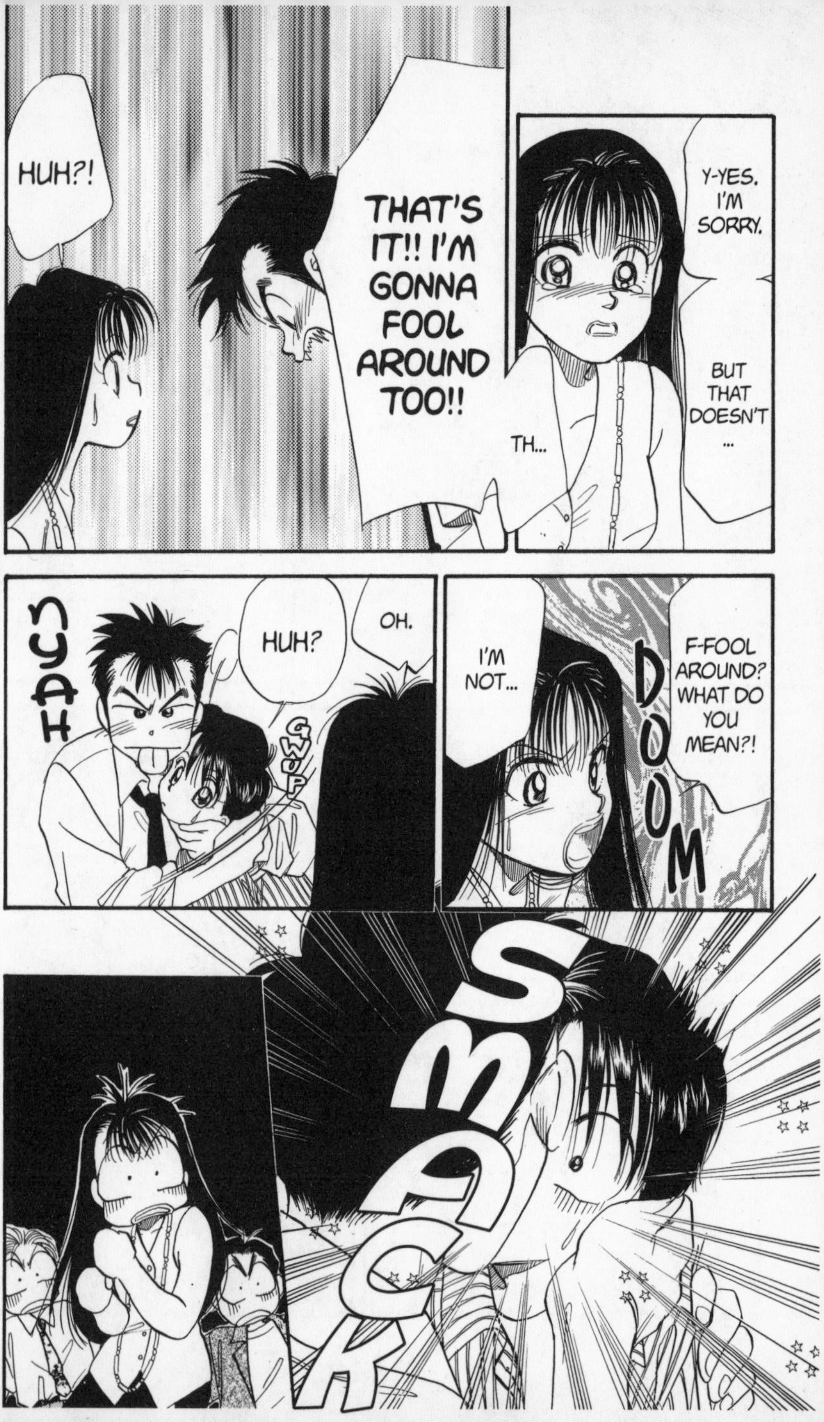
Y-YES. I'M SORRY.
BUT THAT DOESN'T ...
TH...
THAT'S IT!! I'M GONNA FOOL AROUND TOO!!
HUH?!
F-FOOL AROUND? WHAT DO YOU MEAN?!
DOOM
I'M NOT...
OH.
HUH?
GWUP
HYAH
SMACK

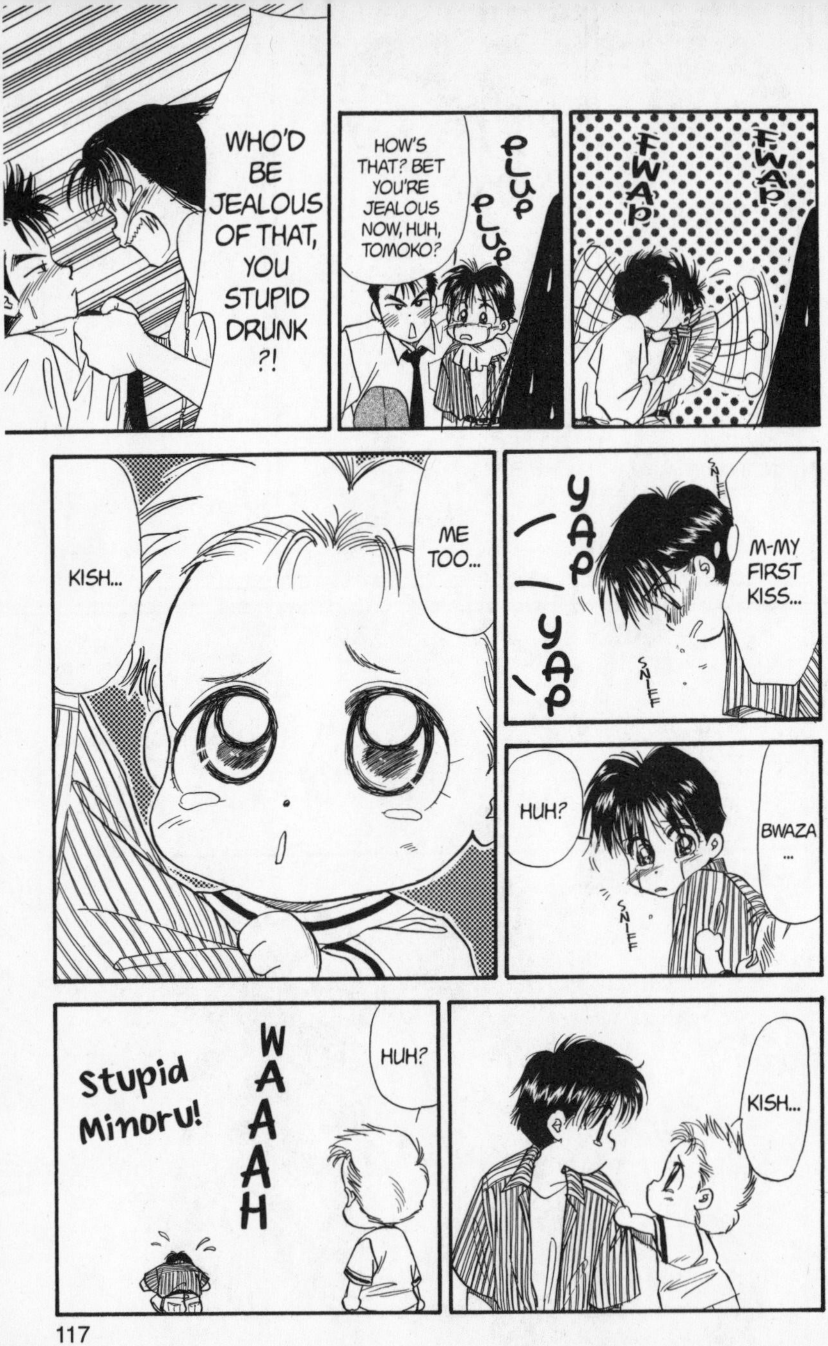
FWAP
FWAP
HOW'S THAT? BET YOU'RE JEALOUS NOW, HUH, TOMOKO?
PLUP
PLUP
WHO'D BE JEALOUS OF THAT, YOU STUPID DRUNK ?!
M-MY FIRST KISS...
SNIFF
YAP YAP
YAP
SNIFF
BWAZA ...
HUH?
SNIFF
ME TOO...
KISH...
KISH...
HUH?
WAAAAH
Stupid Minoru!

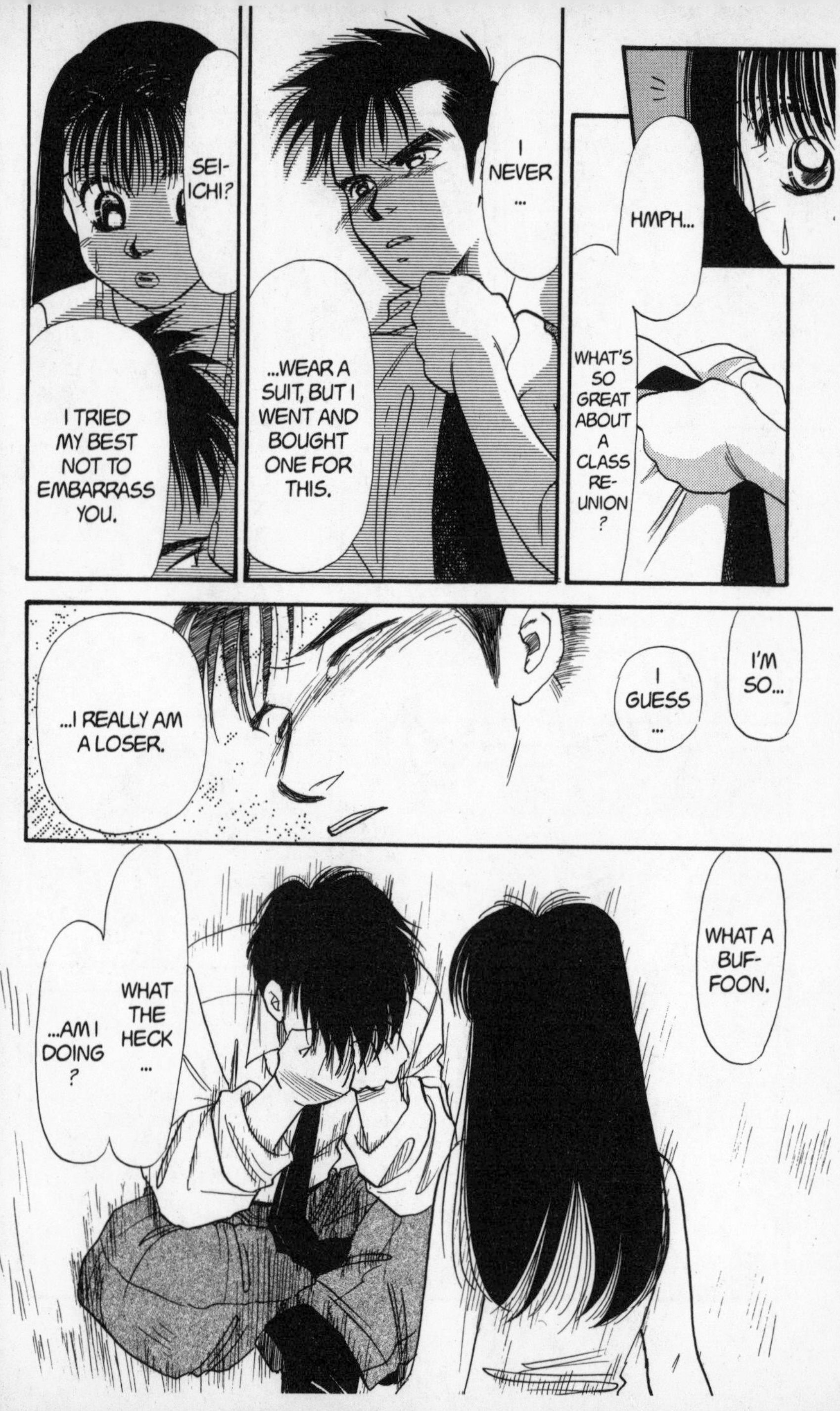
HMPH...
WHAT'S SO GREAT ABOUT A CLASS RE-UNION?
I NEVER...
...WEAR A SUIT, BUT I WENT AND BOUGHT ONE FOR THIS.
SEI-ICHI?
I TRIED MY BEST NOT TO EMBARRASS YOU.
I'M SO...
I GUESS...
...I REALLY AM A LOSER.
WHAT A BUF-FOON.
WHAT THE HECK...
...AM I DOING?

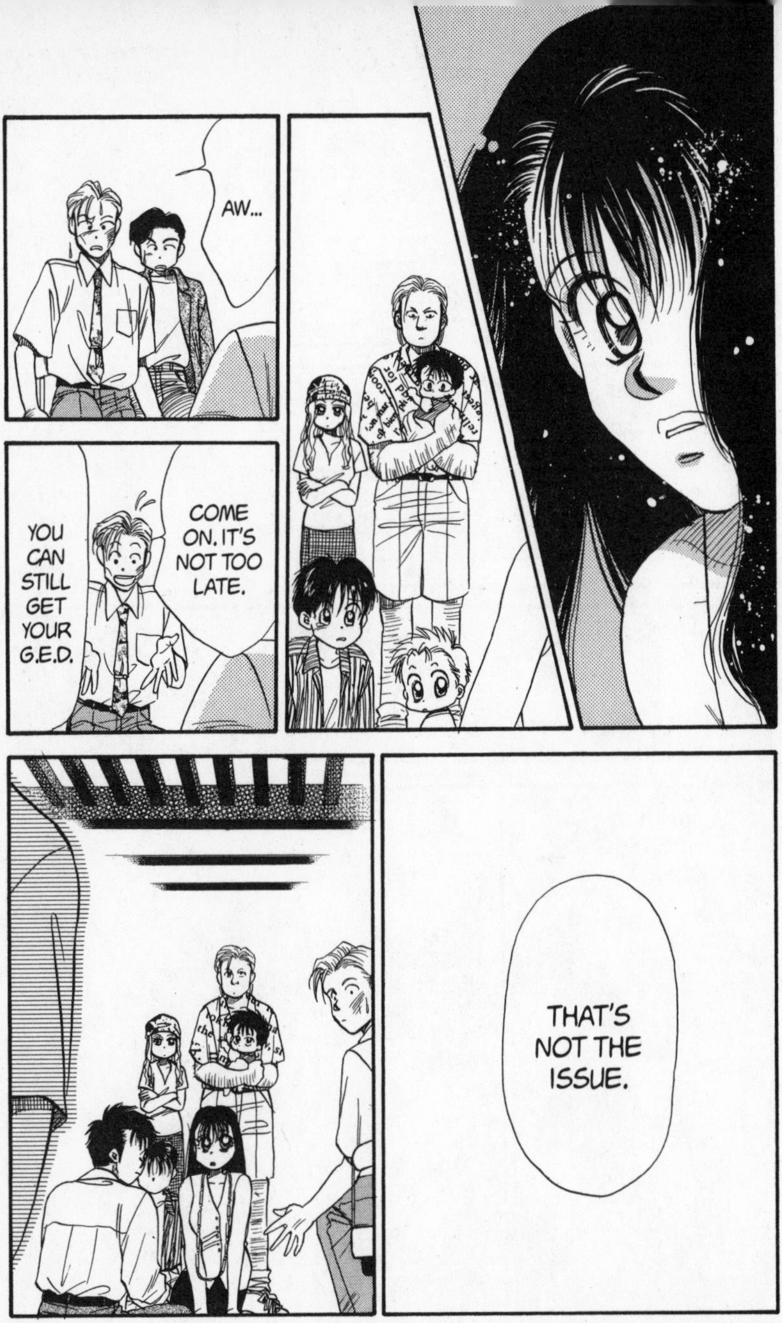
AW...
COME ON. IT'S NOT TOO LATE.
YOU CAN STILL GET YOUR G.E.D.
THAT'S NOT THE ISSUE.

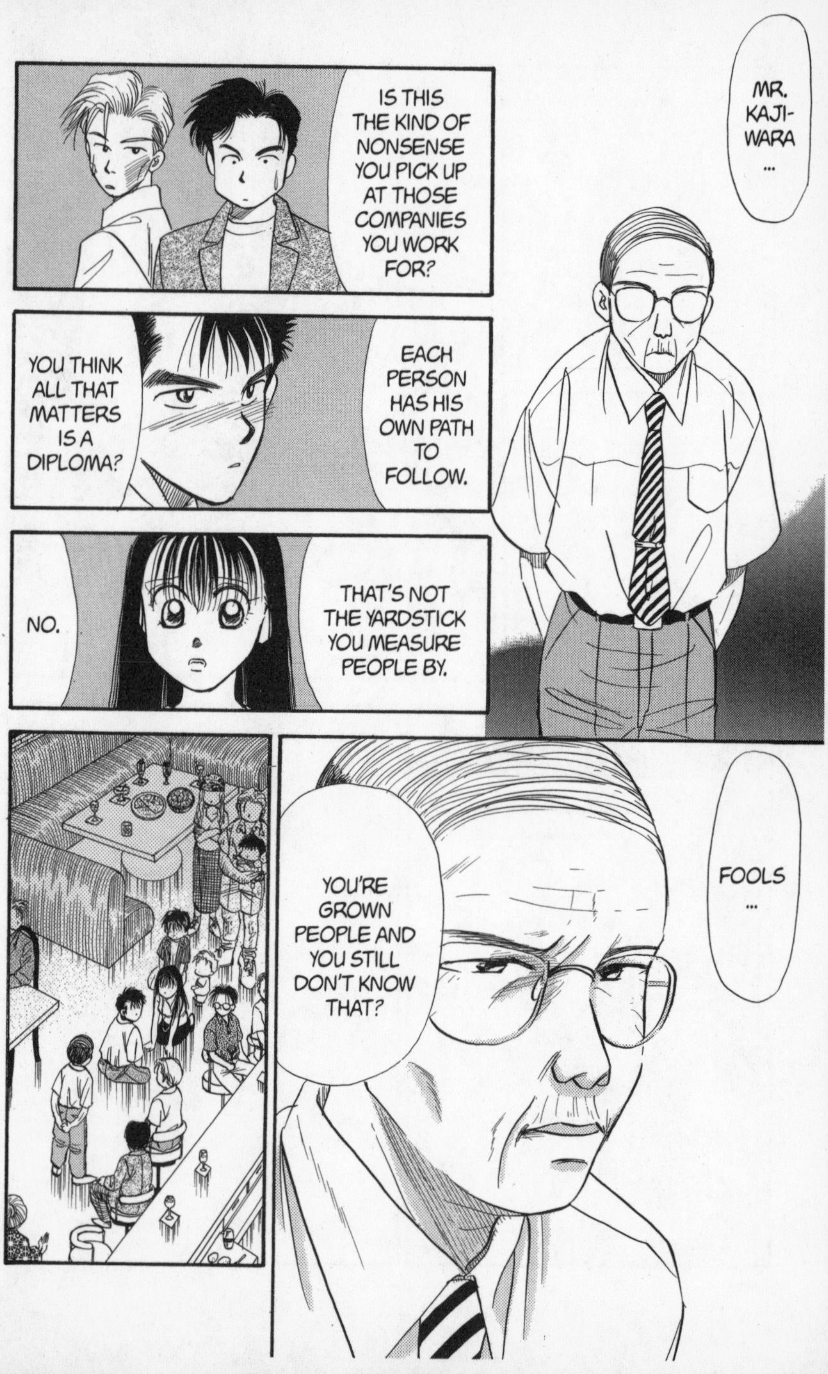
MR. KAJI-WARA ...
IS THIS THE KIND OF NONSENSE YOU PICK UP AT THOSE COMPANIES YOU WORK FOR?
EACH PERSON HAS HIS OWN PATH TO FOLLOW.
YOU THINK ALL THAT MATTERS IS A DIPLOMA?
THAT'S NOT THE YARDSTICK YOU MEASURE PEOPLE BY.
NO.
FOOLS ...
YOU'RE GROWN PEOPLE AND YOU STILL DON'T KNOW THAT?

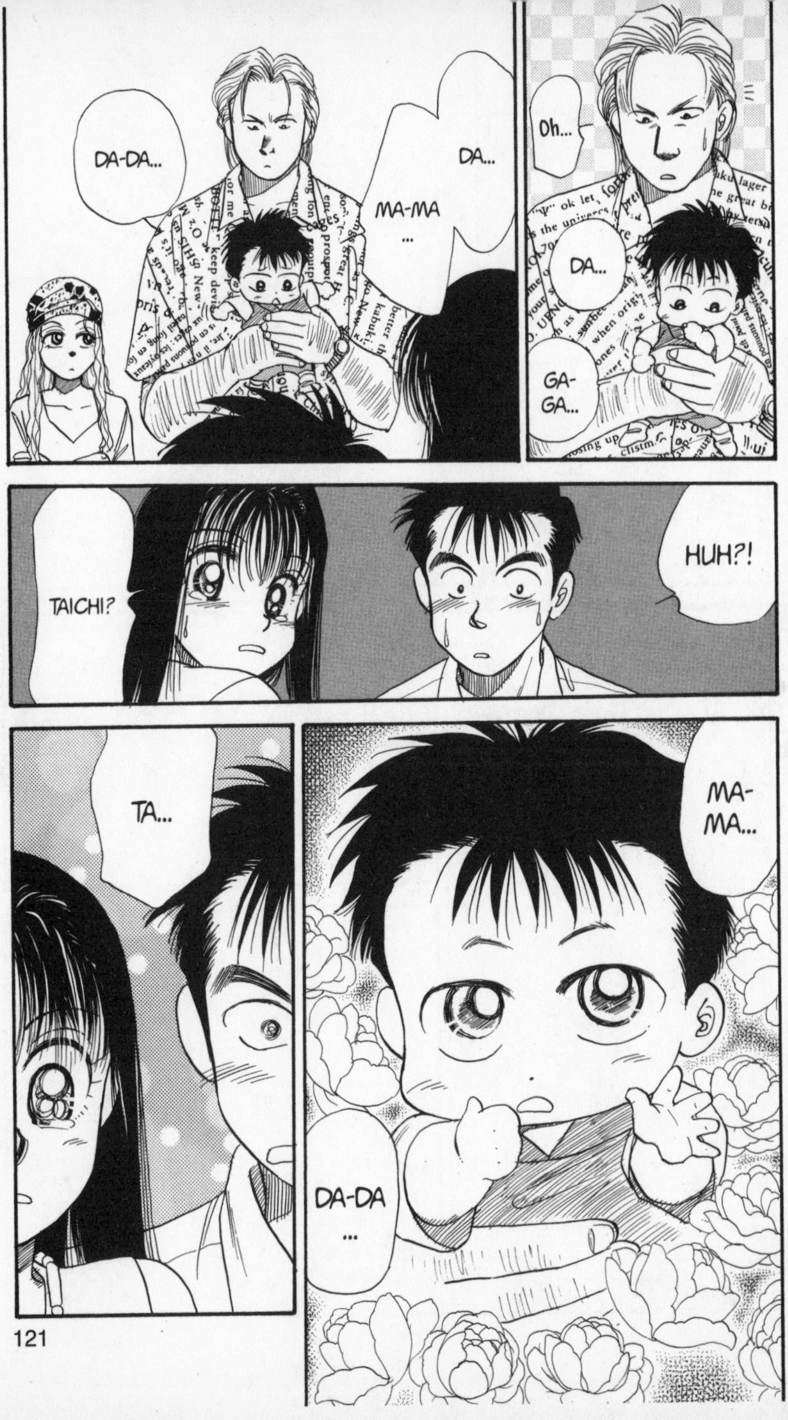
Oh...
DA...
GA-GA...
DA...
MA-MA ...
DA-DA...
HUH?!
TAICHI?
MA-MA...
DA-DA ...
TA...

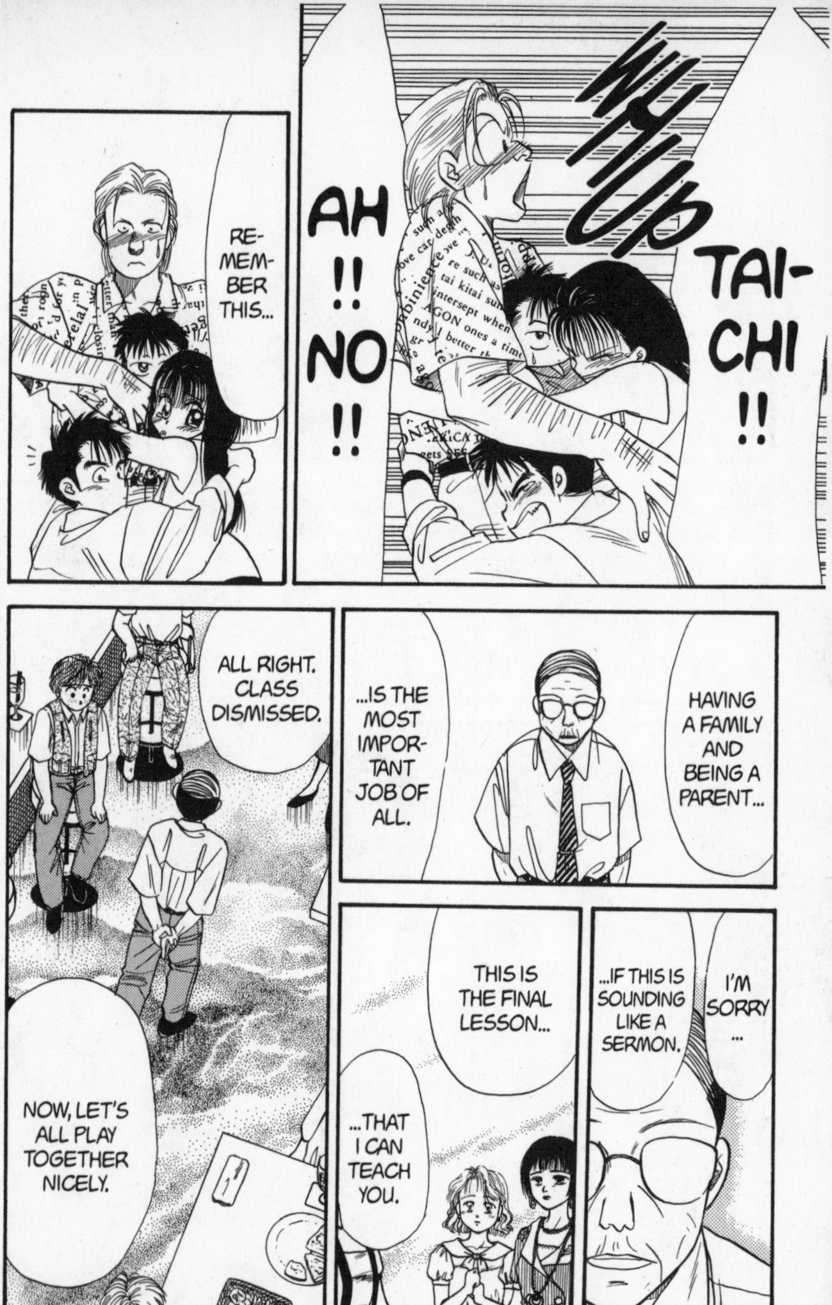
WHUP
TAI-CHI!!
AH!! NO!!
RE-MEMBER THIS...
HAVING A FAMILY AND BEING A PARENT...
...IS THE MOST IMPORTANT JOB OF ALL.
I'M SORRY...
...IF THIS IS SOUNDING LIKE A SERMON.
THIS IS THE FINAL LESSON...
...THAT I CAN TEACH YOU.
ALL RIGHT. CLASS DISMISSED.
NOW, LET'S ALL PLAY TOGETHER NICELY.

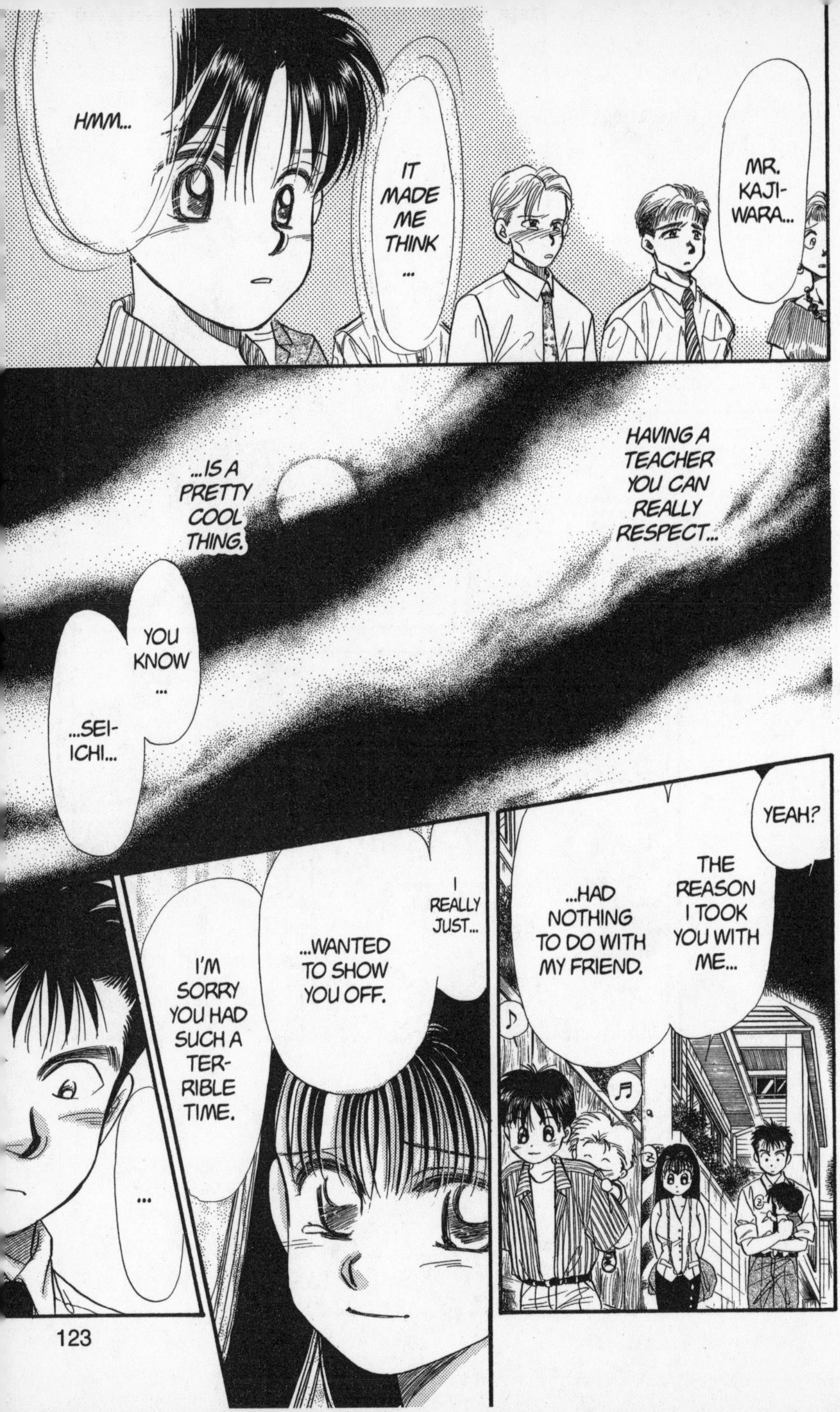
MR. KAJI-WARA...
IT MADE ME THINK...
HMM...
HAVING A TEACHER YOU CAN REALLY RESPECT...
...IS A PRETTY COOL THING.
YOU KNOW...
...SEI-ICHI...
YEAH?
THE REASON I TOOK YOU WITH ME...
...HAD NOTHING TO DO WITH MY FRIEND.
I REALLY JUST...
...WANTED TO SHOW YOU OFF.
I'M SORRY YOU HAD SUCH A TER-RIBLE TIME.
...

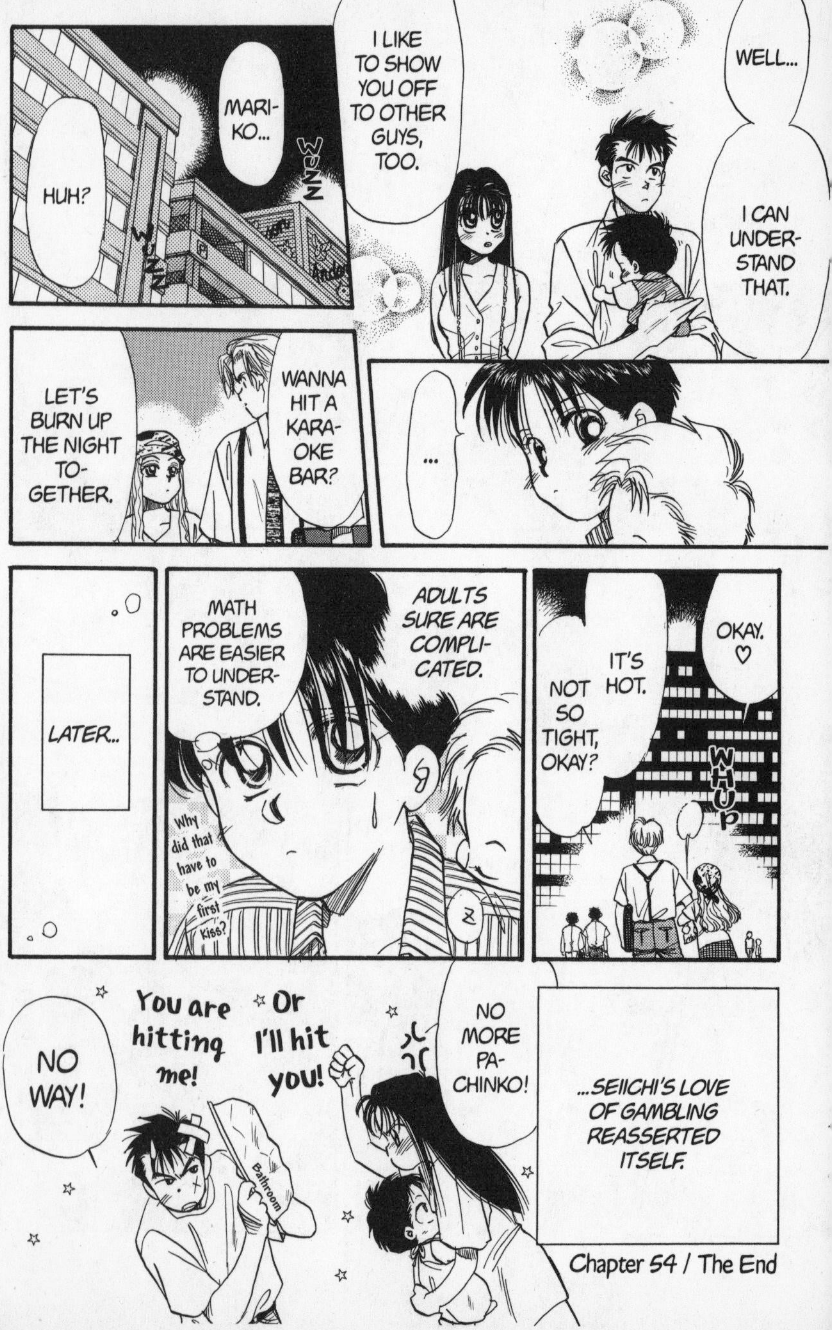
WELL...
I CAN UNDERSTAND THAT.
I LIKE TO SHOW YOU OFF TO OTHER GUYS, TOO.
MARIKO...
WUZZ
HUH?
WUZZ
...
WANNA HIT A KARAOKE BAR?
LET'S BURN UP THE NIGHT TOGETHER.
OKAY. ♡
IT'S HOT.
NOT SO TIGHT, OKAY?
WHUP
ADULTS SURE ARE COMPLICATED.
MATH PROBLEMS ARE EASIER TO UNDERSTAND.
Why did that have to be my first kiss?
Z
LATER...
...SEIICHI'S LOVE OF GAMBLING REASSERTED ITSELF.
NO MORE PACHINKO!
Or I'll hit you!
You are hitting me!
NO WAY!
Bathroom

Chapter 54 / The End

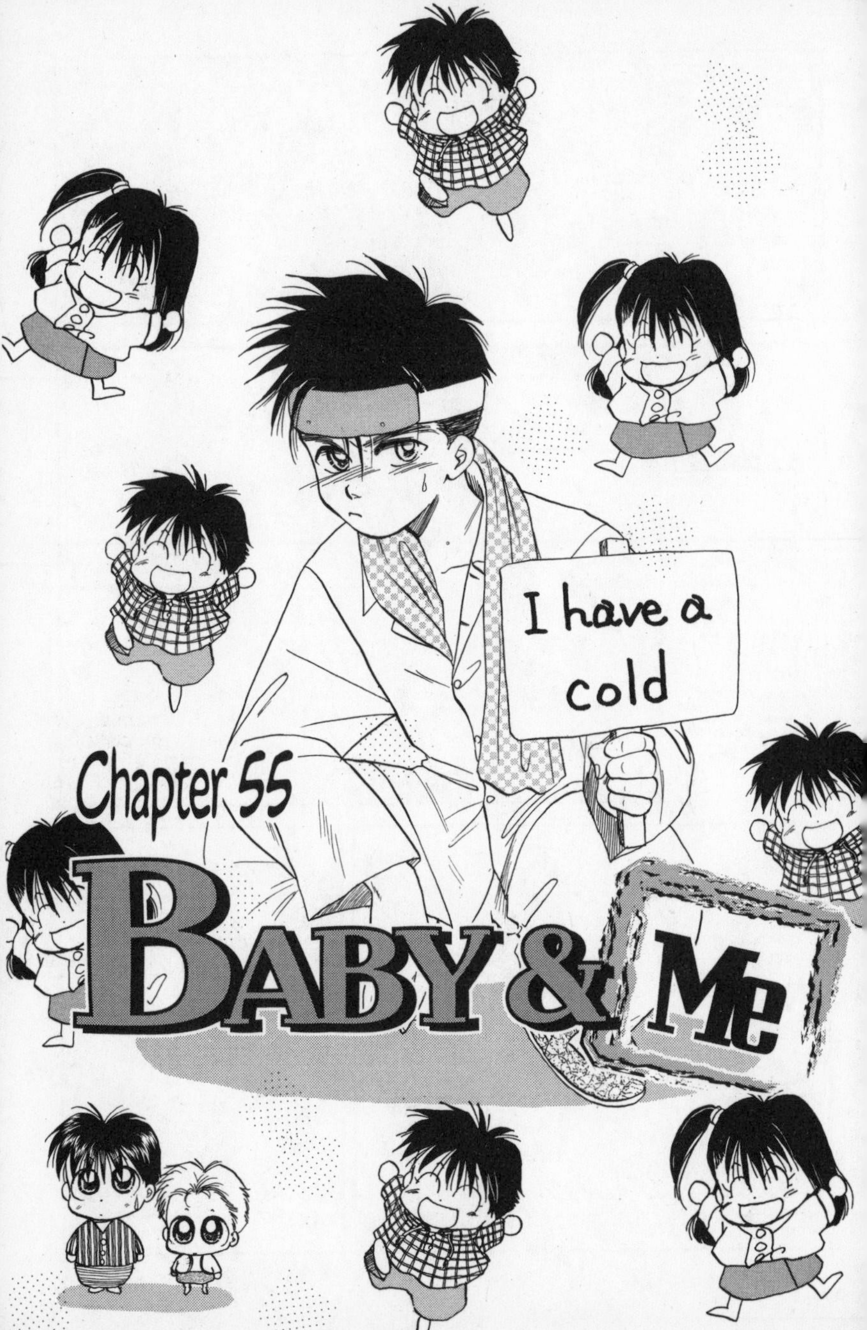
I have a cold
Chapter 55
BABY & ME

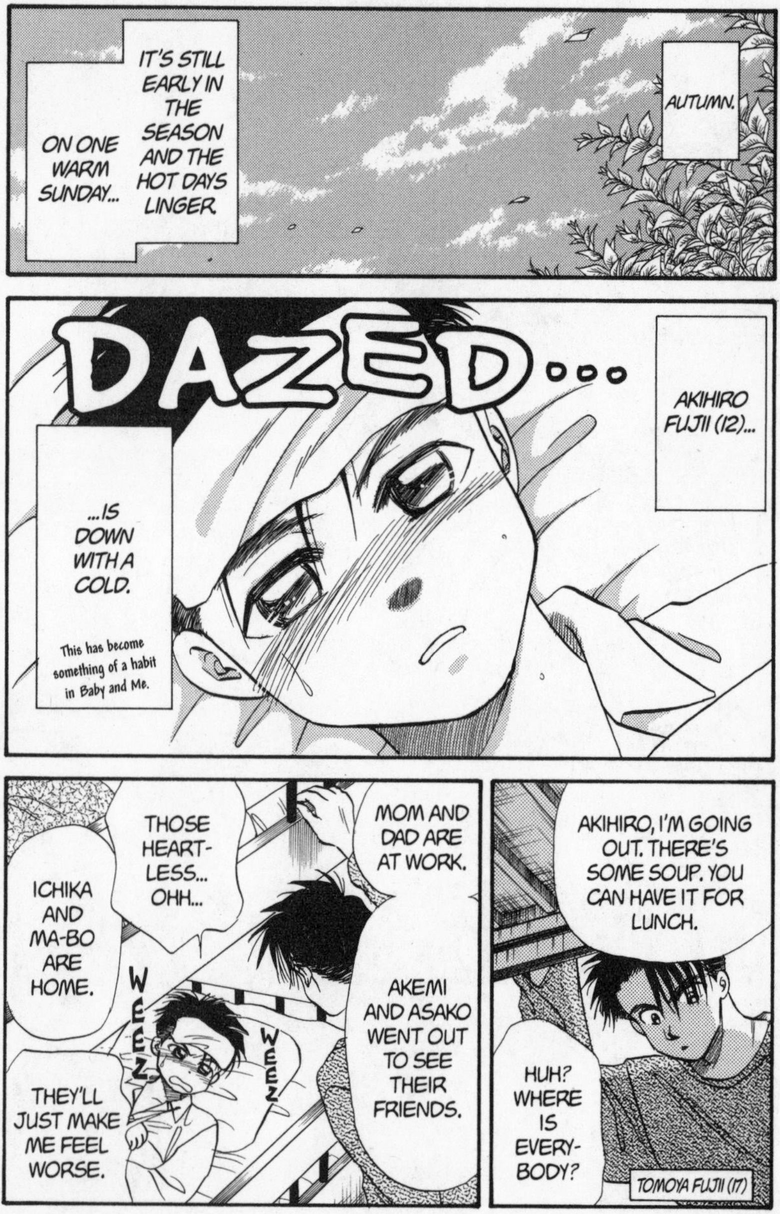
AUTUMN.
IT'S STILL EARLY IN THE SEASON AND THE HOT DAYS LINGER.
ON ONE WARM SUNDAY...
AKIHIRO FUJII (12)...
DAZED...
...IS DOWN WITH A COLD.
This has become something of a habit in Baby and Me.
AKIHIRO, I'M GOING OUT. THERE'S SOME SOUP. YOU CAN HAVE IT FOR LUNCH.
HUH? WHERE IS EVERYBODY?
TOMOYA FUJII (17)
MOM AND DAD ARE AT WORK.
AKEMI AND ASAKO WENT OUT TO SEE THEIR FRIENDS.
THOSE HEART-LESS... OHH...
ICHIKA AND MA-BO ARE HOME.
WEEZ
WEEZ
THEY'LL JUST MAKE ME FEEL WORSE.

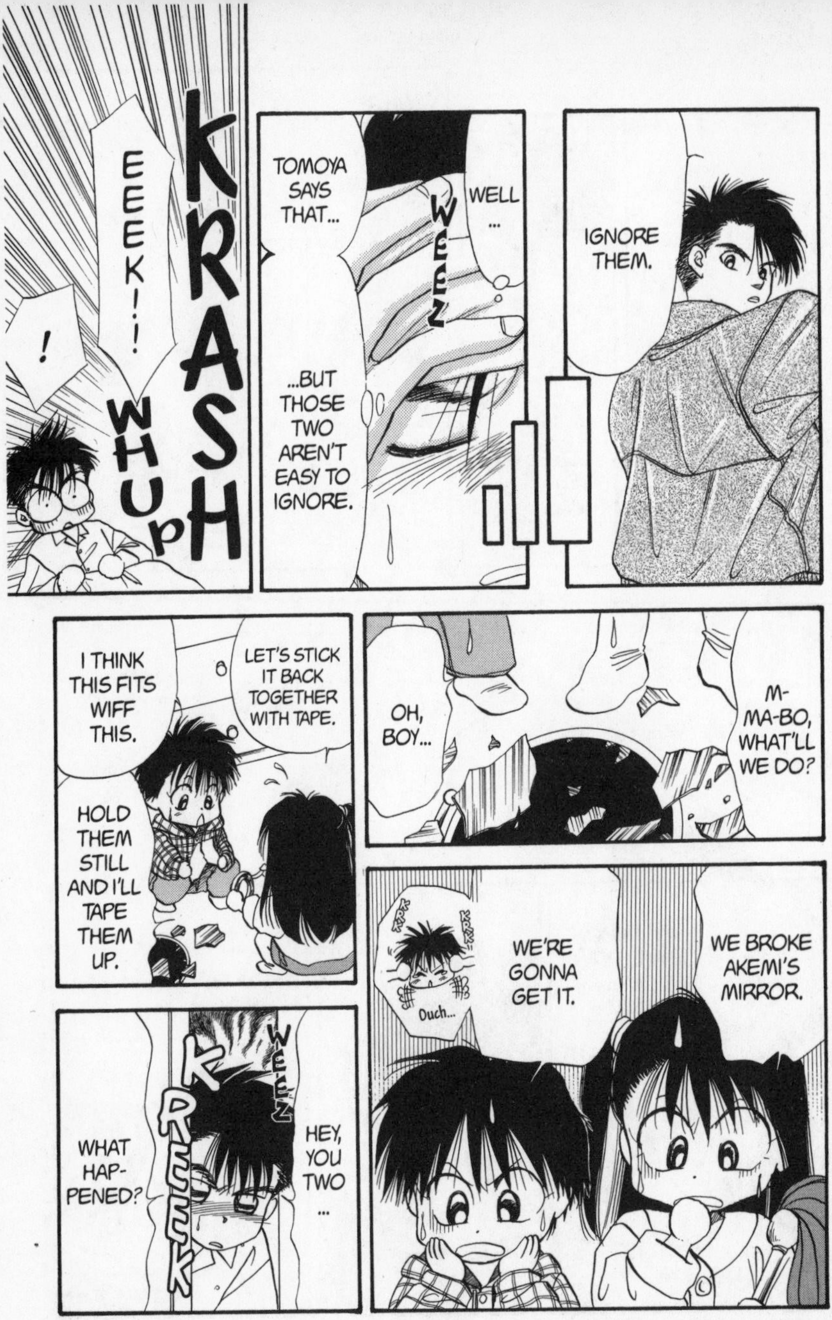
IGNORE THEM.
WELL ...
WEEZ
TOMOYA SAYS THAT...
...BUT THOSE TWO AREN'T EASY TO IGNORE.
KRASH
EEEK!!
WHUp
!
M-MA-BO, WHAT'LL WE DO?
OH, BOY...
LET'S STICK IT BACK TOGETHER WITH TAPE.
I THINK THIS FITS WIFF THIS.
HOLD THEM STILL AND I'LL TAPE THEM UP.
WE BROKE AKEMI'S MIRROR.
WE'RE GONNA GET IT.
KRAK
KRAK
Ouch...
WEEZ
HEY, YOU TWO ...
KREEEK
WHAT HAP-PENED?

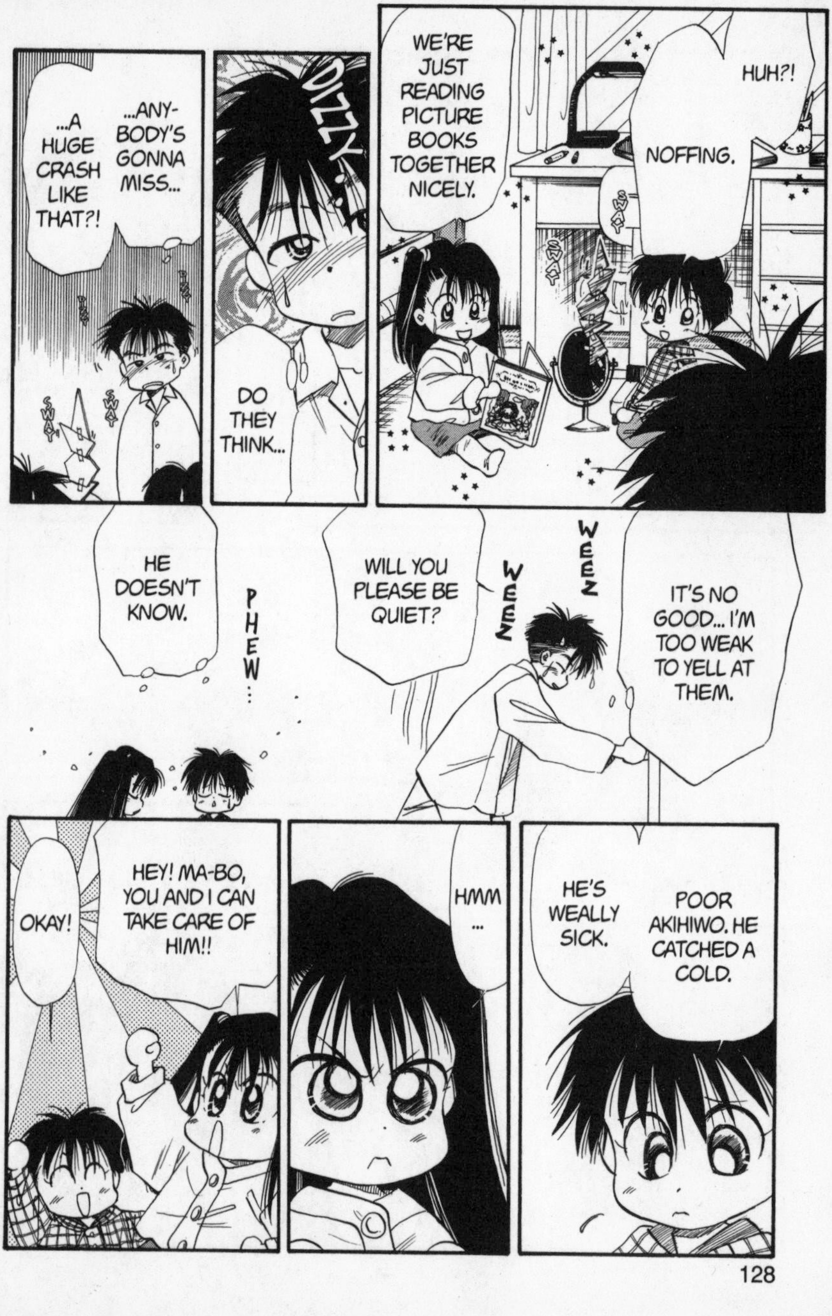
HUH?!
NOFFING.
WE'RE JUST READING PICTURE BOOKS TOGETHER NICELY.
SWAY
SWAY
DIZZY
DO THEY THINK...
...ANY-BODY'S GONNA MISS...
...A HUGE CRASH LIKE THAT?!
SWAY
SWAY
IT'S NO GOOD... I'M TOO WEAK TO YELL AT THEM.
WEEZ
WEEZ
WILL YOU PLEASE BE QUIET?
PHEW...
HE DOESN'T KNOW.
POOR AKIHIWO. HE CATCHED A COLD.
HE'S WEALLY SICK.
HMM...
HEY! MA-BO, YOU AND I CAN TAKE CARE OF HIM!!
OKAY!

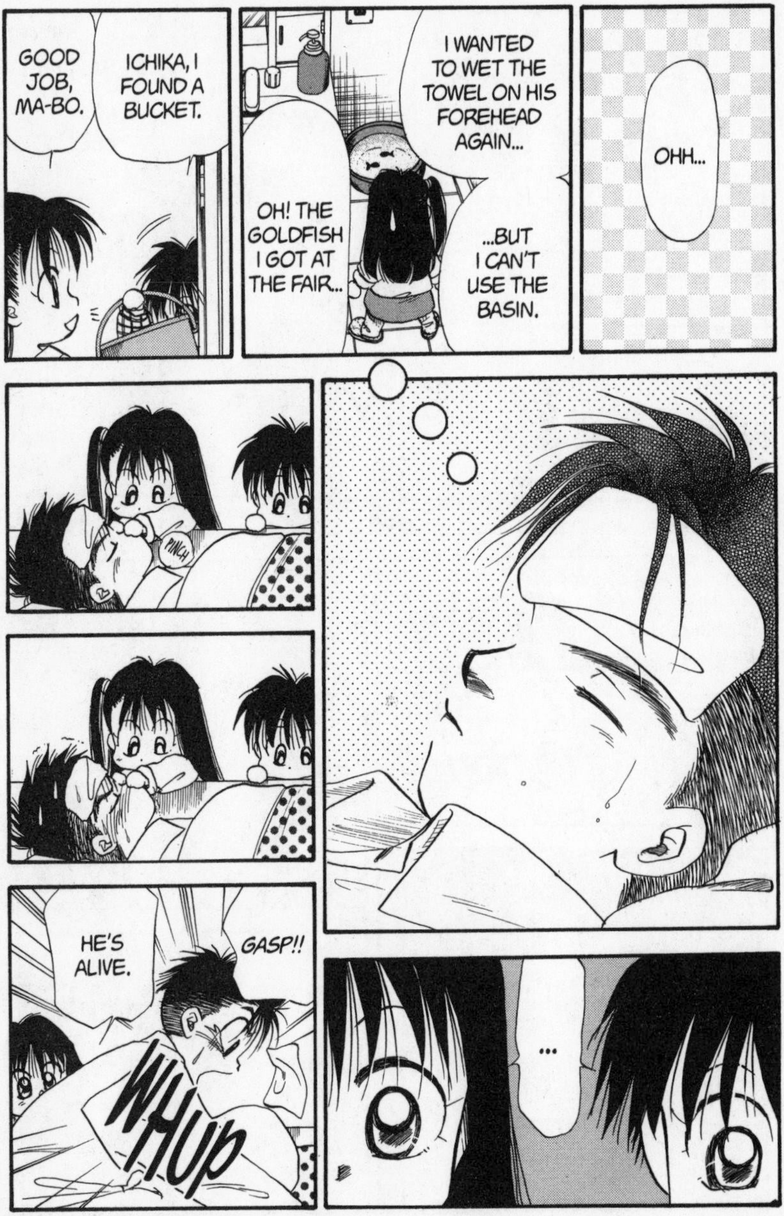
OHH...
I WANTED TO WET THE TOWEL ON HIS FOREHEAD AGAIN...
...BUT I CAN'T USE THE BASIN.
OH! THE GOLDFISH I GOT AT THE FAIR...
ICHIKA, I FOUND A BUCKET.
GOOD JOB, MA-BO.
PINCH
...
GASP!!
HE'S ALIVE.
WHUP

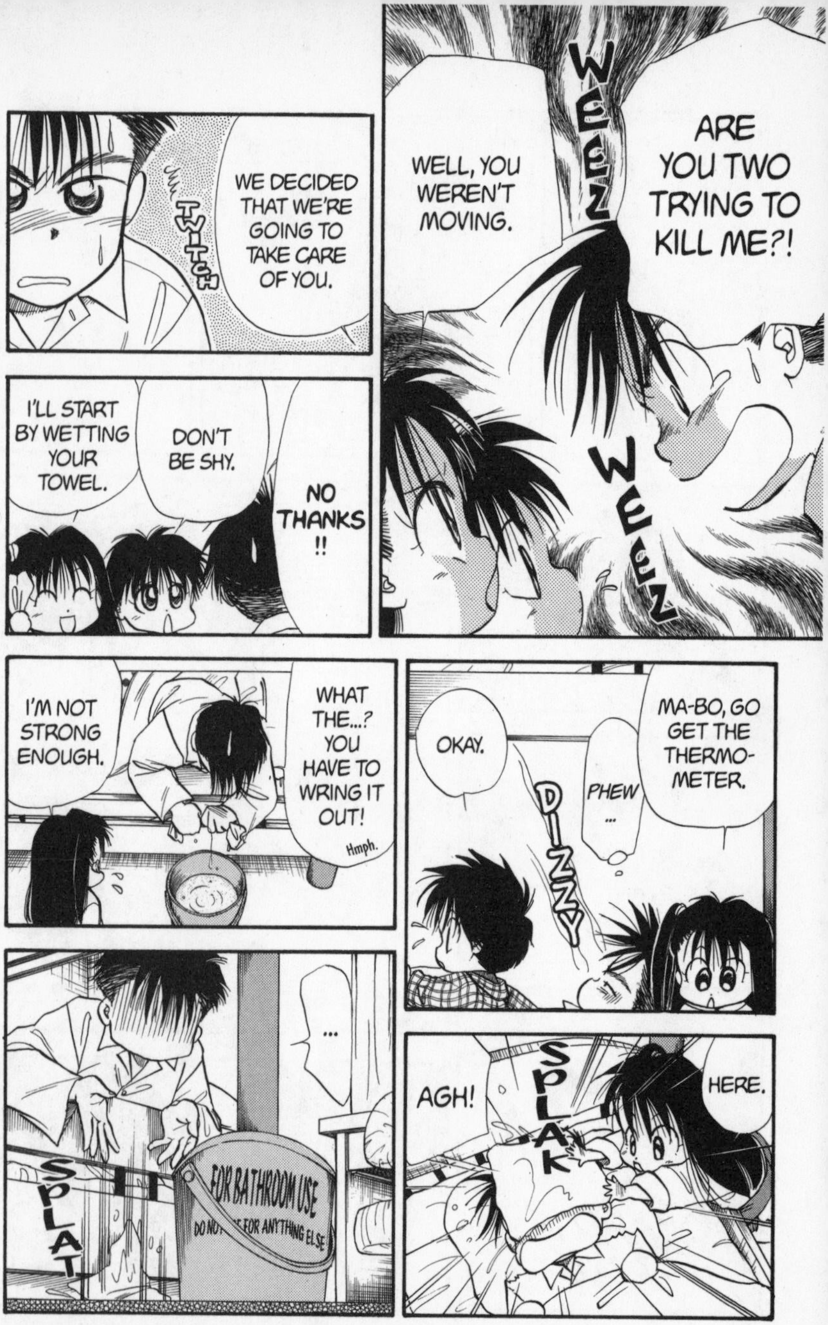
ARE YOU TWO TRYING TO KILL ME?!
WEEZ
WELL, YOU WEREN'T MOVING.
WEEZ
WE DECIDED THAT WE'RE GOING TO TAKE CARE OF YOU.
TWITCH
NO THANKS!!
DON'T BE SHY.
I'LL START BY WETTING YOUR TOWEL.
MA-BO, GO GET THE THERMOMETER.
PHEW...
DIZZY
OKAY.
WHAT THE...? YOU HAVE TO WRING IT OUT!
Hmph.
I'M NOT STRONG ENOUGH.
HERE.
SPLAK
AGH!
...
FOR BATHROOM USE
FOR ANYTHING ELSE
SPLAT

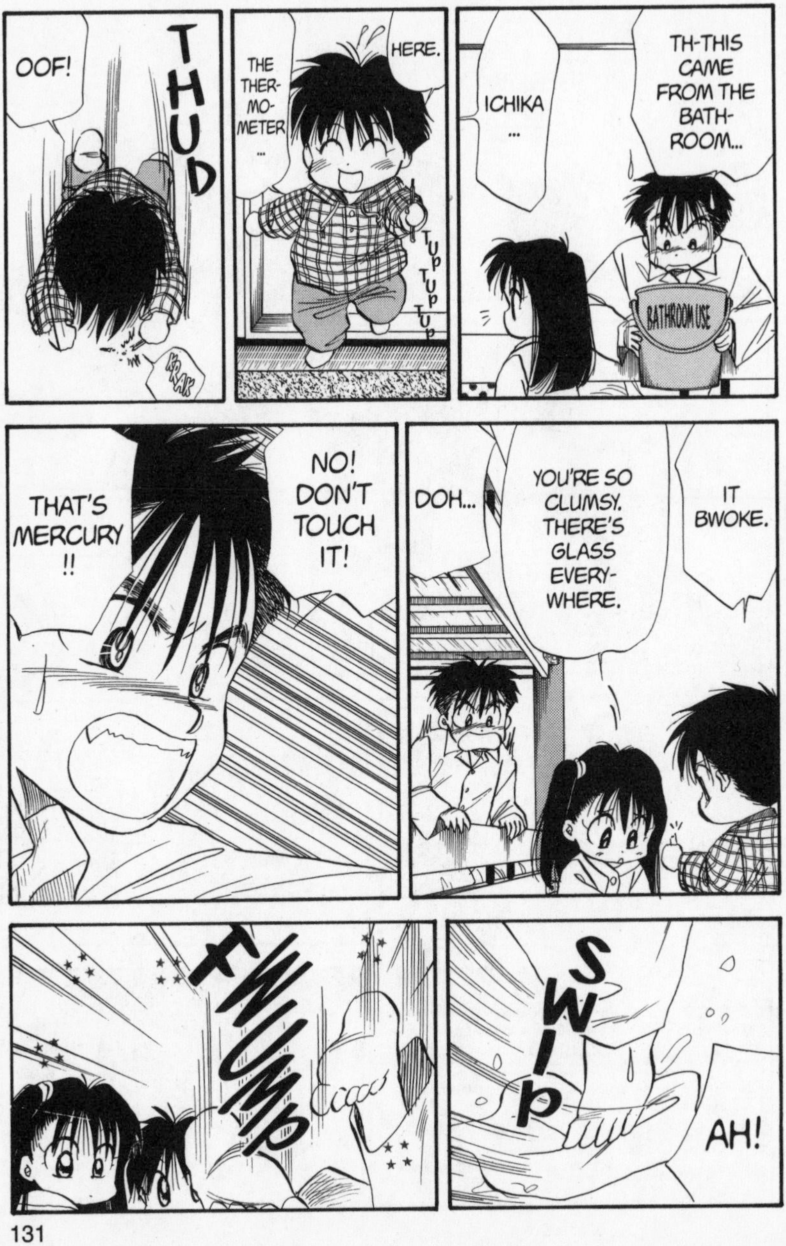
TH-THIS CAME FROM THE BATH-ROOM...
ICHIKA ...
BATHROOM USE
HERE.
THE THER-MO-METER ...
TUP TUP TUP
THUD
OOF!
KRAK
IT BWOKE.
YOU'RE SO CLUMSY. THERE'S GLASS EVERY-WHERE.
DOH...
NO! DON'T TOUCH IT!
THAT'S MERCURY !!
SWIP
AH!
FWUMP

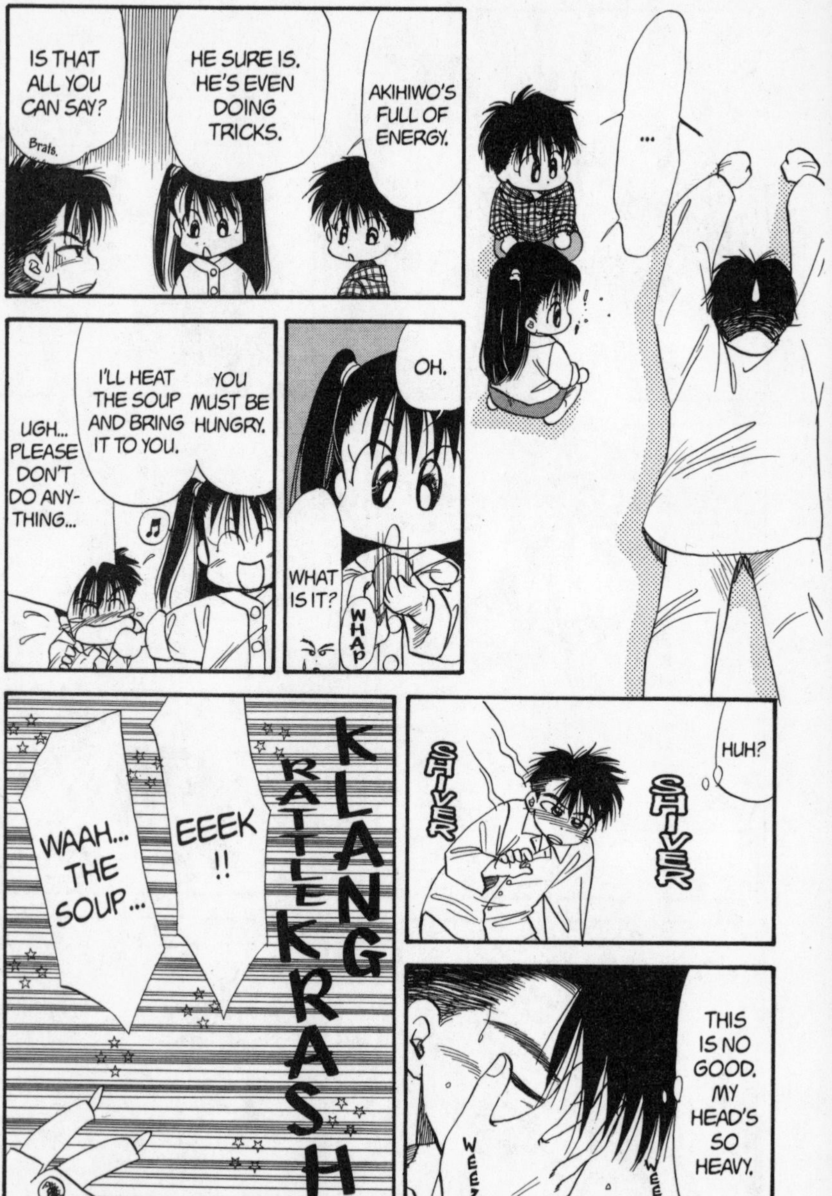
...
AKIHIWO'S FULL OF ENERGY.
HE SURE IS. HE'S EVEN DOING TRICKS.
IS THAT ALL YOU CAN SAY?
Brats.
OH.
WHAT IS IT?
WHAP
YOU MUST BE HUNGRY.
I'LL HEAT THE SOUP AND BRING IT TO YOU.
UGH... PLEASE DON'T DO ANY-THING...
HUH?
SHIVER
SHIVER
THIS IS NO GOOD. MY HEAD'S SO HEAVY.
WEEZ
WEEZ
KLANG
RATTLE
KRASH
EEEK !!
WAAH... THE SOUP...

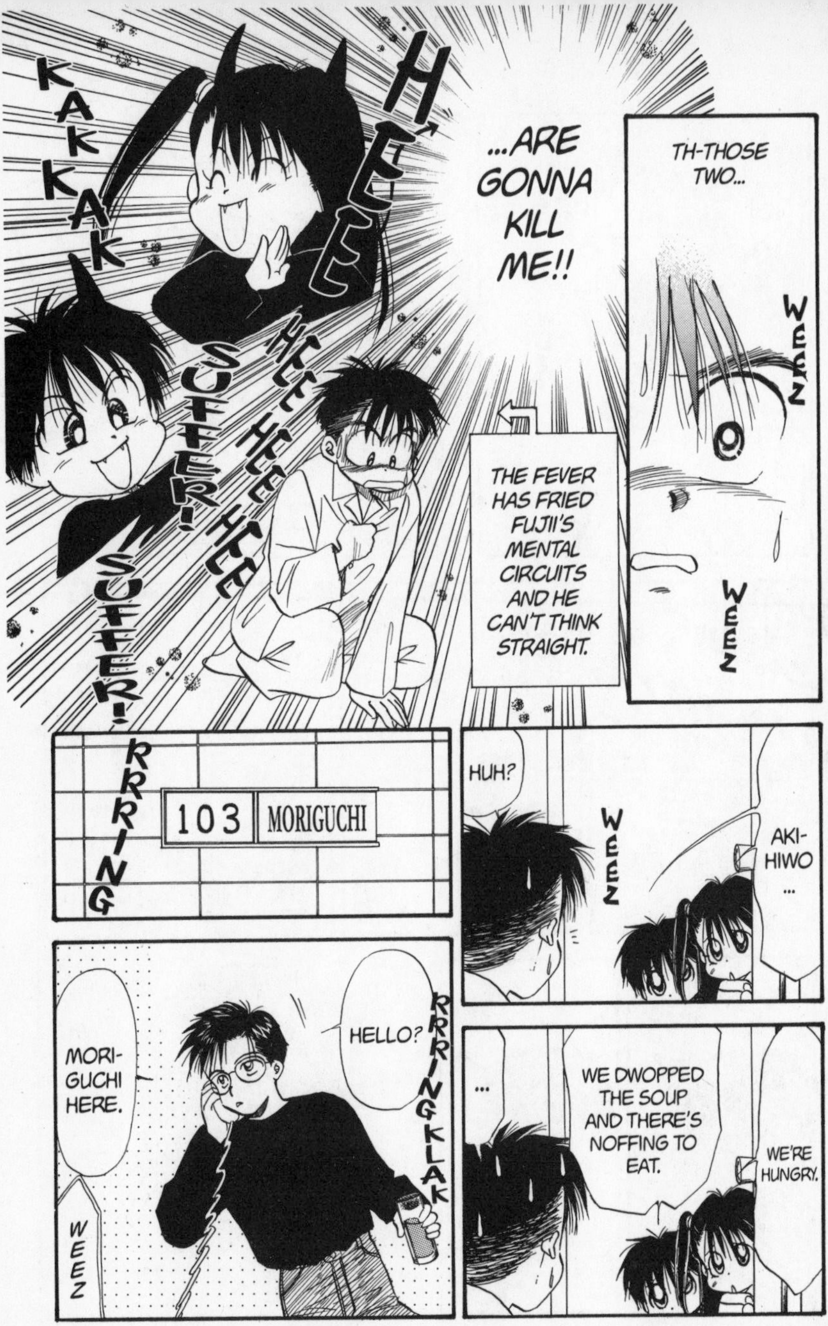
TH-THOSE TWO...
WEEZ
WEEZ
...ARE GONNA KILL ME!!
THE FEVER HAS FRIED FUJII'S MENTAL CIRCUITS AND HE CAN'T THINK STRAIGHT.
HEEE
KAKKAK
HEE HEE HEE
SUFFER!
SUFFER!
HUH?
WEEZ
AKI-HIWO ...
RRRING
103
MORIGUCHI
...
WE DWOPPED THE SOUP AND THERE'S NOFFING TO EAT.
WE'RE HUNGRY.
RRRING
KLAK
HELLO?
MORI-GUCHI HERE.
WEEZ

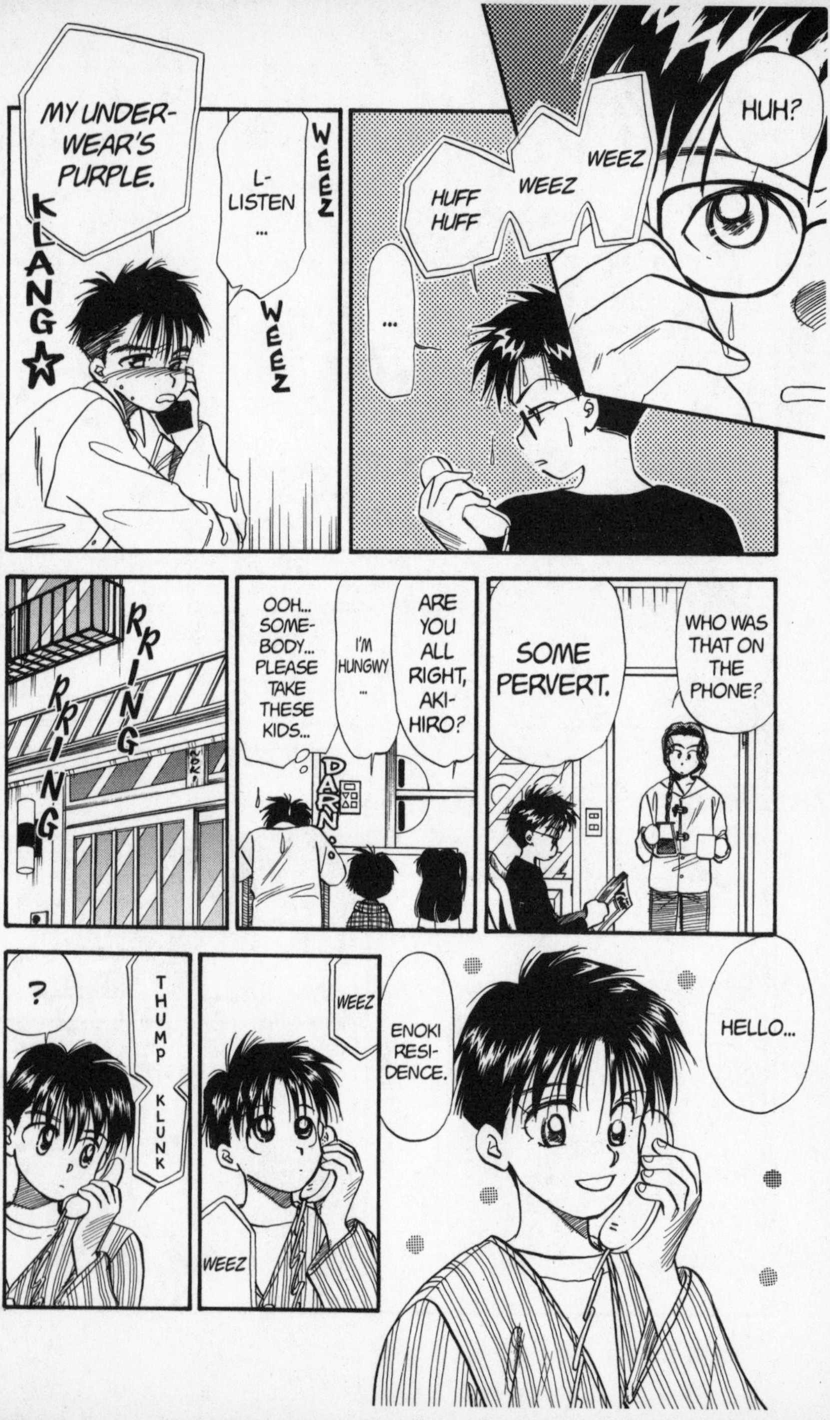
HUH?
WEEZ
WEEZ
HUFF HUFF
...
MY UNDER-WEAR'S PURPLE.
L-LISTEN...
WEEZ
WEEZ
KLANG☆
WHO WAS THAT ON THE PHONE?
SOME PERVERT.
ARE YOU ALL RIGHT, AKI-HIRO?
I'M HUNGWY...
OOH... SOME-BODY... PLEASE TAKE THESE KIDS...
DARN
RRING
RRING
HELLO...
ENOKI RESI-DENCE.
WEEZ
WEEZ
THUMP
KLUNK
?

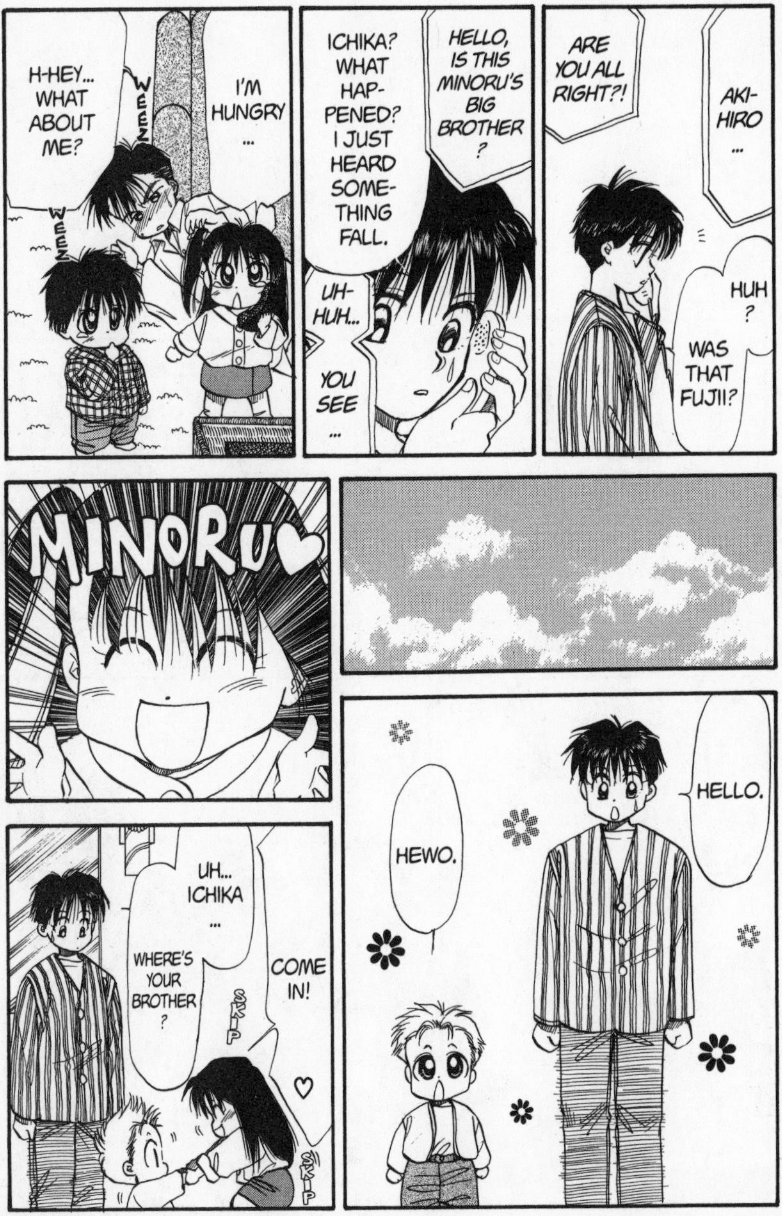
AKI-HIRO...
ARE YOU ALL RIGHT?!
HUH? WAS THAT FUJII?
HELLO, IS THIS MINORU'S BIG BROTHER?
ICHIKA? WHAT HAP-PENED? I JUST HEARD SOME-THING FALL.
UH-HUH... YOU SEE...
I'M HUNGRY...
WEEZ
H-HEY... WHAT ABOUT ME?
WEEZ
MINORU♥
HELLO.
HEWO.
COME IN!
UH... ICHIKA...
WHERE'S YOUR BROTHER?
SKIP
SKIP

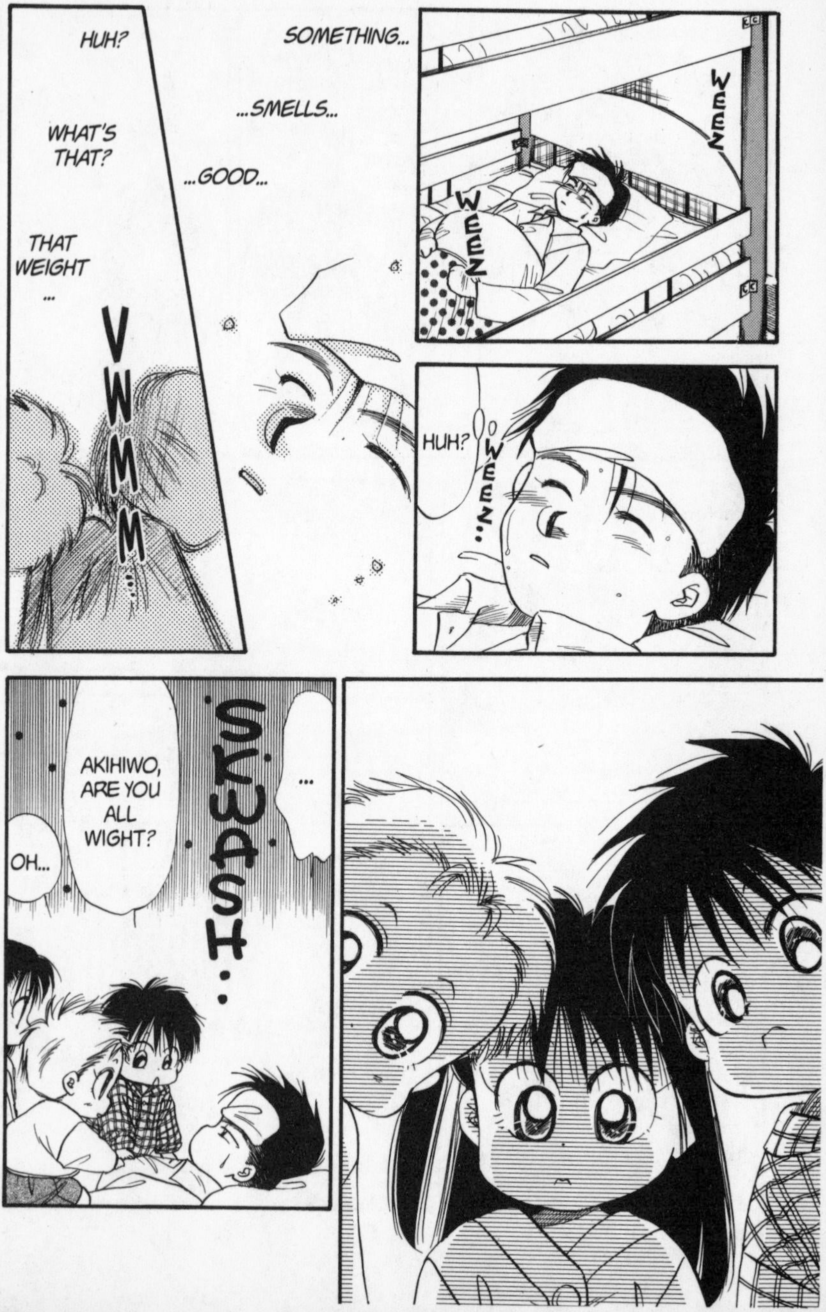
SOMETHING...
...SMELLS...
...GOOD...
WEEZ
WEEZ
HUH?
WHAT'S THAT?
THAT WEIGHT ...
VWMM...
HUH?
WEEZ...
...
AKIHIWO, ARE YOU ALL WIGHT?
OH...
SWASH..

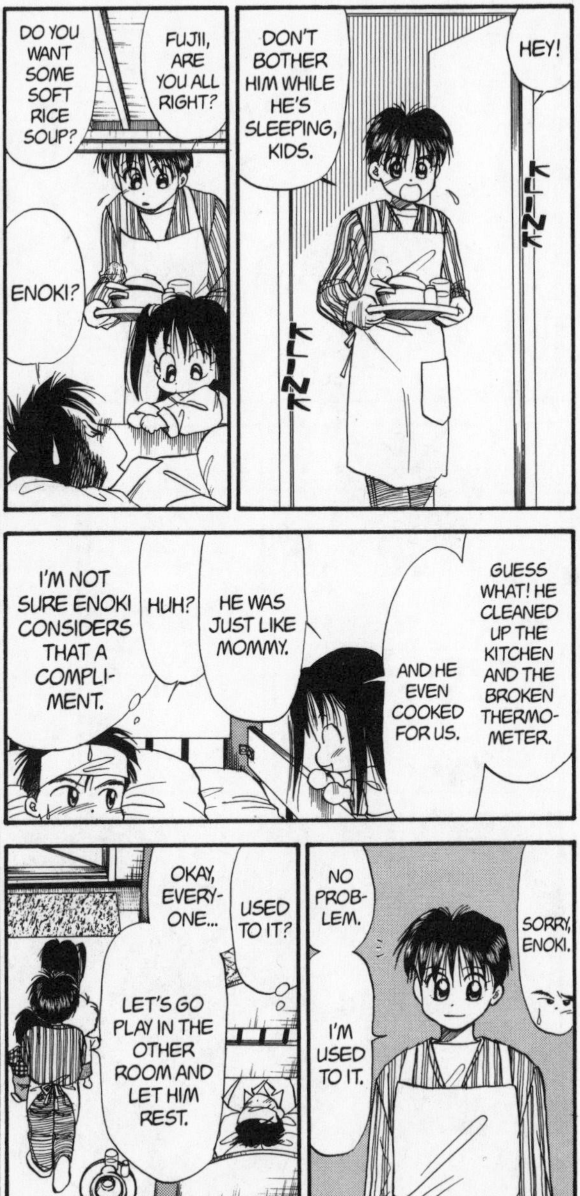
HEY!
DON'T BOTHER HIM WHILE HE'S SLEEPING, KIDS.
KLINK
KLINK
FUJII, ARE YOU ALL RIGHT?
DO YOU WANT SOME SOFT RICE SOUP?
ENOKI?
GUESS WHAT! HE CLEANED UP THE KITCHEN AND THE BROKEN THERMOMETER.
AND HE EVEN COOKED FOR US.
HE WAS JUST LIKE MOMMY.
HUH?
I'M NOT SURE ENOKI CONSIDERS THAT A COMPLIMENT.
SORRY, ENOKI.
NO PROBLEM.
I'M USED TO IT.
USED TO IT?
OKAY, EVERYONE...
LET'S GO PLAY IN THE OTHER ROOM AND LET HIM REST.

Author's Note: Part 5

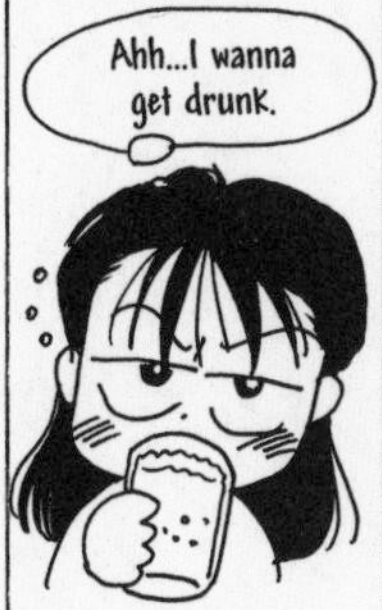
Ahh...I wanna get drunk.

I want to get drunk. I don't know if I can hold my liquor or what, but I drink whatever people pour me. Even if I feel like my speech is slurred and I'm tipsy, the only thing people notice is that my cheeks get hot and a little red, so they think I can hold my liquor well. Is that good or bad?

However, I never forget myself. Even if I get drunk and slur my words, and stagger, and laugh like a fool, my mind is clear as a bell. But sometimes, when things are so bad that I get really sad and sick of everything, I wish I could get drunk enough to forget myself...

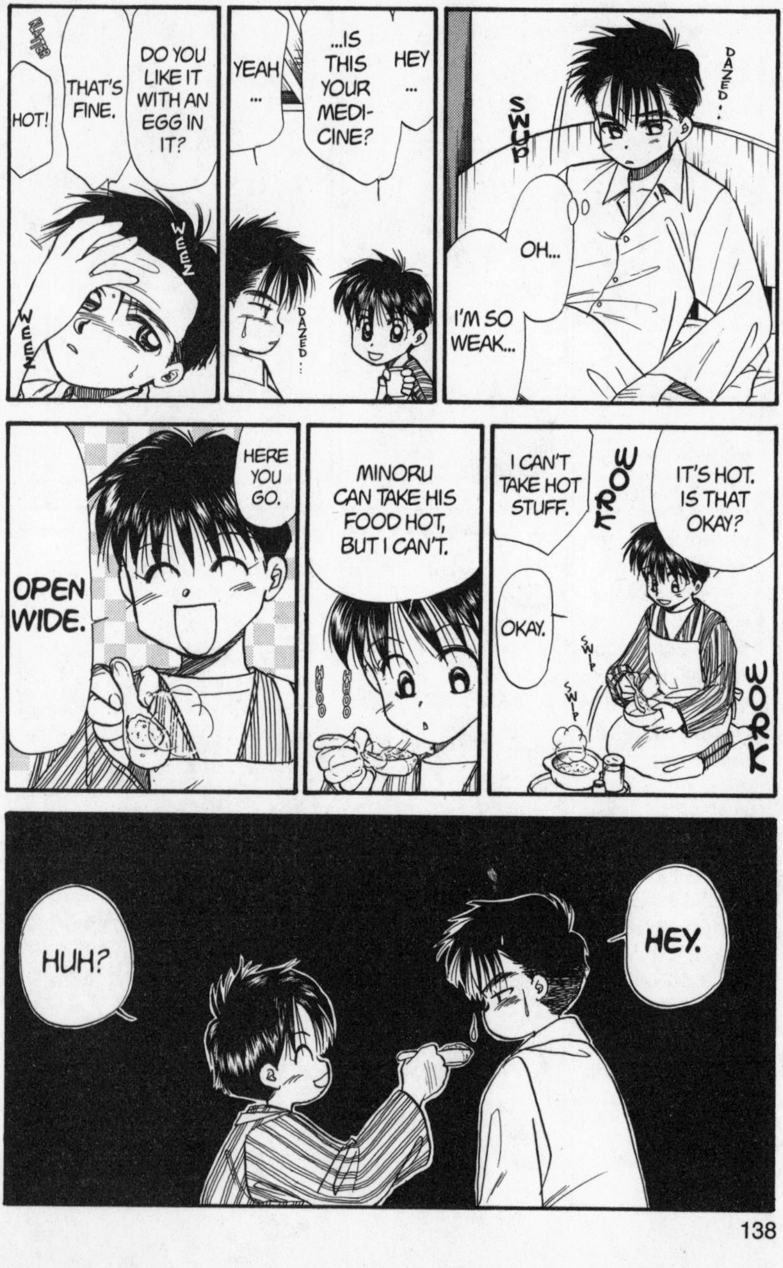
DAZED . .
SWUP
OH...
I'M SO WEAK...
HEY ...
...IS THIS YOUR MEDICINE?
YEAH ...
DAZED . . .
DO YOU LIKE IT WITH AN EGG IN IT?
THAT'S FINE.
HOT!
WEEZ
WEEZ
IT'S HOT. IS THAT OKAY?
WORK
WORK
I CAN'T TAKE HOT STUFF.
OKAY.
SWIP
SWIP
MINORU CAN TAKE HIS FOOD HOT, BUT I CAN'T.
HERE YOU GO.
OPEN WIDE.
HEY.
HUH?

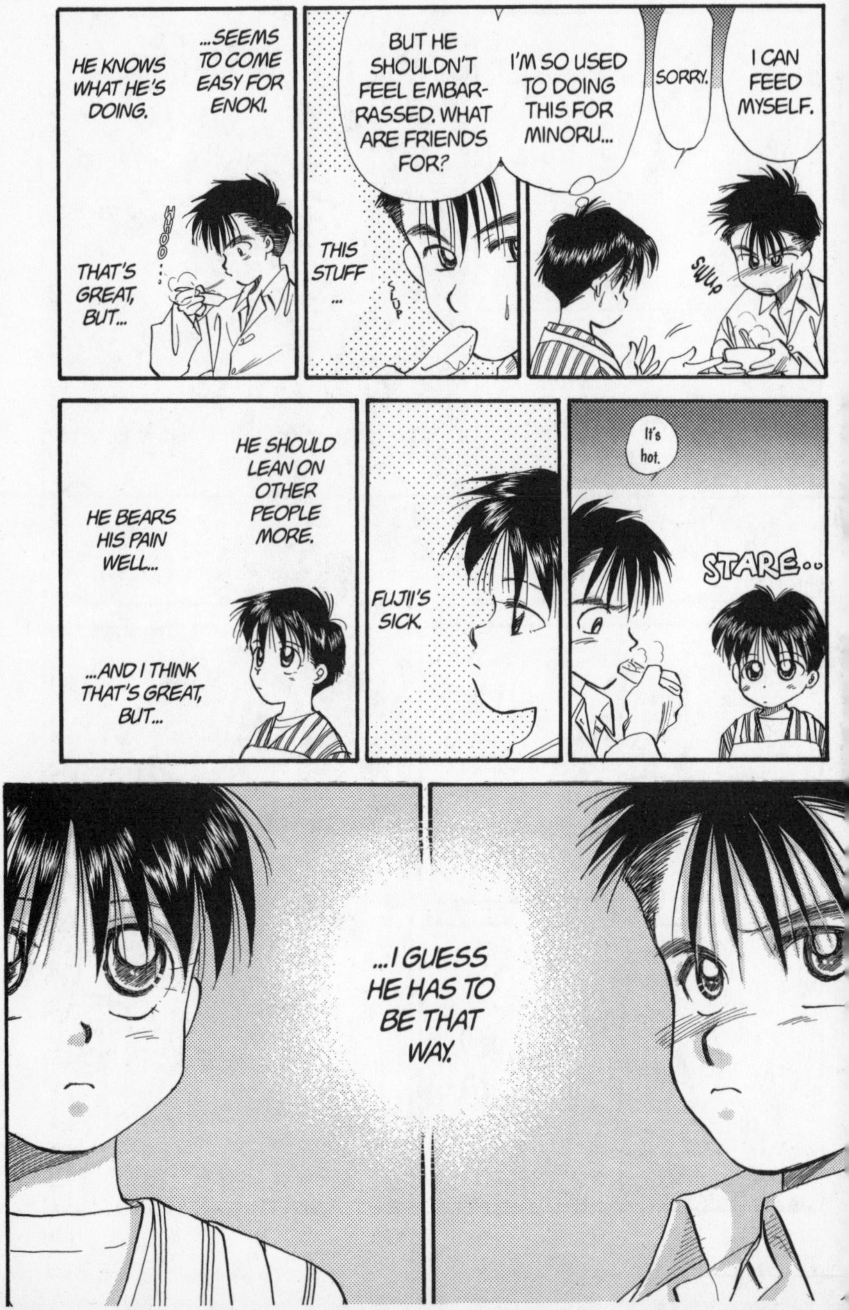
I CAN FEED MYSELF.
SORRY.
I'M SO USED TO DOING THIS FOR MINORU...
SWUP
BUT HE SHOULDN'T FEEL EMBARRASSED. WHAT ARE FRIENDS FOR?
THIS STUFF ...
SLUP
...SEEMS TO COME EASY FOR ENOKI.
HE KNOWS WHAT HE'S DOING.
WHOO...
THAT'S GREAT, BUT...
It's hot.
STARE...
FUJII'S SICK.
HE SHOULD LEAN ON OTHER PEOPLE MORE.
HE BEARS HIS PAIN WELL...
...AND I THINK THAT'S GREAT, BUT...
...I GUESS HE HAS TO BE THAT WAY.

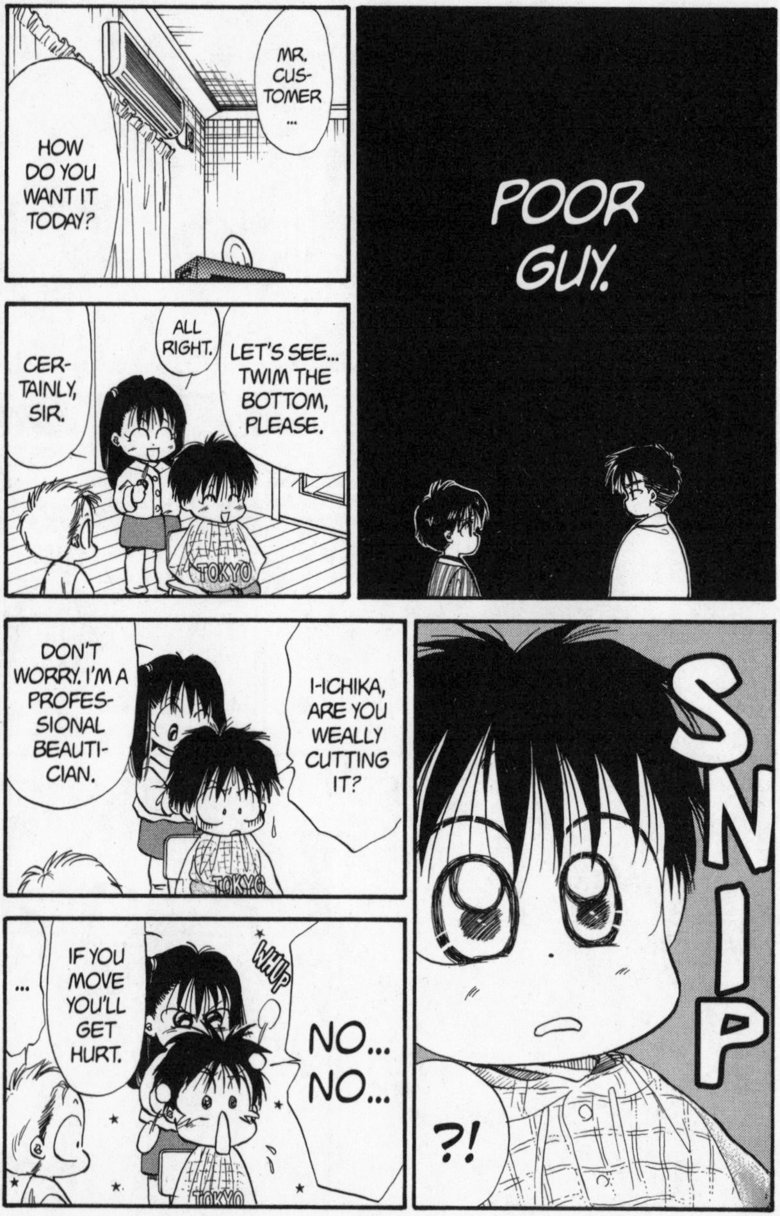
POOR GUY.
MR. CUSTOMER...
HOW DO YOU WANT IT TODAY?
LET'S SEE... TWIM THE BOTTOM, PLEASE.
ALL RIGHT.
CERTAINLY, SIR.
SNIP
?!
I-ICHIKA, ARE YOU WEALLY CUTTING IT?
DON'T WORRY. I'M A PROFESSIONAL BEAUTICIAN.
NO... NO...
WHIP
IF YOU MOVE YOU'LL GET HURT.
...

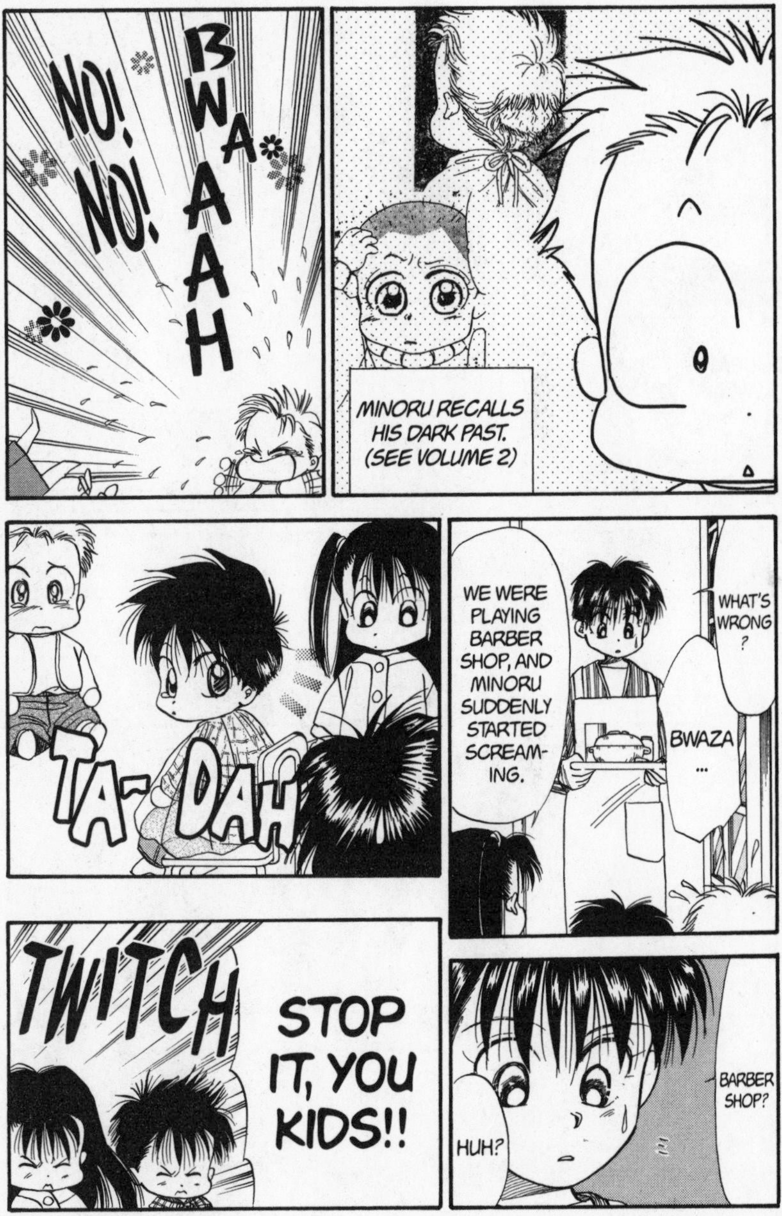
MINORU RECALLS HIS DARK PAST. (SEE VOLUME 2)
BWAAAH
NO! NO!
WHAT'S WRONG?
BWAZA ...
WE WERE PLAYING BARBER SHOP, AND MINORU SUDDENLY STARTED SCREAM-ING.
TA-DAH
BARBER SHOP?
HUH?
STOP IT, YOU KIDS!!
TWITCH

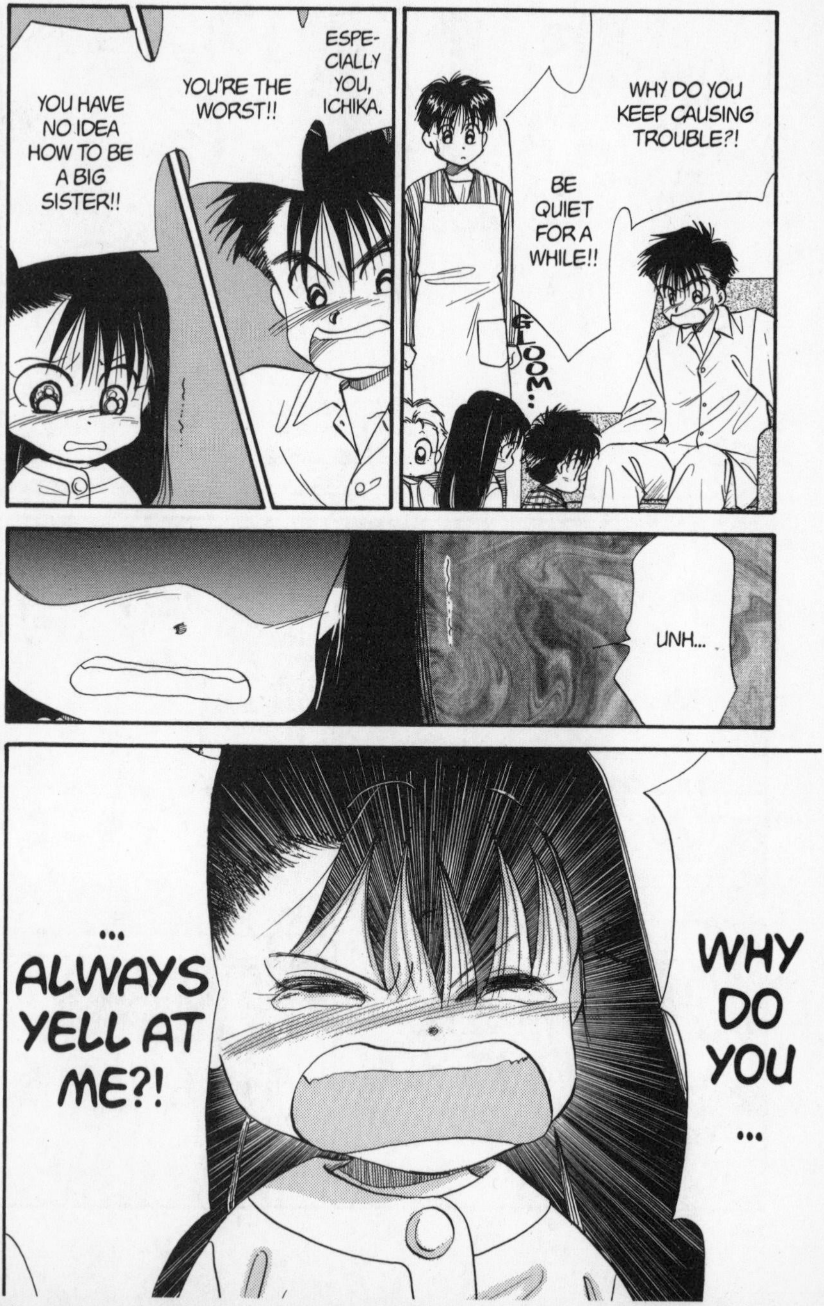
WHY DO YOU KEEP CAUSING TROUBLE?!
BE QUIET FOR A WHILE!!
GLOOM..
ESPECIALLY YOU, ICHIKA.
YOU'RE THE WORST!!
YOU HAVE NO IDEA HOW TO BE A BIG SISTER!!
UNH...
WHY DO YOU ...
... ALWAYS YELL AT ME?!

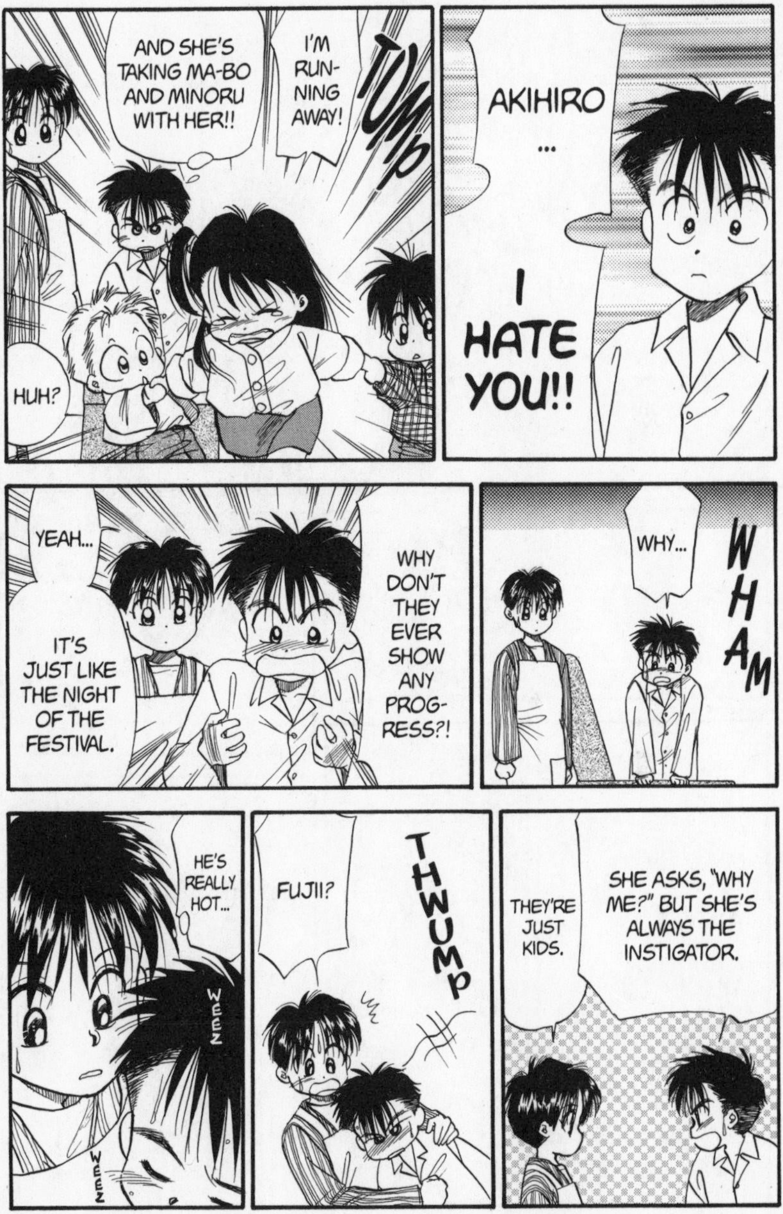
AKIHIRO ...
I HATE YOU!!
TUMP
I'M RUN-NING AWAY!
AND SHE'S TAKING MA-BO AND MINORU WITH HER!!
HUH?
WHY...
WHAM
WHY DON'T THEY EVER SHOW ANY PROG-RESS?!
YEAH...
IT'S JUST LIKE THE NIGHT OF THE FESTIVAL.
SHE ASKS, "WHY ME?" BUT SHE'S ALWAYS THE INSTIGATOR.
THEY'RE JUST KIDS.
THWUMP
FUJII?
HE'S REALLY HOT...
WEEZ
WEEZ

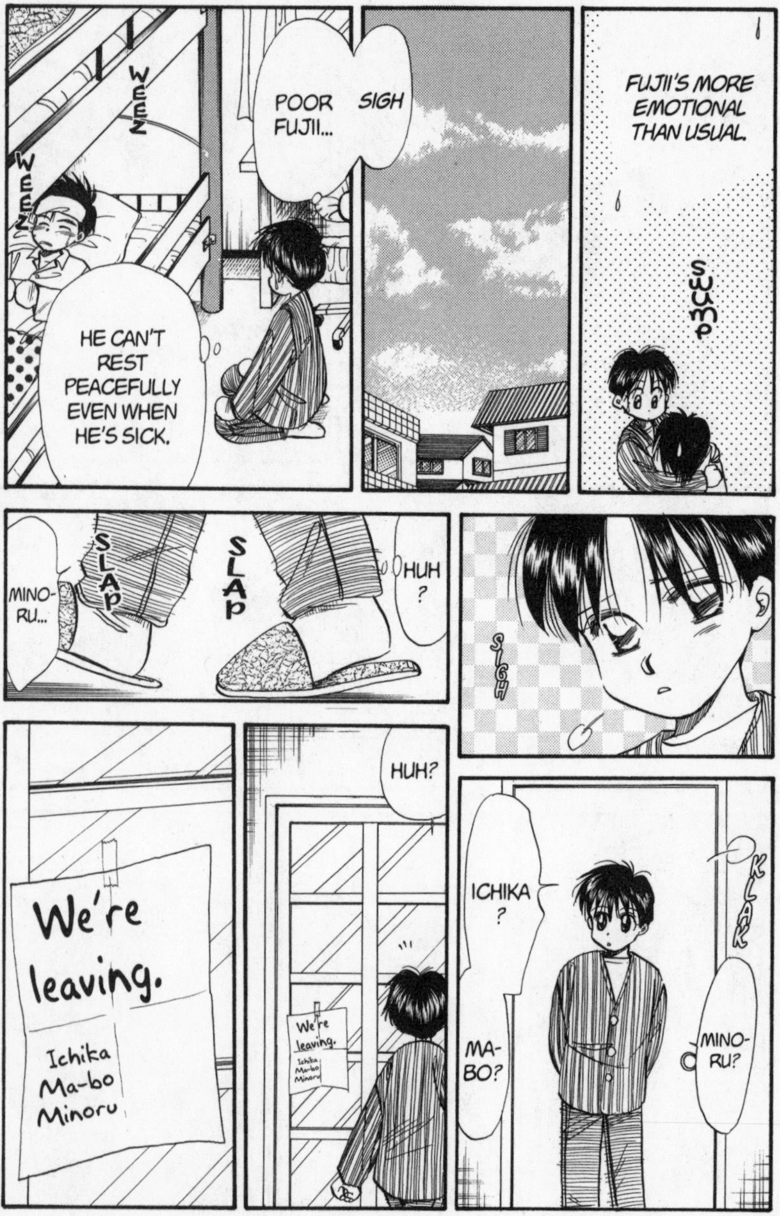
FUJII'S MORE EMOTIONAL THAN USUAL.
SWUMP
SIGH
POOR FUJII...
WEEZ
WEEZ
HE CAN'T REST PEACEFULLY EVEN WHEN HE'S SICK.
SIGH
HUH?
SLAP
SLAP
MINO-RU...
KLAK
ICHIKA?
MINO-RU?
MA-BO?
HUH?
We're leaving.
Ichika
Ma-bo
Minoru
We're leaving.
Ichika
Ma-bo
Minoru

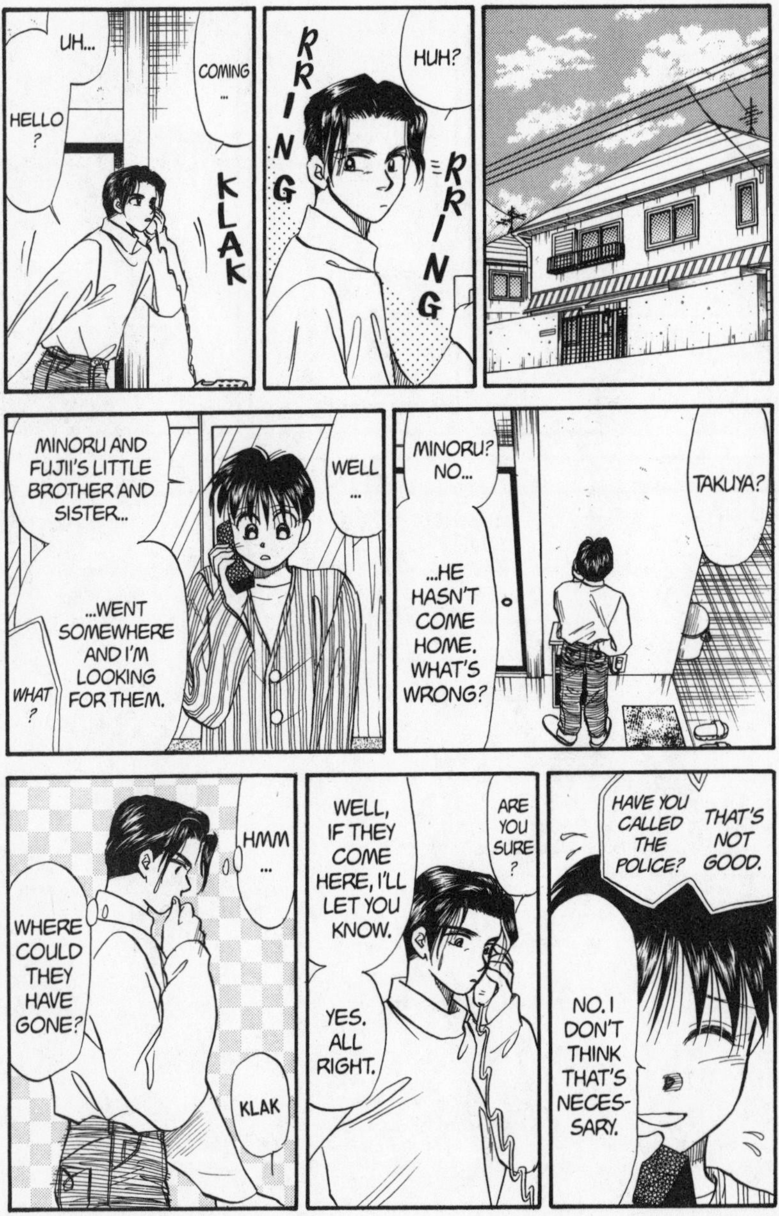
HUH?
RRING
RRING
COMING...
UH...
HELLO?
KLAK
TAKUYA?
MINORU? NO...
...HE HASN'T COME HOME. WHAT'S WRONG?
WELL...
MINORU AND FUJII'S LITTLE BROTHER AND SISTER...
...WENT SOMEWHERE AND I'M LOOKING FOR THEM.
WHAT?
THAT'S NOT GOOD.
HAVE YOU CALLED THE POLICE?
NO. I DON'T THINK THAT'S NECESSARY.
ARE YOU SURE?
WELL, IF THEY COME HERE, I'LL LET YOU KNOW.
YES. ALL RIGHT.
HMM...
WHERE COULD THEY HAVE GONE?
KLAK

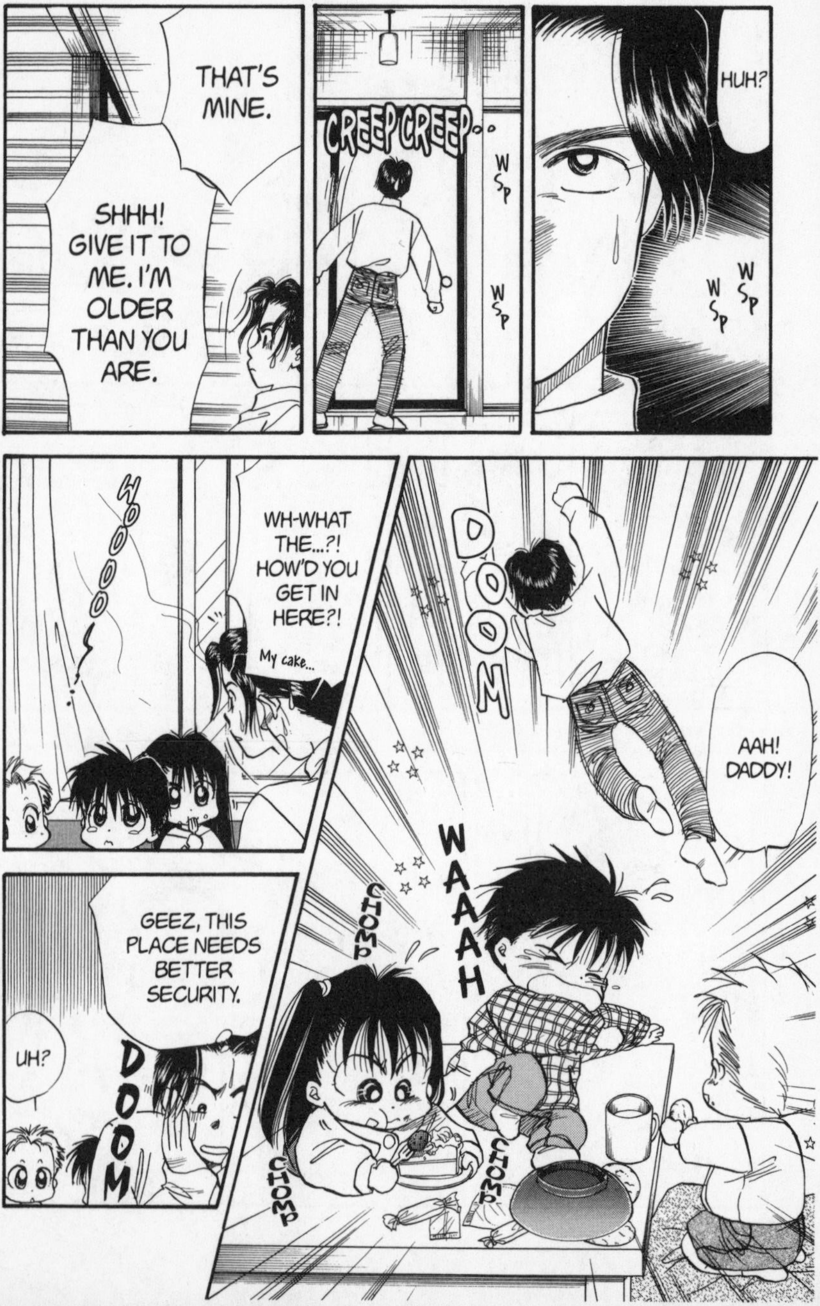
HUH?
WSP WSP
CREEP CREEP..
WSP
WSP
THAT'S MINE.
SHHH! GIVE IT TO ME. I'M OLDER THAN YOU ARE.
AAH! DADDY!
DOOOM
WAAAH
CHOMP
CHOMP
CHOMP
WH-WHAT THE...?! HOW'D YOU GET IN HERE?!
WOOOOO
My cake...
GEEZ, THIS PLACE NEEDS BETTER SECURITY.
UH?
DOOM

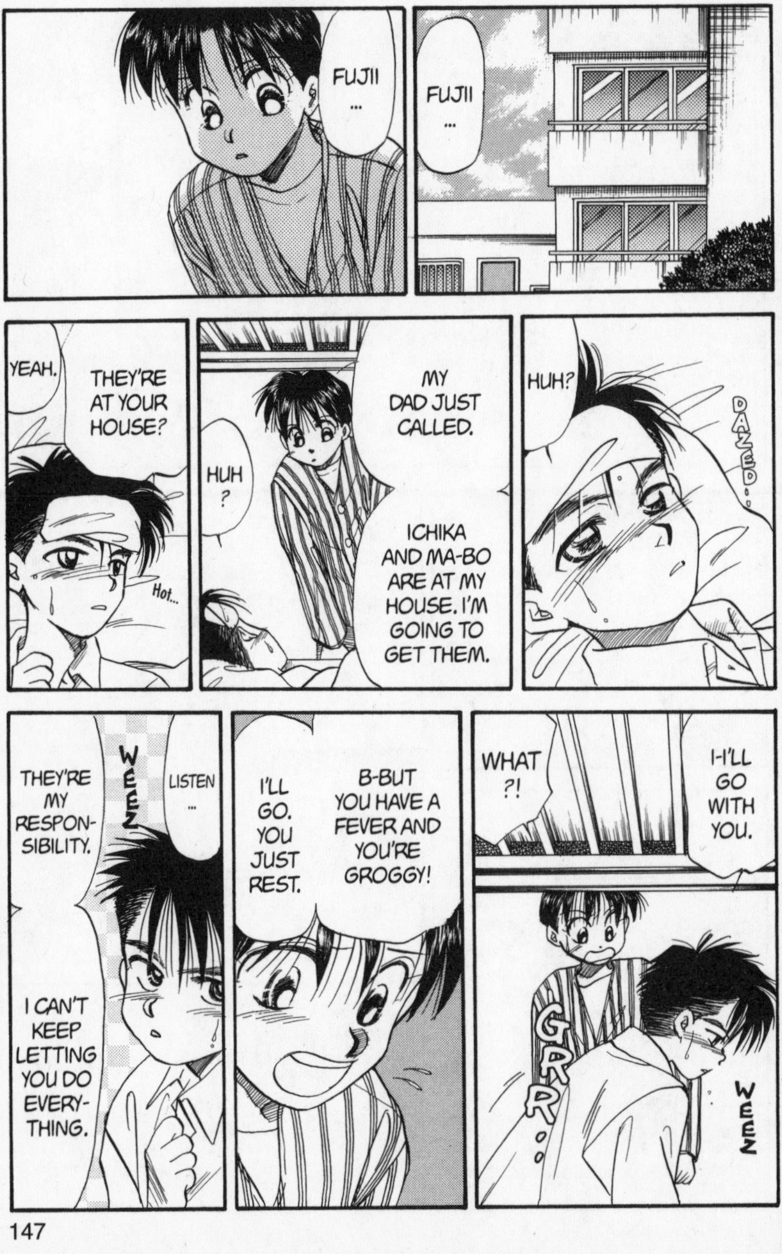
FUJII ...
FUJII ...
HUH?
DAZED...
MY DAD JUST CALLED.
ICHIKA AND MA-BO ARE AT MY HOUSE. I'M GOING TO GET THEM.
HUH?
THEY'RE AT YOUR HOUSE?
YEAH.
Hot...
I-I'LL GO WITH YOU.
WHAT?!
GRR...
WEEZ
B-BUT YOU HAVE A FEVER AND YOU'RE GROGGY!
I'LL GO. YOU JUST REST.
LISTEN ...
WEEZ
THEY'RE MY RESPONSIBILITY.
I CAN'T KEEP LETTING YOU DO EVERYTHING.

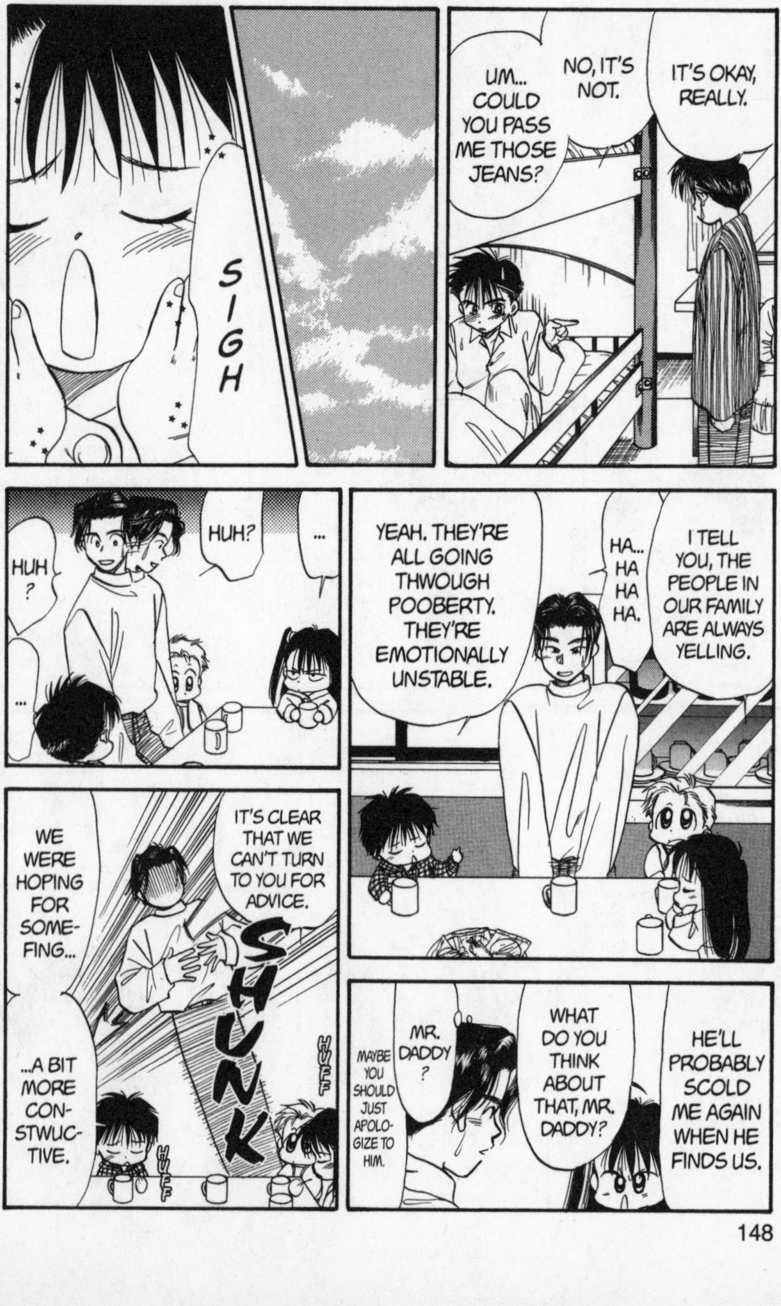
IT'S OKAY, REALLY.
NO, IT'S NOT.
UM... COULD YOU PASS ME THOSE JEANS?
SIGH
I TELL YOU, THE PEOPLE IN OUR FAMILY ARE ALWAYS YELLING.
HA... HA HA HA.
YEAH. THEY'RE ALL GOING THWOUGH POOBERTY. THEY'RE EMOTIONALLY UNSTABLE.
...
HUH?
HUH ?
...
IT'S CLEAR THAT WE CAN'T TURN TO YOU FOR ADVICE.
SHUNK
HUFF
WE WERE HOPING FOR SOMEFING...
HUFF
...A BIT MORE CONSTWUCTIVE.
HE'LL PROBABLY SCOLD ME AGAIN WHEN HE FINDS US.
WHAT DO YOU THINK ABOUT THAT, MR. DADDY?
MR. DADDY ?
MAYBE YOU SHOULD JUST APOLOGIZE TO HIM.

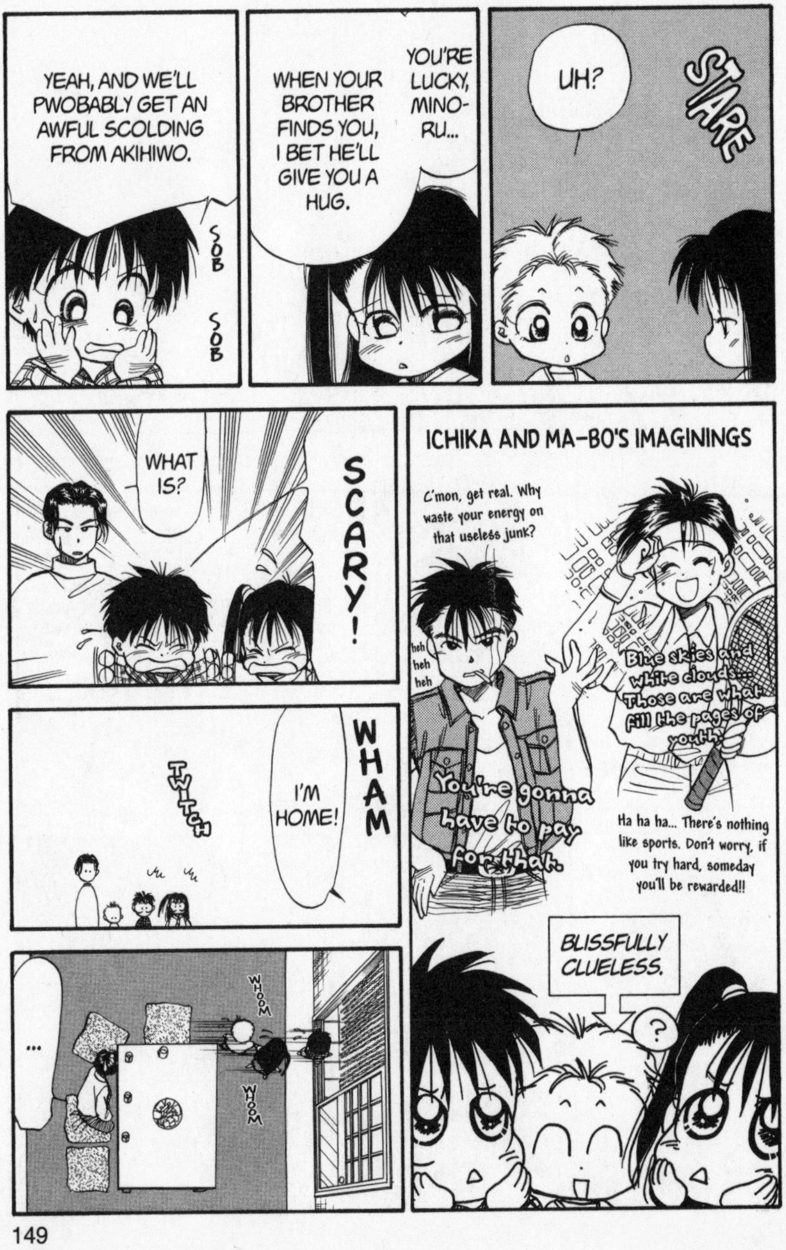
STARE
UH?
YOU'RE LUCKY, MINO-RU...
WHEN YOUR BROTHER FINDS YOU, I BET HE'LL GIVE YOU A HUG.
YEAH, AND WE'LL PWOBABLY GET AN AWFUL SCOLDING FROM AKIHIWO.
SOB SOB
ICHIKA AND MA-BO'S IMAGININGS
Blue skies and white clouds... Those are what fill the pages of youth.
Ha ha ha... There's nothing like sports. Don't worry, if you try hard, someday you'll be rewarded!!
C'mon, get real. Why waste your energy on that useless junk?
heh heh heh
You're gonna have to pay for that.
BLISSFULLY CLUELESS.
?
SCARY!
WHAT IS?
WHAM
I'M HOME!
TWITCH
WHOOM
WHOOM
...

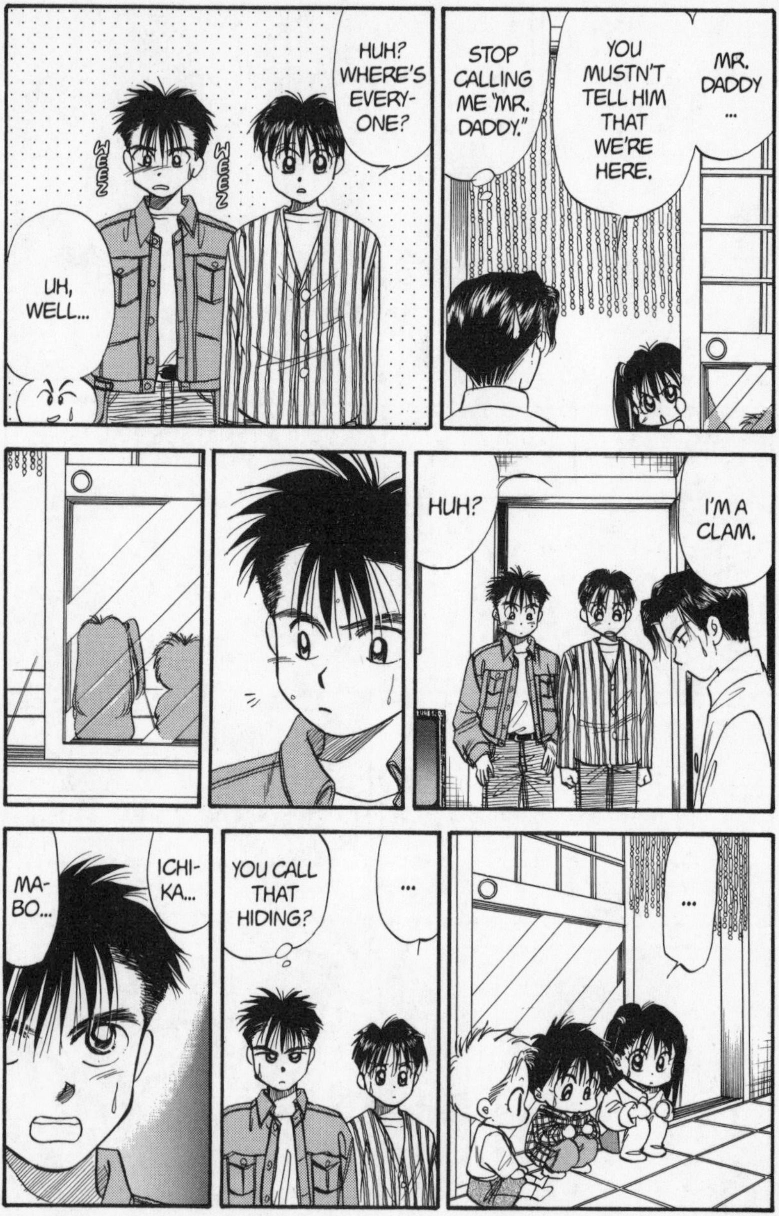
MR. DADDY ...
YOU MUSTN'T TELL HIM THAT WE'RE HERE.
STOP CALLING ME "MR. DADDY."
HUH? WHERE'S EVERY-ONE?
WEEZ
WEEZ
UH, WELL...
I'M A CLAM.
HUH?
...
...
YOU CALL THAT HIDING?
ICHI-KA...
MA-BO...

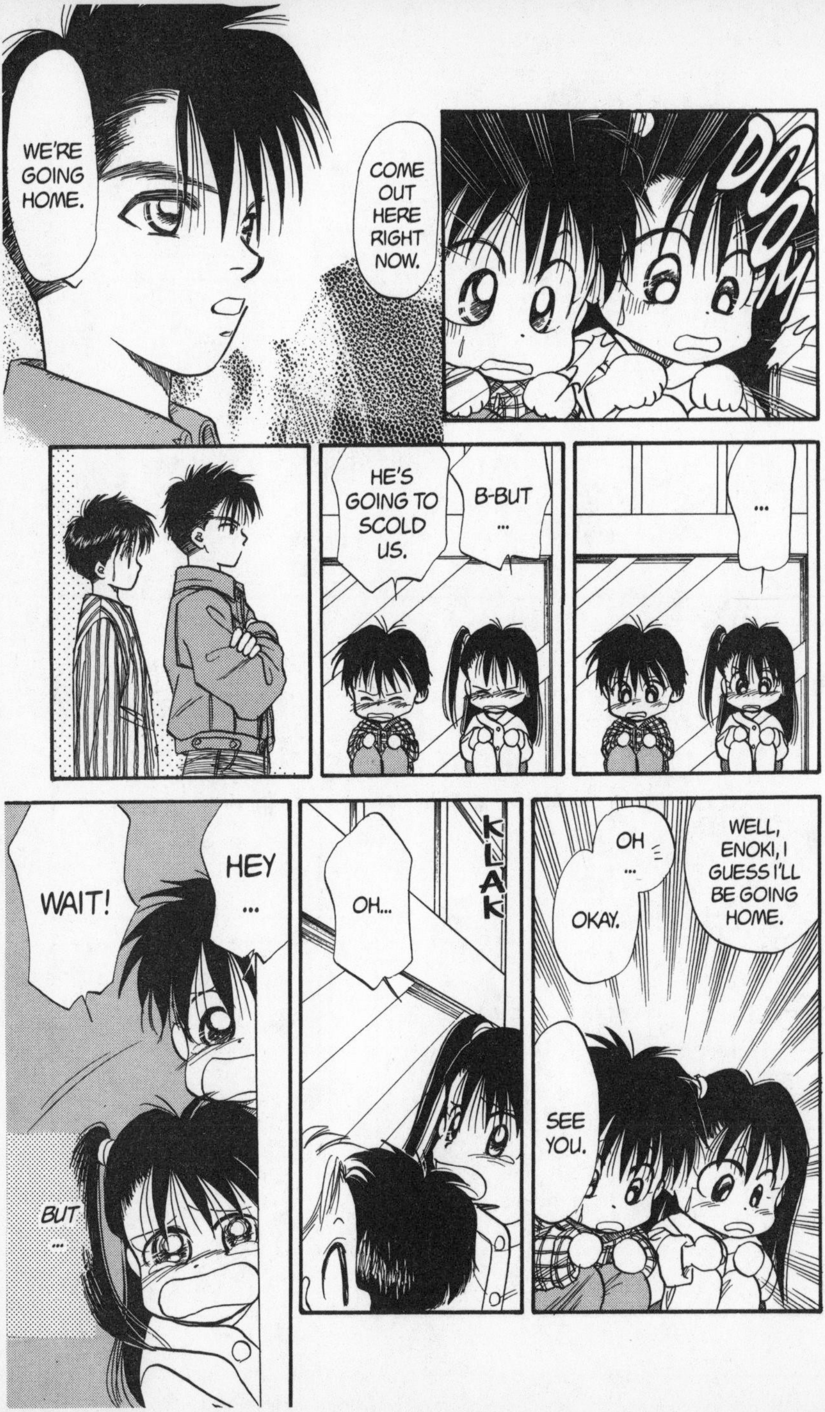
DOOM
COME OUT HERE RIGHT NOW.
WE'RE GOING HOME.
...
B-BUT ...
HE'S GOING TO SCOLD US.
WELL, ENOKI, I GUESS I'LL BE GOING HOME.
OH ... OKAY.
SEE YOU.
KLAK
OH...
HEY ...
WAIT!
BUT ...

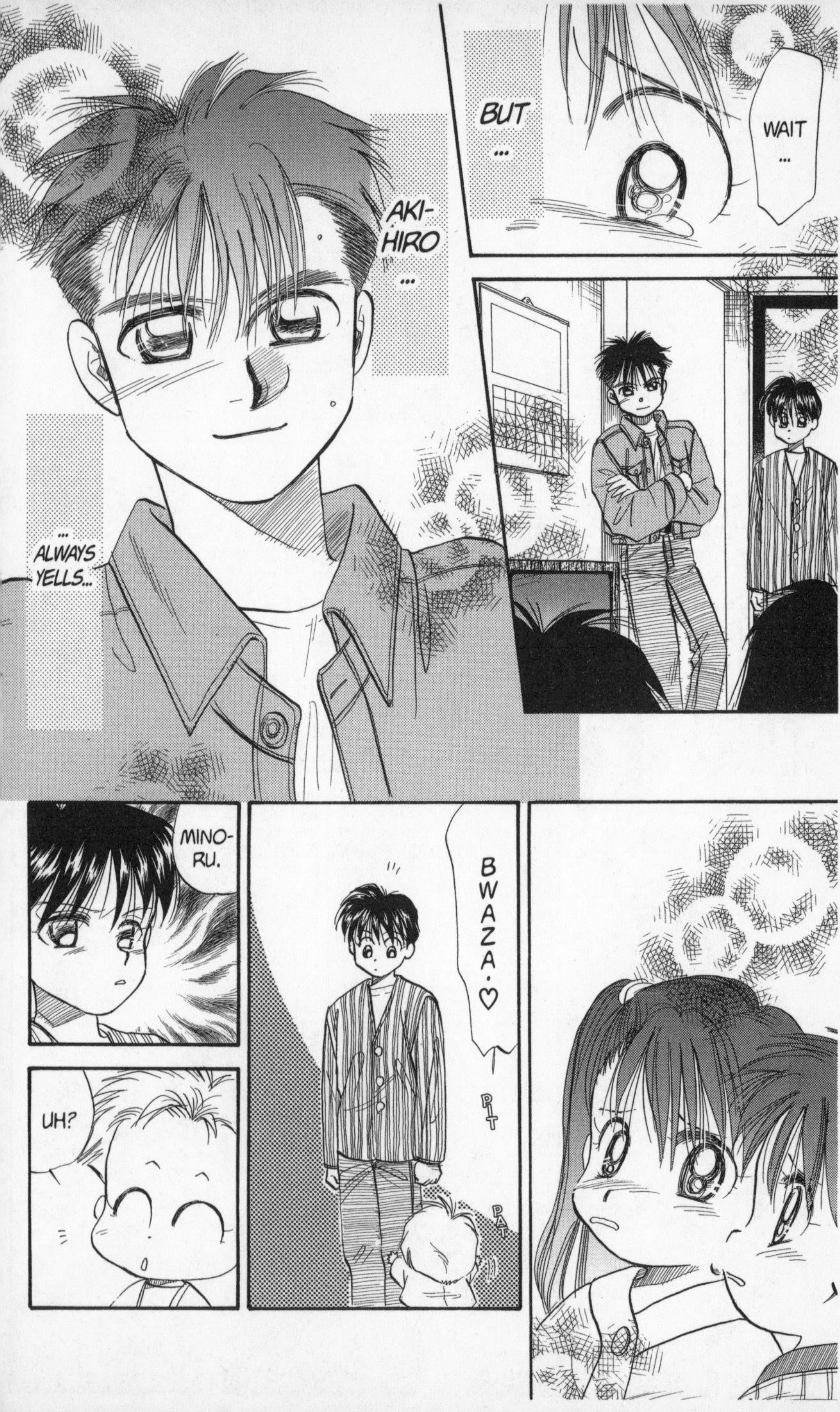
WAIT ...
BUT ...
AKI-HIRO ...
... ALWAYS YELLS...
BWAZA.♡
PIT
PAT
MINO-RU.
UH?

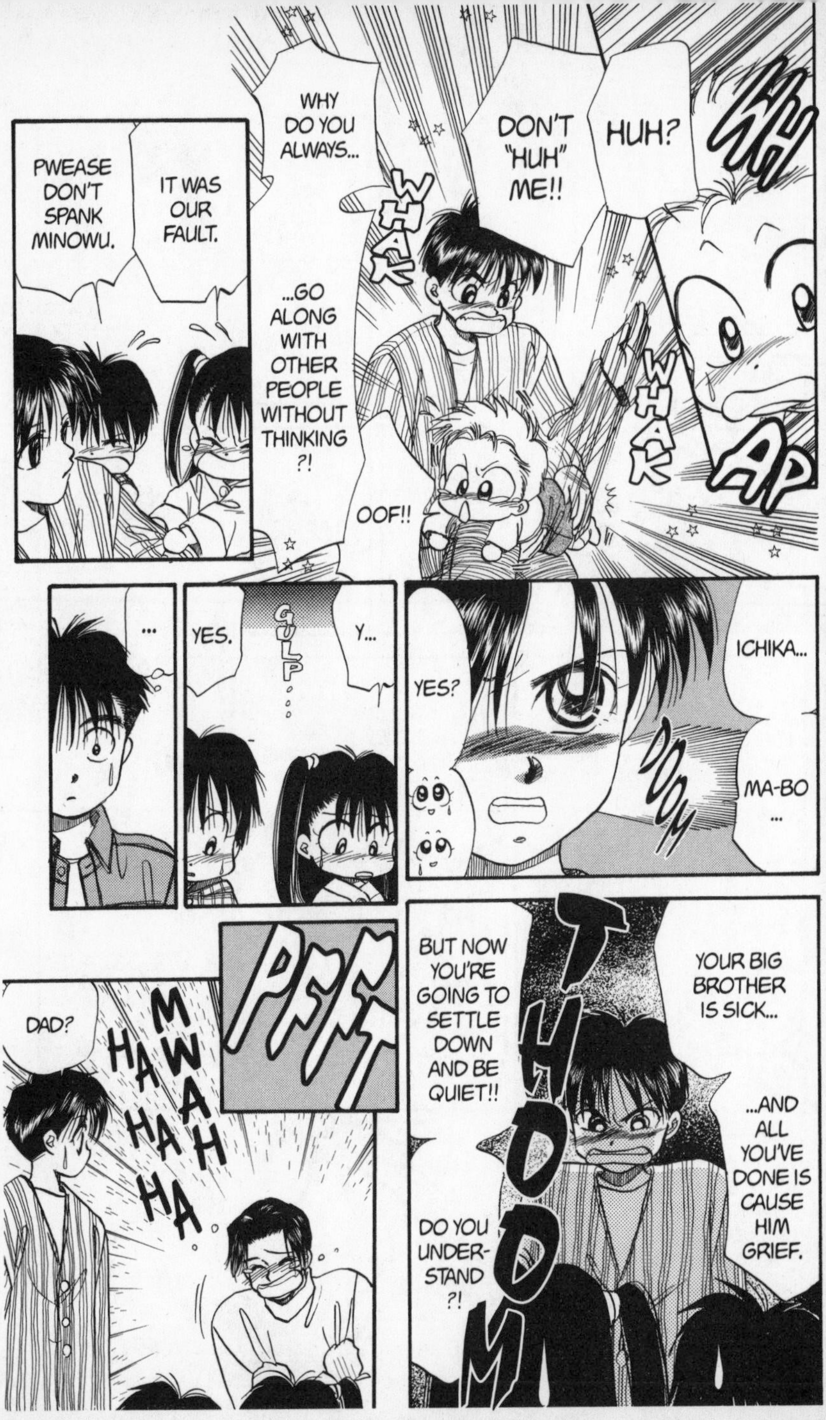
WHAP
HUH?
DON'T "HUH" ME!!
WHY DO YOU ALWAYS...
WHAK
...GO ALONG WITH OTHER PEOPLE WITHOUT THINKING ?!
WHAK
OOF!!
IT WAS OUR FAULT.
PWEASE DON'T SPANK MINOWU.
ICHIKA...
MA-BO ...
DOOM
YES?
Y...
GULP
YES.
...
YOUR BIG BROTHER IS SICK...
...AND ALL YOU'VE DONE IS CAUSE HIM GRIEF.
THUDDOM
BUT NOW YOU'RE GOING TO SETTLE DOWN AND BE QUIET!!
DO YOU UNDER-STAND ?!
PFFT
MWAH HAHAHAHA
DAD?

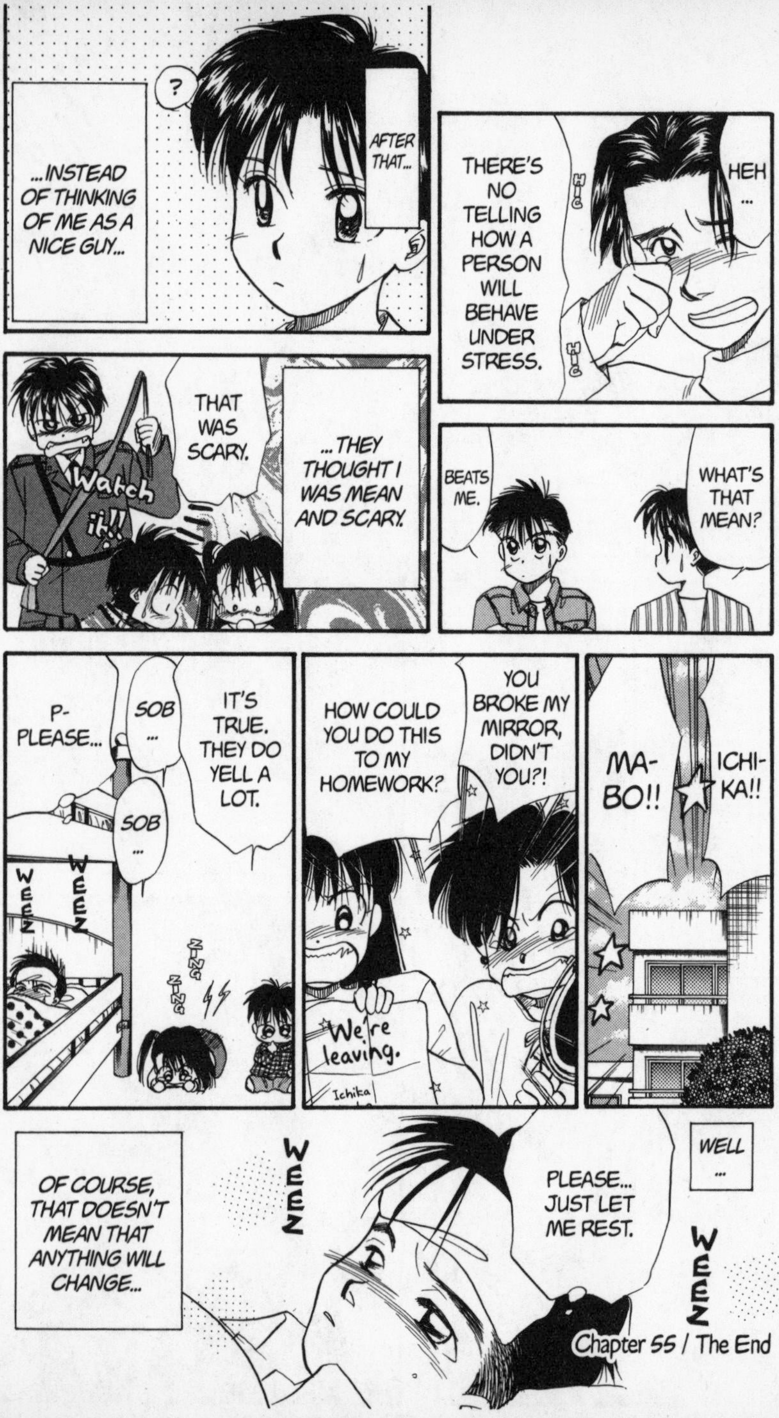
HEH ...
THERE'S NO TELLING HOW A PERSON WILL BEHAVE UNDER STRESS.
HIC
HIC
AFTER THAT...
?
...INSTEAD OF THINKING OF ME AS A NICE GUY...
WHAT'S THAT MEAN?
BEATS ME.
...THEY THOUGHT I WAS MEAN AND SCARY.
THAT WAS SCARY.
Watch it!!
MA-BO!!
ICHI-KA!!
YOU BROKE MY MIRROR, DIDN'T YOU?!
HOW COULD YOU DO THIS TO MY HOMEWORK?
We're leaving.
Ichika
IT'S TRUE. THEY DO YELL A LOT.
SOB ...
SOB ...
P-PLEASE...
WEEZ
WEEZ
ZING
ZING
WELL ...
PLEASE... JUST LET ME REST.
WEEZ
WEEZ
OF COURSE, THAT DOESN'T MEAN THAT ANYTHING WILL CHANGE...
Chapter 55 / The End

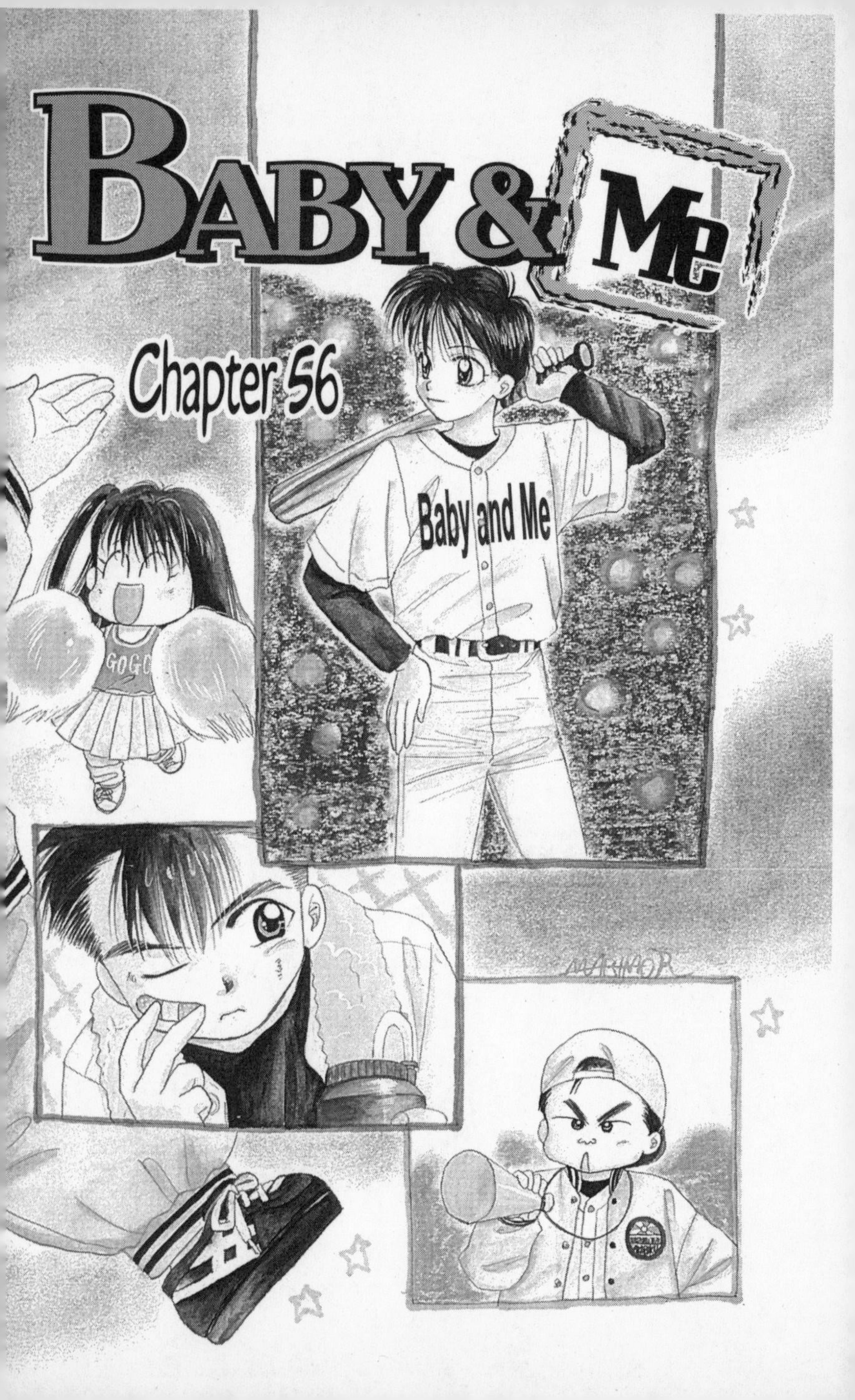
BABY & Me
Chapter 56
Baby and Me

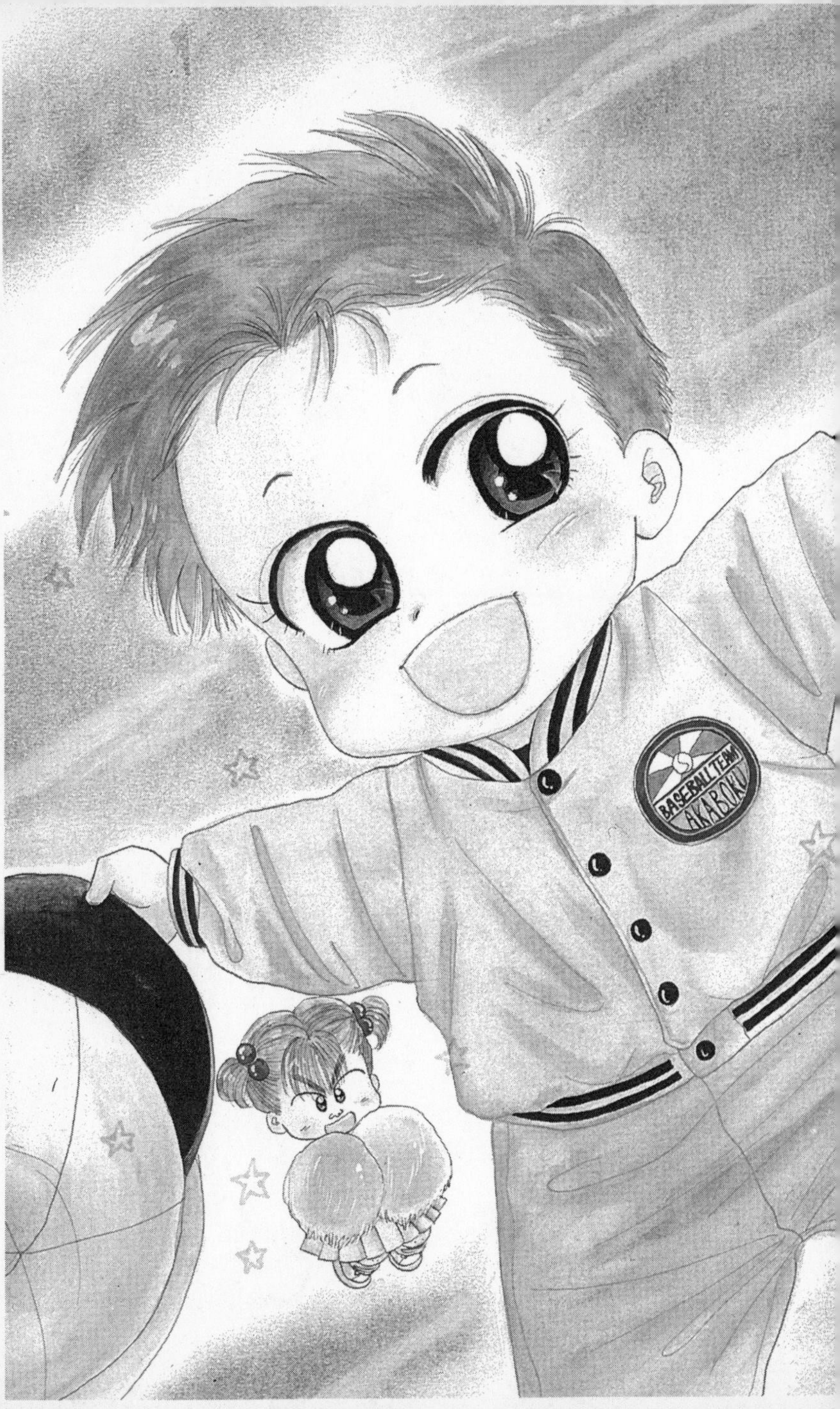
BASEBALL TEAM
AKABOKU

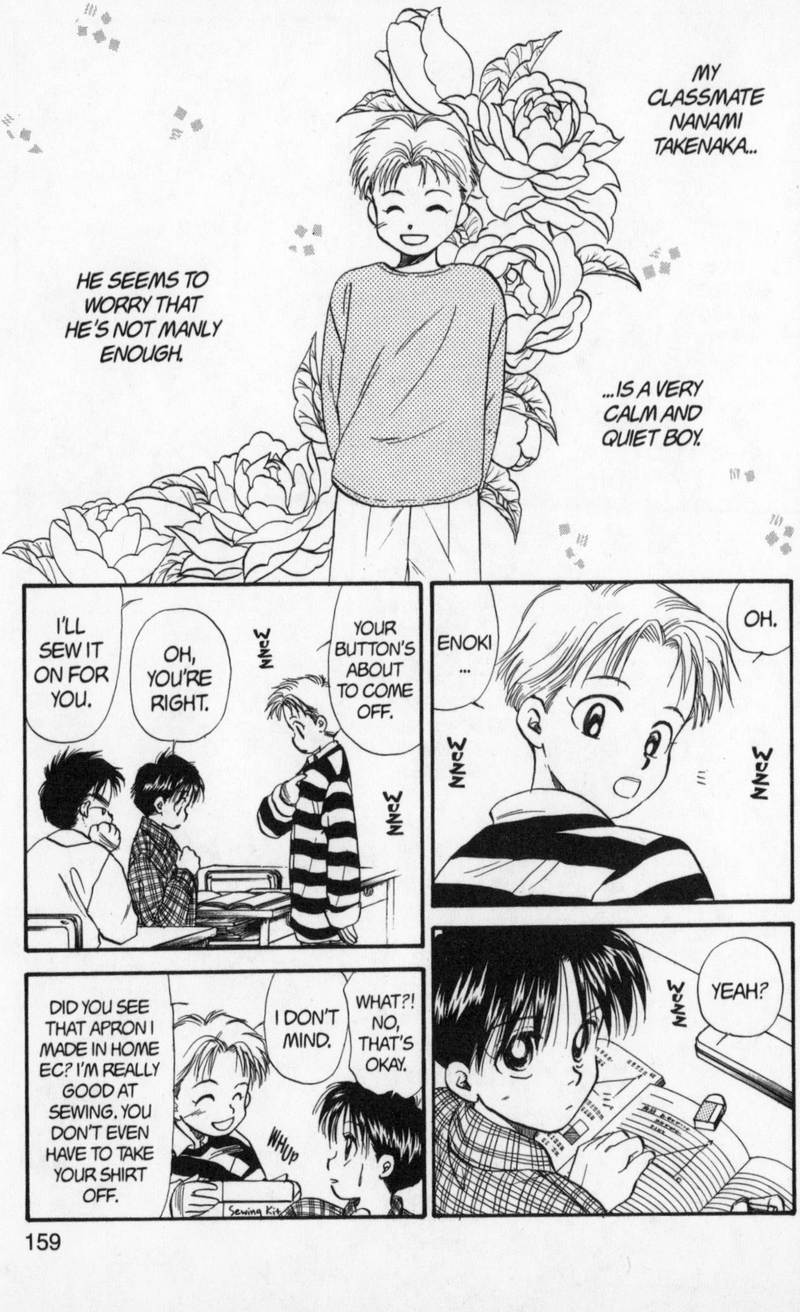
MY CLASSMATE NANAMI TAKENAKA...
...IS A VERY CALM AND QUIET BOY.
HE SEEMS TO WORRY THAT HE'S NOT MANLY ENOUGH.
OH.
WUZZ
ENOKI ...
WUZZ
YOUR BUTTON'S ABOUT TO COME OFF.
WUZZ
OH, YOU'RE RIGHT.
I'LL SEW IT ON FOR YOU.
WUZZ
WUZZ
YEAH?
WHAT?! NO, THAT'S OKAY.
I DON'T MIND.
DID YOU SEE THAT APRON I MADE IN HOME EC? I'M REALLY GOOD AT SEWING. YOU DON'T EVEN HAVE TO TAKE YOUR SHIRT OFF.
WHUP
Sewing Kit

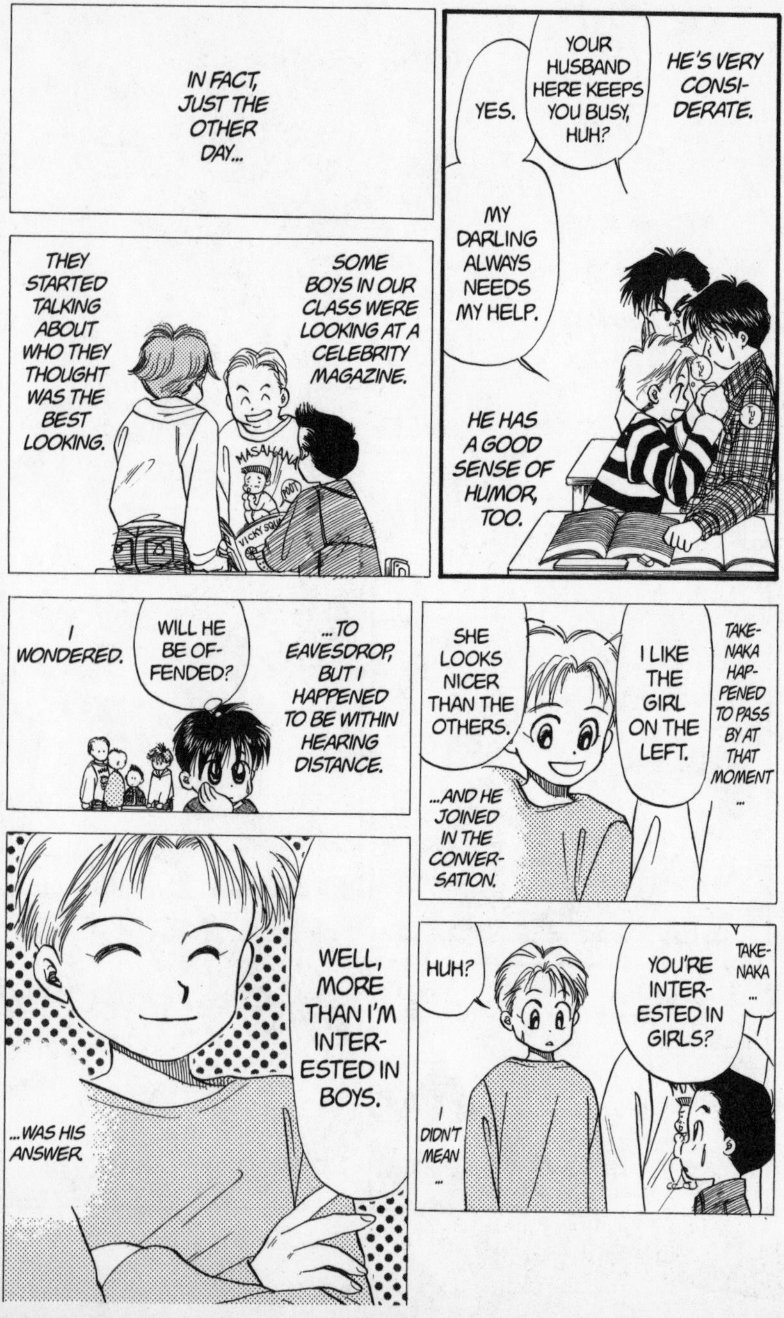
HE'S VERY CONSIDERATE.
YOUR HUSBAND HERE KEEPS YOU BUSY, HUH?
YES.
MY DARLING ALWAYS NEEDS MY HELP.
HE HAS A GOOD SENSE OF HUMOR, TOO.
IN FACT, JUST THE OTHER DAY...
SOME BOYS IN OUR CLASS WERE LOOKING AT A CELEBRITY MAGAZINE.
THEY STARTED TALKING ABOUT WHO THEY THOUGHT WAS THE BEST LOOKING.
MASAHANA
TAKENAKA HAPPENED TO PASS BY AT THAT MOMENT...
I LIKE THE GIRL ON THE LEFT.
SHE LOOKS NICER THAN THE OTHERS.
...AND HE JOINED IN THE CONVERSATION.
...TO EAVESDROP, BUT I HAPPENED TO BE WITHIN HEARING DISTANCE.
WILL HE BE OFFENDED?
I WONDERED.
TAKENAKA...
YOU'RE INTERESTED IN GIRLS?
HUH?
I DIDN'T MEAN...
WELL, MORE THAN I'M INTERESTED IN BOYS.
...WAS HIS ANSWER

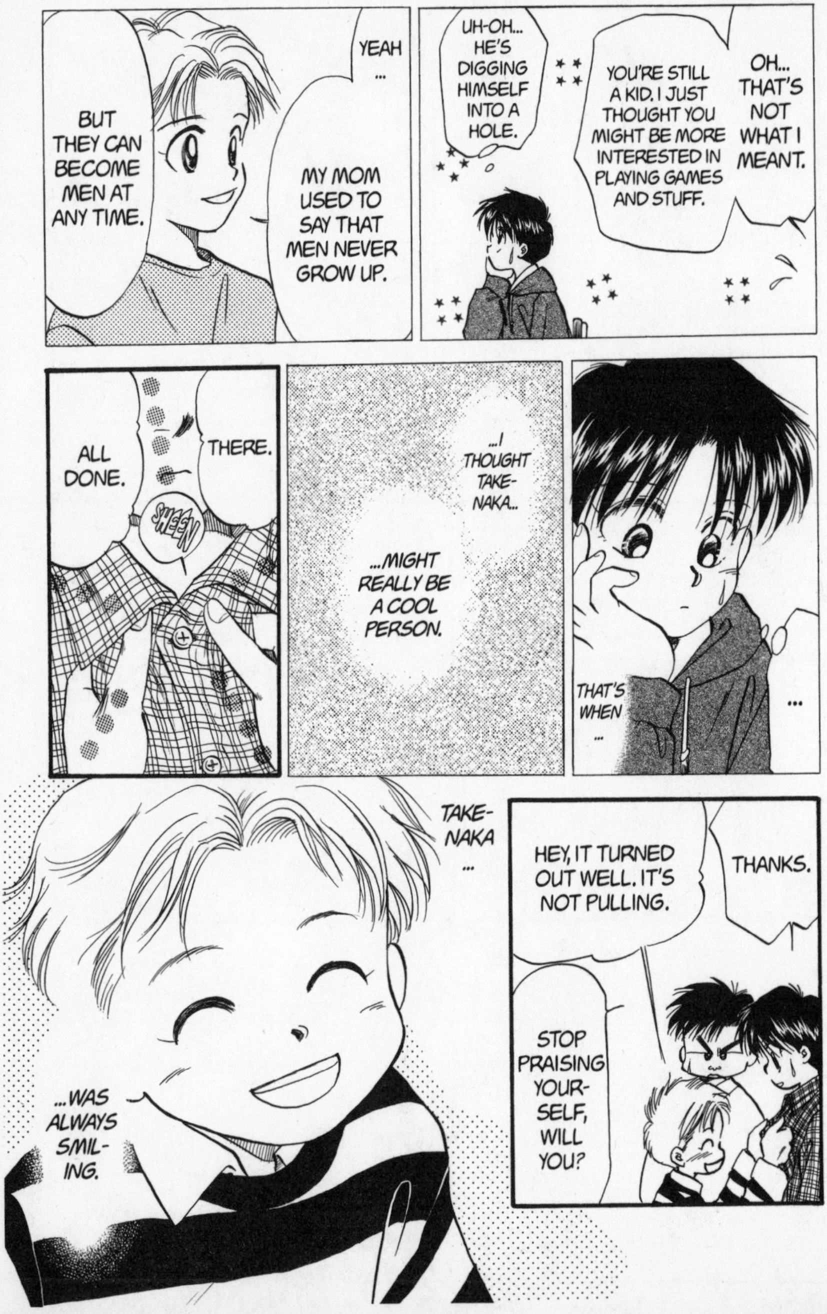
OH... THAT'S NOT WHAT I MEANT.
YOU'RE STILL A KID. I JUST THOUGHT YOU MIGHT BE MORE INTERESTED IN PLAYING GAMES AND STUFF.
UH-OH... HE'S DIGGING HIMSELF INTO A HOLE.
YEAH ...
MY MOM USED TO SAY THAT MEN NEVER GROW UP.
BUT THEY CAN BECOME MEN AT ANY TIME.
...
THAT'S WHEN ...
...I THOUGHT TAKE-NAKA...
...MIGHT REALLY BE A COOL PERSON.
THERE.
ALL DONE.
SHEEN
THANKS.
HEY, IT TURNED OUT WELL. IT'S NOT PULLING.
STOP PRAISING YOUR-SELF, WILL YOU?
TAKE-NAKA ...
...WAS ALWAYS SMIL-ING.

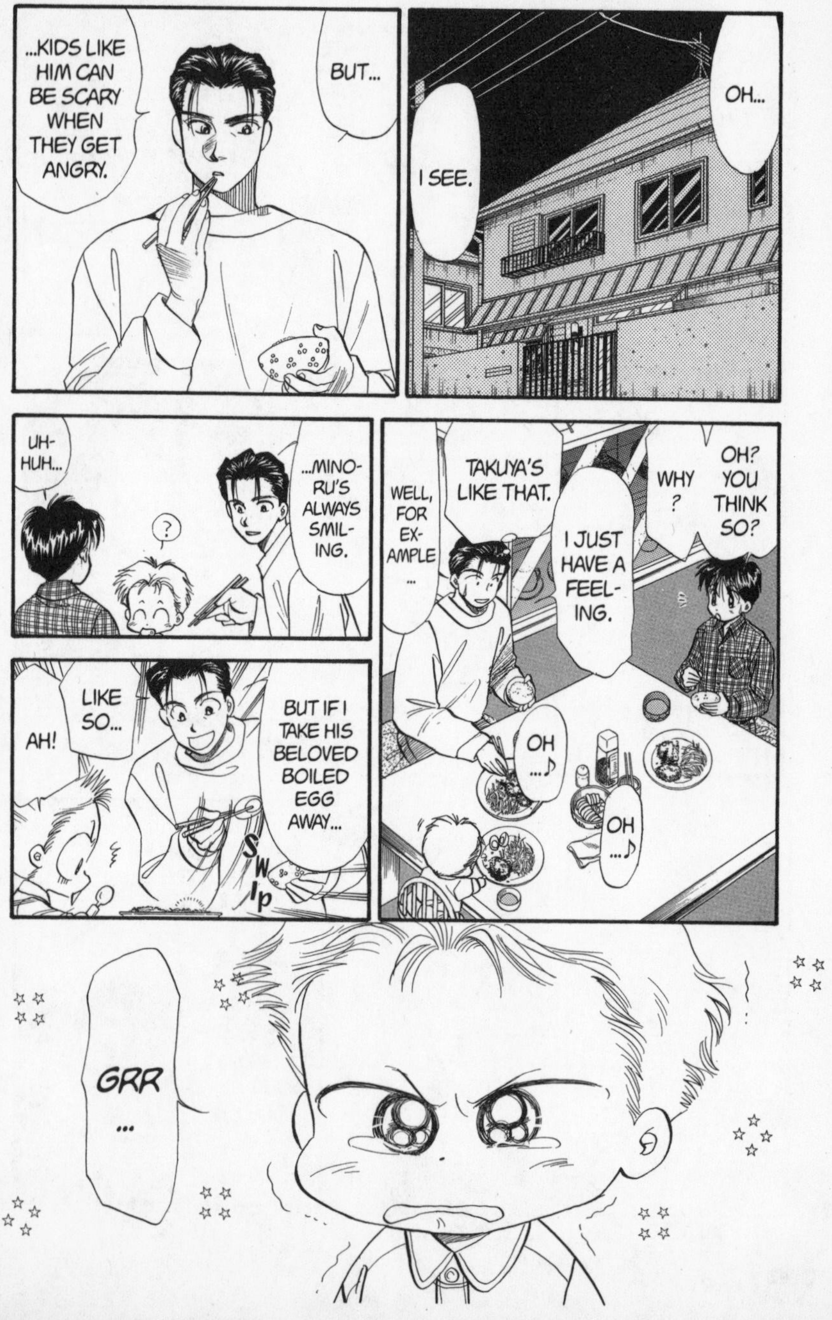
OH...
I SEE.
BUT...
...KIDS LIKE HIM CAN BE SCARY WHEN THEY GET ANGRY.
OH? YOU THINK SO?
WHY?
TAKUYA'S LIKE THAT.
I JUST HAVE A FEEL-ING.
WELL, FOR EX-AMPLE...
OH ...♪
OH ...♪
...MINO-RU'S ALWAYS SMIL-ING.
UH-HUH...
BUT IF I TAKE HIS BELOVED BOILED EGG AWAY...
SWIP
LIKE SO...
AH!
GRR ...

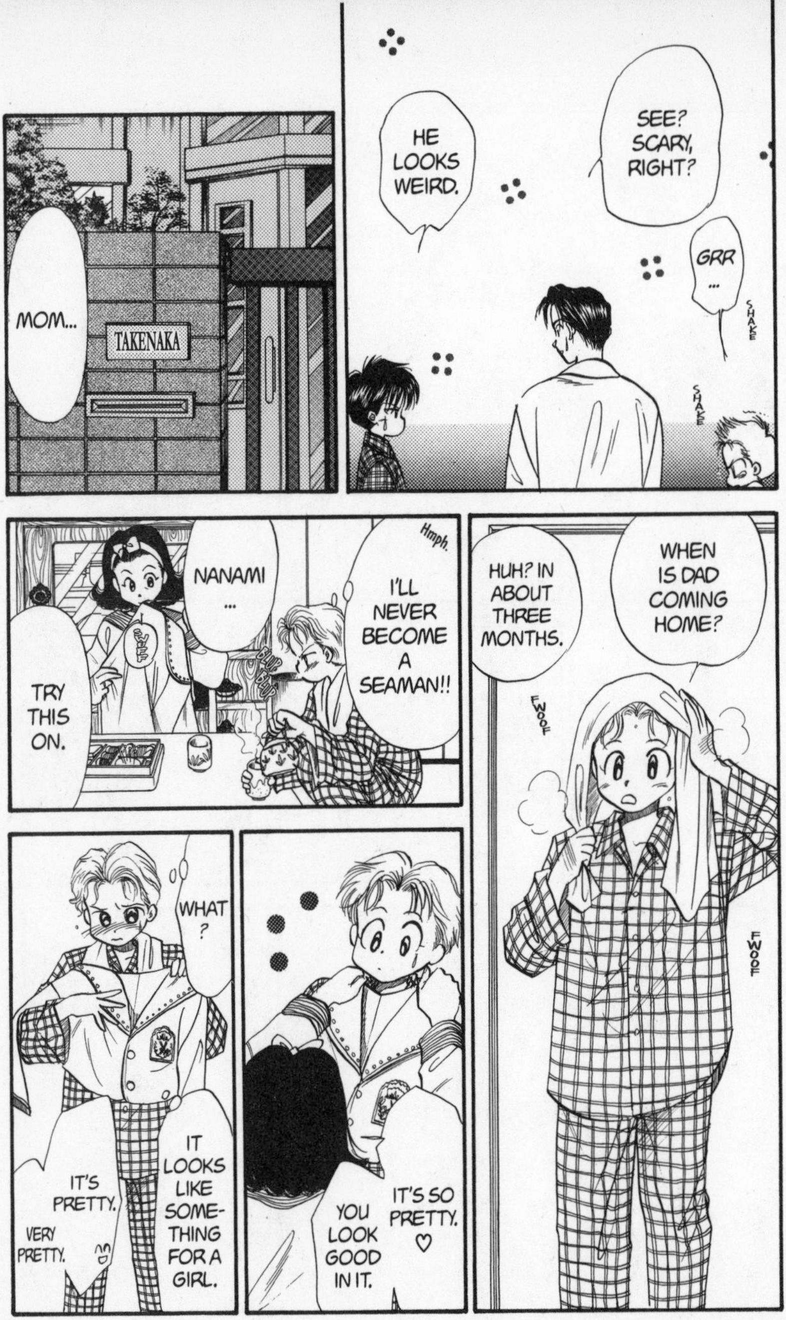
SEE? SCARY, RIGHT?
GRR ...
SHAKE
SHAKE
HE LOOKS WEIRD.
MOM...
TAKENAKA
WHEN IS DAD COMING HOME?
HUH? IN ABOUT THREE MONTHS.
FWOOF
FWOOF
Hmph.
I'LL NEVER BECOME A SEAMAN!!
NANAMI ...
SHUFF
BLUP BLUP
TRY THIS ON.
IT'S SO PRETTY. ♡
YOU LOOK GOOD IN IT.
WHAT?
IT LOOKS LIKE SOME-THING FOR A GIRL.
IT'S PRETTY.
VERY PRETTY.

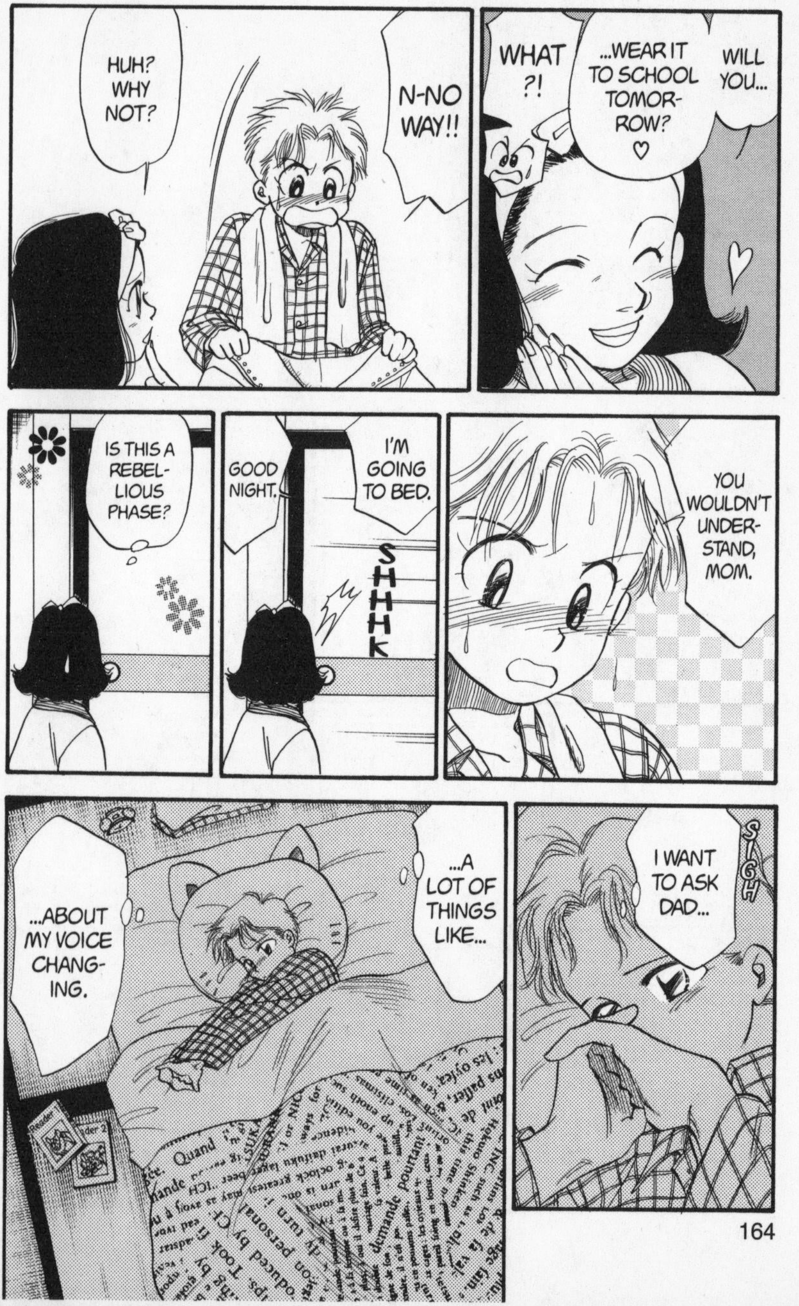
WILL YOU...
...WEAR IT TO SCHOOL TOMORROW? ♡
WHAT ?!
N-NO WAY!!
HUH? WHY NOT?
YOU WOULDN'T UNDERSTAND, MOM.
I'M GOING TO BED.
GOOD NIGHT.
SHHHK
IS THIS A REBELLIOUS PHASE?
SIGH
I WANT TO ASK DAD...
...A LOT OF THINGS LIKE...
...ABOUT MY VOICE CHANGING.

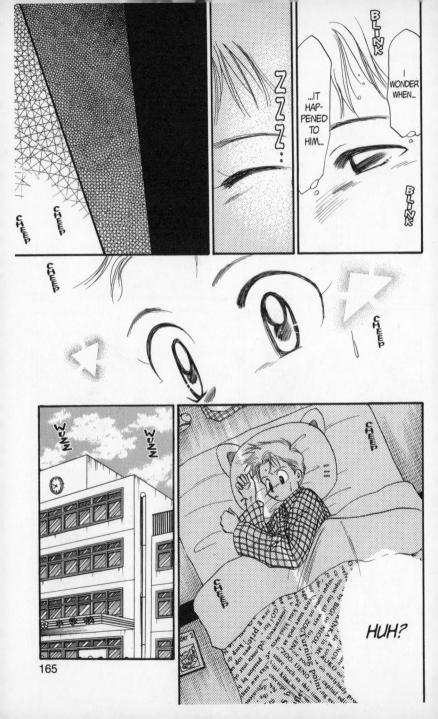

CHEEP CHEEP

CHEEP

ZZZ...

...IT HAPPENED TO HIM...

BLINK

I WONDER WHEN...

BLINK

CHEEP

WUZZ WUZZ

CHEEP

CHEEP

HUH?

165

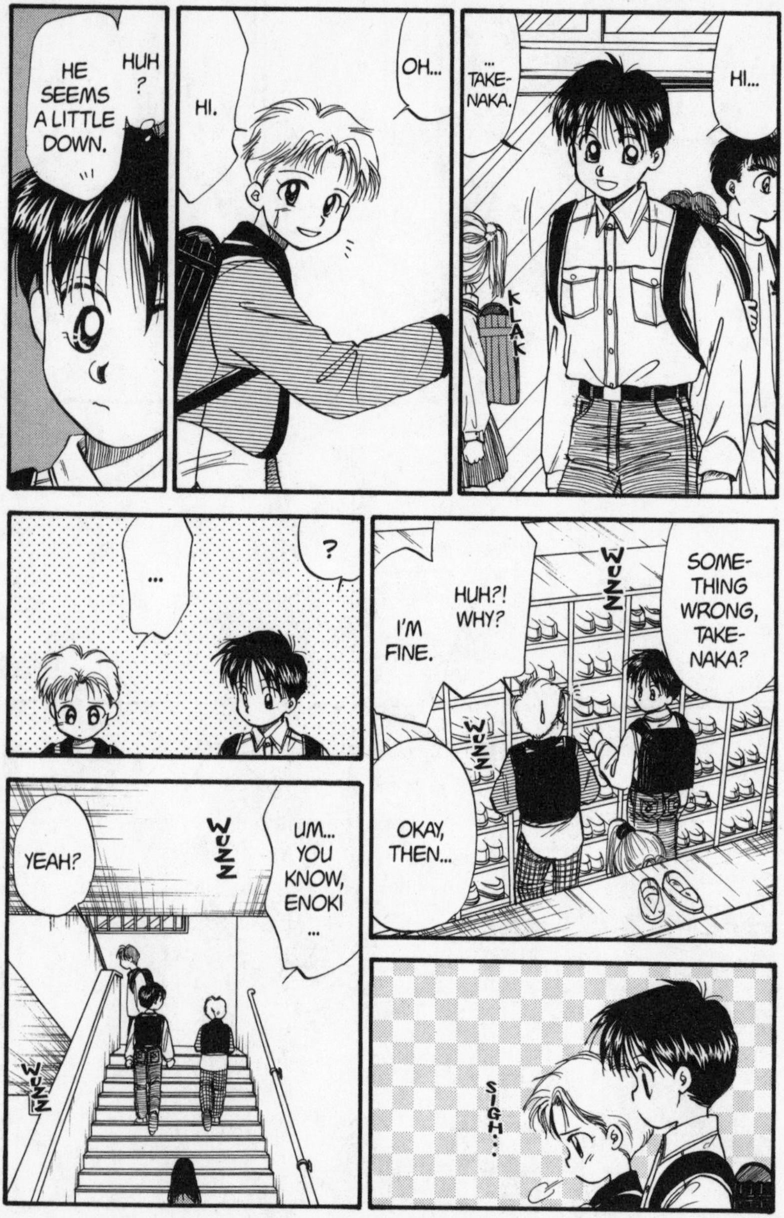
HI...
... TAKE-NAKA.
KLAK
OH...
HI.
HUH ?
HE SEEMS A LITTLE DOWN.
SOME-THING WRONG, TAKE-NAKA?
WUZZ
HUH?! WHY?
I'M FINE.
WUZZ
OKAY, THEN...
?
...
UM... YOU KNOW, ENOKI ...
WUZZ
YEAH?
WUZZ
SIGH...

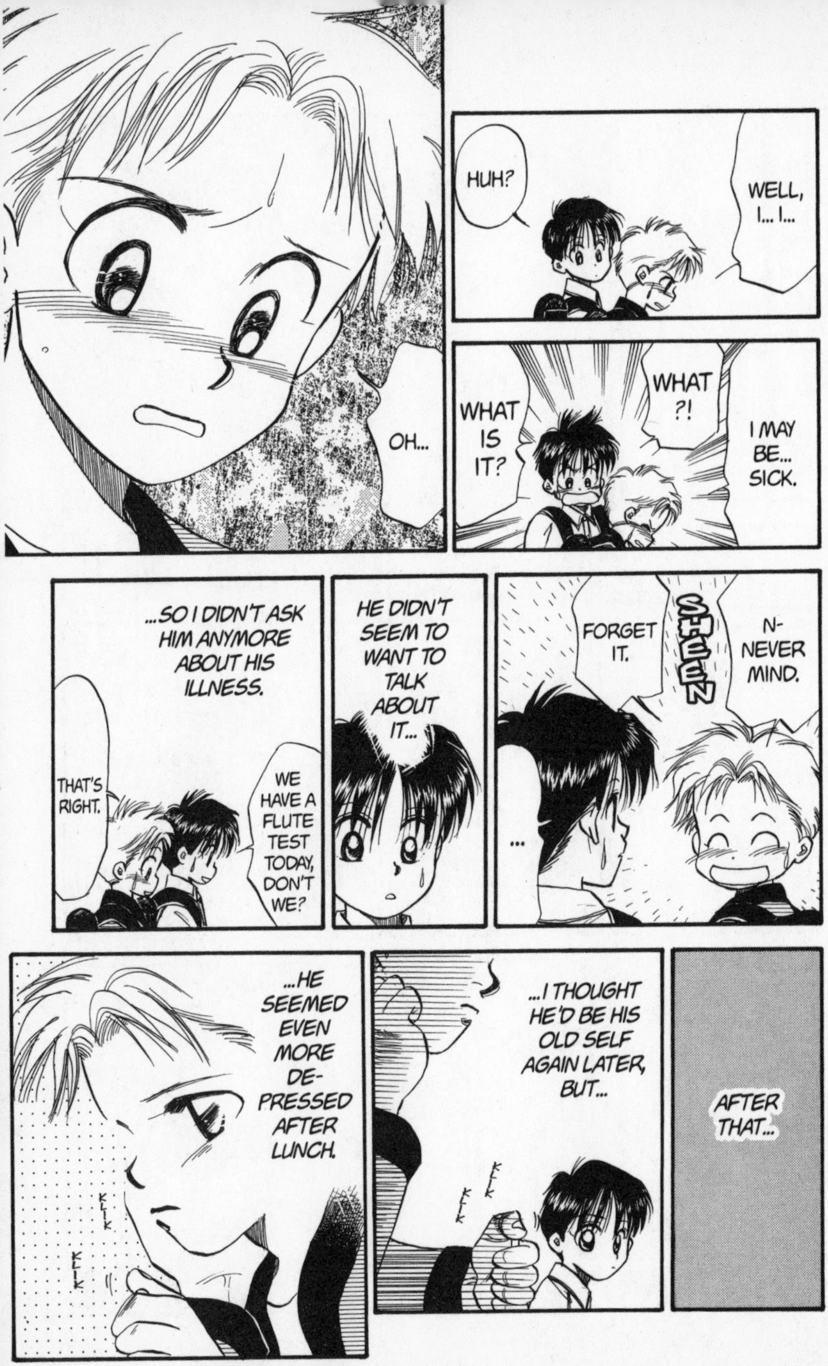
WELL, I... I...
HUH?
I MAY BE... SICK.
WHAT ?!
WHAT IS IT?
OH...
N-NEVER MIND.
SHEEN
FORGET IT.
...
HE DIDN'T SEEM TO WANT TO TALK ABOUT IT...
...SO I DIDN'T ASK HIM ANYMORE ABOUT HIS ILLNESS.
WE HAVE A FLUTE TEST TODAY, DON'T WE?
THAT'S RIGHT.
AFTER THAT...
...I THOUGHT HE'D BE HIS OLD SELF AGAIN LATER, BUT...
KLIK
KLIK
...HE SEEMED EVEN MORE DE-PRESSED AFTER LUNCH.
KLIK
KLIK

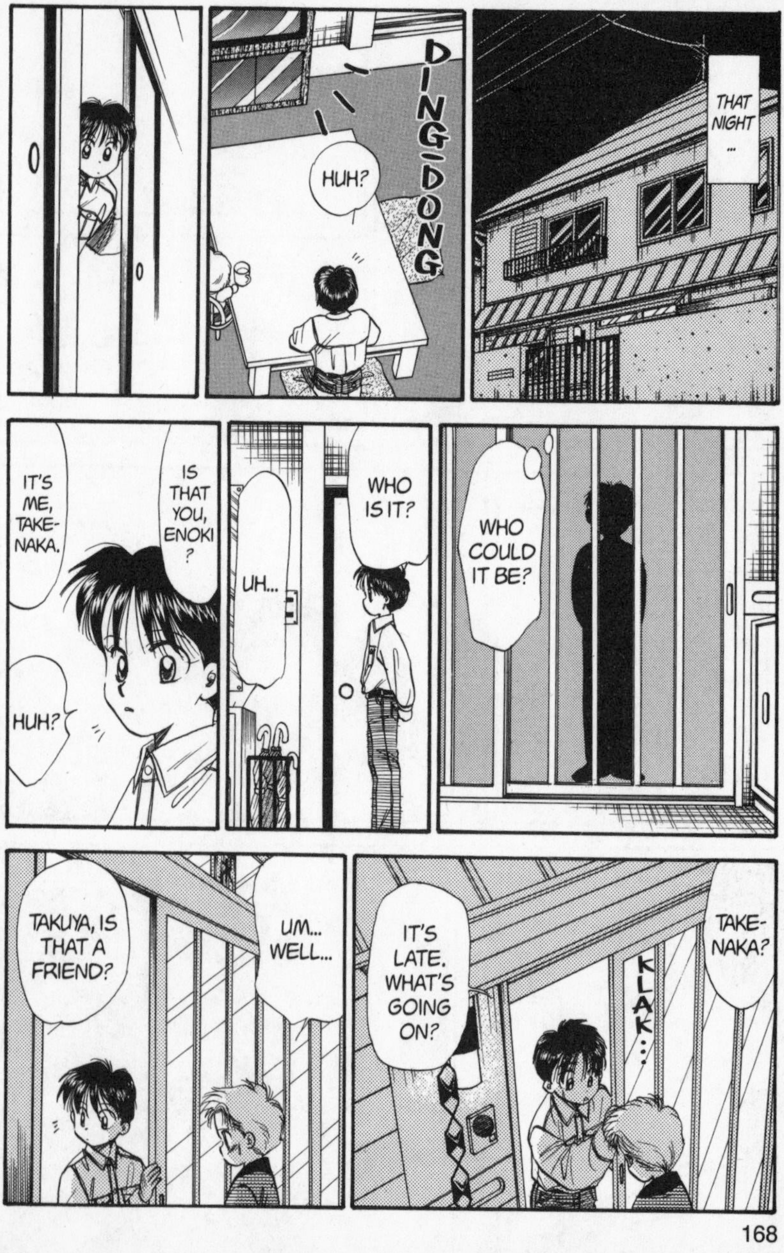
THAT NIGHT ...
DING-DONG
HUH?
WHO COULD IT BE?
WHO IS IT?
UH...
IS THAT YOU, ENOKI?
IT'S ME, TAKE-NAKA.
HUH?
TAKE-NAKA?
KLAK...
IT'S LATE. WHAT'S GOING ON?
UM... WELL...
TAKUYA, IS THAT A FRIEND?

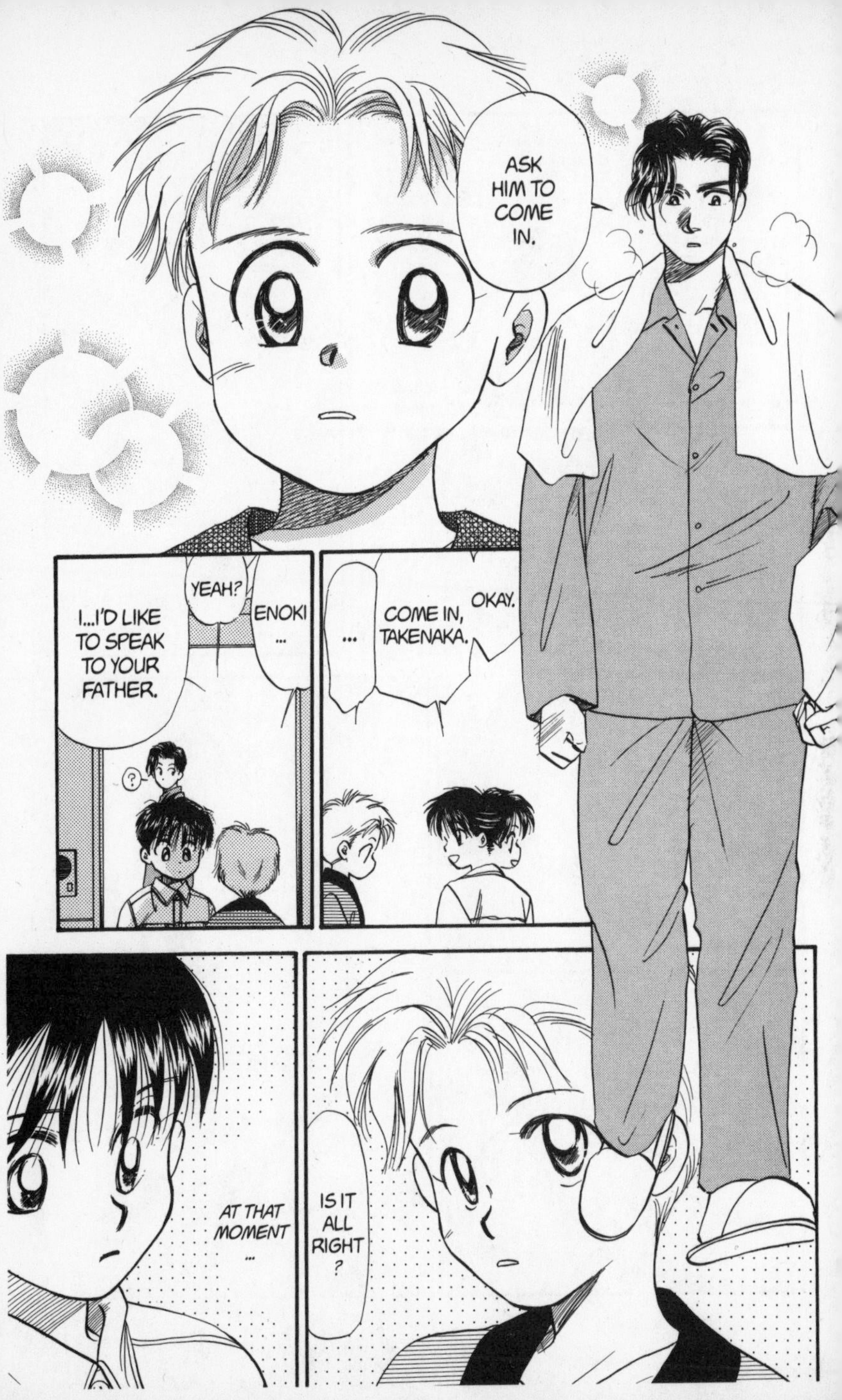
ASK HIM TO COME IN.
OKAY.
COME IN, TAKENAKA.
...
ENOKI ...
YEAH?
I...I'D LIKE TO SPEAK TO YOUR FATHER.
IS IT ALL RIGHT?
AT THAT MOMENT ...

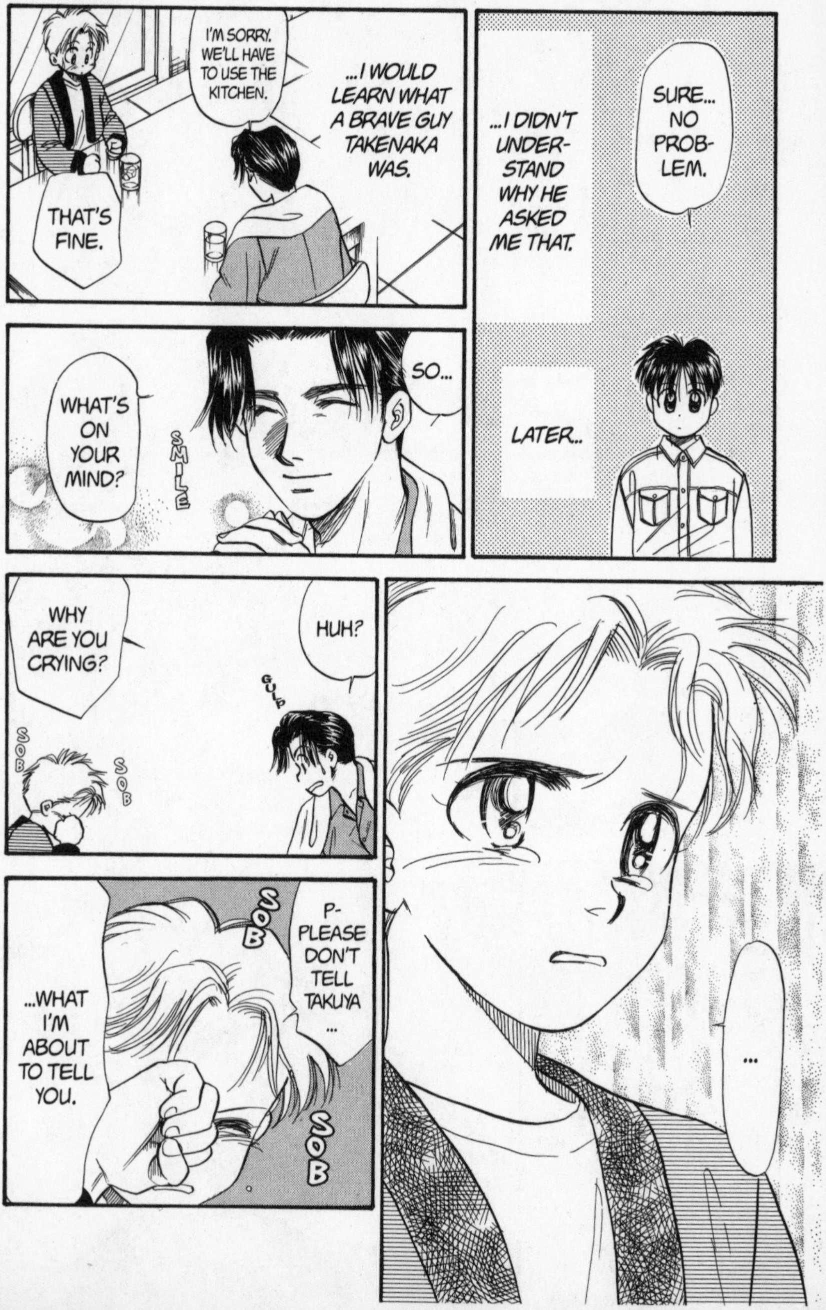
SURE... NO PROBLEM.
...I DIDN'T UNDERSTAND WHY HE ASKED ME THAT.
LATER..
I'M SORRY. WE'LL HAVE TO USE THE KITCHEN.
...I WOULD LEARN WHAT A BRAVE GUY TAKENAKA WAS.
THAT'S FINE.
SO...
SMILE
WHAT'S ON YOUR MIND?
...
HUH?
GULP
WHY ARE YOU CRYING?
SOB
SOB
SOB
P-PLEASE DON'T TELL TAKUYA...
...WHAT I'M ABOUT TO TELL YOU.
SOB

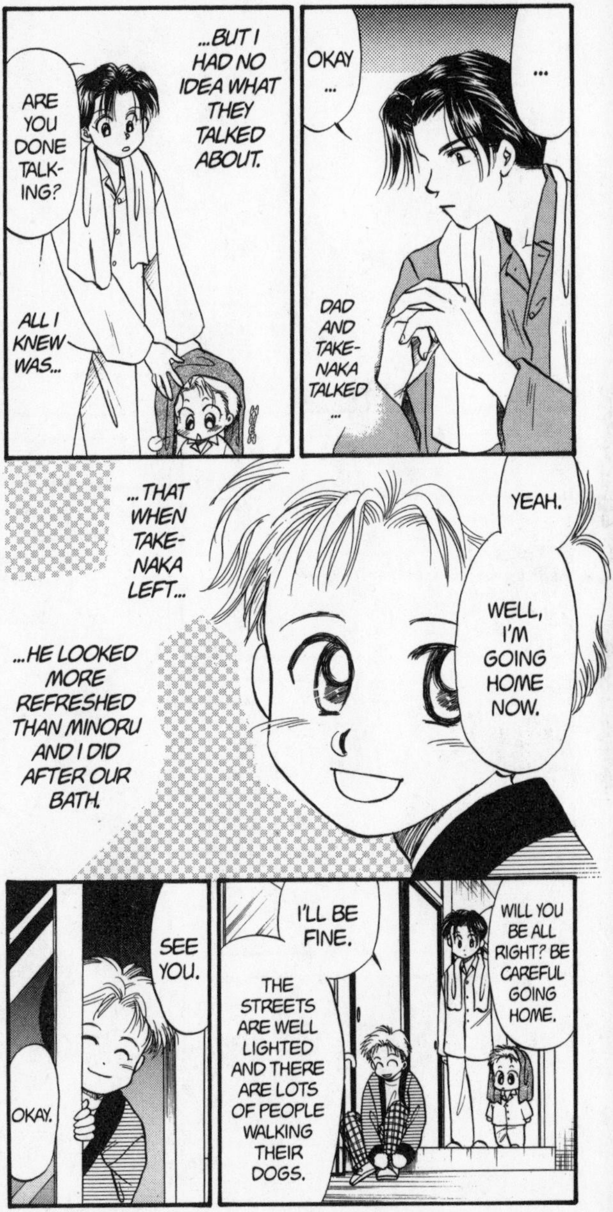
...
OKAY ...
DAD AND TAKENAKA TALKED ...
...BUT I HAD NO IDEA WHAT THEY TALKED ABOUT.
ARE YOU DONE TALKING?
ALL I KNEW WAS...
YEAH.
WELL, I'M GOING HOME NOW.
...THAT WHEN TAKENAKA LEFT...
...HE LOOKED MORE REFRESHED THAN MINORU AND I DID AFTER OUR BATH.
WILL YOU BE ALL RIGHT? BE CAREFUL GOING HOME.
I'LL BE FINE.
THE STREETS ARE WELL LIGHTED AND THERE ARE LOTS OF PEOPLE WALKING THEIR DOGS.
SEE YOU.
OKAY.

Author's Note: Part 6

Hi. This is the last author's note for this volume. In this chapter, Takenaka talks to Takuya's dad about a wet dream he had. Takuya's father tells him, "It is a normal physiological phenomenon." But let me say this for the sake of the little boys who are reading this--some boys never have them. So don't think you're weird if you don't.

I got a lot of flak when I started drawing this chapter, but I stuck to my guns and did it. Now I'm glad I did.

I felt that the problems that girls face, like their budding breasts and menstrual cycles, are dealt with a lot in stories, but boys go through stages too--their voices change, they have wet dreams, and they get body hair as they mature. I was told that this subject would make girls turn away, but I don't think so. What do you think?

See you again in Volume 11! ♡ Goodbye, and thanks!!

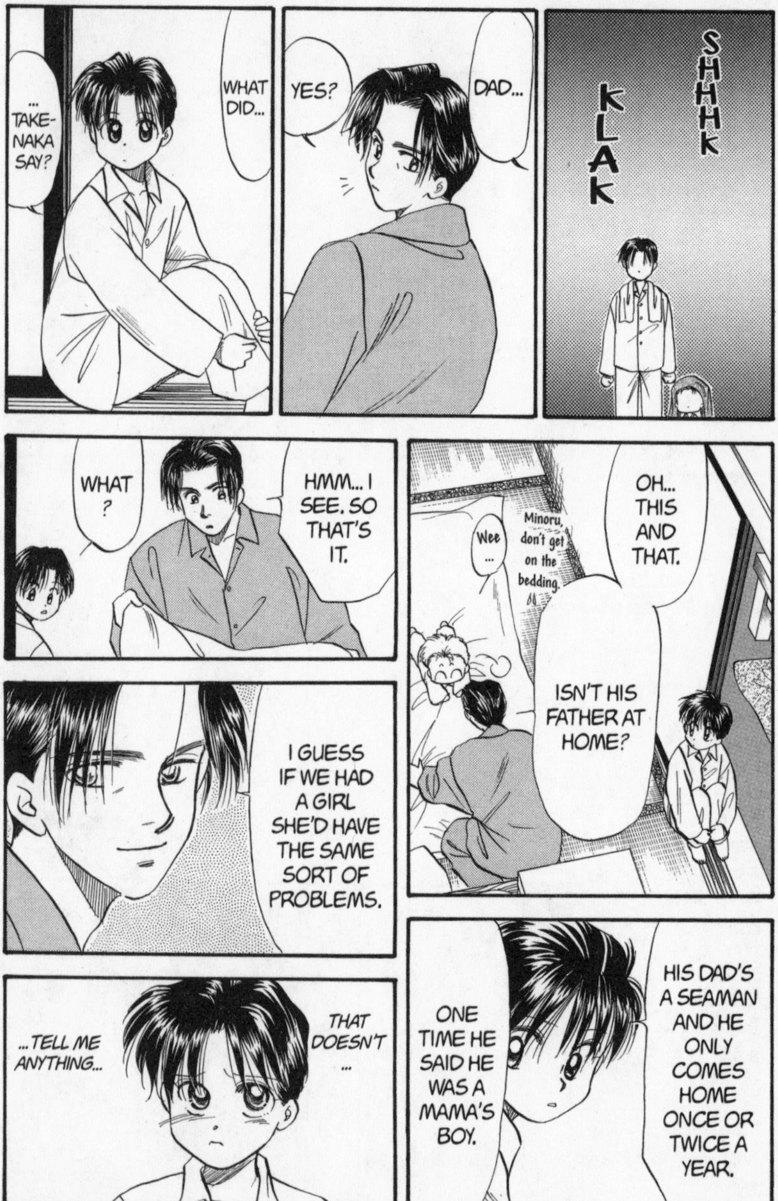
SHHHK
KLAK
DAD...
YES?
WHAT DID...
...TAKE-NAKA SAY?
OH... THIS AND THAT.
Minoru, don't get on the bedding.
Wee...
ISN'T HIS FATHER AT HOME?
HMM... I SEE. SO THAT'S IT.
WHAT?
I GUESS IF WE HAD A GIRL SHE'D HAVE THE SAME SORT OF PROBLEMS.
HIS DAD'S A SEAMAN AND HE ONLY COMES HOME ONCE OR TWICE A YEAR.
ONE TIME HE SAID HE WAS A MAMA'S BOY.
THAT DOESN'T...
...TELL ME ANYTHING...

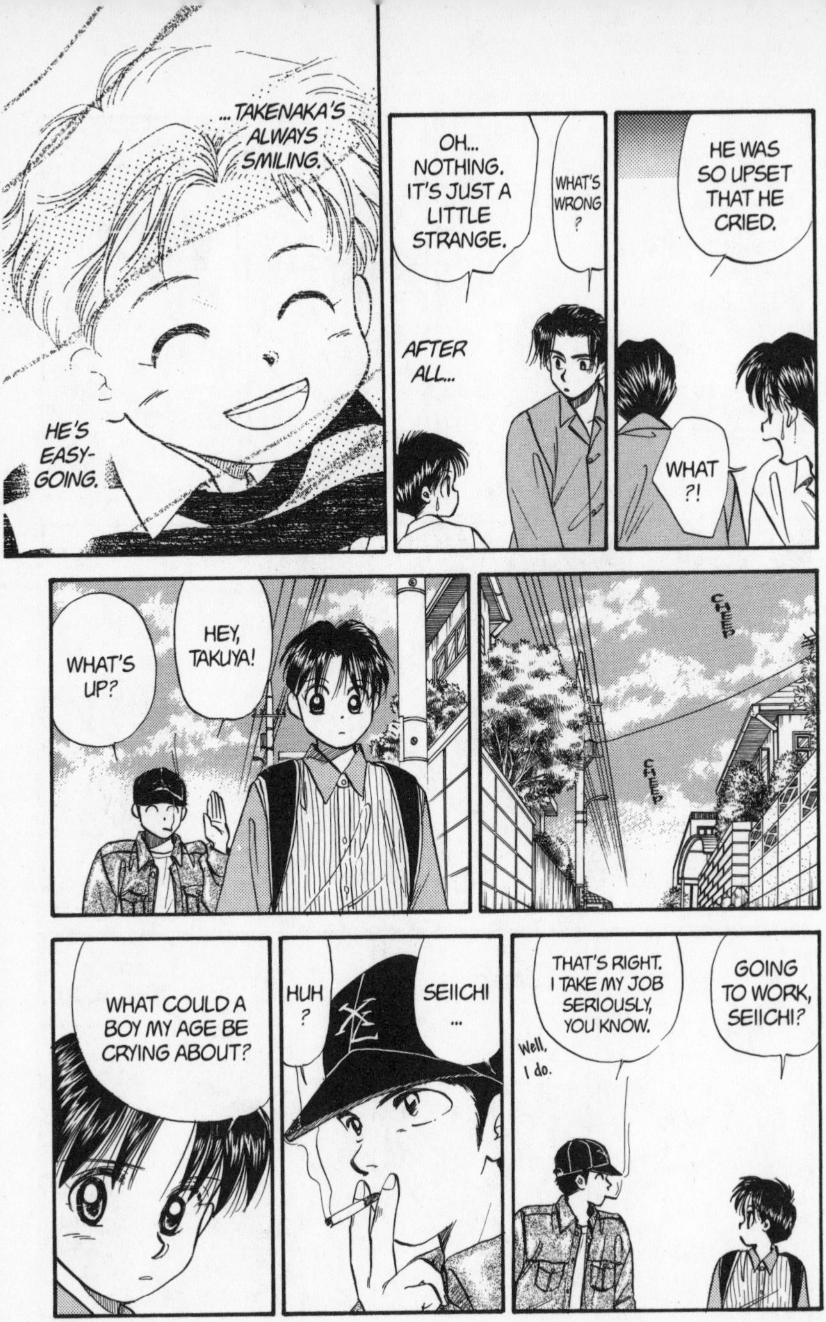
HE WAS SO UPSET THAT HE CRIED.
WHAT?!
WHAT'S WRONG?
OH... NOTHING. IT'S JUST A LITTLE STRANGE.
AFTER ALL...
...TAKENAKA'S ALWAYS SMILING.
HE'S EASY-GOING.
CHEEP
CHEEP
HEY, TAKUYA!
WHAT'S UP?
GOING TO WORK, SEIICHI?
THAT'S RIGHT. I TAKE MY JOB SERIOUSLY, YOU KNOW.
Well, I do.
SEIICHI...
HUH?
WHAT COULD A BOY MY AGE BE CRYING ABOUT?

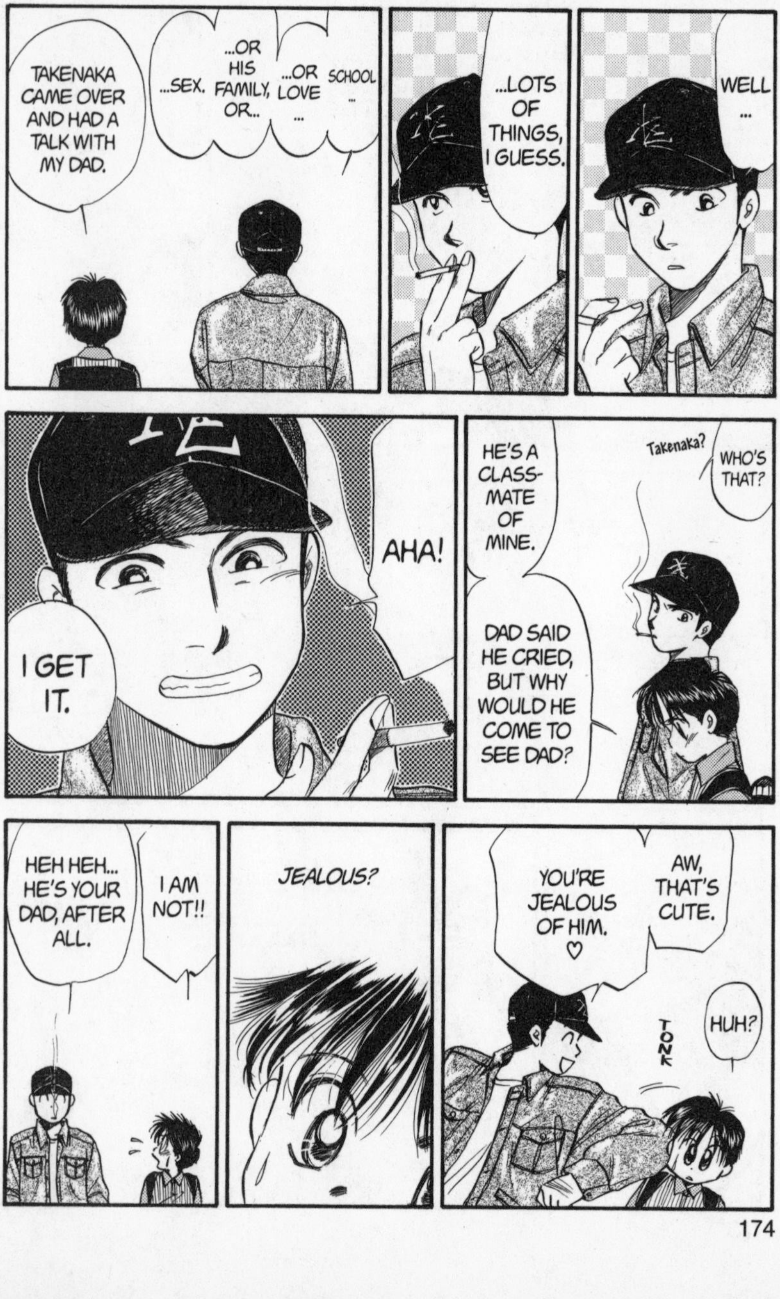
WELL ...
...LOTS OF THINGS, I GUESS.
SCHOOL ...
...OR LOVE ...
...OR HIS FAMILY, OR...
...SEX.
TAKENAKA CAME OVER AND HAD A TALK WITH MY DAD.
WHO'S THAT?
Takenaka?
HE'S A CLASS-MATE OF MINE.
DAD SAID HE CRIED, BUT WHY WOULD HE COME TO SEE DAD?
AHA!
I GET IT.
AW, THAT'S CUTE.
YOU'RE JEALOUS OF HIM. ♡
HUH?
TONK
JEALOUS?
I AM NOT!!
HEH HEH... HE'S YOUR DAD, AFTER ALL.

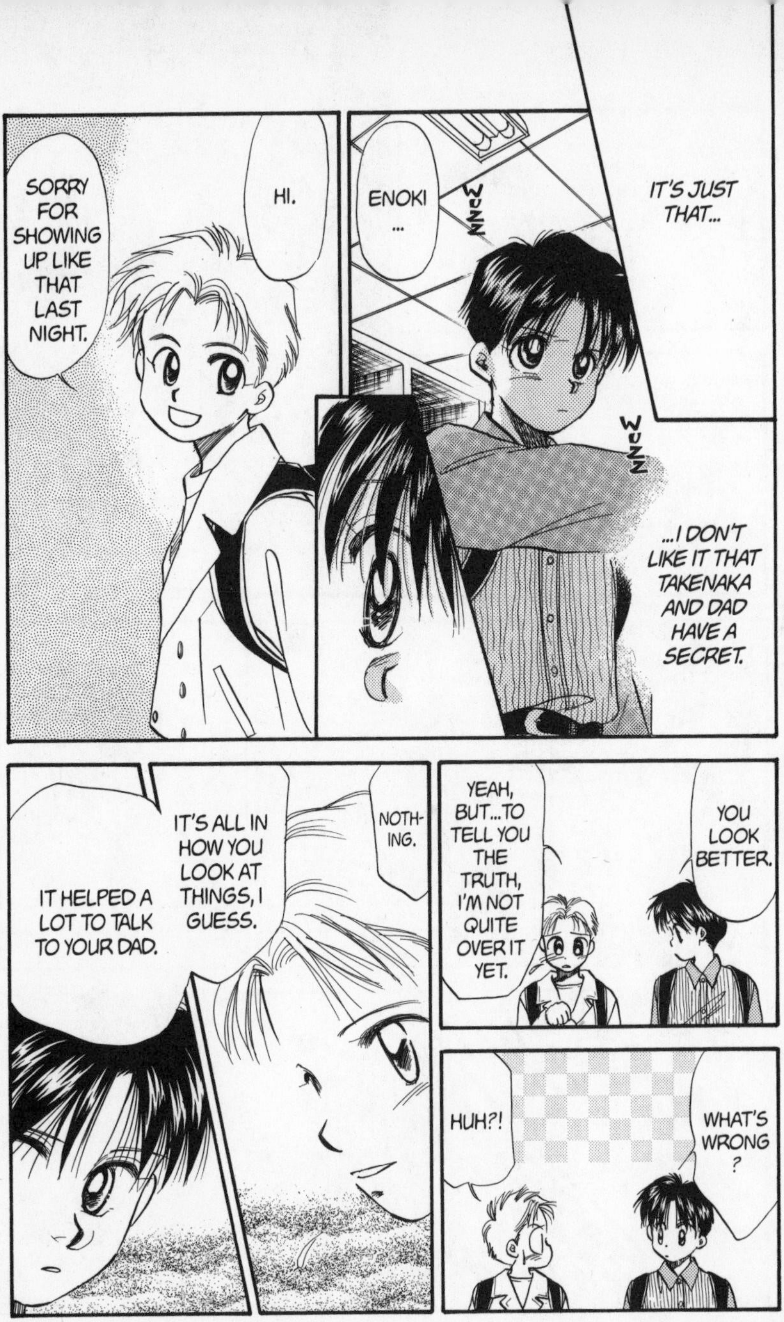
IT'S JUST THAT...
WUZZ
WUZZ
...I DON'T LIKE IT THAT TAKENAKA AND DAD HAVE A SECRET.
ENOKI ...
HI.
SORRY FOR SHOWING UP LIKE THAT LAST NIGHT.
YOU LOOK BETTER.
YEAH, BUT...TO TELL YOU THE TRUTH, I'M NOT QUITE OVER IT YET.
WHAT'S WRONG ?
HUH?!
NOTH-ING.
IT'S ALL IN HOW YOU LOOK AT THINGS, I GUESS.
IT HELPED A LOT TO TALK TO YOUR DAD.

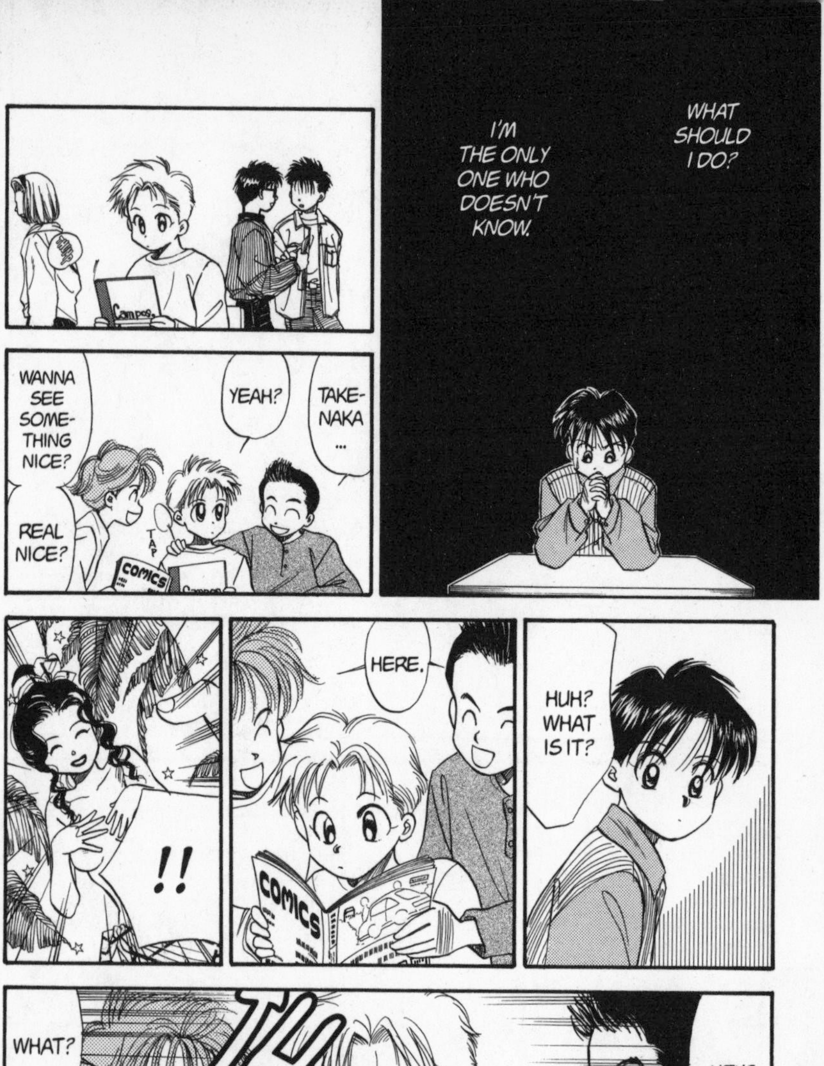
WHAT SHOULD I DO?
I'M THE ONLY ONE WHO DOESN'T KNOW.
TAKE-NAKA ...
YEAH?
WANNA SEE SOME-THING NICE?
TAP
REAL NICE?
HUH? WHAT IS IT?
HERE.
!!
HEY?
THWAP
WHAT?

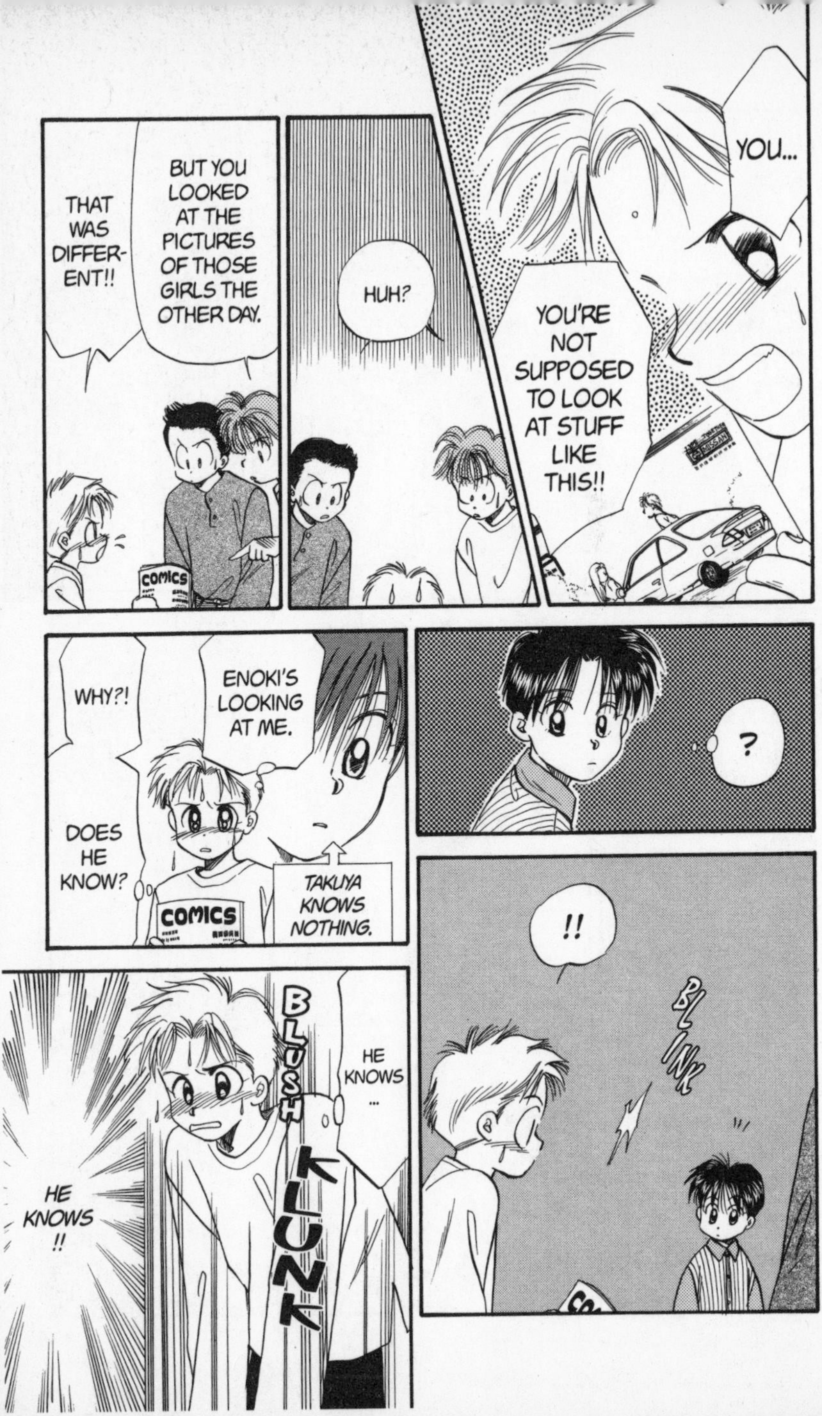
YOU...
YOU'RE NOT SUPPOSED TO LOOK AT STUFF LIKE THIS!!
HUH?
BUT YOU LOOKED AT THE PICTURES OF THOSE GIRLS THE OTHER DAY.
THAT WAS DIFFER-ENT!!
COMICS
?
ENOKI'S LOOKING AT ME.
WHY?!
DOES HE KNOW?
TAKUYA KNOWS NOTHING.
COMICS
!!
BLINK
HE KNOWS ...
BLUSH
KLUNK
HE KNOWS !!

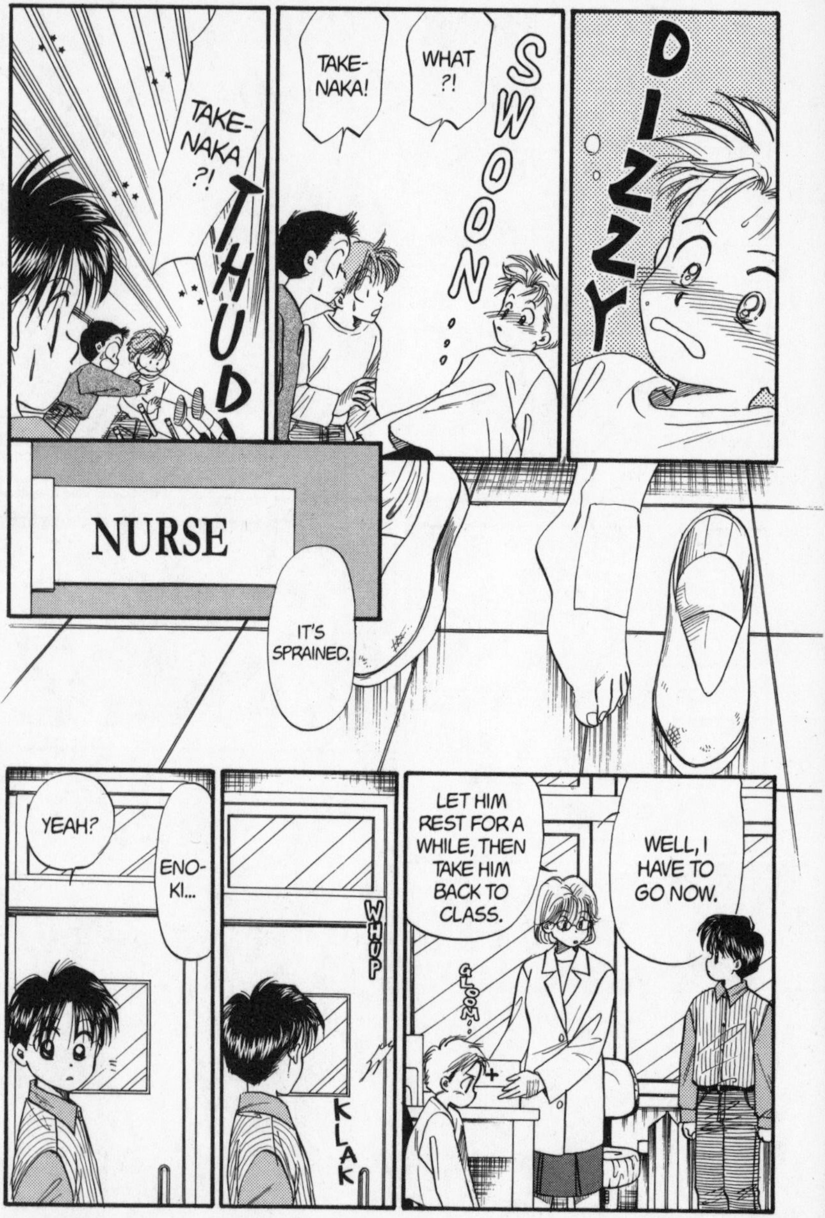
DIZZY
SWOON...
WHAT?!
TAKE-NAKA!
TAKE-NAKA?!
THUD
NURSE
IT'S SPRAINED.
WELL, I HAVE TO GO NOW.
LET HIM REST FOR A WHILE, THEN TAKE HIM BACK TO CLASS.
GLOOM...
WHUP
KLAK
ENO-KI...
YEAH?

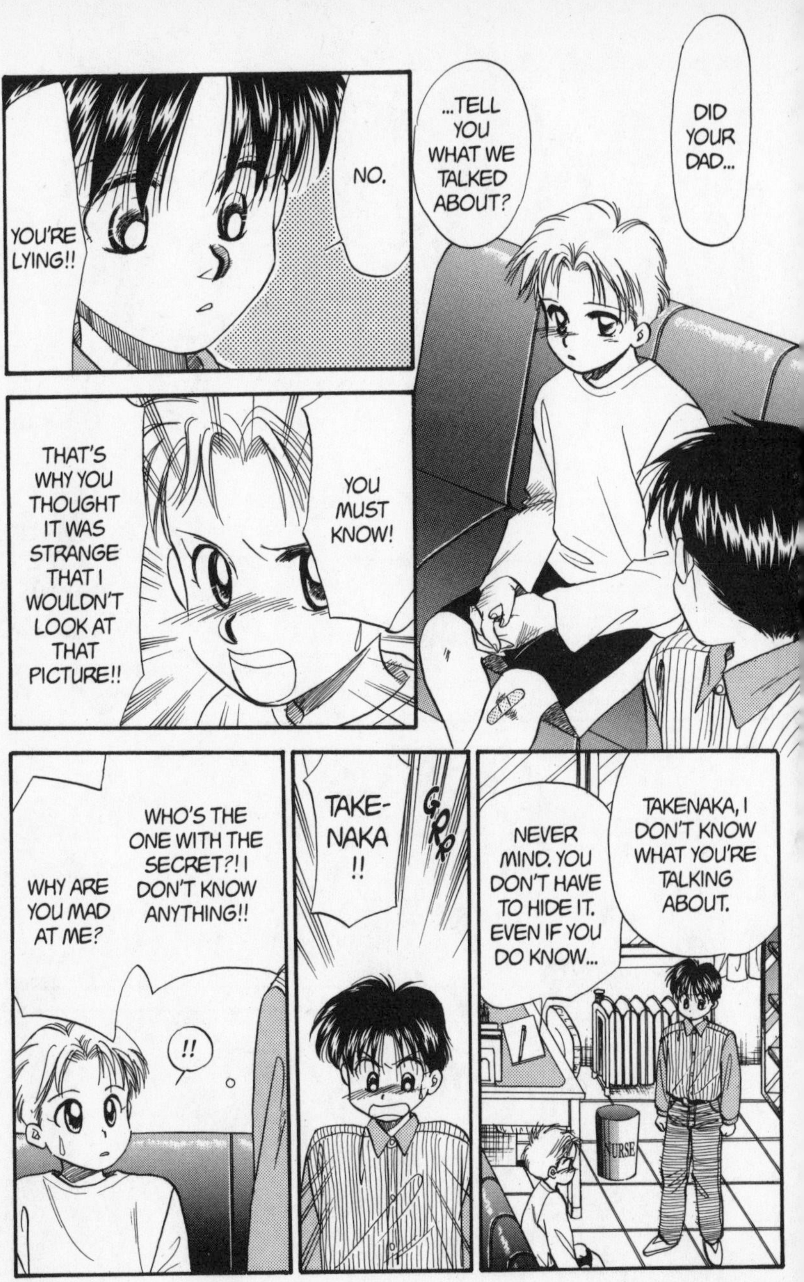
DID YOUR DAD...
...TELL YOU WHAT WE TALKED ABOUT?
NO.
YOU'RE LYING!!
YOU MUST KNOW!
THAT'S WHY YOU THOUGHT IT WAS STRANGE THAT I WOULDN'T LOOK AT THAT PICTURE!!
TAKENAKA, I DON'T KNOW WHAT YOU'RE TALKING ABOUT.
NEVER MIND. YOU DON'T HAVE TO HIDE IT. EVEN IF YOU DO KNOW...
NURSE
TAKE-NAKA !!
GRR
WHO'S THE ONE WITH THE SECRET?! I DON'T KNOW ANYTHING!!
WHY ARE YOU MAD AT ME?
!!

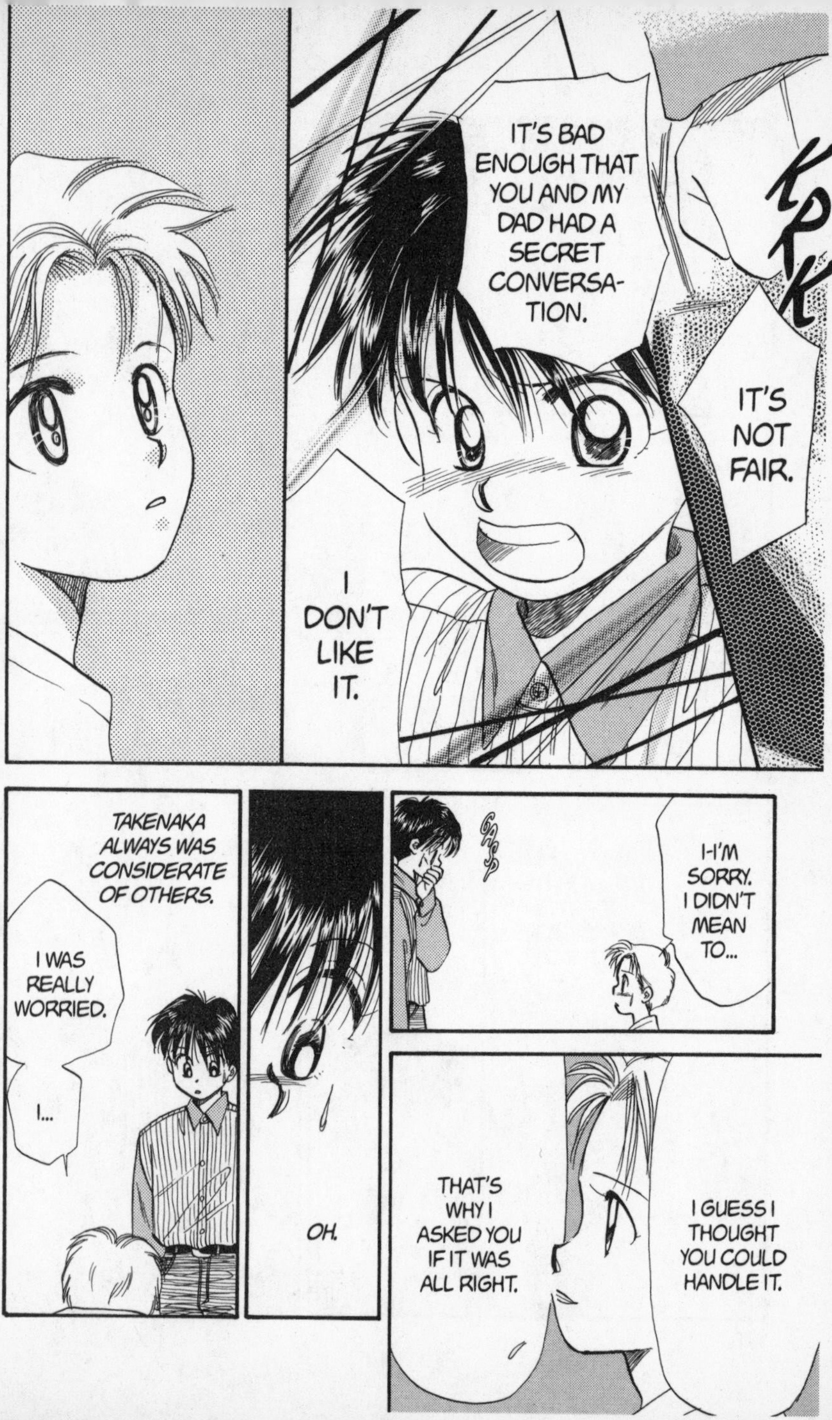
KRK
IT'S BAD ENOUGH THAT YOU AND MY DAD HAD A SECRET CONVERSA-TION.
IT'S NOT FAIR.
I DON'T LIKE IT.
I-I'M SORRY. I DIDN'T MEAN TO...
GASP
I GUESS I THOUGHT YOU COULD HANDLE IT.
THAT'S WHY I ASKED YOU IF IT WAS ALL RIGHT.
OH.
TAKENAKA ALWAYS WAS CONSIDERATE OF OTHERS.
I WAS REALLY WORRIED.
I...

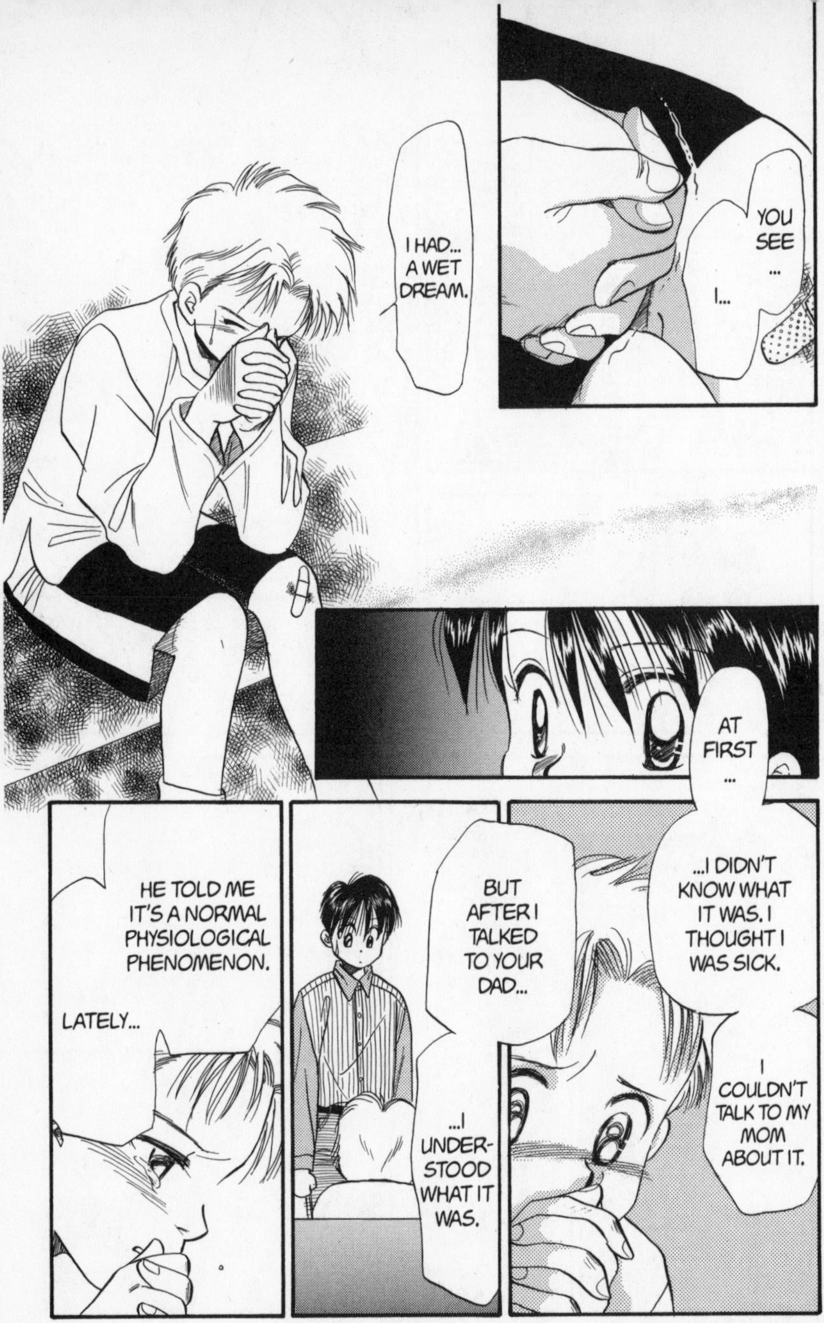

YOU SEE... I...
I HAD... A WET DREAM.
AT FIRST...
...I DIDN'T KNOW WHAT IT WAS. I THOUGHT I WAS SICK.
I COULDN'T TALK TO MY MOM ABOUT IT.
BUT AFTER I TALKED TO YOUR DAD...
...I UNDER-STOOD WHAT IT WAS.
HE TOLD ME IT'S A NORMAL PHYSIOLOGICAL PHENOMENON.
LATELY...

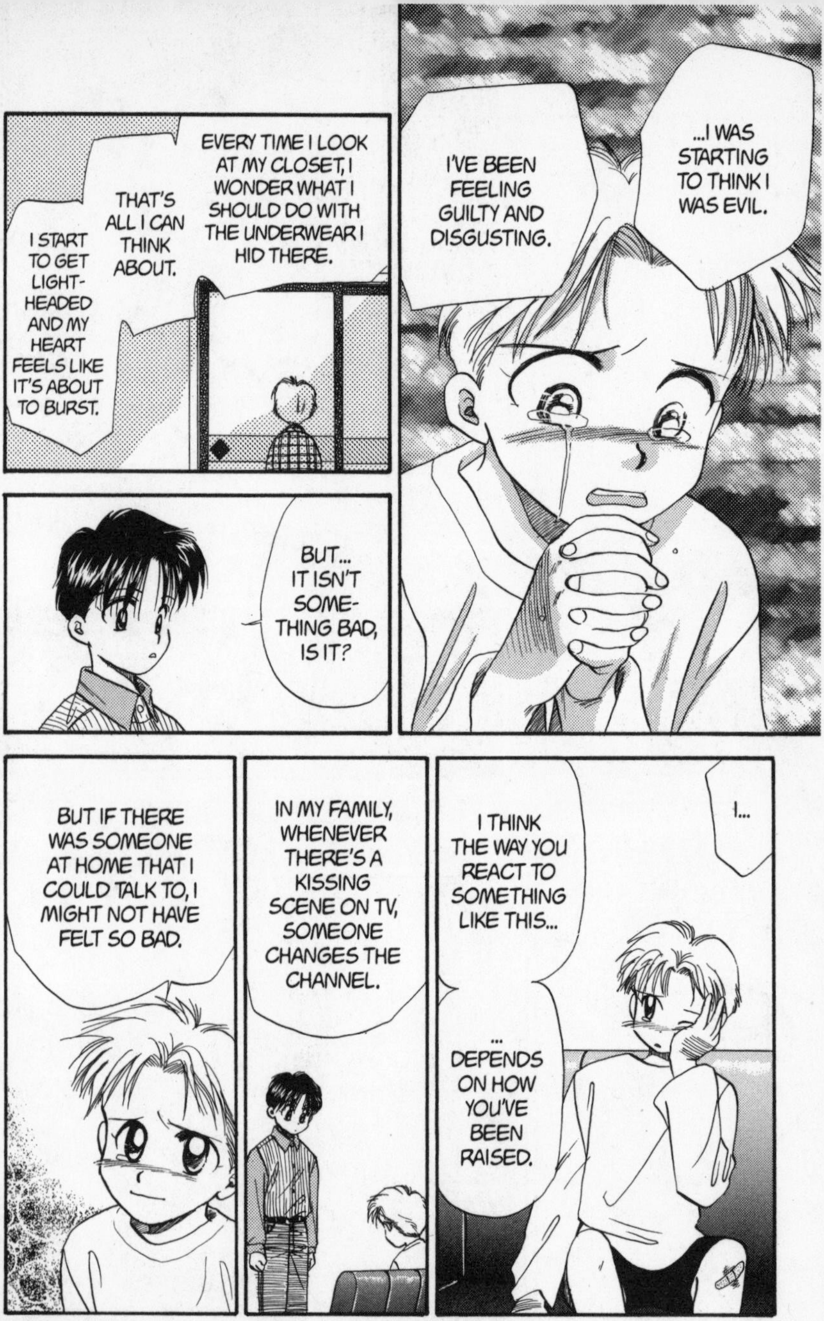
...I WAS STARTING TO THINK I WAS EVIL.
I'VE BEEN FEELING GUILTY AND DISGUSTING.
EVERY TIME I LOOK AT MY CLOSET, I WONDER WHAT I SHOULD DO WITH THE UNDERWEAR I HID THERE.
THAT'S ALL I CAN THINK ABOUT.
I START TO GET LIGHT-HEADED AND MY HEART FEELS LIKE IT'S ABOUT TO BURST.
BUT... IT ISN'T SOME-THING BAD, IS IT?
I...
I THINK THE WAY YOU REACT TO SOMETHING LIKE THIS...
... DEPENDS ON HOW YOU'VE BEEN RAISED.
IN MY FAMILY, WHENEVER THERE'S A KISSING SCENE ON TV, SOMEONE CHANGES THE CHANNEL.
BUT IF THERE WAS SOMEONE AT HOME THAT I COULD TALK TO, I MIGHT NOT HAVE FELT SO BAD.

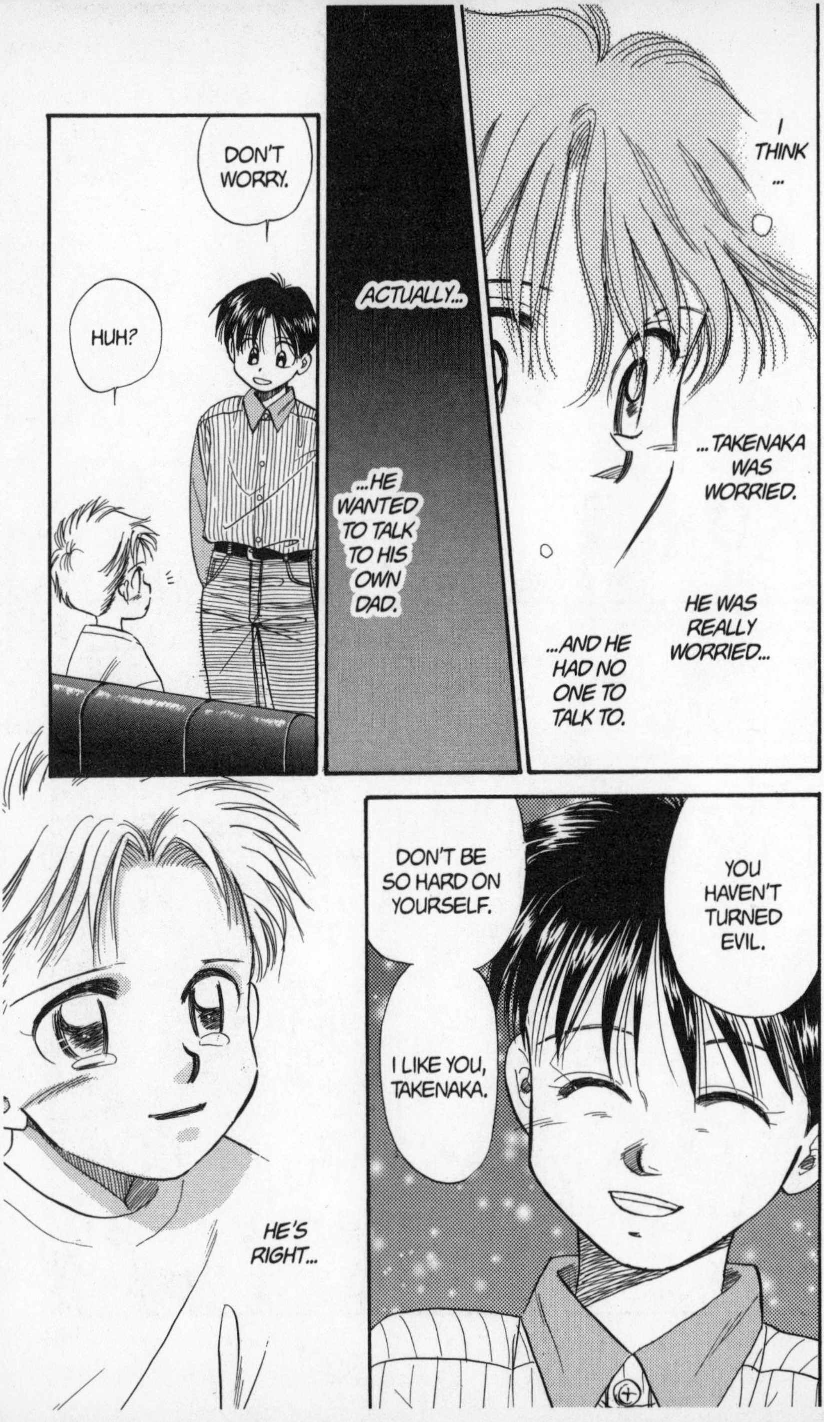
I THINK ...
...TAKENAKA WAS WORRIED.
HE WAS REALLY WORRIED...
...AND HE HAD NO ONE TO TALK TO.
ACTUALLY...
...HE WANTED TO TALK TO HIS OWN DAD.
DON'T WORRY.
HUH?
YOU HAVEN'T TURNED EVIL.
DON'T BE SO HARD ON YOURSELF.
I LIKE YOU, TAKENAKA.
HE'S RIGHT...

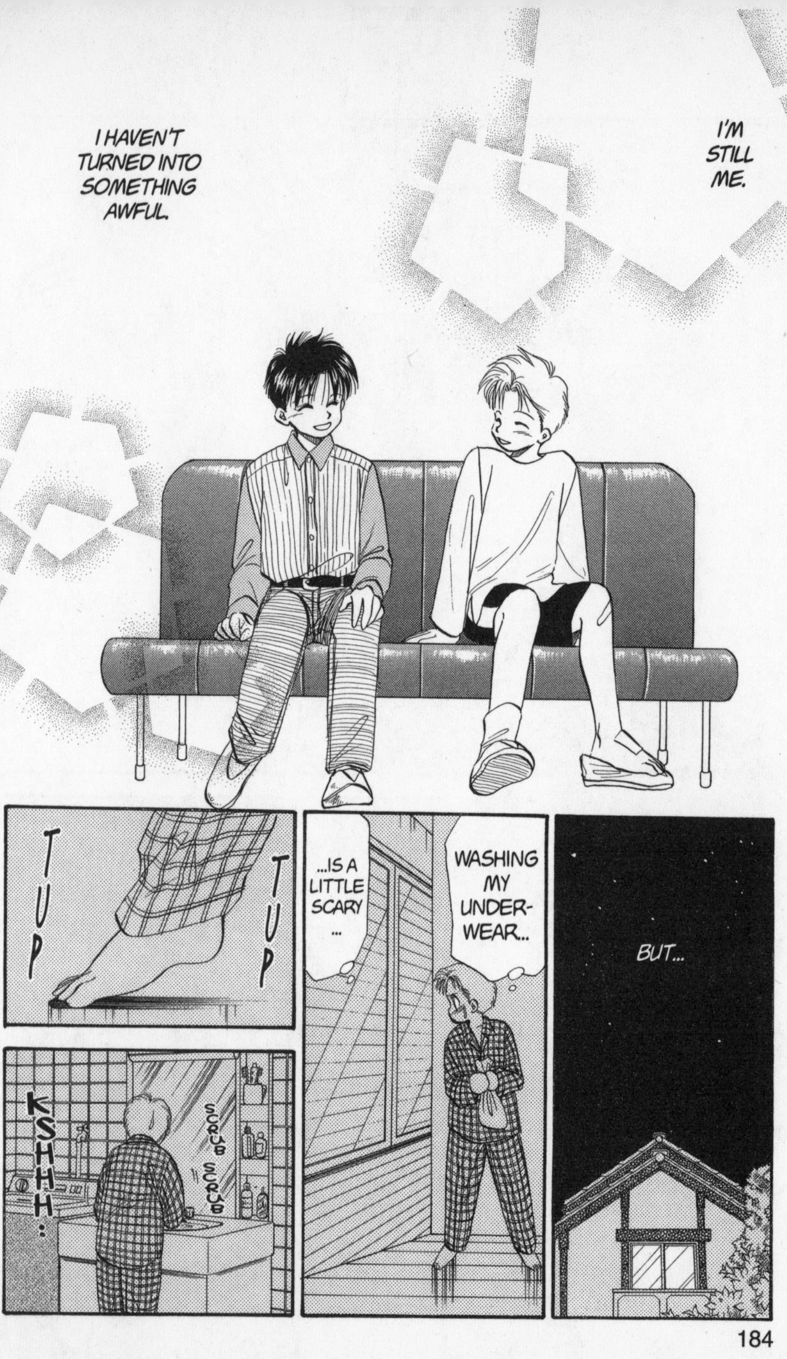
I'M STILL ME.
I HAVEN'T TURNED INTO SOMETHING AWFUL.
BUT...
WASHING MY UNDER-WEAR...
...IS A LITTLE SCARY ...
TUP TUP
KSHHH..
SCRUB SCRUB

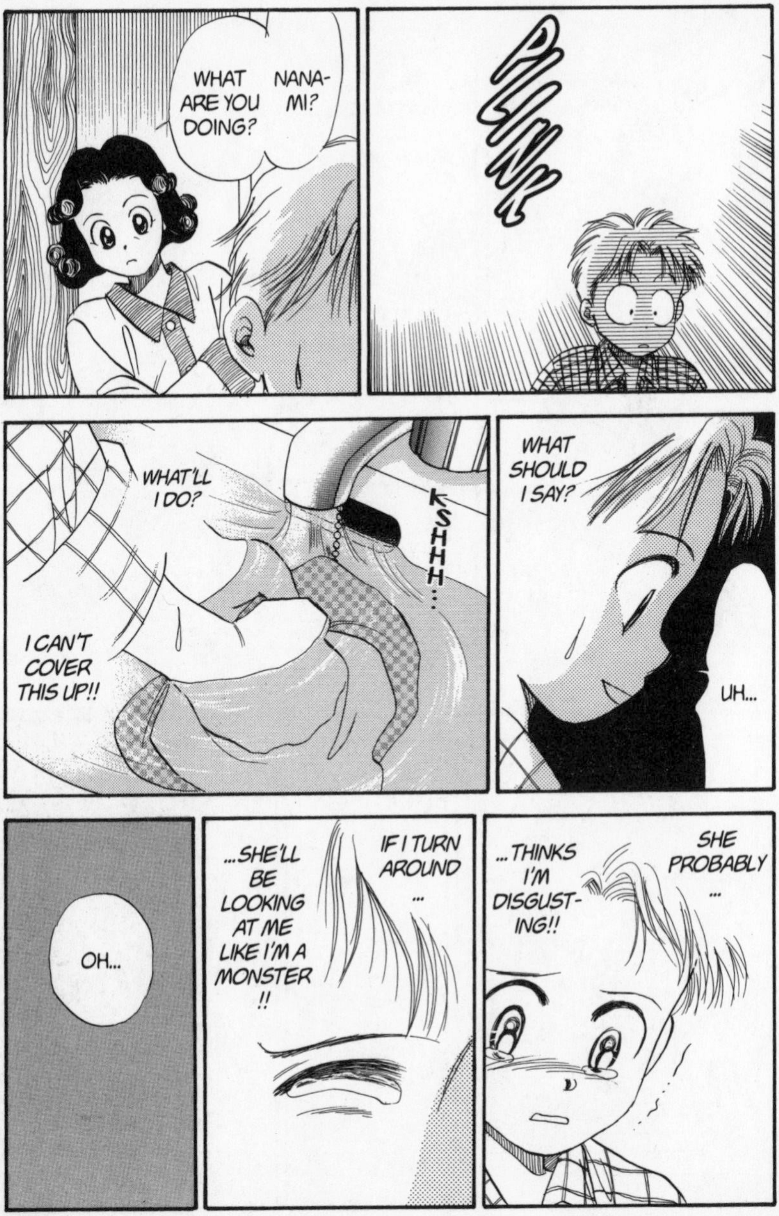
PLINK
NANA-MI?
WHAT ARE YOU DOING?
WHAT SHOULD I SAY?
UH...
WHAT'LL I DO?
KSHHH...
I CAN'T COVER THIS UP!!
SHE PROBABLY...
...THINKS I'M DISGUST-ING!!
IF I TURN AROUND...
...SHE'LL BE LOOKING AT ME LIKE I'M A MONSTER!!
OH...

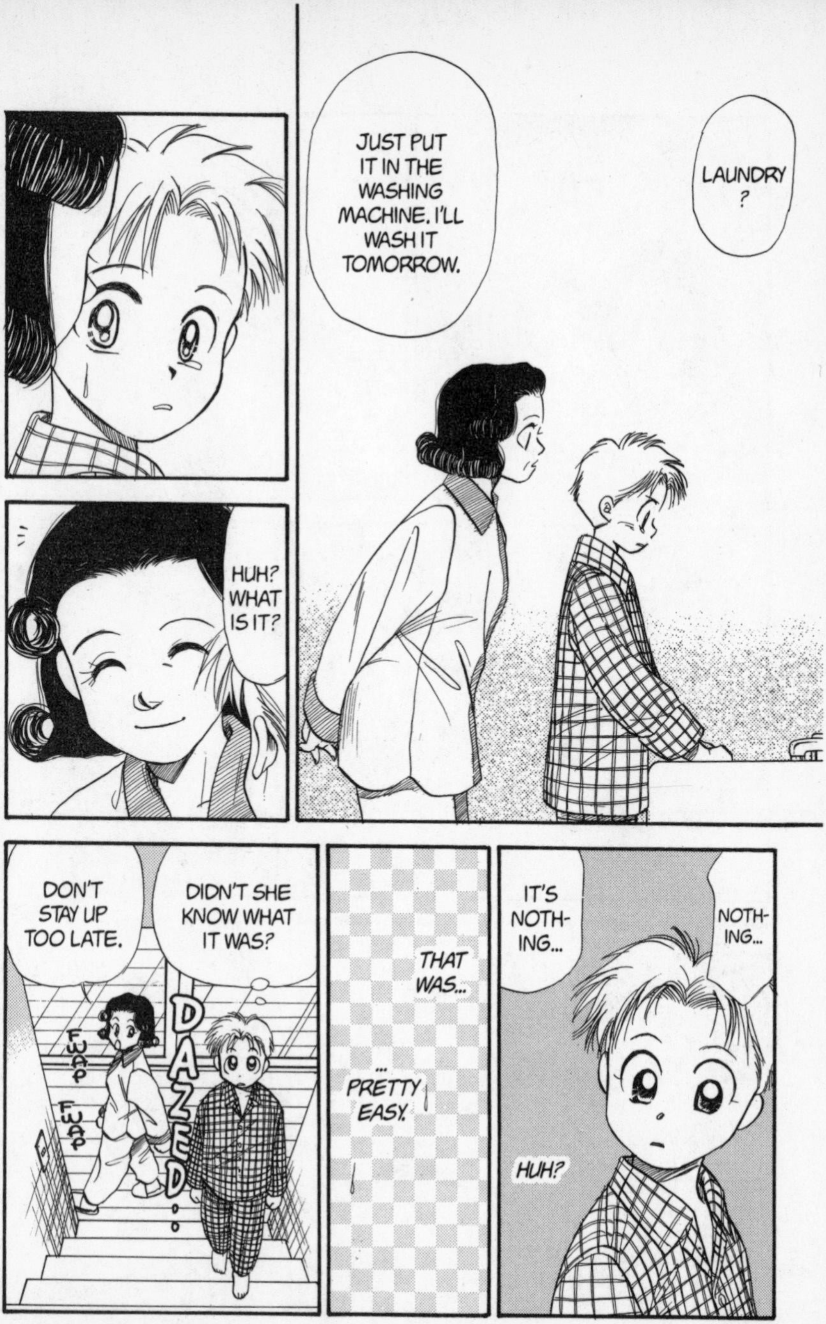
LAUNDRY?
JUST PUT IT IN THE WASHING MACHINE. I'LL WASH IT TOMORROW.
HUH? WHAT IS IT?
NOTH-ING...
IT'S NOTH-ING...
HUH?
THAT WAS...
...PRETTY EASY.
DIDN'T SHE KNOW WHAT IT WAS?
DON'T STAY UP TOO LATE.
FWAP
FWAP
DAZED...

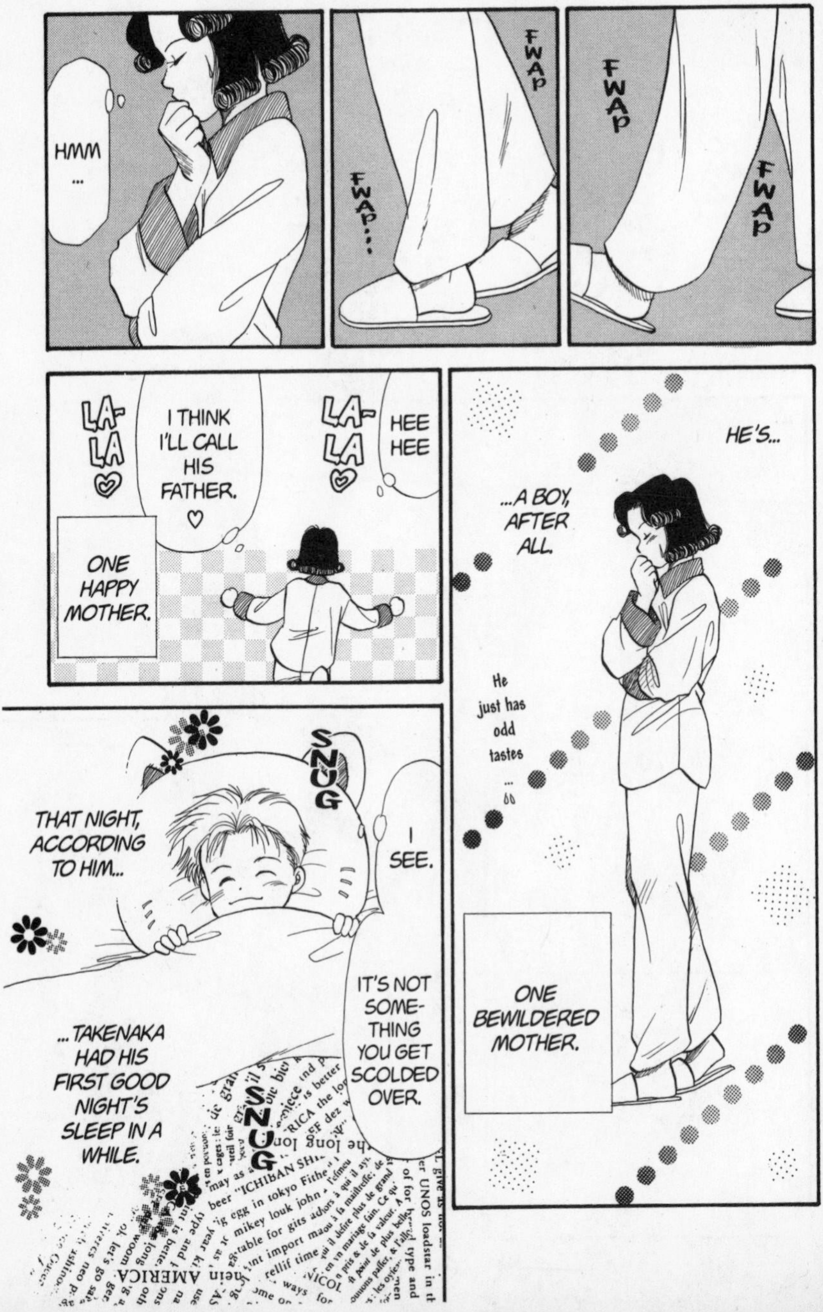
FWAP
FWAP
FWAP
FWAP...
HMM ...
HE'S...
...A BOY, AFTER ALL.
He just has odd tastes ...
ONE BEWILDERED MOTHER.
LA-LA
HEE HEE
I THINK I'LL CALL HIS FATHER.
LA-LA
ONE HAPPY MOTHER.
SNUG
I SEE.
THAT NIGHT, ACCORDING TO HIM...
IT'S NOT SOME-THING YOU GET SCOLDED OVER.
SNUG
...TAKENAKA HAD HIS FIRST GOOD NIGHT'S SLEEP IN A WHILE.

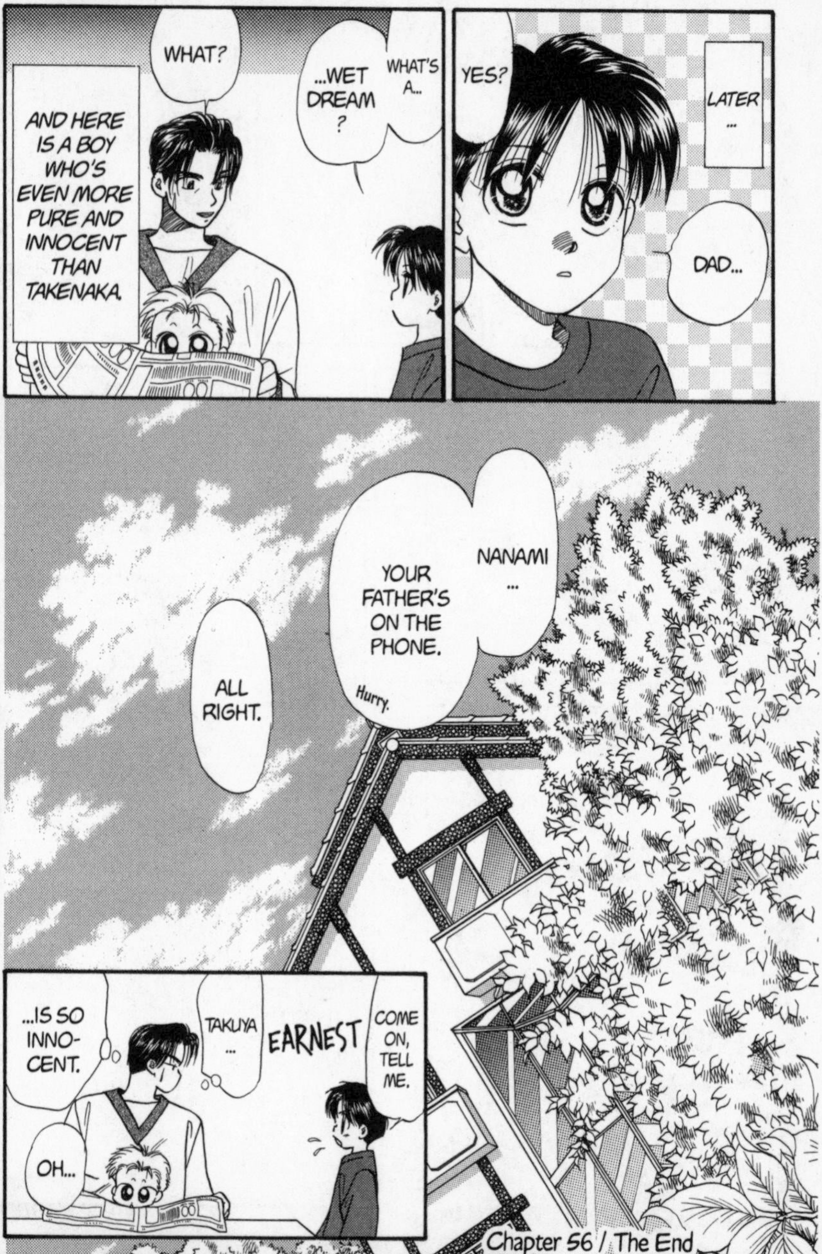
LATER...
DAD...
YES?
WHAT'S A...
...WET DREAM?
WHAT?
AND HERE IS A BOY WHO'S EVEN MORE PURE AND INNOCENT THAN TAKENAKA.
NANAMI...
YOUR FATHER'S ON THE PHONE.
Hurry.
ALL RIGHT.
COME ON, TELL ME.
EARNEST
TAKUYA...
...IS SO INNO-CENT.
OH...

Chapter 56 / The End

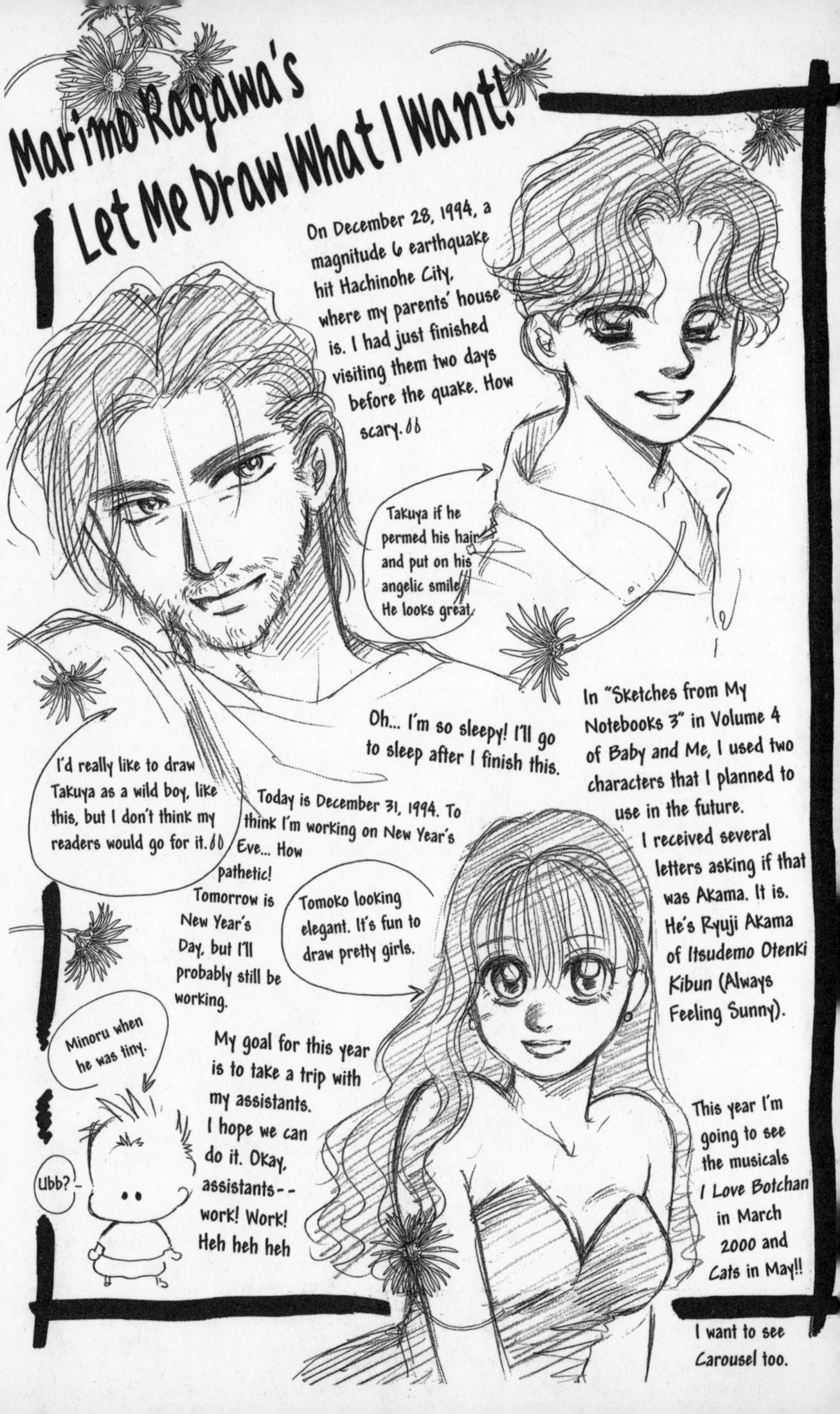
Marimo Ragawa's Let Me Draw What I Want!
On December 28, 1994, a magnitude 6 earthquake hit Hachinohe City, where my parents' house is. I had just finished visiting them two days before the quake. How scary.
Takuya if he permed his hair and put on his angelic smile. He looks great.
I'd really like to draw Takuya as a wild boy, like this, but I don't think my readers would go for it.
Oh... I'm so sleepy! I'll go to sleep after I finish this.
In "Sketches from My Notebooks 3" in Volume 4 of Baby and Me, I used two characters that I planned to use in the future.
I received several letters asking if that was Akama. It is. He's Ryuji Akama of Itsudemo Otenki Kibun (Always Feeling Sunny).
Today is December 31, 1994. To think I'm working on New Year's Eve... How pathetic!
Tomorrow is New Year's Day, but I'll probably still be working.
Tomoko looking elegant. It's fun to draw pretty girls.
Minoru when he was tiny.
Ubb?
My goal for this year is to take a trip with my assistants.
I hope we can do it. Okay, assistants-- work! Work! Heh heh heh
This year I'm going to see the musicals I Love Botchan in March 2000 and Cats in May!!
I want to see Carousel too.

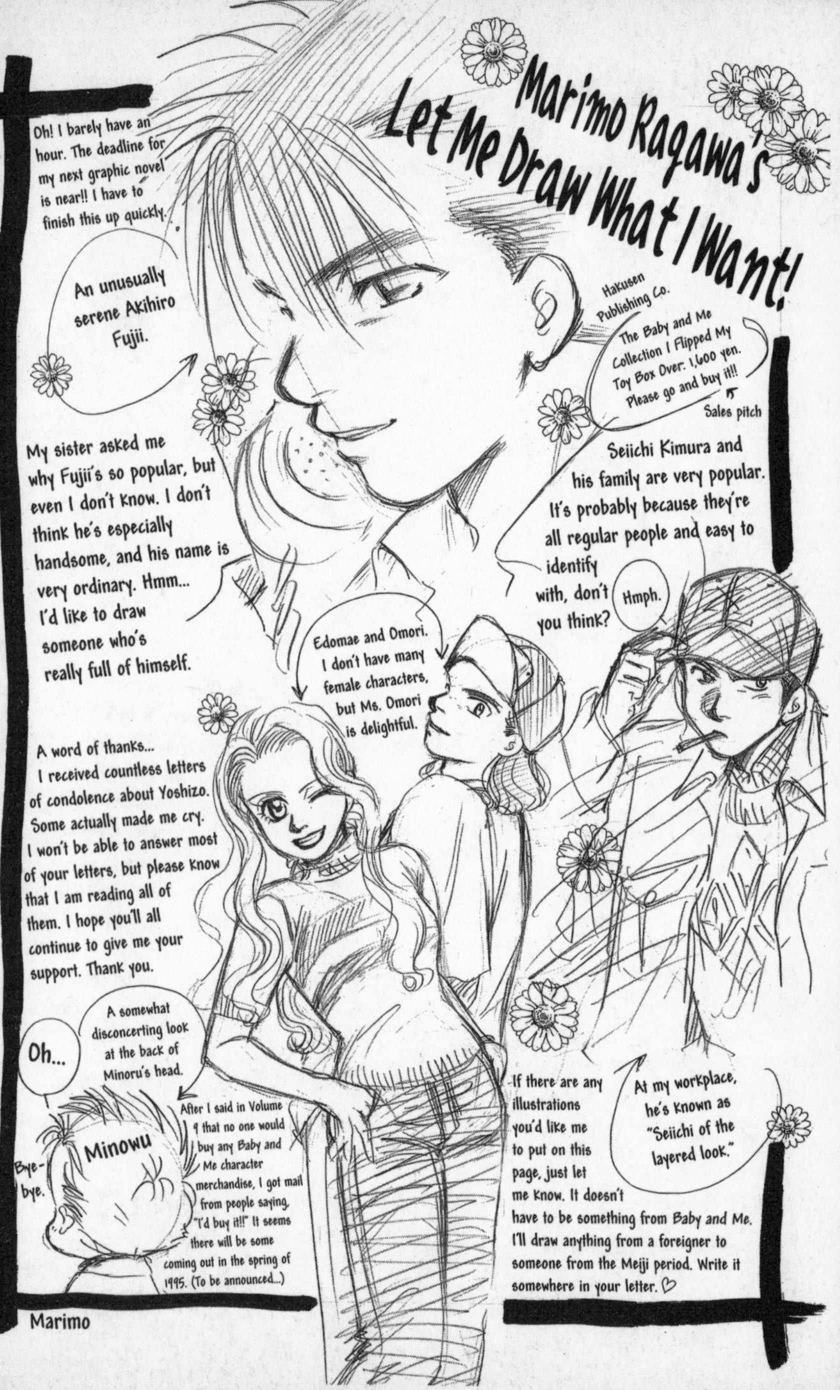

Marimo Ragawa's Let Me Draw What I Want!
Oh! I barely have an hour. The deadline for my next graphic novel is near!! I have to finish this up quickly.
An unusually serene Akihiro Fujii.
Hakusen Publishing Co.
The Baby and Me Collection I Flipped My Toy Box Over. 1,600 yen. Please go and buy it!!
Sales pitch
My sister asked me why Fujii's so popular, but even I don't know. I don't think he's especially handsome, and his name is very ordinary. Hmm... I'd like to draw someone who's really full of himself.
Seiichi Kimura and his family are very popular. It's probably because they're all regular people and easy to identify with, don't you think?
Hmph.
Edomae and Omori. I don't have many female characters, but Ms. Omori is delightful.
A word of thanks... I received countless letters of condolence about Yoshizo. Some actually made me cry. I won't be able to answer most of your letters, but please know that I am reading all of them. I hope you'll all continue to give me your support. Thank you.
Oh...
A somewhat disconcerting look at the back of Minoru's head.
Minowu
Bye-bye.
After I said in Volume 9 that no one would buy any Baby and Me character merchandise, I got mail from people saying, "I'd buy it!!" It seems there will be some coming out in the spring of 1995. (To be announced...)
If there are any illustrations you'd like me to put on this page, just let me know. It doesn't have to be something from Baby and Me. I'll draw anything from a foreigner to someone from the Meiji period. Write it somewhere in your letter. ♡
At my workplace, he's known as "Seiichi of the layered look."
Marimo